Microsoft® Flight Simulator 98

Unauthorized Game Secrets

Microsoft® Flight Simulator 98

Unauthorized Game Secrets

Douglas Kiang

PRIMA PUBLISHING
Rocklin, California
(916) 632-4400
http://www.primagames.com

Project Editor: Brooke N. Raymond

Acknowledgments

This book is dedicated to my father, Lindsey, and my Uncle Beechie for showing me how to fly and for fostering in me a love of All Things Computer. I am enormously grateful to my mother, Gail Woliver, for teaching me to love words. My heartfelt thanks go to my wife, Mary, for all of her love and patience during the creation of this book, even as our living room became an office and the computer keyboard was replaced with an airplane yoke, throttle, and rudder pedals. I owe a great debt of gratitude to Bart Farkas for his boundless support and encouragement, for believing in me, and for showing me through his own example what it means to be a true professional. I am equally grateful to Amy Raynor and Brooke Raymond of Prima Publishing, for their guidance, their suggestions, and their support as I stretched my wings. Additional thanks go to Erin Matuse for having the courage to take off in an airplane with me one summer and land under a parachute. I am also grateful for the support of Bob Woliver, Keiko Woliver, the whole Radlhammer and Brown clan, and Anne-Marie Soulliére. Certainly deserving of a mention is my home away from home, the Blue Sky Ranch in Gardiner, New York. And last but certainly not least, I am grateful to Kyle Michael Bills, simply for being himself.

Table of Contents

Foreword

When I was 14, and growing up in Hawaii, I loved airplanes. Though Hawaii was a beautiful place to live, there was no escaping the fact that we were thousands of miles from the west coast of the United States, and pretty isolated. If you wanted to go anywhere, you had to take a plane. Airplanes awakened the adventurous spirit in me; they were a way to escape from the familiar and venture into the unknown. It was about this time that my uncle got a brand new, state-of-the-art personal computer—an IBM 8088 with a monochrome screen. My dad used to take me to visit, and we would all sit huddled in the dark, peering at the monitor. I got my first glimpse of *Flight Simulator* version 1.0 one evening, and it was quite an experience. My uncle's cat Lucy pricked her ears up at the tinny sound of the engines emanating from the single speaker, and my uncle showed us how we could fly cross-country in real-time, using the autopilot. I was more interested, however, in dogfighting in the Sopwith Camel. While the graphics and sound were nowhere near today's version of *Flight Simulator*, what stays with me most is the feeling of escape I got from flying that very first version of the game. Even though I didn't know how to use all of the dials and navigation instruments, we would literally fly for hours, traveling far beyond the walls of that small apartment, over the round top of the hill, into the darkness of the night, and onward through the sky.

Microsoft Flight Simulator 98 is several generations beyond that very first version of the game. This newest version combines great graphics and sound with absolute realism. Additional hardware acceleration and force feedback technology truly put you in the pilot's seat, surrounding you with audio, visual, and tactile feedback. Much of the scenery was developed from real photographs of the actual locations, and the stereo sound effects are digitized from the real sounds you would hear if you were sitting in a real cockpit. All of the dials look exactly the way they would in real life—right down to the grease stains! The planes handle very realistically, which means they *feel* very real—flying a 737 is hard! This version of *Flight Simulator* features three new aircraft—two more advanced versions of the Cessna and the LearJet, and the Bell 206B JetRanger III helicopter, which is every bit as inherently unstable as the real thing. It will take every ounce of your skill simply to keep this two-ton rotary wing aircraft in a stable hover. Yet, even with all of these additions, *Microsoft Flight Simulator 98* runs very smoothly on most computers because it has been optimized for Windows 95, and takes advantage of its DirectX 5. If you own an add-on hardware accelerator card, you are in for a real treat—fully texture-mapped landscapes and transparent cloud effects, all running at speeds so smooth you may actually get motion sickness! *Flight Simulator's* built-in online help makes it easy to learn more about the various instruments and dials while you fly. There are movies and interactive lessons that will help you perfect your skills. With *Microsoft Flight Simulator 98: Unauthorized Game Secrets* by your side, you have everything you need to explore the sky, practice your bad-weather landing skills, navigate cross-country, succeed at all of the built-in challenges and adventures, and even create your own flights and challenging situations. You can even fly with a friend over the modem or the Internet. Read a little, fly a lot, don't be afraid to explore and experiment, and above all, enjoy yourself!

—Douglas Kiang

C H A P T E R

1

Flight Plan

FLIGHT SIMULATOR IS FUN!

This book is about having fun in the air. You won't have to wade through miles of aeronautical charts, take any written exams, or pass any tests. The bottom line is that *Microsoft Flight Simulator 98* is supposed to be fun, and you should be free to have fun with it without having to spend hours wading through dense text. This book is designed to get you in the air quickly, and to introduce you to some of the most amazing features of *Flight Simulator*.

THIS BOOK WILL BE FUN TO READ!

The very best thing about *Flight Simulator* is flying—that feeling you get when you soar through a misty layer of clouds into the rose-tinted blue of the sky as the sun sets. This book focuses primarily on how to fly and have fun in the air. We won't spend as much time fiddling with such nuances as manifold pressure, exhaust gas temperature, propeller pitch, or the proper fuel mixture for different flying conditions. If you want to customize these things, you can do it quite easily. You can just as easily turn off certain options and let the computer worry about keeping the engine running. I like to fly this way because it allows me to escape and relax without fretting over all the sweaty little details. If this means we have to buzz a few air traffic towers, so be it.

The second best thing about *Flight Simulator* is its realism and attention to detail. You can customize *Flight Simulator* to make it as close to flying the real thing as possible. You can request take-off and landing clearances from the tower, keep to landing patterns and assigned altitudes, crash your plane if you hit parts of the scenery, have your engine run out of fuel and basically simulate all those nitty gritty details that can sometimes make real life such a pain.

THE BEST WAY TO LEARN HOW TO FLY IS TO FLY

There is no other way to put it. The more you fly, the more you learn. So feel free to put the book down from time to time and experiment on your own. I will provide an introduction to many of *Flight Simulator*'s features in a step-by-step approach that will have you flying as soon and as much as possible. Bart Farkas, our *Flight Simulator* expert, has completed all of the flight challenges that are included with *Flight Simulator*, and he gives you his tips on how to beat all of them.

Flight Simulator is a very detailed simulation with many features, and I have focused on the features that you will use most often. But there is much more to *Flight Simulator*, so once you get comfortable, start exploring. Poke around the controls and see what does what. Take off during some of the step-by-step flights to do some experimenting on your own. Push the limits of your aircraft—it's educational and fun! All of the flights I set up for you will be saved from the Flight menu, so you can always go back to them.

HOW TO USE THIS BOOK

This book is divided into six chapters, representing different stages of a flight career. Feel free to skip around and choose whatever interests you. If you haven't flown before, you would probably do best to start with Chapter 2, "Flight Student." People who have used earlier versions of *Flight Simulator* might want to look at chapters 5 and 6 for information on the new planes and features. If you want to jump right to some wacky tips and tricks, check out the end of Chapter 3, as well as the "*Flight Simulator* Secrets" section of Chapter 5.

Chapter 1: Flight Plan

This chapter explains how this book is organized and gives you a glimpse of the exciting adventures that are in store for you as you explore the world of *Microsoft Flight Simulator 98*. You will also find descriptions of the various types of tips and hints that I will provide throughout the book.

Chapter 2: Flight Student

How do you fly this thing? Take a no-frills, introductory flight and discover the basics of flying using no more than a few key instruments. You'll find how to start out at a different airport than Chicago's Meigs Field, and you'll get a first look at some of the stunning photorealistic scenery that *Microsoft Flight Simulator 98* features. You will also learn some of the physics behind flight: What keeps this thing up in the air, anyway? Later, you'll get a full briefing on all of the Cessna's flight instruments, and make a few flights in which you will learn how to takeoff, land, and even stall the plane. Finally, I'll provide tips and hints on finishing all of the built-in lessons with flying colors.

Chapter 3: Pilot's License

In this section, you will learn some of the finer points of making turns, you'll find out how to get yourself into a spin (and get out of one), and you'll even find out how to control the weather and give yourself the kind of flying conditions you really want. You can't do that in real life! I'll teach you to land in nasty weather conditions, then take a cross-country flight using the Cessna's instrumentation to navigate. Next, for a change of pace, you'll test fly a Learjet. Finally, I'll show you how to take revenge on your instructor in my section on "Stupid Cessna Tricks."

Chapter 4: Commercial Pilot

Ever wanted to fly a Really Big Jet? How about a Boeing 737? Learn how to fly passengers and bring them safely in for a landing in a jet that weighs over 75 tons. Get tips from a real pilot on how to solve such catastrophic challenges as an engine flameout or hydraulics failure at 10,000 feet. You'll also find out how to communicate with the tower and how to talk like a bona fide pilot.

Chapter 5: Barnstormer

Go over the edge! If you have ever dreamed of being a stunt pilot, this is your section. Learn how to fly the Porsche of stunt planes—the nimble, aerobatic Extra 300S. Find out how to soar through the sky with the greatest of ease, and learn all sorts of aerobatic maneuvers. Master how to fly without an engine in the Schweizer

Sailplane, and buzz tall buildings in a Sopwith Camel. Finally, you will find tips on solving every one of the built-in Challenges, which are the ultimate tests of your *Flight Simulator* prowess.

Chapter 6: Chopper Pilot

Take a break from fixed-wing aircraft and try your hand at flying the Bell 206B JetRanger III helicopter. Learn the basics of helicopter flight, find out how to succeed at the built-in lessons, and even learn how to shut off the main rotor, autorotate to a landing, and walk away from the wreckage pieces. Finally, you'll find the preflight briefings for all 20 of the *Flight Simulator 98* Adventures.

The Wild Blue Yonder

At the end of the book, you will find lots of useful information on expanding your *Flight Simulator* world. Appendix A is an interview with the pilots of a 767 passenger jet. Appendix B contains information on how to see the best sights and appreciate the finer parts of the many new cities included with *Microsoft Flight Simulator 98*. Appendix C features a tour of Hawaiian volcanoes during a major eruption. Appendix D provides some hints, ideas, and information on using the multiplayer features. Appendix E provides you with a comprehensive list of every single *Flight Simulator* action that can be controlled from the keyboard. Appendix F provides VOR charts and other navigational information that you'll want right at your fingertips. Finally, the glossary will explain any unfamiliar terms.

CONVENTIONS USED IN THIS BOOK

Microsoft Flight Simulator 98 offers a number of ways to control your aircraft. In the descriptions in this book, for consistency and for simplicity's sake, I will refer to the controls in an actual aircraft. For example, when I say "pull back on the yoke," it means to perform the appropriate action using your keyboard, mouse, joystick, or yoke. On the keyboard, you would press keypad [2] to accomplish this. On a mouse, you would drag the mouse toward you. With a joystick or a yoke, you would pull them back toward you.

"Keep back pressure on the yoke" means to pull the yoke back. Conversely, "keep forward pressure on the yoke" means to push the yoke forward. I use these terms throughout the book, and soon you'll be using them, too, no matter what you're actually doing to accomplish the action. Sometimes I might tell you to "keep the nose of the plane level with the horizon." You will need to play with the controls a bit in order to get the plane to do what you want.

ACRONYMS AND ABBREVIATIONS

You will find many acronyms for specialized equipment and procedures in *Microsoft Flight Simulator 98*. I have provided a list in Chapter 2 of some of the more common acronyms, and I have used these acronyms throughout the book. Refer to this list if you are unsure of what something stands for, or use *Flight Simulator's* built-in online help feature to identify any gauge or dial by right-clicking on it with the mouse.

VIDEOS

One of the best ways to learn new maneuvers or become familiar with flight instruments is to view the videos and animations that are included with *Microsoft Flight Simulator 98*. These are sprinkled throughout the online Flight School, and they are an excellent preview to the topics covered in this book. I have searched through every page of the online manual and have found all of the videos for you. As you read this book, I will mention any relevant videos and tell you where they are located. For example, when you start

Video: Meet Patty Wagstaff

Location: Flight School → Aerobatics Course → Aerobatics Course: Introduction → Your Instructor: Patty Wagstaff

learning how to fly aerobatic maneuvers in the Extra 300S try checking out the videos featuring Patty Wagstaff by following this note:

PROPELLER-HEAD TIPS

Every so often, you'll find a tip or hint off to the side with some added information or a cool tip to enhance your flights. I have indicated these tips with a picture of a propeller beanie.

This is a propeller-head tip. Notice the snazzy icon.

These Are a Few of Our Favorite Things . . .

Just gotten *Flight Simulator*? Don't know where to begin? Bart and I sat down and tried to figure out some of our favorite features of *Microsoft Flight Simulator 98*.

Doug:

Hardware acceleration. Wow. With an add-on 3D accelerator card such as the Diamond Monster 3D, *Flight Simulator 98* becomes a whole new game. The graphics and textures are much smoother, the frame rate speeds up tremendously, and transparent effects such as clouds and mist become enabled. All of the screen shots in this book were taken *without* the benefit of hardware acceleration, so if you think these graphics are good, you have got to get yourself a 3D card to see them look even better. Trust us, it's worth it. See Chapter 5 for details on setting up hardware acceleration.

If you like a challenge, the helicopter is for you. I have had more fun flying the brand-new Bell 206B JetRanger III helicopter than any of the other aircraft. It's difficult to learn, but immensely rewarding to master. I like to take the helicopter on early morning jaunts across New York City, hopping from building to building. I also like to start out on the very edge of the World Trade Center helipad, then base jump from the top of the tower, kill the engine, and autorotate to a landing. Check out Chapter 6 for everything you need to know to become a chopper pilot.

Another favorite feature of mine is the Land Me feature, which automatically hands the controls over to the computer to land the plane. Besides being very handy while you're learning, it can be great fun when used as an instrument of torment for the computer instructor. Press ⓧ to activate Land Me when you are near an airport that supports this feature, like Meigs Field. You can also use the new auto-throttle feature in the 737, in conjunction with the autopilot, to land the plane automatically! See Chapter 5 and Appendix A for details.

Finally, I have had lots of fun with the carrier landings at different levels, especially the Mastery landings using a crosswind. I always liked to imagine I was a fighter pilot, until I found out just how difficult it is to land on a carrier deck and walk away in one piece! Check out my tips in Chapter 5 on solving the Carrier Challenges.

Bart:

You know, to me there's nothing quite like pulling a 737 through a loop without crashing it into a thousand pieces. In fact, activating the "Crash and Damage from Stress" realism can make for some interesting moments in the 737. I like to make everything as realistic as possible, then see if I can fly in between the World Trade Centers or land on a short strip like Meigs Field.

The other great feature is the ability to make your aircraft unreliable. If you're looking for some fun, set the reliability to "unreliable," then take one of the jets up for a spin. Undoubtedly you'll have at least one system fail while you're in flight, and this can stretch your piloting capabilities to the max.

Finally, I think some of the most entertaining things in *Flight Simulator* involve the impossible. That's the beauty of a program like this: if you want to land a 737 on a carrier, you can try (and fail). Likewise, if you want to fly under the Golden Gate Bridge in a Learjet, you can! I recommend experimenting with all the permutations and combinations a great simulation like this affords you. Enjoy!

CHAPTER
2

Flight Student

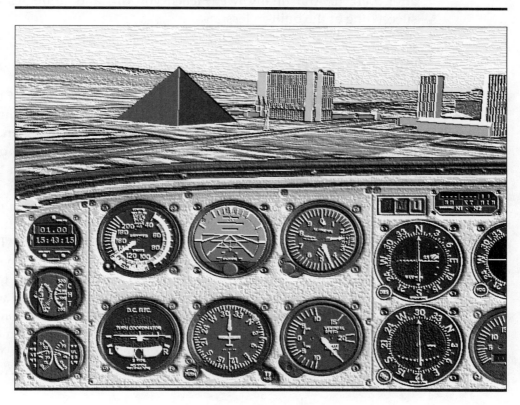

The best way to learn how to fly is to get up in the air and start flying. Even if you crash, you can look at the flight analysis graph and learn what not to do next time. That's one advantage Microsoft Flight Simulator 98 has over real life. In this section, you will take an introductory flight to get a feel for what it's like to fly an airplane. Next, we'll show you what's really going on behind the scenes: What actually keeps an airplane up in the air, anyway? And what are all those dials and gauges for? You'll learn the finer points of landing an airplane and walking away from the pieces after a crash. And finally, we'll teach you tips and strategies for succeeding at the built-in lessons.

WELCOME TO VEGAS!

After escaping the crowds and journalists at the front door of the casino, you slip into a waiting limousine and travel at breakneck speed to an airfield on the edge of town, casting nervous glances back over your shoulder the entire way. After all, it isn't every day that somebody walks into a Vegas casino and leaves with the largest jackpot in casino history. Everyone knows your face now, all sorts of people you don't recognize are claiming to be your old friends and relatives, and at any moment, the IRS will start sniffing around; you realize you aren't going to get a minute's peace. The sooner you can get out of Las Vegas and into the air with your new-found wealth, the happier you will be. You have succumbed to a longtime dream—to fly an airplane. In just a few minutes, you will get that chance. The flight instructor opens the gate and welcomes you in. You peer around some oil drums and gaze upon your most recent purchase: a shiny new Cessna Skylane, fueled up and ready to carry you out of the desert and into a world of new horizons. . . .

Setting Everything Up

Although it's early, you might want to make sure the machine is properly configured for 3D graphics if you have a 3D card. Well, we're just trying to keep this interesting. Let's get into the air and see what this thing can do. Start up Microsoft Flight Simulator 98, if you haven't done so already, and click the "Fly Now" button at the main menu to place yourself in Chicago, where all adventures begin (well, Flight Simulator ones, anyway). Before we start off on our maiden voyage, let's configure the controls in Flight Simulator to operate correctly.

If you're using a joystick, flight yoke, or rudders, make sure you have configured them properly in the Windows 95 Game Controllers control panel. From the Aircraft menu, choose Select Aircraft. Choose the Cessna Skylane 182S and click OK to close this box.

Next, go to the Aircraft menu and choose "Aircraft Settings." At the top of the realism window you will see a slide bar entitled Flight Realism; this controls how difficult flying the plane will be. In Flight Simulator, the Cessna's flight model is really quite accurate and realistic, so why not experience it more fully? Move the bar from "Easy" to somewhere in the middle. It's always a good idea to start flying using a more difficult flight model because if

If you're getting tired of seeing the Microsoft movie every time you start up, you can get rid of it by deleting the file called MSLOGO.AVI in the *Flight Simulator* directory, or by adding the line ShowLogo=0 in the "MAIN" section of your FLTSIM98.CFG file.

Figure 2-1 Clicking the Fly Now button takes you immediately to your default flight.

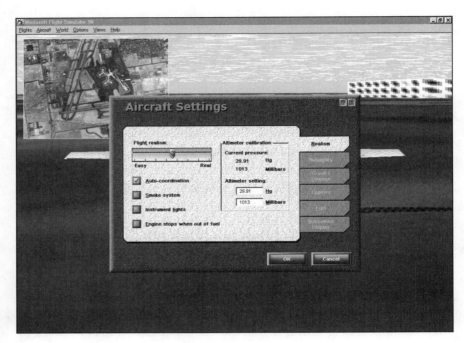

Figure 2-2 Set the flight control to medium.

you learn to fly on an unrealistically simple setting, it's easy to pick up bad habits that are hard to unlearn. Besides, Flight Simulator offers many other features that make it easier to fly, such as an automatic landing option and an indestructible plane. We'll show you those features while you're learning to fly. Click OK to close this box.

Go to the Options menu and choose "Preferences." Click on the Display Tab. Click the Display Options button. Make sure that "See own aircraft from cockpit" is checked. Close the Preferences box.

Getting to Vegas

Now, to set the stage. First, we'll place your Cessna in Las Vegas. Choose "Go to…" and "Airport" from the submenu. You will see a list of all the airports in the Flight Simulator world. You can narrow down your search by choosing North America from the Global Region menu, then United States from the Country menu, and finally, Las Vegas from the City menu. This gives you a list of the airports in that city. Click on McCarran Intl, and select Runway 7L from the list of runways. When you click OK, you will be transported to that dusty runway in the desert.

Pull down the World menu. Choose the Airport/Facilities directory. This is a listing of every airport that Flight Simulator supports—over three thousand of them around the world. You used to have to get all of this information from a separate table. Now it's all available online. Neat, huh? Click USA, then choose Nevada, in the Southwest region of the United States. Scroll down the list of airports until you find Las Vegas, NV – McCarran Intl.

In this listing you will find tons of useful information, such as radio frequencies (ATIS), latitude and longitude, and runway information. You'll also see an identification code listed for every airport, so if your lost luggage ever comes back stamped VGT, you'll know it went to Vegas without you. We're most interested in the latitude and longitude information, however, because if you type those exact coordinates into the Set Exact Location dialog box under the World menu, that's exactly where you'll go. Before you close this box, notice the buttons in the upper right corner. Clicking the Navaids button will show you additional information about these airports, such as VOR and NDB frequencies, which are important for navigation. Not all airports will have the newest navigation equipment, so it's important to plan ahead by consulting the chart.

Okay, close the Airport/Facilities directory, and go to the World menu. We need to do a few more things before we take off. Go to the World menu and choose "Time & Season." Select Day as the time of day. Click OK. If you have a faster computer, you may want to increase the scenery complexity. Go to the World menu and choose Scenery Complexity. From the Image Complexity pulldown menu, choose anything from Normal to Very Dense. Click OK. Next, go to the World menu and choose Dynamic Scenery. This controls the number of other objects whizzing around in the air. Turn on as many as you dare, and change the Scenery Frequency to anything from Normal to Very Dense, depending on the speed of your system. If things seem too slow, you can always turn some of these options off or reduce the image density. Click OK. Whew, that was a lot of work. Choose Save Flight from the Flight menu, call it Vegas Test Drive, and click OK. Now, if anything happens to you, you can always choose Select Flight from the Flights menu and refly this scenario with all your options intact.

The Preflight Check

Now, let's preflight this baby and get it off the ground. First of all, take a look at the instrument panel. You should see two rows of dials in the center panel. Let me introduce them to you. On the top row, from left to right, you have the airspeed indicator, the attitude indicator, and the altimeter. In the second row, from left to right, meet the turn coordinator, the heading indicator, and the vertical speed indicator, or VSI. These are your six primary instruments, and you will find them on just about any aircraft. They are indispensable. Learn to use them as much as you use your eyes and ears. The instrument names pop up, and you can also right-click Help for name information. The other two dials are used for navigation and for monitoring the status of the different systems

Figure 2-3 You can use the different views to look around your aircraft.

Video: Airplane Flight Controls

Location: Flight School → Ground School → Aerodynamics → The Axes of Flight

of the airplane. For this introductory flight, you should be fine as long as you pay attention to the airspeed indicator, the altimeter, and the VSI. We'll get to the other instruments, and explain them in more detail, after your first flight.

Above your instrument panel you should be able to see out the front of the plane. You can also look out the different windows if you want a different view. Let's look out the left window. Press Shift-4 on the keypad. The "Hat" switch on many joysticks change views, too. You should see your left wing. Get in the habit of using the different views to look around. On some lessons, for example, the instructor will tell you to "clear final" and start your turn, which basically means to look in the direction of your turn before you actually put your plane in that airspace. Press Shift-8 to return to the front view. Take another look at your instrument panel. Between your attitude indicator and your altimeter, you can see the aileron, rudder, and elevator indicators. Try moving the yoke left and right to move the ailerons. The indicator should move accordingly. (If you don't see this, go to the Options menu, choose Preferences, and find out which Controls are selected.) Pull back on the yoke, and you're working the elevators. Look out the rear window by hitting Shift-2 and you can see the tail, where the rudder is located. Try holding down the shift key and pressing all the keypad keys clockwise from Shift-8 to get a 360° view from your plane. Shift-5 lets you look straight down.

How to Look Around

To look Straight Ahead, press Shift-8

To look Right Front, press Shift-9

To look Right, press Shift-6

To look Right Rear, press (Shift)-(3)

To look Rear, press (Shift)-(2)

To look Left Rear, press (Shift)-(1)

To look Left, press (Shift)-(4)

To look Left Front, press (Shift)-(7)

To look Straight Down, press (Shift)-(5)

The Spot Plane View

Let's try taxiing around the runway to get a feel for how the aircraft handles on the ground. Normally, the control tower may tell you to taxi to a particular runway for takeoff, or even to wait in line for takeoff clearance. Today, you own the whole airport, so let's take our time and look around.

Go to the Views menu and choose View Options. Click on the Spot Plane button. In the View Options screen, drag the end of the red line to the back of the plane, just behind the tail. Deselect the "Gradual transition" option. Click OK. The spot plane is an imaginary plane that constantly follows you at a specified distance and altitude. Think of it as your own personal movie camera. It's much easier to maneuver on the taxiways from the spot plane view, so use this view when you're lining yourself up for takeoff. If the spot plane view doesn't show itself when you close the View Options box, hit (S) three times to see your plane from the back.

As part of our preflight check, let's make sure the flaps are working. Press (F7) to extend the flaps 10°. You should be able to see the flaps working (look toward the rear of the wing). Now, let's check out the rudder and yoke. Try moving the yoke left and right to move the ailerons. You should see the ailerons moving up and down on the trailing edge of the wing. (If you don't see this, go to the Options menu, choose Preferences, and find out which Controls are selected.) Pull back on the yoke to work the elevators on the tail. Look on the vertical stabilizer and you can see the rudder move when you press (0) and (Enter). Press (.) to disengage the parking brakes and increase throttle about 10 percent, until you start to move. Use the yoke to steer yourself back and forth, and

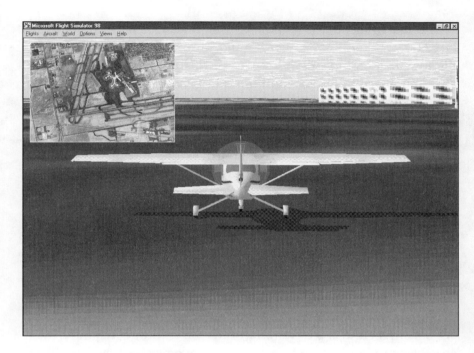

Figure 2-4 The map view makes it easier to find your way while on the taxiway.

control your speed with the throttle. Take a look at the entire airport. See if you can find the refueling area, which is a big yellow F surrounded by a square. Try to stay on the taxiway or the runway, but don't worry too much about veering off; the whole state is practically one big runway, after all. When you want to return to the cockpit view, hit Ⓢ again.

Takeoff!

Now it's time to take off. Get yourself to one end of the runway and face the right direction (that's with the long part in front of you). Press ⟨.⟩ to release the parking brakes. Make sure you're pointed down the center of the runway. If not, increase the throttle to about 20 RPM and steer with the yoke until you are centered. Make sure your flaps are extended 10°, then increase the throttle to full. As the plane builds up speed, make small corrections with the yoke to keep the aircraft pointed down the runway centerline. Add a little back pressure; otherwise the airplane accelerates past

If you hear a beep-
ing sound and see
the letters O, M, or
I light up, don't
worry. The naviga-
tion system alerts
you when you are a
fixed distance from
the airport. It took
me several panic-
stricken flights to
figure out what
that alarm was!

sound takeoff speed. When the Cessna reaches takeoff speed (usually 60 to 70 knots), the nose should lift off the runway, and your
plane will rise gracefully in the air. If this doesn't happen for you,
and you are getting close to the end of the runway (for example,
you can read the numbers on the other end and see mice hiding in
the grass), then pull gently back on the yoke to lift off.

Stay on a nice gentle climb. Keep your nose up slightly, and
climb at about 80 knots. After you pass the end of the runway,
retract your flaps. This reduces drag and helps your plane present
a more streamlined shape to the relative wind. Notice that your
airspeed rises. Reduce the throttle a little bit. Congratulations—
you're flying!

You should continue to climb until you reach an altitude of
2,000 feet. We're going to practice flying straight and level right
now. Try changing the pitch of the nose to keep the needle on the
VSI near zero. Try to maintain an altitude of 2,000 feet. Make
small, smooth corrections to your flight path. The airplane controls
are sensitive, and it's easy to fall into the trap of constantly overcorrecting up and down to match the movements of the VSI. Pilots
call this "chasing the needle." Make a correction first, then wait to
see if the needle settles down. It's better to make a series of small
corrections rather than overcorrecting and having to swing back
the other way.

Pitch Controls Your Airspeed, Throttle Controls Your Altitude

Once you've gotten the hang of flying straight and level, try
pitching the nose up above the horizon by pulling back on the
yoke. Notice what happens to your airspeed. Now, pitch the nose
below the horizon. Watch your airspeed climb back up. In an airplane, your pitch is the primary control of your airspeed. Now,
return to straight and level flight again. This time, keep your
pitch the same, and reduce the throttle to 1,500 RPM. Watch what
happens to your altitude. Pitch the nose up slightly to maintain a
constant altitude, then increase the throttle to 2,500 RPM. What
happens to your altitude? The throttle is your primary control of

altitude. If you increase the throttle, you will ascend. Decrease the throttle, and you descend. This is much more evident when you're maneuvering at minimum airspeeds, such as when you are trying to land the plane. Knowing how to make adjustments in the pitch and the throttle to maintain a steady descent rate is the key to controlling your aircraft.

Tired of flying straight and level? Let's try some turns. The standard rate of turn is shown on the turn coordinator. Take a look at the artificial horizon. At the top of the ball is a little white triangle. Directly above the triangle is a series of white marks in 10° increments. When the horizon is level, the triangle is centered. As you turn, the white marks move above the triangle indicating your degree of turn. Try a 20° left bank. You must refer to the turn coordinator to set a standard rate turn. In a turn, you generally need to pull back slightly on the yoke in order to maintain a consistent altitude. Notice how your heading changes on the compass as you turn. Try to stop at 90°. If you overshoot, turn back the other way and try leveling out from the turn a little early. Try to time it so that you stop at exactly 90°. As you turn the yoke, look at the control indicators and notice how the rudder and ailerons are coordinated. Now swing back the other way and try a banking turn in the other direction. If you feel adventurous, try steeper turns while attempting to maintain your altitude.

If you like, fly into downtown Las Vegas and check out all of the casinos. If you get close enough (and you have Detailed Scenery turned on in the Preferences), you can actually read the names of the hotels! Can you find the hotel where Siegfried and Roy are playing? There are also a couple of well-known musical groups playing in town . . . can you find out who they are? How about the Luxor Pyramid? Don't forget to reduce your throttle to about 75 percent, and watch your altitude—don't crash into anything! When you get near McCarran Airport again, choose "Land Me" from the Aircraft menu and have the instructor land the plane for you. We'll get to landings next time; you've already done quite a lot for this introductory flight! Watch the instructor carefully, particularly how he lines the aircraft up to land on the runway. You'll have to do this soon!

Figure 2-5 Buzzing the Luxor Pyramid

EVERYTHING YOU ALWAYS WANTED TO KNOW ABOUT FLIGHT BUT WERE TOO BUSY FLYING TO ASK

"My observations have since only convinced me more firmly that human flight is possible and practicable. It is only a question of knowledge and skill just as in all acrobatic feats."

—Wilbur Wright, 1899

The Wright Stuff

OK, now that you've had a taste of what it's like to fly a Cessna, let's find out a little about what's going on behind the scenes . . . or above the wings, in this case.

Not Everything That Goes Up In the Air Is Flying

Many different things go up in the air. Some glide, some float, some are pushed. In 1783 the Montgolfier brothers constructed the world's first hot-air balloon and demonstrated it before the prestigious Academy of Sciences in Paris. Their balloon, which floated for eight minutes over a distance of nearly two miles, was the first manned flight. Today's space shuttle, on the other hand, is pushed by rockets into orbit, and when it reenters the atmosphere it glides to a landing.

But how do things actually fly? An engine may get a plane moving, but in fact it's air pressure that keeps it in the air. Air has pressure—14.7 pounds per square inch at sea level. That means that on the top of your head, air exerts a pressure of nearly 800 pounds. On the wing of a four-hundred-ton jumbo jet there is a pressure of 350,000 pounds on both the top and the bottom surfaces.

However, air pressure is virtually the same on all sides of an object at rest. Because of this, the forces of pressure are balanced and we do not feel them in any direction. But if some of the pressure on top of an object (such as an airplane wing) could be lessened while the air pressure on the bottom surface remained the same, the greater pressure on the bottom would eventually be enough to counteract the force of gravity and lift that object in the air. This is flight, and as I'll explain further below, lift is accomplished by the shape of the wing and the speed of the plane.

So, from this definition we can say that anything that uses a difference in air pressure to gain lift is flying. A rocket may go up in the air, but it is not "flying" any more than a rock is "flying" when thrown. Thrust in a vertical direction, whether generated by engines or by the motion of your throwing arm, does not generate lift; for that, something is needed to cause a difference in pressure. It wasn't until the Wright brothers put thrust, wings, and a control method together that the world's first airplane flew at Kitty Hawk, North Carolina, in 1903.

The Four Forces of Flight

Besides the force of lift, however, there are three other forces acting on an object in the air—gravity, thrust, and drag. So an

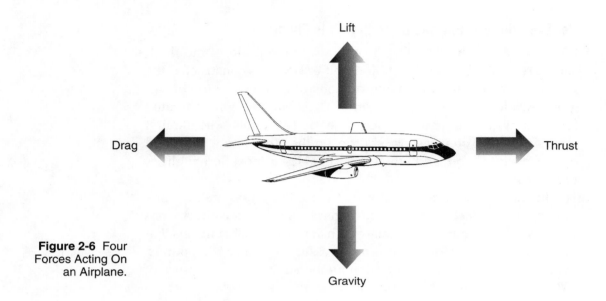

Figure 2-6 Four Forces Acting On an Airplane.

airplane has a force acting in each of four directions—up (lift), down (gravity), forward (thrust), and backward (drag).

Total drag includes induced drag, a byproduct of lift. Drag is caused by friction of the air over the skin of an airplane, and thrust is usually supplied by an engine. When an airplane is flying straight and level, the opposing forces are balanced. Lift equals weight; thrust equals drag. There is enough thrust to both overcome the drag and produce enough airspeed to create enough lift to counteract gravity. However, lift is the force directly responsible for flight.

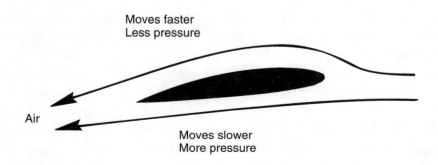

Figure 2-7 As air flows over an airfoil, faster air on top has less pressure.

Video: How a Wing Works

Location: Flight School → Ground School → Aerodynamics → How Wings Work

Wings and Things

Every wing has a curved surface. This shape is known as an airfoil. Lift is created as the wing moves through the air. As the airstream moves over the curved surface of the wing, it speeds up, causing a lower pressure than that on the bottom of the wing. The force resulting from this difference in pressure is lift. This is partially explained by the Bernoulli Principle, formulated by a Swiss mathematician named Daniel Bernoulli (1700–1782). Bernoulli observed that fluids in pipes accelerated as they went around bends, and as they did so they exerted less pressure on the sides of the pipe. On an airfoil, because the air passing over the curved top surface of the wing is traveling faster than the air underneath the wing, it exerts less pressure on the top surface.

An airplane's wings generate additional lift by deflecting air downward. The angle at which an airplane's wings meet the oncoming air is called the angle of attack. As the air hits the bottom of the wing it is deflected downward, resulting in a "push" upward. This is explained by Newton's First Law of Motion, which states that for every action there is an equal and opposite reaction. You have probably felt this "push" yourself if you have ever stuck your hand out of a car window: hold your hand parallel to the road, and nothing happens; increase the angle of attack, and you'll feel lift. This also explains why balsa wood gliders with flat wings can still fly if thrown at an angle. When you extend the flaps in the Cessna, they actually angle downward from the rear edge of the wing and deflect more air down, giving you an added amount of "push" to compensate for a reduced airspeed or greater rate of descent.

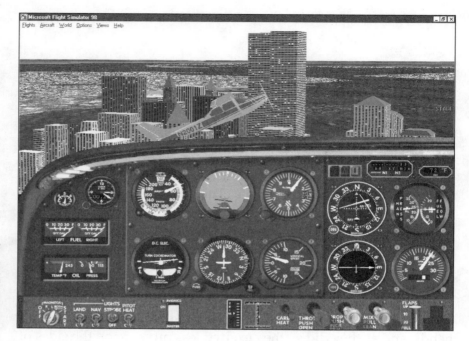

Figure 2-8 Shortly after this Cessna demonstrated its critical angle of attack, it was being salvaged for scrap metal.

The greater the angle of attack, the more lift that's created—to a point. If a wing is tilted too much, the air passing over the top of the wing begins to separate from the surface, creating turbulence and destroying the lift. This condition is known as a stall.

The amount of lift a wing generates depends on several factors—the speed of the airplane, the angle of attack, the shape of the wing, and the surface area of the wing. In the next sections of this book, you will learn how to constantly shift the balance between these factors as conditions change to achieve the most efficient and effective lift possible.

Pitch

The elevator controls your pitch. Pitch refers to the angle of the airplane's nose to the horizon. You pitch the nose of the aircraft up by pulling back on the control yoke. You pitch the nose down by pushing forward on the yoke. When the nose is pitched down, the aircraft's speed increases. When the nose is pitched up, the

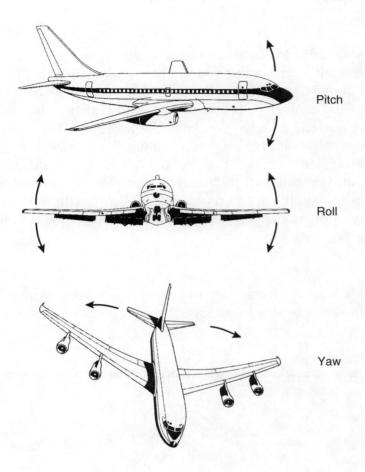

Figure 2-9 The three basic components of airplane movement.

aircraft's speed decreases. See how complicated this gets? You'll hear a lot more about pitching too high when we discuss stalls, but for now remember that you control the aircraft's speed primarily by changing the aircraft's pitch relative to the horizon. Pitch the nose down to pick up more airspeed if you're going too slowly.

Video: The Horizontal Component of Lift

Location: Flight School → Ground School → Aerodynamics → Turns

Roll

The ailerons control your roll, or bank angle. When you turn the yoke to the left or the right, you are causing the aircraft to roll. From the outside, when you roll left, the left wing dips down and the right wing comes up. The direction of lift is perpendicular to the wing's surface, so when you bank the wing, you are decreasing the amount of vertical lift you're getting. The horizontal component of lift is what makes the airplane turn. If your bank angle is too great, you can stall the plane. Consequently, in a normal banking turn, you'll want to coordinate your roll with the elevator and the rudders to maintain your altitude and give you a nice, smooth turn.

Yaw

The rudder is used primarily to overcome yaw effects caused by engine, propeller, or slipstream. Technically, yaw is rotation about

Figure 2-10 How to lose your license by buzzing the Statue of Liberty.

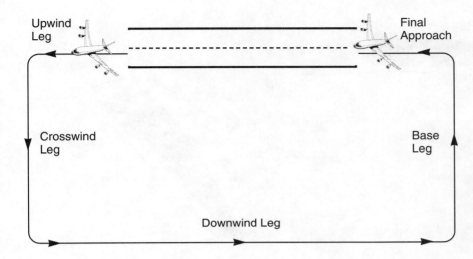

Upwind Leg

Final Approach

Crosswind Leg

Base Leg

Figure 2-11 The landing pattern is a pattern that all airplanes fly when approaching an airport.

Downwind Leg

the plane's vertical axis. In practice, you'll need to learn how to use the rudder to coordinate your turns and to come in for a landing approach in a crosswind. If you've ever seen a plane fly sideways, the pilot was using the rudder opposite the ailerons to keep the plane on a constant heading.

A Little about Stalls

A stall, in general, is a bad thing. It occurs when the wings are no longer providing lift, and without lift, the plane falls. The wing's curved shape allows air to flow smoothly along its top surface, but if the angle of attack becomes too large, this property is destroyed. The air begins to separate from the surface of the wing, creating turbulence and disrupting the smooth airflow, and this destroys lift. This condition is known as a stall.

Video: Stalling an airplane's wing

Location: Flight School → Ground School → Aerodynamics
→ Stalls

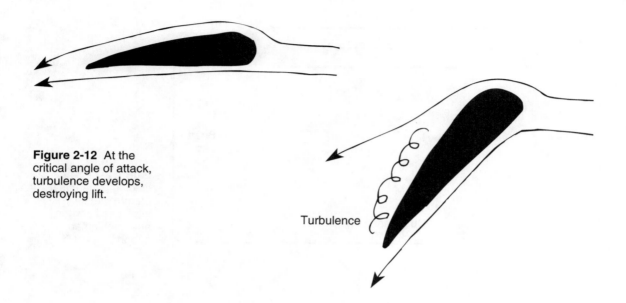

Figure 2-12 At the critical angle of attack, turbulence develops, destroying lift.

Turbulence

Any wing will stall, regardless of how fast or how slow you're going. Every wing has a critical angle of attack. When you exceed this angle, you will stall, but depending on your altitude or situation, this condition won't be fatal and may even be desired. You can recover from a stall if you have enough altitude. Stalling on takeoff or while descending on a landing approach could prove disastrous. But if you're making a picture-perfect landing, you intentionally stall the plane just as it touches the ground. In that case, stalling at just the right moment is ideal. In the next section, you will become very familiar with the stall point of the Cessna by learning how to intentionally stall your aircraft, how to recover from a stall, and how to land the aircraft low and slow and silky smooth—using your new best friend, the stall. . . .

An Introduction to the Cessna Cockpit

Climbing into the cockpit as a new pilot, you are confronted with banks and rows of dials, instruments, and gauges. While this sight can be initially overwhelming, soon you will become very familiar with these instruments and learn what each one does in which situations. For now, though, I'll give you a brief description of each one and let you know when they come in handy. Certain instruments, like the altimeter, are absolutely necessary for each and every flight. Others, like the manifold pressure gauge, you may never have to worry about unless you want everything to be absolutely realistic. Some instruments will be covered in much greater detail later on. If you start to get lost with all the acronyms, refer to the chart of acronyms in this section.

Are You Normal?

Compass headings can get confusing once you start getting into more advanced navigation, so let's clear up some basic aeronautical issues right away. First of all, pilots are not normal people. They love to spend their time in a little aluminum cabin thousands of feet above solid ground, so right away their judgment should be suspect. Second, when explaining how to get somewhere, they use a complicated lingo of phonetic alphabets and numerical information. As you learn Flight Simulator, you will not only begin to understand and speak this language, you will learn to find your way around as a pilot does, and sooner or later you might even enjoy the prospect of sailing through the sky far above the earth.

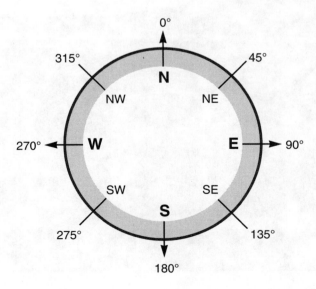

Figure 2-13
360° of movement

TIP

To find out the name of a particular instrument, position the mouse cursor over it and in a few seconds a label will appear. To find out more information, click the right mouse button and choose "What's this?"

A Few Words about Basic Navigation

With that warning out of the way, here are a few words about how pilots find their way. Where we might refer to directions using north, east, south, and west, pilots use numerical headings. The compass on your instrument panel shows 360°, which correspond numerically to the words normal people use. A heading of 0° means you are heading due north. A heading of 90° means you are heading due east. 45° is northeast. Being able to recognize that a heading of, say, 270° is due west will help you greatly when it comes to navigating using nothing more than a map and your wits (OK, for some of us, using just a map).

We might use traffic lights, stores, and other neighborhood landmarks in order to give someone directions. Pilots take a similar approach. Perhaps it isn't quite the same as "head west until you see the mountains, turn left at the second cactus, turn right at the pond, and you're there," but pilots do look for specific landmarks when using a chart and compass. This tells them whether or not they are still on course. Pilots call this form of navigation pilotage. It's a valuable skill to learn.

Figure 2-14 The Instrument Panel On a Cessna

There are two banks of instruments on the Cessna. The left side contains all the dials, and the right side contains numerical displays, for the most part. Let's take a look at these instruments in detail.

The Ones with Dials

Airspeed Indicator

The airspeed indicator is marked off in knots. The green arc indicates safe operating airspeed for the Cessna. If the needle goes into the yellow or red zone, you are in danger of overstressing the aircraft. If the "Aircraft receives damage from stress" option is checked in the Preferences dialog, the plane will literally fly apart if you go too fast. Try it sometime—it's a blast. Don't extend your flaps outside of the first white arc. The Cessna can display true airspeed or indicated airspeed. True airspeed corrects for air density at altitude, indicated airspeed doesn't. Pilots use indicated air speed.

Video: The Attitude Indicator

Location: Flight School → Ground School → Flight Instruments → Gyro Instruments → Attitude Indicator

Attitude Indicator

The attitude indicator, also called the artificial horizon, is a ball that rolls as you bank the wings and raise or lower the nose. It indicates your bank and pitch angles relative to the horizon. In conditions under which you cannot see the actual horizon, such as a night approach, the artificial horizon is your best friend. If you ever feel yourself disoriented (such as during a stall), get in the habit of checking the attitude indicator immediately to get your bearings. The white lines around the circumference indicate bank angles of 10°, 20°, 30°, 60°, and 90°, respectively. The black lines in the center of the ball indicate your attitude, or pitch angle, and are marked off in 10° increments.

Altimeter

The Flight Simulator altimeter is marked off in thousands of feet. By reading the long hand, you can get a reading accurate to one hundred feet. As an example, the altimeter in this figure indicates an altitude of almost 2,740 feet. It is important to remember that the altimeter indicates your altitude above sea level (MSL, or mean sea level), not above ground level (AGL). This means that you need to pay attention to the elevation of the runway where you're landing. In Denver, Colorado, for example, by the time your altimeter reads 5,000 feet, you're already on the ground (or buried in it!).

VOR Indicator 1 (OBI 1)

The VOR indicator, or OBI, is used with your radio to establish your position relative to a station broadcasting at a certain frequency. It is crucial for long-distance navigation. The horizontal needle centers when you are on the glide slope, and the vertical needle centers when you are on the proper course. Press V, 1, and the + or − key to adjust the setting.

VOR Indicator 2 (OBI 2)

This is your second OBI, or omnibearing indicator. You can tune each OBI to a different frequency and find your position along your flight path. When you are traveling toward a station (TO), the white triangle points up. When you are traveling away from a station (FROM), the white triangle points down. Press V, 2, and the + or − key to adjust the setting. The Cessna Skylane RG has only one VOR indicator.

Video: Turn Coordinator

Location: Flight School → Ground School → Flight Instruments → Gyro Instruments → Turn Coordinator

Turn Coordinator

The turn coordinator indicates the roll rate of the aircraft. It also shows the rate of turn and quality of turn. There are marks on the left and right side of the turn coordinator that indicate the rate of a turn. You will probably find the turn coordinator most useful, however, as an indicator of whether you are skidding or slipping through a turn. When you turn off autocoordination in the Aircraft Settings dialog, the ailerons and the rudder move independently of one another. The little ball at the bottom of the turn coordinator should stay in the center of the tube during a turn if the rudders and ailerons are coordinated with each other. Unlike the attitude indicator, the turn coordinator does not indicate pitch.

Heading Indicator

This instrument indicates your heading when it's properly set. You calibrate the heading indicator using your magnetic compass by pressing D. By clicking the right knob you can move the red mark, or heading "bug," to mark a desired heading.

Vertical Speed Indicator (VSI)

The vertical speed indicator is marked off in hundreds of feet per minute and indicates your rate of climb or descent. When the needle is pointing to zero, you are neither gaining nor losing altitude. When the needle falls below the zero and points to the number five, you are descending at a rate of 500 feet per minute. Sometimes the needle takes a few seconds to catch up to what you're doing, so make gentle corrections and don't "chase the needle."

Automatic Direction Finder (ADF)

A nondirectional beacon, or NDB, transmits a signal that you tune in with your automatic direction finder, or ADF. The ADF needle always points in the direction of the NDB. To fly to an NDB signal, turn the aircraft until the needle is at zero, indicating the NDB is directly in front of you. The ADF simply displays the NDB's location in relation to your airplane. It does not directly indicate a magnetic heading like a compass does.

Lights

These switches indicate the status of strobe lights, running lights, and pitot heat. You should turn your lights on at night. You can turn all of these on by clicking the appropriate switch with the mouse. Turn on pitot heat when the outside temperature is near freezing and you're flying in clouds to ensure the airspeed indicator gives you an accurate reading. The left wing light is red, and the right wing light is green. At night, when you see a set of lights in front of you, if red is on the right, it means the plane is headed toward you!

The Cessna
Skylane 182S

Fuel Gauges

When you have selected the "Engine stops when out of fuel" option, you will have to refill your aircraft regularly or risk a long hike back to the airfield. In order to refuel, you will need to land your aircraft at an airport and drive around the taxiways until you find a big yellow box with an F in it. Drive into this box, and your fuel tanks will be refilled.

The Cessna Skylane
182R RG

When I was in high school, my biology teacher was an avid pilot and flew almost every weekend. When we started studying about vision, we were astonished to find out that he was color blind. How could he possibly have gotten a pilot's license allowing him to fly at night, if he couldn't distinguish between the red and green lights on the tips of the wings? It's simple, he explained to us. If you see a set of lights in front of you and they're getting closer together, no problem. If they're getting farther and farther apart, then you hurry up and get out of the way.

The fuel selector switch in the Aircraft Settings box indicates whether the engines are drawing fuel from the left tank, the right tank, or both. Make sure you check this switch when you're running low on gas. In one recent incident, an airplane ran out of fuel and crashed. An investigation found that the right tank was still full! The flight crew had missed setting this switch during their preflight check.

EGT/CHT Gauge

The left gauge monitors the exhaust gas temperature (EGT), which indicates the fuel/air mixture. In general, as you climb you should lean the mixture to provide the best fuel economy. The EGT is the primary control for adjusting the mixture. The CHT (cylinder head temperature) gauge helps you monitor engine temperature.

Manifold Pressure and Fuel Flow Gauge

The manifold pressure gauge indicates what power setting you have set with the throttle. The fuel flow reflects how much fuel is being sent to the engine, controlled by the throttle and mixture knobs.

Oil Temperature and Pressure Gauge

Watch the temperature and pressure gauge carefully to prevent overheating or damage to your engine. If either of the needles approaches the red, you should land at the nearest airport.

The Cessna Skylane
182R RG

The Cessna
Skylane 182S

Doug's Handy Comprehensive Chart of Acronyms (or DHCCoA)

ADF	Automatic Direction Finder
AGL	Above Ground Level
ALS	Approach Lighting System
AOA	Angle of Attack
ATC	Air Traffic Control
ATIS	Automatic Terminal Information Service
DME	Distance Measuring Equipment
EFIS/CFPD	Electronic Flight Instrument System/Command Flight Path Display
EGT	Exhaust Gas Temperature
GPS	Global Positioning System
GUMP	Gas, Undercarriage, Mixture, Propeller
IFR	Instrument Flight Rules (navigating using instruments)
ILS	Instrument Landing System
MBI	Magnetic Bearing Indicator
MSL	Mean Sea Level
NDB	Nondirectional Beacon
OBI	Omnibearing Indicator
VFR	Visual Flight Rules
VOR	Very-high-frequency Omnidirectional Range
VSI	Vertical Speed Indicator
XPDR	Transponder

The Ones with Numbers

The Bendix/King radio stack contains the displays for your radio communications, as well as the controls for the autopilot. You can show or hide the radio stack by clicking the master avionics switch at the bottom of the instrument panel, or you can select it from the Instrument Panel submenu under the Views menu.

COMM and NAV Displays

The COMM 1 display shows what frequencies your COMM radio is tuned to. When you're near an airport, you can receive useful information on weather conditions and approach information from the ATIS, or Air Traffic Information Service. You can find ATIS frequencies in the Airport/Facility directory under the World menu. You use the NAV 1 and NAV 2 radios to tune in VOR beacons. You then use the course selector knob in

your VOR Indicator, or OBI, to find out what your location is relative to that station. You'll find more information on VOR navigation in the Pilot's License section of this book.

OMI Display

This indicator displays a light for the outer, middle, and inner beacons that you encounter on an ILS approach to an airport. These beacons will sound a repeating tone as you pass over them and help you determine your position along the ILS and the DH.

DME Indicator

This display shows your distance in nautical miles from the station you have tuned in on NAV 1. It is very accurate and comes in handy when you're planning a landing approach (if there's a VORTAC or ILS–DME at the airport you're heading for). It also shows your ground speed and your estimated time of arrival in

The DME display located on the instrument panel

minutes if you're heading directly to or from a VORTAC. The display on the instrument panel itself can be impossible to read on all but the highest resolution settings. A switch on both displays allows you to switch between NAV 1 and NAV 2.

The DME display located on the Bendix/King radio stack

TIP

On real transpon-
ders, certain
emergency codes
will set off alarms
at the radar
facility. 7500 is
the code for a
hijacking. 7700 is
the code for an
emergency. 7777 is
the code used for
military interceptor
operations.

ADF Display

This allows you to tune your automatic direction finder, or ADF radio. Watch the ADF indicator to home in on an ADF signal.

Transponder Display

In the same way that Christmas becomes Xmas when you don't have enough space left on the card, XPDR stands for transponder. When you request clearance for takeoff, the tower will tell you to "squawk 0123" or some other four-digit number. When you tune this into your transponder, your aircraft will transmit this signal, which tells air traffic controllers information about your plane. In Flight Simulator, entering the code into the transponder doesn't really do anything. Set it to your birthday, if you like.

Autopilot

The autopilot can maintain heading, altitude, or follow a VOR radial or ILS localizer and glideslope. To control the autopilot, click the AP switch in the lower left, or press Z to turn it on.

Autopilot Setting	Keystroke
Wing Leveler (LVL)	Ctrl-V
Altitude Hold	Ctrl-Z
Heading Hold	Ctrl-H
Attitude Hold	Ctrl-T
NAV 1 Hold	Ctrl-N
ILS Lock (APP)	Ctrl-A
Localizer Lock	Ctrl-O
Back Course Lock	Ctrl-B
Yaw Damper on/off	Ctrl-D
Airspeed Hold	Ctrl-R
Arm Autothrottle	Shift-R
Set Takeoff power/go-around	Ctrl-Shift-V

Compass

You can show the compass from the Views menu by choosing "Instrument Panel" and "Compass." The compass shows what direction your airplane is facing. Note that depending on the winds, the direction you are facing may not be the direction you are traveling! Make sure to keep an eye on the compass as you turn, and start leveling the plane out when you are 10° from your desired heading. Note that this shows your magnetic heading. Variation can cause a large difference between a magnetic compass heading and a true heading.

Temperature Gauge

This displays the outside air temperature. Cold weather or hot, excessively humid temperatures will cause your plane to handle

differently. Learn how the aircraft handles under various weather conditions. Icing on the wings of the aircraft disrupts the airflow and the wing's ability to provide lift. My own personal method for preventing ice buildup is to fly in the Caribbean or Hawaii. Watch your problems melt away.

Throttle Control, Propeller Pitch, Mixture Control

These three knobs help you control how efficiently your engine is working. The throttle knob allows you to set your throttle. Check the manifold pressure

indicator to get an idea for how much throttle to set. To control the throttle using the keyboard, you use the F1 through F4 keys. F1 cuts the throttle, F2 or keypad 3 decreases the throttle, F3 or keypad 9 increases the throttle, and F4 sets it to full. Next to the throttle control are two other sliders that change the pitch of the propeller and the fuel mixture. Pushing the prop knob in will decrease the pitch angle of the blades and set highter RPM, giving them more "bite" and pulling the prop knob will increase the blades' pitch and decrease RPM. You might use this while cruising at high altitudes. For takeoffs or landings, you should decrease the propeller pitch, thereby increasing manifold pressure. The mixture control allows you to maximize fuel economy.

RPM Indicator

This shows how much you're revving the engine, in revolutions per minute. During flight lessons, if your instructor tells you to set the throttle at 2,400 RPM, this is where you want to look as you increase or decrease the throttle. Normal Cessna cruising RPM is 2,100 to 2,400 RPM.

Landing Gear Indicator

The Cessna Skylane RG is equipped with retractable landing gear. Press G to toggle the landing gear. Three green lights mean that your gear is down. After takeoff, once you see that there isn't enough runway to make an emergency landing if your engine quits on you, you can go ahead and raise the landing gear. This provides less air resistance and will make it easier to gain altitude. On the way back, landing after forgetting to lower your gear again is very embarrassing, and it can stick you with a huge repair bill. Check this indicator as part of your normal takeoff and landing procedure. If the gear is stuck, hit Ctrl-G to pump the gear down.

Flaps Indicator

This indicator displays how many degrees of flaps are extended. Each time you press F7, you extend your flaps by 10°, up to 30°. You can also click the corresponding mark on the indicator. When your flaps are extended, you can take off at a lower airspeed, and when you are landing, your flaps allow you to descend at a steeper angle without building up too much speed.

Magnetos

Magnetos provide the electrical energy to the spark plugs.

Suction Gauge

The gyroscopic heading indicator and the attitude indicators both use a vacuum pump which provides the force that drives the gyros. When the vacuum pump is operating within normal limits, the needle will be in the green area. Check this indicator if your instruments are acting up, or if you no longer hear that giant sucking sound.

Clock and Simulation Rate

Yes, the clock tells you what time it is. But that's not all. When you change the time to midnight, the sun actually disappears and it gets pitch black outside. That's some clock! To change the time, you need to go to the World menu and choose "Time & Season." The numbers behind the clock hands represent the simulation rate. To make time go faster, click the numbers to increase them. This comes in handy on long flights.

EVERYBODY SING AFTER ME: WE'RE GOING TO JAMAICA . . .

One of my favorite features of Flight Simulator is the number of airports all over the world. So why restrict your flight training to the same airfield day in and day out? Never let anyone say your flight instructor didn't let you have any fun. For your first landing flight, we're going to Jamaica. Grab your sunglasses and sandals, and let's go!

Booking Your Tropical Vacation

1. First, go to the Aircraft menu and choose "Select aircraft."
2. Choose the Cessna Skylane 182S from the dialog box. Press OK to close this box.
3. Go to the Aircraft menu and choose "Aircraft Settings." Set the flight control to halfway between easy and real. Turn auto-coordination on. Click OK to close this box.
4. Go to the World menu and choose "Go to..." and "Airport" from the submenu.
5. Choose "Caribbean" from the Global Region pull-down menu. Select "Jamaica" from the Country menu.
6. Choose "Sangster Intl" from the Airport pull-down menu, and choose Runway 7. Click OK to close this box.
7. Now, go to the World menu and choose "Time & Season."
8. Click on the Set Time of Day button and choose Day from the pull-down menu.
9. Click OK to close this box.
10. Go to the Views menu and choose "View Options."
11. Click on the "Set Spot Plane" button.
12. Drag the red line so that you are looking directly at the right side of the airplane.
13. Close this box, and press ⓢ to put yourself back in the cockpit.
14. Now, choose Save Flight from the Flights menu, and title it (perhaps, "Fun In the Sun In Jamaica").

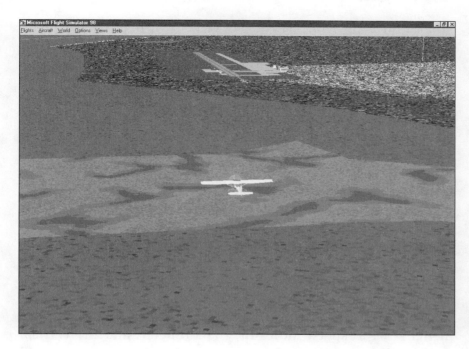

Figure 2-15 A View of Beautiful Jamaica

Landing the Plane: A Crash Course

Navy fighter pilots who routinely have to land on aircraft carriers often refer to that type of landing as "a controlled crash." While landing on the deck of a pitching, rolling carrier is probably one of the most difficult kinds of landings (and you can try it yourself by choosing Carrier Landings from the Challenges menu), even landing on a runway is no piece of cake: It involves controlling your airspeed and descent rate to guide a several-ton aircraft to a safe, gentle landing on a long, narrow strip of asphalt. Ideally, you want to come in at a low speed and nose-high attitude and stall the aircraft only at the last phase of landing.

Landing the plane is the most difficult part of the entire flight. There is no substitute for practice, practice, practice. You may crash the Cessna numerous times, but the great thing about Flight Simulator is that you can always reset the flight and try again. The more landings you attempt in the Cessna, the better you will get at controlling your descent rate and keeping the aircraft lined up with the runway centerline. Before long, you'll be pulling off landings that are so smooth your passengers will be on the ground before they even realize that your wheels have touched down.

Rather than present you with an exhaustive list of airspeeds, altitudes, and formulas, we will concentrate on getting you on the ground in one piece for your first landing. After that, as you make more landings (successful and otherwise) you will develop a better feel for such factors as proper airspeed, descent rate, and distance from the runway. The right approach will "look right" to you, and you will recognize when you should abort a landing and go around for another try. But to do that, first you need to get up in the air, so grab the keys and let's go!

Ready for Takeoff

When landing, we will be primarily concerned with three instruments—the airspeed indicator, the altimeter, and the vertical speed indicator, or VSI. As you get better at landing, you will probably be able to sense changes in the VSI out of the corner of your eye and be able to correct your descent rate without having to focus on the controls. On this flight, we will practice low power and no-power approach stalls at 2,000 feet, and then we will bring the aircraft in for a landing at picturesque Sangster airport in Montego Bay, Jamaica.

Add a zero to the end of any runway number to find out what heading the runway faces. For example, if you take off from Runway 7, as below, you'll be oriented to 70°.

The Takeoff Leg

You're starting out on Runway 7 at Sangster Intl, Montego Bay, Jamaica. Take off as normal and climb to 2,000 feet. You should be on a heading of about 70°. As you climb, use the other views to look around and admire the scenery. Take a look out the rear window, in particular, and watch the runway receding in the distance with the blue of the water and the white sand. Beautiful!

We are going to follow a left-hand traffic pattern and position ourselves for a landing. Along the way, we'll find out how the plane handles during a low power approach, stall it a few times, and generally scare the locals on the beach. Hey, it's only a simulation, and

Video: Traffic Pattern

Location: Flight School → Ground School → Navigation
→ Procedure Turns

you'll learn a lot about how the plane handles. Ensure that the flaps are retracted and throttle back to 2,200 RPM.

The Crosswind Leg

We are going to turn left 90°. We're on a heading of 70°, so what heading do you need to turn to? On the compass, 70° minus 90° is actually 340°. It's Flight Simulator math. Practice makes perfect. Watch your altitude during the turn, don't bank more than 30°, and pull back slightly on the yoke to maintain your altitude. Don't forget to start leveling out about 10° short of your desired heading, so you don't overshoot.

The Downwind Leg

Take a look out the window. Press Shift-4 or Shift-1, and you should see the airport off to the left. Get used to using the external views to line yourself up for a landing. Continue on this heading for a little while, then turn left 90° to start our downwind leg.

Pitch and Power Control Airspeed

Once you're holding a consistent heading and altitude, reduce the throttle to 1,700 RPM, and bring the nose up. Watch what happens to your airspeed as you pull back on the yoke. When the needle gets to 40 knots, gently ease the yoke forward, bringing the nose back down toward the horizon. See how the airspeed picks back up again? By controlling the pitch of the nose and the power of your airplane, you control your airspeed. Now try to keep a constant heading and altitude at this throttle setting.

At low airspeeds, maintaining straight and level flight takes

Figure 2-16 Flying
Low and Slow over
Montego Bay

practice. You will find that you need to pitch the nose up in order to maintain level flight. This is exactly the proper attitude when coming in for a landing. Remember, even though the airplane's nose may be pointing above the horizon, the plane's actual flight path may be very different. Once you have yourself stabilized, press S three times to change to the spot plane view and take a look at how you're flying.

Press S to return to the cockpit. OK. Time to stall the plane. This time, bring the nose up until you hear the stall warning sound. Keep pulling back on the nose until the airplane begins to stall. You will see your airspeed decrease, the VSI will drop, and the nose of the aircraft will drop back down toward the ground. While you're leaning back in your seat watching the waves get bigger, relax your grip on the yoke and apply full power until the plane picks up enough airspeed to get out of the stall. Then, pull back smoothly on the yoke to bring yourself back to straight and level flight. Resume a climb, then return to level flight when you're back at the original altitude.

Figure 2-17 In this picture of a plane flaring just before landing, the nose is pitched up, but the plane is actually still descending.

Attitude Adjustment Hour

That was fun, wasn't it? Check your heading and make sure you're still heading parallel to the runway. A quick look out the left window ([Shift]-[4]) should let you know right away. If necessary, correct your heading to 250° and climb to at least 1,500 feet.

Minimum Controllable Airspeed

This time we will practice a low and slow landing approach and practice landing on that big, fat runway in the air. Throttle back to 1,800 RPM, and extend your flaps all the way. Keep an eye on your VSI and keep your descent rate around 500 feet per minute. Try to stay on heading as well. Don't forget to make small adjustments with the yoke; large, swinging turns or pitching up and down can get you into trouble at low altitudes. You are maneuvering at what they call "minimum controllable airspeed." Your airspeed should be around 60 knots, your nose is pitched up, and

Sometimes the plane's wings and tail will obscure your view of the runway. Go into the preferences and deselect "see own aircraft from cockpit." Now you know why Wonder Woman used an Invisible Jet.

Checklist for Recovering from a Stall when the stall alarm goes off:

1. Smoothly increase throttle to 100 percent.

2. Push the yoke forward to pitch the nose down and gain airspeed.

3. Roll your wings level with the horizon (use the artificial horizon if the real one isn't available) and bring the nose up smoothly.

4. Once you are flying straight and level, you can reduce the throttle again.

you have a nice, positive attitude about landing this plane. (Want proof? Hit ⑤ three times for the spot plane view and check out that positive nose-up attitude you're flying.)

As your wheels are about to touch down on the Runway of Make-Believe, you will want to flare, which means bringing the nose of the plane up even farther just as the wheels are about to touch the ground. As you just experienced, bringing the nose of the plane up at a low airspeed will stall the aircraft. However, if your timing is right, you can flare just before you touch down, which will slow down your descent rate and provide a nice, smooth landing. It's not easy, and it requires practice, but once you get the feel for the flare you will have no trouble at all with it (and neither will your passengers.) Here, though, you want to watch your altitude and practice recovering from the stall.

The Base Leg

Once you've had enough practice, it's time to get ready for the real thing. Retract the flaps. Hold an altitude of 1,500 feet, and turn left to a heading of 160° for our base leg. Keep back pressure on the yoke to maintain your altitude, and watch your bank angle to ensure you don't stall the plane.

Figure 2-18 When the runway looks like this out your left window, it's time to start your final approach.

After you are flying level, press [Shift]-[4] and [Shift]-[7] to look out your left window. You should see the runway coming into view as you cross over the beach. While you're looking out your left window, wait until the runway is just about lined up as you see in Figure 2-18. Depending on how long you took the downwind leg, the runway may not be in view yet, but turn for your final approach anyway since you'll have plenty of time to line yourself up.

Aircraft On Final Approach!

Turn left 90° as you cross over the beach. Again, watch your bank angle and maintain your altitude. Make a nice, smooth turn and start lining yourself up with the runway.

As you approach the runway, set the throttle at about 2,000 RPM and slow the aircraft to 70–80 knots. Your descent rate should be between 500 and 1,000 feet per minute. Try to keep a nice, steady descent rate and make small corrections in your flight path to keep yourself lined up with the centerline of the runway.

Remember what we taught you in ground school: Your pitch controls your airspeed, and the throttle controls your altitude. This is most important here. If you are descending too quickly, increase the throttle a little bit. A common mistake is to pull the nose up to gain altitude. This will actually decrease your airspeed, causing you to descend even faster. You may even stall the plane if you pull the nose up too much. The ideal approach to the runway has the nose of the Cessna slightly below the horizon.

What Goes Up . . .

Keep a nice steady descent. At about 1,000 feet, extend the flaps all the way and lower the landing gear. You will notice that the plane's attitude will change, and you may descend slower. Be sure to adjust the throttle to keep yourself on a nice, even path to the runway.

Figure 2-19 This is what a good approach looks like. Note that the speed here is 72 knots

If you are looking short (you might land before you reach the runway), increase the throttle to flatten your glide path. You can decrease the throttle again when you get to the proper point in the glide slope.

If you are looking long (you might overshoot the runway), decrease the throttle to increase your descent rate and give you a steeper glide slope. Don't dive toward the runway. You may have to pitch the nose up slightly to maintain a descent rate under 1,000 feet per minute. If you're really overshooting, increase the throttle to full power and go around for another pass. You can keep setting up for an approach as often as you like, but you can only crash the plane once.

If you're coming in too high, don't be afraid to cut the throttle entirely and glide the rest of the way in. It's important to get a feel for the glide angle of the Cessna; this knowledge may save your life if you ever have an engine failure and need to glide to a landing.

Figure 2-20
Now is the perfect time to flare. Note the nearly level pitch altitude.

. . . Must Come Down!

You should be coming in low and slow, with a positive attitude. When you get close enough to the runway to see all the tire tread marks, get ready to flare. Just before you touch the ground, ease back on the yoke to bring the nose up. Your airspeed will drop, your descent rate will decrease until it's close to zero, and ideally you should touch down. When you hear the squeak of the wheels on the runway (oh, what a welcome sound!), ease the pressure on the yoke. If you continue to pull back on the yoke, you may bounce back into the air a few times before you come to a stop. Cut the throttle, and apply the brakes. Steer with the yoke to keep yourself tracking the runway centerline.

The Eagle Has Landed!

Whew! Wipe your brow and pat yourself on the back. You've just successfully landed your first plane. If something went wrong, simply take off and try again. You can use the slew controls to quickly place yourself in the right position for a landing. Press Y to activate slew, then press Q to gain altitude. Use the mouse or the yoke to move around laterally. Turn off slew by pressing Y again.

Practice Makes Perfect!

At most airports, unless otherwise specified, follow a left-hand traffic pattern.

To practice landings, you can do what we call a "touch-and-go" landing, which simply means that as soon as you touch the ground, you give it full throttle, retract the flaps, and roar off into the sky again. Once you get up to about 1,500 feet, make a 90° left-hand turn to enter the traffic pattern again, then another 90° left turn to start your downwind leg. This will give you valuable practice in locating the runway and setting yourself up for a nice final approach. Don't forget to use the different views frequently to keep tabs on where you are in relation to the airport.

Alternately, you can always practice landings someplace where it's flat, such as Waco, Texas, or Cheyenne, Wyoming. Simply take off and land as often as you wish, wherever you choose.

As far as you're concerned, the whole state is one big runway. You won't win any points with the local authorities, but it should make you a better pilot.

Another way to learn the proper glide slope for landing is to make a series of landings using the ILS, or instrument landing system. Not every airport will be equipped with an ILS, so you should learn how to land without it. Still, if an ILS is available, it can make your life a whole lot easier, especially when you're landing in bad weather conditions. See the section on ILS landings for more information.

TIPS ON THE BUILT-IN LESSONS

Flight Simulator 98 offers a number of lessons to help you learn basic skills, such as landing in a crosswind, maintaining a predetermined heading and altitude, and dealing with stalls. To access these lessons, choose Lessons from the Flights menu. Be forewarned: Not all of these lessons are easy to complete. On some of them, the instructor is strict, and if you deviate from the flight plan, he has a disconcerting tendency to disappear from the plane, leaving you on your own for a spontaneous solo flight. If you've flown the introductory flights in this book, however, you're well prepared for these lessons. Here are some more helpful tips for dealing with many of the situations.

Want to see your plane from the outside? Hit S once for a view from the virtual cockpit, hit S again for a view from the tower, and hit S a third time for a view from the spot plane, an imaginary plane that follows you at a specified heading and distance. Think of the spot plane as your own movable camera, and learn where to place it for the most dramatic shots and angles.

Action	Keystroke
Restart the lesson	Ctrl-R
Exit the lesson	Ctrl-U
Repeat the last instruction	Ctrl-M

Introductory Flight: Cessna Skylane RG at Meigs Field

Meet your flight instructor. He chewed up the last four students before you, and guess what? He's still hungry. Listen to the flight instructor, and try to keep up with his instructions. This flight will take you through takeoff, the flight pattern, and landing. Remember to keep your banks smooth and controlled, and remember to start leveling out when you are 10° from your desired heading. The flight plan calls for an altitude of 1,527 feet, and if you go too low or too high, the instructor will bail out on you.

After the instructor gives his initial instructions, feel free to throttle up and take off. As you hit 60 knots, the instructor will call out, "Rotate!" This is your signal to pull back gently on the yoke to take off. The ideal rate of climb for the Cessna is 79 knots, so adjust your pitch attitude to maintain this airspeed.

On your downwind leg, the instructor will announce, "You are abeam your touchdown point." This means that if you look out your left window by pressing [Shift]-[4], you will see that you are right across from the point at which you will want to touch down when you are on final approach.

As you turn for your base leg, you will hear the instructor tell you, "Don't forget your GUMP check." This is an acronym to

Figure 2-21 Rotate! Pull back on the yoke to take off.

remind pilots to check their gas, undercarriage (make sure the gear is down), mixture (full rich), and propeller (high RPM). And don't forget your box of chocolates, either.

ILS Approach with Procedure Turn: Cessna Skylane RG

This is a good first or second lesson, since the instructor is unusually helpful, giving you key commands for the various controls as well as a number of useful tips. To succeed in this lesson, remember to keep your altitude at 1,900 feet and pull back on the yoke during a banking turn to maintain your altitude.

Introductory Flight, Day VFR: Cessna Skylane 182S

In this lesson, you will take off from one airport and land at another one nearby. After you have reached cruising altitude, you will probably have to keep pulling back on the yoke to stay level, but you can use the trim tabs to adjust the yoke so you don't have to sit there and hold the yoke back. Press keypad ⨪1⨪ and keypad ⨪7⨪ to adjust the pressure on the yoke, a little at a time.

As you make your final approach, watch the glide slope needle to maintain your descent. The glide slope is an imaginary line descending through space to the runway that represents the ideal descent rate. The glide slope needle helps you follow this ideal path by moving up or down to show you how far off the glide slope you are. When you are on the glide slope, the needle stays centered. If the needle is high, you are below the glide slope, and you need to increase your RPM to decrease the descent rate. If the needle is low, you are too high, and you need to decrease your RPM to increase the descent rate.

The vertical needle gets much more sensitive as you get closer, so don't ruin your approach by trying to "chase the needle." Once you have the runway in sight, concentrate on lining yourself up visually with the runway and on matching your glide slope with the horizontal needle.

If you forget your assigned heading, look on the heading indicator for the set of red marks, known as the "bug," that will tell you which heading to turn to.

Figure 2-22 When the glide slope needle drifts up, you are low.

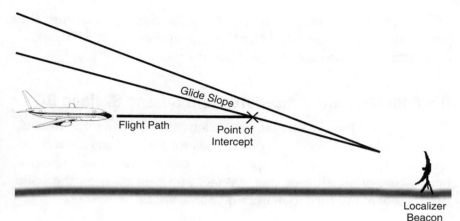

Figure 2-23 If you're too low, wait until you intercept the glide slope and then work on matching your descent rate by adjusting the throttle.

Normal Landing: Cessna Skylane RG

In this flight you will fly a standard traffic pattern from takeoff to landing. On your descent, if the instructor warns you that you're too low, don't make radical adjustments to climb back up again. If you decrease your descent rate, you will probably intercept the glide slope at some point.

15-Knot Crosswind Landing

Of the lessons, this is one of the more difficult. You must make a landing at Meigs Field in a strong crosswind, and the instructor doesn't really tell you how to do it, although he is fairly crabby in this lesson. You'll probably want to check the preflight briefing for this one, located in Pilot's Help under the Help menu.

First of all, I highly recommend a set of rudder pedals or a joystick with rudder control, because trying to complete this lesson using just the keyboard makes it even more difficult than it already is. Keep your altitude at 1,527 MSL all the way until you turn for your base leg. If the instructor warns you that you're too low, just hold your altitude anywhere above 1,000 feet and you'll intercept the glide slope. When the instructor tells you to "clear

Crabs and Slips

- **Crabbing:** When the plane's nose is pointed to one side of the actual flight path. You would crab when approaching a runway in a crosswind. Pointing the plane's nose to one side helps compensate for the crosswind. Auto-coordination can be on or off to perform this maneuver.

- **Slipping:** Just before touching down, you want your nose to be pointed straight down the runway. To accomplish this, you can bank the wings into the wind to compensate for the crosswind. You apply opposite rudder to keep the plane from turning. Auto-coordination must be off to perform a slip.

final and start your approach," check out your left window first before you turn. Don't turn too early, or you'll won't be lined up on the runway!

As you approach, line yourself up with the runway well ahead of time, then turn your nose slightly to the left. Your flight path should still be carrying you straight in to the runway. If you're floating to one side or the other, make small corrections in the yoke. Turning your nose slightly into the wind is called crabbing, and it will help keep your flight path straight.

Climbs, Turns, and Descents: Cessna Skylane RG

Watch your descent rate. Make sure to keep it at about 500 feet per minute (5 on the VSI dial). Wait to hear the target heading and altitude before starting your turn. The instructor will wait to give the next command until you have matched both proper heading and altitude. For example, if you come out of a descending turn and

Figure 2-24 I know this looks weird, but the plane really is traveling straight toward the runway. Honest.

you're still high, maintain your heading and continue a smooth, slow descent rate. Remember not to "chase the needle"—wait a little bit to see what the effect of your control input is before you correct for it. When the instructor corrects you, make sure you don't "snap to" his commands and jerk the plane around. Make smooth, controlled corrections to avoid losing control of the airplane.

Maneuvering at MCA: Cessna Skylane RG

MCA stands for minimum controllable airspeed, which means: How slow can you fly and still be able to control the airplane? It will pay to keep that in mind because in this lesson the instructor doesn't tell you what throttle setting to fly at. It's assumed that you will decrease the throttle as much as you can while still being able to hold your heading and climb or descend to the proper altitude. As you climb or descend, watch the pitch of the nose. If you pitch up too much, you'll stall the plane. If this happens, add more throttle and decrease the pitch. You'll still be able to climb.

Figure 2-25 When the runway looks like this out your left window ([Shift]-[4]), start a 30° turn to a heading of 180° and you'll be perfectly lined up.

At low airspeeds (below 50 knots) you may need to pitch the nose down to build up some airspeed before you start your climb again. The trick to MCA is finding that balance between using as little throttle as you possibly can and pitching the nose just far enough so that you don't stall. These skills will help make your landings smooth and teach you how the throttle controls your altitude and descent rate.

Stalls: Cessna Skylane RG

When the instructor says, "Watch your altitude," it can mean you are too low or too high. On the takeoff stall, when the instructor tells you go to full power, something he neglects to tell you is that you have to pitch the nose up in order to induce a stall. If you follow his exact instructions and fly straight and level at full throttle, you are, of course, never going to stall the plane. Once you have successfully stalled the plane, the instructor will shout at you, "Recover!" and the lesson will continue.

Night Landing: Cessna Skylane RG

The runway is off to the left, and although it's lit up, you may have to look carefully to see it. You can also watch the course correction needle on the VOR 1 indicator to give you an idea of where you are in relation to the airport.

Introductory Flight, Day VFR: Cessna Skylane 182S

When the instructor tells you to pitch the nose up about 10°, that's to the first black mark. You may need to pitch up a little bit more to maintain the proper airspeed.

CHAPTER

3

Pilot's License

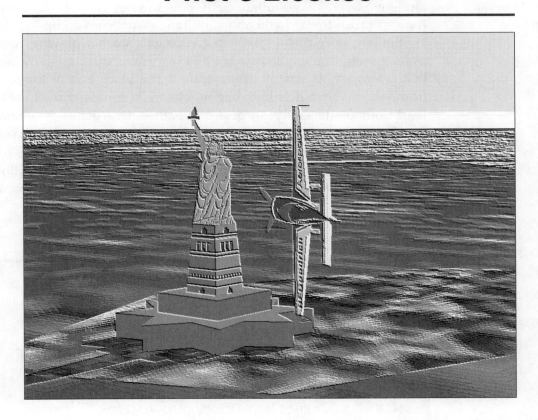

When I started studying the martial arts, a wise Japanese sensei explained the following to me: "When you pass your proficiency trials," he intoned, "we will have a simple but elegant ceremony in which we will present you with a certificate entitling you to wear the black belt, the highest belt we offer." I listened in rapt attention as he described the revered, traditional ceremony that would lead up to my first demonstration as a black belt aikido expert. "After the ceremony," he continued, "you will enter a hall with some of our most advanced and knowledgeable black belt students, who will simultaneously bow to you. Then, on a signal, they will rush toward you and simultaneously beat you up."

Shortly after this, I gave up aikido and started playing computer games. The whole point of this story (and this unusual black belt ceremony) is simply to illustrate that a black belt or a pilot's license is merely a license to begin to learn. You now know how to land your plane safely, in perfect weather. Instructors feel comfortable taking a ride with you to teach you the finer points of navigation and maneuvering. They make their lunch reservations for after the flight without hesitating. You are a safe and capable pilot. Now, you can really begin to learn how to find your way around and have fun in the air.

Are you getting tired of constantly changing the Realism & Reliability settings every time you crash? Want to be a French citizen and start out each day in Le Bourget, Paris, instead of old Meigs Field? Go to the runway of your choice, change all the settings the way you like them, and save the flight. Then, go to the Options menu and choose Preferences. Click on the Select Flight button, and highlight your flight. Click the button that says, "Make this the default flight." Click OK, and from now on *Flight Simulator* will default to this location and those settings.

ADVANCED MANEUVERS

In this section, you will learn how to use the rudders and the ailerons separately to control your airplane in a turn. You'll pick up some useful hints on practicing your turns, and you'll find out how to use the turn coordinator.

You Don't Have to Be Coordinated to Fly Without Auto-Coordination

Now that you're comfortable with banks and turns, let's throw a monkey wrench into the works and turn off auto-coordination. Don't worry, this isn't as frightening as it sounds. Enabling the rudders and the ailerons to move separately will allow you more control over how your plane handles, and it will make it much easier to land on a runway when it's windy. To start with, let's get up in the air so we can try this out.

We're Going Where??

Ah, yes. I am reminded of my driving school instructor, who on my very first day took me onto the expressway because, she reasoned, "if you can handle this kind of traffic, you can handle anything." I handled it, all right. I nearly froze up on the entrance ramp. Once I got going, though, I actually did all right. In this case, I knew more than I gave myself credit for. Such is the case with your skills as a new pilot. Sure, there's still a lot to learn, but you also are starting to develop that elusive "feel" of how to handle the controls properly. Today we'll practice turns, banks, and rolls in that most spectacular of American landmarks, the Grand Canyon.

Setting Up the Flight

We're going to start out with auto-coordination turned on, and then we'll turn it off once you're up in the air. Watch how the rudders move in coordination with the ailerons when you turn the yoke.

1. Go to the Flights menu and choose "Create Flight."
2. Click the "Select Aircraft" button, and choose the Cessna Skylane 182S. Click OK.

For best results, calibrate your game controllers from within *Flight Simulator* instead of the Windows desktop. Choose "Custom Controls" from the Options menu. Click the Calibrate button. In the Game Controllers dialog box, highlight your game controller, and click the Properties button to Calibrate it. Close all the dialog boxes, and you are ready to fly.

3. Click the "Select Airport" button. Enter "Grand Canyon National Park" as the airport name. Click OK to close this box.

4. If it isn't daylight outside, choose "Time & Season" from the World menu.

5. Click the "Set Time of Day" button and choose Day from the pull-down menu. Click OK to close this box.

6. Click OK and you will be transported to the Grand Canyon.

7. Go to the Aircraft menu and choose "Aircraft Settings." Make sure that Auto-coordination is checked.

8. Set the flight realism to halfway between easy and real. Click OK.

9. Go to the Views menu and choose "View Options." Click on the "Set Spot Plane" button.

10. Drag the end of the red line to the back of the airplane.

Figure 3-1 The entrance to the Grand Canyon.

11. De-select the "Gradual Transition" box. Click OK to close this box.

12. Now, choose Save Flight from the Flights menu, and title it "Banking at the Grand Canyon."

Takeoff

You begin the flight sitting on runway 3, at an elevation of 6,600 feet. Set flaps at 10°, release the parking brakes, point the nose of the aircraft down the runway, and go to full throttle. Once you're airborne, retract the flaps. Turn to a heading of 10°. Straight ahead of you, you will see a break in the mountains. This is the mouth of the Grand Canyon. To learn how the plane handles in uncoordinated flight, we'll gain some altitude and then turn that option off. Climb to about 10,000 feet, or if you're in a hurry, set that altitude in the "Set exact location" option under the World menu.

Roll a Few Banks

Take a look at the aileron, elevator, and rudder indicators on the instrument panel. When auto-coordination is on, the rudders are coordinated with the ailerons, giving you a nice clean turn. Watch the ball in the turn coordinator as you bank. Notice that the ball stays in the center of the tube as the wings tilt. This is a coordinated bank. Make a few more banks, and watch the turn coordinator. When the tip of your wing is aligned with the white line, you are at a standard rate of turn, which means that you'll turn 360° in two minutes. The ball stays in the middle of the tube no matter how you turn, indicating that you are, indeed, very coordinated. Try a few more banks, then turn off auto-coordination in the Aircraft Settings box.

Now make a 20° bank turn to the left, with just the yoke (leave the rudders alone for now). Pull back on the yoke and maintain altitude. Watch the turn coordinator. As the aileron creates drag on the wing surface, the tail tends to yaw. The ball in the turn coordinator shows how the tail is yawing. If the ball moves opposite the turn, the airplane is skidding. If the ball moves inside the

Figure 3-2 This is a standard rate of turn. The wing tips are lined up with the white marks in the turn coordinator.

Figure 3-3 In an uncoordinated turn, the ball in the turn coordinator slides toward one side or the other, indicating, in this case, that the airplane is slipping. Use the rudder to keep the ball centered.

> **Video:** Turn Coordinator
>
> **Location:** Flight School → Ground School → Flight
> Instruments → Gyro Instruments → Turn Coordinator

turn, the airplane is slipping. Either way, you're looking pretty uncoordinated.

Add Some Rudder to that Turn

Now, let's make some coordinated turns. This time, as you turn the yoke, try adding some rudder in the same direction as your bank (if you're turning left, add some left rudder, and vice versa). When the yoke returns to center, ease off on the rudder, too. When you apply opposite pressure to the yoke to stop the bank, remember to do the same to the rudder. Keep an eye on the indicators and make sure you're applying the same amount of pressure to both. Keep back pressure on the yoke to maintain your altitude, and don't forget your stall recovery procedures. Try making a coordinated turn 360° to the right or the left. Then, try switching direction. Once you get the hang of coordinating all these things, try watching the turn coordinator as you bank, and try to keep the ball in the middle. Pilots call this "stepping on the ball." I call it "works well after a lot of practice." To keep your turns coordinated, "step on the ball," or step on the side of the ball that is exposed. Keep making coordinated turns, and practice stopping on a heading. Remember to start leveling out 10° short of your desired heading. It's a lot more difficult when you're trying to coordinate the rudder, too, isn't it?

> **Video:** Performing S = Turns Across a Road
>
> **Location:** Flight School → Ground School → Aerodynamics
> → Turns

This is a 10° bank.

Figure 3-4 Use the white triangle on the artificial horizon to judge your bank angle.

This is a 20° bank.

This is a 30° bank.

This is a 60° bank.

Truthfully, you may not notice a whole lot of difference flying in uncoordinated mode. The turns are a little mushier, but you can still turn with the yoke. You'll probably notice that the plane tends to slide around a bit more, but you can still pull off a passable turn and get to the heading you want without using the rudders. Flying with auto-coordination off gives the plane a little more realistic feel (and if you're using actual rudder pedals, it feels very realistic), and it allows you to perform some maneuvers that would otherwise be impossible, such as the slip. To line up with the runway, use coordinated turn, then establish crab or slip to maintain counterline.

Slip Out the Back, Jack

All right, now it's time to give everybody the slip. This is a very cool maneuver that shows people you're a hot pilot. It also helps you land in a crosswind.

Go back to straight and level flight. To perform the slip, you apply pressure to the rudder opposite from the direction of the yoke. Try a gentle bank to the right at first, and apply a little left

At the drop zone where I skydive, we own a Twin Otter that routinely has to make crosswind landings on the tiny airstrip. The pilot approaches with the nose of the plane pointing toward the wind, which often makes it look as if it is coming down sideways. Just before he touches the ground, the pilot brings the nose back to the center and banks the plane. This takes real skill to pull off, and looks very scary from the ground. Many a new skydiver has gone running in fear from the plane, preferring to stay on the ground rather than jump with a crazy pilot.

rudder. This should keep your plane on the same heading, even though you're tilted to the right. Your plane is actually sliding to the side, though you're still pointing in the same direction. You can land successfully in a crosswind by using the slip, which is also called the "wing low" method (see "Landing in a Crosswind" later on in this chapter).

Putting a New Spin On Things

Similar to the stall, the spin is a dangerous situation you may unwittingly get yourself into as you experiment with auto-coordination turned off. First, let's learn about the spin, then cause an intentional spin high up in the air and practice stopping it. Since you'll need to be able to use the rudders independently from the control yoke, make sure auto-coordination is turned off.

What Causes a Spin?

A spin is bad news, and it requires quick thinking on your part to correct. In a spin, the aircraft plummets to the earth, nose down, spinning like those paper helicopters you might have made as a child.

Spins occur during stalls, when the aircraft yaws to one side or the other. First, both wings of the airplane stall, then one wing stalls less than the other wing. This causes a spin as the plane falls to the ground. If the plane spins near its center of gravity, you might encounter a flat spin, in which the nose remains relatively level with the horizon and the plane spins parallel to the ground. It can be impossible to recover from a flat spin.

On an aerobatics plane like the Extra 300S, if you bank the plane 90° and give it full opposite rudder, you can fly sideways. This is useful for flying between the World Trade Center towers in New York.

Video: Wake Turbulence Dangers

Location: Flight School → Ground School → The Flight Environment → The Airport Environment

Figure 3-5 A spin
is a stall with a
bad attitude.

Getting Out of a Spin

When the plane goes into a spin, first push forward on the yoke to break the stall. It's also important to correct for the spin by applying opposite rudder from the direction of the spin. When you begin to recover from the spin, center the rudder. You don't want to yaw the plane into a spin in the opposite direction.

Taking the Cessna for a Spin

Warning! Intentionally causing a spin in a plane that is not rated for spins is not only illegal, it's mighty dangerous as well! That's why we're going to get up in the air and spin *Flight Simulator*'s Cessna to our heart's content. What fun!

To practice spinning the Cessna, start high. I like to start at about 10,000 feet AGL, so if you're still in the Grand Canyon, put yourself at 16,000 feet MSL by going to the World menu and choosing "Go to Exact Location." Enter 16,000 in the altitude box, then click OK and level the plane.

Decrease the throttle to about 1,500 RPM, and pitch the nose up to induce a stall. As the stall warning buzzer sounds, and the nose begins to drop, keep back pressure on the yoke and apply full rudder to one side or the other to start a spin in that direction. As the spin develops, you can recover by pushing the yoke forward and applying rudder in the other direction. Watch your altitude, and don't start a spin too close to the ground, or the fun will end really quickly. Try watching the plane from the Tower view (press Ⓢ once, then ⊞ to zoom in) to really see what's happening in a spin.

Buzzing the Grand Canyon

Before you land the plane again, try flying into the Grand Canyon. Try to stay low, and use your new skills at turns and banks to follow the contours of the canyon walls. You can use the Map view, accessed by pressing Ⓢⓗⓘⓕⓣ-⑴, to keep track of your location. For real fun, try flying your plane from the spot plane view by pressing ⑤ three times. When you've had enough fun for one day, return to the airport and land the plane. For a real challenge, try landing the plane from the spot plane view. (Hint: Depend on your instruments to tell you your orientation and descent rate.)

HOW TO CHANGE THE WEATHER

"Milo said, 'I thought you were the Weather Man.' 'Oh no,' said the little fellow. 'I'm the Whether Man. It's more important to know Whether there will be Weather than what the Weather will be.'"

from *The Phantom Tollbooth* by Norton Juster

Have there ever been days when you have looked up at an overcast sky and wished it were sunny? Or watched a thunderstorm approach, wishing the skies would clear up, and the storm would dissipate? So far in your *Flight Simulator* career, you have been blessed with perfect, 75° days, clear blue skies, and no wind or turbulence. But one of the most fun things about *Flight Simulator* is its ability to customize the weather. For some of you, it may be the first time you've actually wished for stormy weather and thick, dark ground fog. Luckily, terrible, turbulent weather is only a click of the mouse away!

Adding Weather Conditions

As any pilot will tell you, a landing approach in windy, low-visibility weather is a white-knuckle experience indeed, one that will truly test your landing skills. On the other hand, there is nothing like taking off from Chelan or Meigs Field at sunset. *Flight Simulator*'s impressive graphics capabilities and its photorealistic scenery are truly showcased by the rosy hues of the setting sun glowing off banks of soft clouds. The Weather dialog box is the place to start to add a whole new dimension to *Flight Simulator*.

Figure 3-6 Great weather conditions are only a click of the mouse away.

There are a number of ways you can customize the outside conditions:

1. Time
2. Season
3. Cloud cover
4. Wind conditions
5. Temperature
6. Visibility

Time

While not technically a weather condition, this is probably the easiest way to get a change of scenery. You can change the time by choosing "Time & Season" from the World menu, or by clicking on the digits of the clock on the instrument panel. By choosing dawn or dusk, you can see some really impressive color effects, particularly if there are clouds in the sky. Don't forget that the time of year makes a difference, too; the sun sets later in the summertime.

Season

Clicking on the Seasons tab in the "Time & Season" option under the Options menu lets you change what season it is. This really affects the temperature and the time the sun rises and sets, more than anything else.

Cloud Cover

Clouds will probably have the greatest impact on you as a pilot. Flying through clouds can be disorienting because suddenly you can't see, and you have to depend on your instruments to tell you where you are in relation to the ground. Certain types of clouds can also contain wind, ice, and turbulence that will test your skill as a pilot. *Flight Simulator* allows you to create clouds of varying type, thickness, and altitude. The following sections contain

If you're having trouble changing the weather, check to see if the Weather Generation option is turned on in the Preferences dialog box. *Flight Simulator* has the ability to automatically generate random weather patterns, and to change them over time. If the Weather Generation option is turned on, the "Add Layer" buttons will be grayed out. To add weather layers, go to the Options menu, choose "Preferences," and turn Weather Generation off.

Figure 3-7 How to make a cloud salad— a layer of cumulus, with a sprinkling of cirrus, and a cumulonimbus or two. . . .

tips on creating some different types of clouds, from picturesque Maxfield Parrish clouds to really nasty, Pilot's Nightmare types of clouds. The real fun, however, is in creating and experimenting with your own layers of clouds, then flying through them (or sending your hapless instructor to forge ahead with a landing). Have fun, and don't be afraid to try out different layers of clouds to see what works well. When you come up with a recipe that you like, go to the Flights menu and choose "Save Flight" so you can go back to it next time.

Fair Weather, Friends

The basic weather generation box is pretty self-explanatory, offering pre-programmed effects such as Haze, Light Clouds, or Heavy Clouds. If the "Use Advanced Weather Dialog" box is checked in the Preferences menu, you have even more options available to you. Let's learn how to use the Advanced Weather dialog to create some beautiful cloud effects.

1. Go to the Flights menu and choose "Select Flight."
2. Choose "Meigs Take Off Dense Scenery" (or your favorite airport).
3. Go to the Options menu and choose "Preferences." Make sure the "Use Advanced Weather Dialog" box is checked. Make sure the "Weather Generation" box is not checked. Click OK.
4. Go to the World menu and choose "Weather."
5. From the Cloud Type box, choose "Cirrus."
6. From the Coverage box, choose "Few 2/8."
7. Click OK to view the results of your efforts.

You should see a sky filled with cirrus clouds, also called "mare's tail" clouds. These clouds are wispy and very high up, and they sometimes forecast good weather. For a really nice effect, change the time of day to Dusk or Dawn. Try changing the cloud type to Cirrostratus, Stratus, Cirrocumulus, or Cumulus. Watch how the coverage characteristics change, as well as the altitude and thickness of the clouds.

Cloud altitudes are given in terms of their height above sea level, not their height above the ground. Take into consideration the elevation of the runway when creating the cloud base.

Really Nasty Cloud Effects

While beautiful, clouds can also be dangerous. In *Flight Simulator*, you can create low cloud layers that hide the runway to test your skill at making an ILS approach. There's nothing like the feeling of trusting your instruments to guide you to the runway, then breaking through the clouds to find yourself right where you're supposed to be, a hundred feet from touchdown. It's very exciting. Almost as exciting as breaking through the cloud cover to find yourself a hundred feet over the water, and not at all where you're supposed to be. Still, it's those moments that keep *Flight Simulator* enjoyable long after you've mastered landing approaches in perfect weather.

Figure 3-8

The one type of cloud that earns the most respect from pilots is probably the cumulonimbus, or thunderstorm. These hulking, malevolent clouds hover about and are associated with such dangerous conditions as icing and wind shear. Most prudent pilots avoid flying near thunderstorms at all cost. Then again, we're playing with *Flight Simulator*, so we are entitled to moments of imprudence from time to time.

Video: Life-Cycle of a Thunderstorm

Location: Flight School → Ground School → Aviation Weather → Thunderstorms

CREATING GROUND FOG

1. Go to the World menu and choose "Weather."
2. From the Cloud Type box, choose "User Defined."
3. From the Coverage box, choose "Overcast."
4. In the Cloud Base box, type in a value at or near the ground elevation of the airport (at Meigs Field, I use 650 feet).
5. In the Cloud Top box, type in the altitude you want the top of the layer to be. I use 1650 feet. At Meigs Field, you can see the blimp and the tops of the tallest towers poking out above the clouds.
6. Now, take off, go around the pattern, and then hit X to have the instructor land the plane (Meigs Field doesn't have an ILS; if you want to try a landing yourself, set this up somewhere that is ILS-equipped).

CREATING A THUNDERSTORM

1. Go to the World menu and choose "Weather."
2. From the Cloud Type box, choose "Cumulonimbus."
3. From the Coverage box, choose "Dense."
4. Click OK and get out your umbrella.

Fly Through a Thunderstorm

Thunderclouds can hide some pretty rough weather, such as severe turbulence and airframe icing. Make sure your seat belt is fastened, then head straight for the thundercloud (you can use the slew function to get closer). If you fly directly through the thundercloud, you and your plane will experience quite a wild ride! You also will lose visibility inside the thundercloud, so watch the attitude indicator to keep yourself level.

How to Add Cloud Layers

You can add different types of clouds to the same weather area to add some variety. In the Weather dialog box, click "Add Layer"

Figure 3-9 Attack of the thunderclouds

and specify Cloud Type and Coverage. The new layer of clouds
will appear above or below the existing layer. You can see the
upper layer of clouds when you climb above the top of the lower
layer of clouds. One thing I like to do is add an Overcast layer
with a base of 1,000 feet and a top of 3,000 feet. Then, I add a layer
of cirrus clouds with "Scattered 1/8" coverage, and set the time of
day to dusk. I take off into an overcast sky, then break through the

Wind shear is a sudden change of wind speed and/or direction. The
most dangerous shear is the shift from headwind to tailwind

Icing Do's and Don'ts

There is more information like this in the Pilot's Training section of Help.

- When climbing out through an icing layer, climb at an airspeed a little faster than normal to avoid stalling as ice accumulates.

- Be alert for erroneous readings from your airspeed indicator, rate-of-climb indicator, and altimeter. Make sure you turn on the carb heat.

- In stratiform clouds, try descending to warmer air or climbing to air colder than 15° F (-10° C).

- In freezing rain, climb or descend to find a layer of warmer air. Freezing rain always indicates warmer air above.

- If you decide to climb, do so quickly. If you descend, you must know the temperature and the terrain below.

- Avoid cumuliform clouds.

- Avoid abrupt maneuvers when your aircraft is coated with ice because the aircraft has lost some of its aerodynamic efficiency.

- When "iced up," fly your landing approach with power.

- Help your fellow pilots by sending pilot reports (PIREPS) when you encounter ice or when icing is forecast but not encountered.

cloud cover to see a beautiful, clear pink and blue sky with a few cirrus clouds floating around. It's quite a sight!

Wind Conditions

Wind conditions go hand in hand with severe weather. Once you have created a front of thunderclouds, for example, you could create a layer of turbulent winds making it difficult to land. You can add several layers of winds coming from different directions and of varying strengths. If you want to practice crosswind landings at your favorite airport, it's as easy as clicking on the Winds tab in the Weather box, then choosing a 15- or 20-knot surface layer coming from a heading 90° to the runway. See "How to Maneuver in Heavy Winds" below for advice on how to fly in these conditions.

Temperature

It's harder to maintain lift in hot weather. Why? Cold air is denser than warm air. If you take a beach ball outside on a hot day, blow it up so it's nice and tight, then take it back inside your house; you may notice that the sides tend to sag a little bit, almost as if your beach ball has sprung a leak. What's actually happening is that as

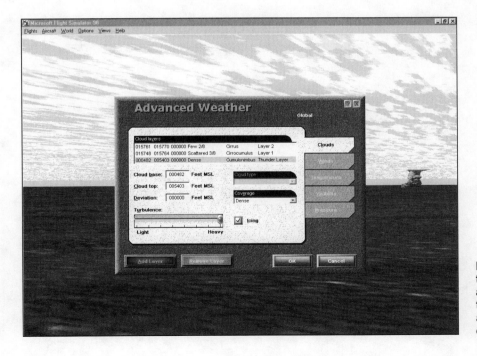

Figure 3-10 When three cloud layers are active, one of them needs to be a cumulonimbus cloud type.

the air inside the ball cools, it takes up less space. The air molecules get closer together.

You can create different temperature layers at different altitudes by clicking the "Add Layer" button in the "Temperature" tab of the Weather dialog box. You can also make the temperature automatically drop at night by clicking on the Day/Night option and setting a variation range for how much colder it should get when night falls.

Visibility

If your video card driver supports the "With haze" option, you can reduce the visibility for a particular area. Feel nostalgic for Los Angeles smog? Not a problem: Select the Visibility tag in the Weather dialog box, and you can change the visibility to anything from unlimited to 1/16 of a mile! Less dramatic visibility changes (say, 20 to 40 miles) make the horizon look very realistic at the higher detail levels.

Figure 3-11 Los Angeles International with Visibility Set to 10 Miles

Figure 3-12 Los Angeles International with Visibility Set to 5 Miles

Figure 3-13 Los Angeles International with Visibility Set to 1 Mile

Setting Global and Local Weather Areas

The "Weather Areas" option under the World menu allows you to create and save weather conditions for various areas of the country. Global weather areas affect everything, and local weather areas are defined by latitude and longitude. You could, for example, take off under an overcast sky in Chicago and land in the middle of thunderstorms in Pittsburgh. You can also set a direction and speed for local weather areas, so you could create a front of thunderstorms approaching from the west at 30 knots.

How to Maneuver In Heavy Winds

Heavy winds make it difficult to navigate and to land the plane. Combined with low visibility, these adverse conditions become an extremely challenging test of your flying skills.

Wind Drift Can Blow You off Course

A course is the path over which you're moving. A good example is a line on a map. Heading is the compass direction in which the longitudinal axis of your aircraft (your nose) is pointing. It is important to realize that a crosswind can blow you off course, even though the compass shows you are keeping the same heading (somewhat like facing north while walking sideways).

Over long distances, you can correct for this by using VOR signals along the way. When you drift from your course, the needle on the VOR indicator will drift off center. Pay attention to the needle and keep it centered so that you are constantly flying along the proper radial, and you should be fine.

Landing In a Crosswind

A crosswind is a wind that blows at any angle to the runway heading. It makes landings difficult because at the same time that you are trying to line up your aircraft with the runway centerline and watch your descent rate, the wind is pushing you sideways. The best way to deal with a crosswind landing is to approach the runway with your nose pointed slightly into the wind so that you can maintain a track that is more or less straight ahead. This is called crabbing. In strong winds you may even need to use another view (right front or left front) in order to keep your eyes on the runway.

Just above the surface of the runway, you need to yaw the nose back toward the center and bank one wing slightly into the wind, while correcting with the opposite rudder. This is called slipping, and it helps keep you straight as the wheels touch down. Make small, smooth corrections with the rudder and yoke, so you don't end up slipping all over the place. Auto-coordination must be off in order for the rudder to work independently from the yoke. Although it is possible to make a crosswind landing without performing a slip (try some of the Crosswind Landing Challenges), you will probably find it much easier to make a crosswind landing with auto-coordination off. You can change this setting at any time during the flight, so if you're more comfortable flying with auto-coordination on, you can always turn it off just when you're about to make a landing.

Crosswind landings are much easier to manage with a set of rudder pedals, such as the Pro Pedals from CH Products.

Crosswind Landing Flight Example

To see how a crosswind landing is done, choose one of the challenges and watch as the instructor lands the plane. If you like, try your hand at flying the Crosswind Landing (Difficult) challenge first, then follow the instructions below to set it up for the instructor.

1. Go to the Flights menu and choose "Challenges."

2. Choose Crosswind Landing (Difficult) from the list of challenges and click OK.

3. As soon as the challenge appears on your screen, press P to pause the simulation.

4. Change COM1 (click on the display) by one digit to stop the on-screen message scroll.

5. Go to the Views menu and choose "View Options."

6. Click on the Set Spot Plane button and drag the end of the red line to the back of the plane.

Figure 3-14 An Example of Crabbing to Stay Even with the Runway While Landing In a Crosswind

Figure 3-15 An Example of Slipping to Keep from Getting Blown to the Side While Landing In a Crosswind

7. Enter a distance of 175 feet and an altitude of 30 feet, so we can see more of the runway, and click OK to close the box.

8. Hit P to unpause the simulation, then press X to let the instructor take over.

Setting Up Your Own Challenges

You can set up your own crosswind situation by choosing an airport, then creating a surface wind layer of 10 to 20 knots, blowing 90° from the runway heading (add a zero to the end of the runway number to find out its heading.) If you want to save this situation as a flight, remember to choose "Save Flight" from the Flights menu. When taking off in a crosswind, you may need to add some aileron or rudder to keep the airplane on a straight course. When you approach the airport for a landing, you can always hit X to have the instructor land the plane, then switch to an external view. This is a great way to learn how to do a crosswind landing.

MORE ON NAVIGATION

You have learned to navigate using your compass, a map, and visual landmarks to help you find your way. Pilots actually refer to this as visual navigation. This is accurate enough for sightseeing around a local airport, but to fly to different airports or to fly in bad weather, you will need to learn how to navigate using the radio. (This doesn't mean calling up the tower and asking for directions!) You can also navigate using a chart showing latitude and longitude along with the global positioning system (or GPS, see "A Word About GPS" below).

Latitude and Longitude

You can find your position anywhere in the world if you know your latitude and longitude. If you look at a world map, you will see that the entire earth has been marked with a grid. On a map, the longitude lines run vertically, and the latitude lines run horizontally. These lines are numbered by degrees, which make it

Note that not every airport supports the Land Me option.

At any point during an instructor's landing, you can press X again to resume control of the aircraft and fly the landing the rest of the way.

Video: Tracking a VOR radial

Location: Flight School → Ground School → Navigation → VOR Navigation

possible to locate a particular spot on the earth by stating its latitude and longitude, much like X and Y coordinates on a graph. For example, if you wanted to find N44 W70, you would follow the latitude lines north until you came to N44. Then, you would follow the longitude lines west until you located W70. Follow the intersection of these lines, and what do you know, you come to a point just outside Portland, Maine, home of sportsman William Sandberg and other luminaries. Similarly, if you were navigating outside of the range of VOR beacons (such as on a transoceanic flight), you could still track your progress on a map with the aid of a GPS, which displays your current latitude and longitude. In *Flight Simulator*, you can access this data by pressing Shift-Z. At the risk of oversimplifying a very complex process, it is certainly possible to find your way cross-country in the *Flight Simulator* world with nothing more than a world atlas and some knowledge of the wind speed and direction at altitude.

Help Me, OBI 1—You're My Only Hope!

VOR stands for very-high-frequency omnidirectional range. VOR stations are sometimes located near airports, and they broadcast a series of signals that radiate out from the VOR station like the spokes of a wheel. These spokes are called radials. Each radial corresponds to a degree on the magnetic compass, with the zero degree radial leading from the VOR station to magnetic north. When you tune in a particular frequency on your NAV 1 radio, the VOR indicator (or OBI) can determine a number of useful things:

1. Your position relative to a particular radial.
2. Your position relative to the VOR station.

3. Which heading you need to fly toward to reach the VOR station.

Here is an example. Let's imagine you are lost in the countryside. You are trying to get to, say, Camelot. You are miles and miles away from the castle, and you don't know how to get there. You have a compass, and you know that all roads lead to Camelot (like spokes on a wheel), but you can't see the roads and you wouldn't know which direction to follow even if you found one. Even if you knew the exact compass heading of Camelot from where you stood, you probably couldn't find it without a road, since you might easily drift right or left while maintaining your heading, and you'd wind up passing it on either side.

Then a friendly stranger offers to come along and help. He tells you what direction the nearest road is. If you keep going in that direction, sooner or later you will come across the road. After all, it's much easier to intercept a line than a point. Once you find the road, though, your friend explains which direction leads *to* the castle and which direction leads *from* the castle, so that you know which way to go. And once you've established all of these things, your friend helps you to continue straight down that road, so you don't veer off to the side and end up in a ditch somewhere. When you get to the castle, you will probably want to go straight to the tavern and buy your friend a big mug of ale. Think about how much time you've saved!

The OBI (omnibearing indicator) and the VOR indicator are the same instrument.

The OBI Is Your Friend

When you tune in a VOR frequency, the OBI interprets the VOR signal and can tell you instantly which radial (numbered 0 through 359) you are closest to, and whether that radial leads to or from the VOR station. Once you intercept that radial and have turned to that heading, the needles on the OBI will help keep you aligned so that you maintain your course toward the VOR station. You have one more display, the DME (or distance measuring equipment) that tells you exactly how far from the VOR station you are. All of these instruments work together to keep you on course. And you don't even have to buy them a drink.

However, the OBI can be confusing if you don't pay attention because it shows your position relative to the VOR station, regardless of your heading. Once you have tuned in to a VOR station, you can choose to fly inbound or outbound on a radial. The OBI will line you up on the correct radial, but it won't indicate your direction of travel. You can select the radial heading to the station, and you can see a white triangle pointing up, and the OBI needle can line up exactly, but you might still be heading in the exact opposite direction. Obviously, keeping an eye on the DME (which indicates if you are getting closer or farther from the VOR station) is one way to avoid this unfortunate situation—though you can't always rely on this, since not every airport supports DME.

Since this can be confusing, let me give you another example. When I moved to Boston, I had to learn how to use the subway system. The hub of the Boston subway system is Park Street station, and almost all of the subway trains pass through Park Street. At every subway station on every subway line, there are two platforms—one for inbound trains, meaning trains that are going toward Park Street, and one for outbound trains, meaning trains that are coming from Park Street. This confused me to no end. I had a knack for finding a subway station and getting on the wrong platform, so I ended up going in the opposite direction. What took me a long time to realize was the fact that you can get on an Inbound train to Park Street, pass through Park Street, and all of a sudden the train changes. It's still the same train, and it's still going in the same direction, but it's now an outbound train.

Radials work the same way. Similar to a subway line or a two-laned road, radials have two directions, and you need to choose one of them with the course selector knob on the OBI. Once you pass through the VOR station, the *to* radial (white triangle pointing up) becomes a *from* radial (white triangle pointing down), and vice versa, but either heading will center the needle. Your heading doesn't make a whit of difference to the OBI. So, just remember that if you want to fly to a VOR station, be sure that you select the radial that makes the white triangle point up (to), and if you want to fly from a VOR station along a particular radial, be sure that the white triangle points down (from). Just remember to watch your compass heading and the DME along with the OBI to make sure you're not just on the right road but headed in the right direction.

VOR Has Some Limitations

VOR navigation has some drawbacks. First of all, it has a limited range. You need to be within about 100 nautical miles before you can tune in a signal from a VOR station. If you're out of range, the OBI will simply remain off. It doesn't turn itself on until you're in range of the VOR station that is tuned in on NAV 1. Second, VOR stations are strictly line-of-sight. This means that the VOR signals can be blocked by mountains or buildings. It also means that you have to be at a minimum altitude in order to pick up the signal. Finally, VOR navigation can give you a headache if you think about it too much. So, without any further delay, let's try actually using VOR navigation to fly from New York's La Guardia airport to Bridgeport, Connecticut.

EXAMPLE FLIGHT: NEW YORK TO BRIDGEPORT (AND BEYOND)

On this flight, we'll learn how to tune in a VOR beacon, select the proper radial, and fly directly to Bridgeport, passing over parts of New York and scenic Connecticut on the way. When we land at Bridgeport, we'll use the ILS to make a picture perfect landing. Dust off your aviator's hat, and let's fly!

Setting Up the Flight

1. Go to the Flights menu and choose "Create Flight."
2. Click the Select Aircraft button, and choose the Cessna Skylane 182S. Click OK.

Figure 3-16 La Guardia is one of the two major airports serving the New York City area.

3. Click the Select Airport button. Type "La Guardia" as the airport name and choose runway 4. Click OK.

4. Click the Select Time of Day button and choose Day from the pull-down menu.

5. Click OK to place yourself on the runway in New York.

6. Go to the Aircraft menu and choose "Aircraft Settings."

7. Make sure that auto-coordination is checked. Set the flight realism to halfway between easy and real. Click OK.

8. Now, choose Save Flight from the Flights menu, and title it "Escape from New York."

How to Tune In the VOR Frequency

On this flight, we'll navigate using the radio and the New York Aeronautical Map that's located in the back of your *Flight*

Simulator 98 manual. It will be a lot easier to understand this stuff if you are looking at a map, so get out that manual. In the future, you can look up just the VOR frequencies in the Airport/Facilities directory under the Help menu.

OK. Take off as normal, and climb to an altitude of 2,000 feet. We're going to fly to Sikorsky Memorial Airport, so we need to find the VOR frequency for Bridgeport. Hit P to pause the simulation, and take a look at your map.

First of all, we're flying from La Guardia Airport in New York, which is in the bottom left corner of the map, northwest of Kennedy Airport. Bridgeport/Sikorsky Memorial Airport is to our northeast, in Connecticut. Both airports are circled, with numbers corresponding to radial degrees, with zero being magnetic north. The number you see in the box with the name of the airport is the VOR frequency for that particular airport. Click the Avionics switch on the instrument panel to open the radio stack. Find the VOR frequency for Bridgeport/Sikorsky, and enter it in your NAV 1 radio by clicking on the digits in the display with the left mouse button. Once you have entered the frequency, you can put the radio display away by clicking the Avionics switch again. The VOR frequency for Bridgeport is 108.8.

Now that you are tuned to the right station, we'll use the OBI to find out where the closest radial is. Take a look at the map, and let's begin with a little common sense. Bridgeport is to our northeast, which means our heading should be around 45°. Let's see if we can get an even better estimate before we go to the OBI. We're still pretty close to La Guardia, so if you take a ruler or some other straight edge and draw a line connecting those two airports, you'll see that the ruler ends up crossing that big circle around Bridgeport just past the number 6. The 6 stands for 60°, so our desired heading will actually be pretty close to 60°, perhaps a little more. That means that one of the radials you are probably closest to right now is radial 60 or 65, or something pretty close to that. Press P again to unpause the simulation, and turn the plane toward Bridgeport. Watch your compass heading and turn to a heading of 60°. Pretty good—you should see the Connecticut coastline stretching out in front of you.

OK, now let's check out the OBI. At the lower left corner of the OBI you will see a little round knob, called the course selector knob. The numbers around the OBI represent radials you are flying to or from, and don't change unless you turn the knob and select a different radial. Think of it as tuning in a station. The needles on the OBI will change to tell you if you are still on the radial you have selected. Use the mouse button to click on the knob to change the numbers in the OBI. We're looking for the radial that is closest to our position, and we know the one we want will be around 60 or 65. You'll know when you find it because the vertical needle will center itself on the dial.

When you have tuned in the VOR station and the needle is centered, take note of the number at the top of the dial. That is the number of the radial that is closest to your position. It's also the heading that you should turn to in order to go to Bridgeport, so turn your plane to correct your heading if necessary. Now, check out the To/From indicator. The white triangle should be pointing up, letting you know that you are flying inbound on the radial heading to Bridgeport.

Don't change your heading. Take a look at the number at the bottom of the OBI. This number is always 180° from the number on the top (your selected radial). Keep flying toward Bridgeport, and click on the course selector knob on the OBI to change the selected radial to the number that was on the bottom. It should be around 240 or so. Hey, wait a second! The needle is lined up again! If you look at the To/From indicator, you will see that the white triangle points down. You're tuned into the Bridgeport VOR; does this mean you're now flying away from the airport? No, because you know you haven't changed your heading. Common sense tells you you're still headed the right way. The radial you're tuned to right now is already heading away *from* the VOR station. It's outbound. Look at the map again. If you were approaching Bridgeport from the opposite direction—from Madison, perhaps—and had tuned into this radial, the indicator would be pointing up. If you were to continue on this heading until you passed right over the VOR station, the white triangle would

Figure 3-17 Lined up on Bridgeport

switch and be pointing down because the radial tuned in to the OBI would now be an outbound radial. If you were to continue through to La Guardia, the indicator would still point down. Sooner or later you would get to the location you're at now.

So, to make a long story short, when you're flying to a VOR station, always select the radial in the OBI that points straight up. If you've pointed your aircraft in the general direction of the station, and the heading on the OBI is 180° from the direction you're heading, you've got the wrong one selected on the OBI. Keep clicking that knob until you get to the radial that makes sense.

Click the course selector knob on the OBI until you have once again located the radial heading to Bridgeport. Turn to that heading, and watch the needle. If the needle drifts left, you need to turn left to stay on course, and vice versa. Throttle back to about 2,200 RPM, and adjust the trim settings by pressing keypad ①, keypad ⑦ to keep you level.

If you are flying from a VOR station along a radial and the triangle is down, the corrections will be reversed. If the needle drifts left, you need to turn right to stay on course.

The autopilot operates with a maximum rate of 4x. You can tell the autopilot to hold a heading and altitude, then turn the autopilot off and increase the simulation rate as much as 64x.

Not every VOR is equipped with distance measuring equipment, which tells your DME display how far you are from the station. Bridgeport is one of those VORs that doesn't support DME; this is why the DME display doesn't show a reading. VORs that are DME equipped are called VORTACs. Sometimes you'll see them referred to on charts as VOR/DME. You do have a second radio, called NAV 2, which you can tune in to La Guardia and find out how far you have flown. Tune NAV 2 to La Guardia's VOR/DME frequency, which is 113.1. If the DME doesn't show a reading, click the switch at the bottom to change radios. Your DME display does double duty, with the ability to show data from either of your NAV radios. Don't worry about the OBI; just keep an eye on the DME so you'll know when you're getting close to Bridgeport. Bridgeport is about 40 nautical miles from La Guardia.

Continue flying toward Bridgeport, and enjoy the scenery along the way. Maintain an altitude of about 3,000 feet. If you like, you can set the autopilot to fly along your assigned course by choosing Autopilot from the Aircraft menu. Turn the autopilot on by clicking "Autopilot Active." Choose "NAV - NAV 1 Course Hold" from the Navigation Mode pop-up menu. Click on "Altitude Hold" and specify 3,000 feet MSL in the altitude box. You can also click on the Rate display to increase the simulation speed and make your flight time shorter. (Don't you wish you could do this in real life?)

Bridgeport is right on the coast. You'll know when you see it because you'll see the green runway beacons. When you spot the Bridgeport airport, turn off the autopilot and return the simulation to its normal rate of speed. (Make sure all seat backs and tray

Video: ILS Approaches

Location: Flight School → Ground School → Navigation → Instrument Landing System

Figure 3-18
Bridgeport from
the Air

tables are in their full upright and locked position.) We're going to turn on the EFIS/CFPD display to tune in to the ILS beacon at Bridgeport. This system will guide us in for a nice landing on the runway.

ILS Landings, or—How to Land When You Can't See the Runway

First, you need to set your NAV 1 to the ILS/Localizer frequency at Bridgeport airport. You can find the ILS frequency in the Airport/ Facilities directory under the World menu. Click on the NAV 1 radio to tune in the ILS frequency (110.7), and then choose "Navigation" from the Aircraft menu. Click on the EFIS/CFPD tab. Turn the EFIS Master Switch on. Choose "Rectangles," "Thin Density," "Long Range," and select "Lock to ILS/LOC" for landing approach. Click OK.

Figure 3-19 This is an ideal ILS descent using the EFIS/CFPD.

You should see a long line of rectangles stretching out from the airport. You need to reduce your throttle to 1,700 RPM, and match the heading and descent rate that the rectangles indicate. If you fly through all the rectangles, you will be flying the perfect glide slope for a landing approach to this airport. Remember to constantly adjust the throttle to maintain the proper descent rate, and your attitude should be slightly nose-up. Make your final approach with 30 to 40° of flaps, and 60 to 70 knots. Good luck, and we'll see you on the ground. Incidentally, when landing in heavy fog or in conditions that otherwise interfere with your view of the runway, the ILS is your best friend.

To Infinity . . . and Beyond!

In this flight you have learned to find your way using your brain, your eyes, and finally, your navigation equipment. Any pilot will tell you that your brain is the most important instrument on the plane. Never become so dependent on the instruments in front of you that you forget to think about what you're doing. Constantly evaluate your readings: What makes sense? What doesn't quite add up? By constantly measuring your instrument data against your growing base of knowledge and flight experience, you will be able to recognize if any of your instruments are malfunctioning, and you'll be able to take appropriate action.

Visit Martha's Vineyard!

You've flown from New York to Bridgeport on your own, and the day is still young! If you would like to continue your flight, line up on the runway again, and take off. How does dinner on Martha's Vineyard sound? *Flight Simulator 98* includes detailed scenery of the entire island. It's a beautiful place to end your day. See if you can find your way to the island completely on your own. Note that Martha's Vineyard is a VOR/DME station, so you can use your DME display to let you know how far you are from the airport. For more of a challenge, use the VOR to navigate to Providence,

Can *Flight Simulator* Improve Your Marriage?

When you decide you want your flights to be more realistic, you can selectively cause certain instruments to malfunction. One *Flight Simulator* player says that, to make his evenings more interesting, he has his wife choose "Instrument Display" in the Aircraft Settings box to make certain instruments inoperative. He then spends the evening flying a long-distance route, first trying to figure out which of the instruments is bad, then compensating for the loss of that instrument. Asking your spouse to do this may make you a better pilot. Asking your spouse to do this a lot may make you divorced.

Rhode Island. There's a big airport there with VORTAC, and from there you can fly southeast to Martha's Vineyard, keeping track of your distance from Providence as you go. Use the simulation rate display to shorten your travel time. As you approach Martha's Vineyard, switch to the ILS localizer frequency and make an ILS landing on the runway. By now, you should be getting a feel for the proper glide slope for a landing. Try turning off the ILS as you get within the Middle beacon for an extra challenge. As you fly over the beach, enjoy the sight of the water and the sand; with the Very Dense scenery option selected under Preferences, the scenery is simply breathtaking.

Catch a Show In Boston

If you would like to get a taste for night flying, try flying from Martha's Vineyard to Boston. You can catch a show, or see the Celtics play in the Fleet Center. Set the time of day to evening or night, take off from Martha's Vineyard, and tune in the VOR frequency at Logan International Airport. You'll cross right over

Panning Your View

Here is one way to put your IFR (instrument flight rules) skills to the test: Try to land your plane using only your instruments. You can hit ⎡⎤ from the cockpit view to blacken the screen. Use the ILS localizer to aid you in your descent down the glide slope. If you keep the VOR needle centered perfectly right down to the ground, you should land right in the middle of the runway. It helps to know the elevation of the airport where you are landing. Good luck. (Note that this is also a great way to really speed up the frame rate on slower systems.)

Cape Cod, fly up the South Shore, and see all the city lights glittering in the night. It's quite a view! Switch to the spot plane view to fully appreciate it. As you approach Logan, be sure to tune in the ATIS so you can find out which runway is being used for takeoffs and landings. The ATIS will also tell you the proper localizer frequency for that runway. Use the EFIS/CFPD to light your way to the runway. Logan International is so lit up, you might even try turning off the EFIS as you approach the Middle or Inner beacon. Stay on the same glide slope and descent rate, and you should be fine. It's a big, long runway. Happy flying!

A Word about GPS

The GPS, or Global Positioning System, is a relatively recent development. The GPS can tell you your exact location anywhere in the world, accurate to a few hundred feet, by picking up signals from satellites overhead. The GPS was used with great success by American troops during Desert Storm to navigate in the desert. Even at night, with no visible landmarks, you can always tell where you are by using GPS. The system even works in bad weather, when other forms of radio navigation are affected. Though the GPS is an electronic device, and you shouldn't rely solely on it for your safety, in *Flight Simulator 98* you can simulate a GPS by pressing Shift-Z. This tells you your exact latitude, longitude, and altitude.

PANNING YOUR VIEW

Pan Up	Shift - Backspace
Pan Down	Shift - Enter
Pan Right	Ctrl - Shift - Enter
Pan Left	Ctrl - Shift - Backspace
Straight and Level	Scroll Lock

LEARJET 45

The Learjet—now you're playing with power. Since the mid-sixties this twin-engine aircraft has been *the* symbol for the jet-set power players of the world. Although the Learjet 45 operates on the same basic principles (maneuvered around the three axes of pitch, roll, and yaw) and uses the same flight controls as the Cessna, the similarities end there.

The Learjet has a functional ceiling of around 45,000 feet, and it has a maximum Mach (speed of sound) of .81. With twin turbo-fan engines providing a total of 7,000 pounds of thrust, the Learjet can climb at a rate of over 4,300 feet per minute. Suffice it to say, this is not your mother's airplane. Indeed, it's an entirely different animal that's an order of magnitude more complicated than any of the propeller-driven aircraft in *Flight Simulator*. For starters, in real life, the Learjet requires two pilots to operate safely. So, are you ready to rumble? Let's get started.

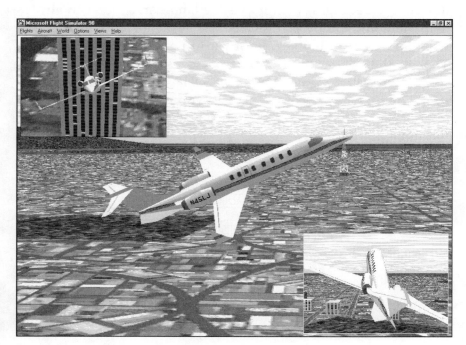

Figure 3-20 The Learjet in action, captured using the different view options

Fly Before You Buy

From the Flight menu, select "Adventures," pick the "Learjet 45: Fly Before You Buy" adventure, and get ready to learn the ropes. You'll be managing a takeoff, cruising down Puget Sound, then landing at Boeing Field, all with the help of a friendly copilot. The tower will instruct you as to what to do, but in case you don't hear them clearly (which is entirely possible), you need to take off and turn to a heading of 200° at an altitude of 3,000 feet. You will soon see the red boxes you will be following into Boeing Field, but that's not to say you can't joy ride a little. If you contravene any of the Learjet or FAA regulations, you will be sternly reminded. Gear and flaps must be up over 200 knots, and you cannot exceed 250 knots under 10,000 feet. In this first flight, you might find it highly beneficial to keep your controls set on auto-coordination. The Learjet has a substantially different "feel" from the Cessna, and if you start fiddling with rudders, you might just find yourself sleeping with the fishes.

The Main Differences

The fundamental differences between the Cessna and the Learjet can be summarized in a few brief points—speed, the type of engines, speed, the number of engines, speed, the system's complexities, the handling characteristics, and of course, speed. Beyond the basics of flight, these two aircraft are markedly disparate, and as you might have guessed, speed plays a major factor in the equation.

Two Engines (and Different Engines at That)

While having two engines provides an added measure of safety, it also creates an additional chore for the pilot to monitor and operate. Surprisingly, a twin-engine aircraft can also present some interesting problems for the pilot if something goes wrong. As previously noted, flying with both engines in the Lear provides a great deal of performance; however, losing one engine will degrade the performance of the aircraft by more than half and create problems in overall control. Although the Learjet's engines are placed fairly close together on the tail, having one quit will create a huge displacement in yaw, causing multiple headaches for controlling the plane. By comparison, if the Cessna loses an engine, it becomes a glider, and it still handles basically the same way it did when the engine was running.

Having two engines also affords you the luxury of surviving in the face of catastrophic engine failure. Although it's certainly no walk in the park, you can definitely land safely on one healthy engine. Though the jet engine is powerful, you'll notice that it's slow to spool up to speed when compared to the prop. As a result, if you get yourself into a "must have power now" situation, you're probably headed toward a world of hurt. Also, because the jet engine basically sucks vast amounts of air into its intake, it's much more susceptible to FOD (foreign object damage), such as birds, gravel, trash, and so on. If a bird takes a shortcut through the turbine, you can kiss that engine goodbye.

There have been many instances of commercial airliners having to make emergency landings after losing an engine to a flock of seagulls.

Bipolarism

If you really have a hankering for mayhem, take the Learjet up to about 10,000 feet and set up a comfortable cruising speed. Set the throttle to 100 percent in the left engine and full reverse thrust in the right engine. Welcome to hell. The resulting push/pull will make any landing (or, indeed, any maneuver) an adventure you won't soon forget.

All Things Speed

While the Cessna is designed to operate mostly at low altitudes and airspeeds, the Learjet is just the opposite. The Lear does not handle as well at low speeds as the Cessna. The Cessna cruises along comfortably letting the pilot leisurely navigate his or her way, using a road map if nothing else. The Learjet, on the other hand, operates at such high speeds that navigation becomes much more complex. In the real world, FAA regulations prohibit flying at more than 250 knots below 10,000 feet.

The higher the performance of the plane, the higher your level of planning must be to operate the aircraft safely, and the Learjet is a prime example of this. When you first take the Learjet up, you'll be struck with several observations. First, the aircraft is much more "touchy" and can be put into a fatal spin with greater ease. This is the least of your worries.

Figure 3-21
The Learjet
instrument panel

Second, when coming in for a landing, you'll quickly notice the disturbing speed at which the runway looms large in your windshield. When flying the Learjet, it can be easy to fall into the euphoria created by the raw power at your fingertips, but you must think much further ahead than you would in the Cessna. As the saying goes, you must always "stay ahead of the game!"

Landings and Takeoffs

While the Cessna can use just about any airport, the same is positively not true for the Learjet. In the real world, runway length, temperature, wind, and aircraft weight must always be considered before each takeoff and landing. Likewise, flap settings and take-off speeds must always be carefully calculated and set properly. Fortunately, in *Flight Simulator* it's not quite as complicated. Basi-

If you find yourself climbing into the misty realms of overspeed in your Learjet, there are several things you can do to slow down. First, reduce your throttle, although this alone won't have any immediately substantial effect on your velocity. Second, pull back on the stick and let good old gravity take the edge off—though this technique isn't of much help if you're trying to land. Last, you can use the Learjet's secret speed weapon, the spoiler. Press the / key to engage the spoiler, which acts like an air brake. Used in combination with one or more of the other techniques, it will get you slowed down in a jiffy. Remember, sometimes you can push your jet too far, and the result can be stress damage or an uncontrolled spin to terra firma. The moral of the story: Don't be a lead foot if you want to live.

cally, you can take off in a fairly short distance by applying full power and extending the flaps to 8° or 20°. This makes takeoff a snap compared to landing. Landing the Lear requires much more planning. Landing speeds are usually much higher, making it more important to be "in the slot" and stable for landing. This is also more important due to the fact that the Lear does not handle as well at slow speeds, and the engines will not respond as quickly to power adjustments. Always take into consideration the wing tip clearance in crosswinds, tire hydroplaning on wet runways, and braking factors from the higher touchdown speeds.

Reverse Thrusters

After you manage to touch your Learjet down on the tarmac, your battle is only partially over. You must now find a way to stop the substantial weight of your jet from forcing you right off the end of the runway. The answer? Reverse thrusters. If you've ever flown in a commercial jet airliner, you no doubt remember the very loud roar the engines emit just after touchdown on the runway. This loud rumble is the result of the reverse thrusters snapping into action. Basically, the reverse thrusters do exactly what their name implies, slowing the craft down dramatically. In conjunction with prudent braking and spoiler management, reverse thrusters enable you to land your Learjet on much smaller runways than you might think possible. Just after your wheels hit the runway, drop the throttle to zero by hitting the F1 key, deploy the spoilers with the / key, and press F2 to engage the reverse thrusters. Voilá! Once your jet has slowed to 60 knots, turn the reverse thrusters off by hitting F3 or you'll end up doing a "wheelie" with your $8 million jet.

STUPID CESSNA TRICKS

One of the best things about *Flight Simulator* is its extensive support for airports all over the world. With a world atlas, a list of VOR frequencies, and the onboard GPS (Shift-Z), you can set up your own flight routes and travel anywhere you want to go. By now, you know how to navigate using visual or electronic navigation, you know how to read a map, how to set the autopilot for those long flights, how to speed up time, and how to change the weather. Now, this is all well and good for real pilots, but we've reached the point in our *Flight Simulator* training when it's time to have some real fun—the kind you won't find in any pilot's manual. Here are some fun flights, stunts, and challenges you can try on your own.

Fly from Meigs to Champaign

This is a great relaxing flight. The Chicago area in *Flight Simulator 98* is tremendously detailed, so you can really enjoy the scenery. Turn on the Weather Generation option in the Preferences box, so

Figure 3-22 This is the building in Champaign, Illinois, that was the headquarters for the company that designed the original version of *Flight Simulator*.

you will encounter random weather patterns. Place yourself at Meigs Field for takeoff, then climb to 2,000 feet and have a look around. Use nearby VOR stations to plot a course inland, to Champaign, Illinois, where the original version of *Flight Simulator* was born.

To see the crew that designed the original *Flight Simulator*:

1. Choose the Boeing 737-400.

2. Go to the World menu and choose "Go to Exact Location."

3. In the Aircraft Position area, enter a latitude of N40*8.71'.

4. In the Aircraft Position area, enter a longitude of W88*12.23'.

5. Enter an altitude of 743 feet.

6. Enter a heading of 173°and an airspeed of 0 knots. Click OK.

7. You will find yourself in front of a billboard with pictures of the BAO team.

The Rocket Cessna

Just how fast can a Cessna go in free fall? You can boost yourself as high as 100,000 feet into the upper stratosphere by using the "Go to Exact Location" option, and dive toward the earth at terminal velocity. You can try flying around, but be careful—the air's mighty thin up there! In fact, it's so thin that the amount of air molecules rushing past your aircraft is hardly enough to register on your indicators. You can fix this by going into the Preferences dialog box and turning off "Display Indicated Airspeed." This gets the airspeed indicator to display your true airspeed, which is how fast your plane would be going from an observer's standpoint. It isn't easy, but you can actually break 1,000 knots in the Cessna with the right combination of maneuvering and judicious use of the "Go to Exact Location" box. Don't forget your oxygen mask!

Figure 3-23
Over 1,000 knots
in a Cessna?

Practice Your VOR Skills

Hidden way out in the Arizona desert is an aerobatics box that you can use for competition in the Extra 300S. You can find it using your VOR navigation skills. Just take off from Avra Valley, Tucson, and fly away from the Tucson VOR (116.0) on the 297° radial. Keep an eye on the DME: You'll find it about 21 nautical miles away.

Stump the Instructor

The instructor is quite good at landing the plane—so good that he gives you grief every time you take a lesson. Now it's time to take revenge. Use the Weather dialog box to create a nightmare situation of low visibility and dueling crosswinds, then hand it off to your instructor and have him land the plane. If he does

Figure 3-24
Mysterious crop markings in the Arizona desert, left here by aliens so you can practice your aerobatic skills

manage to pull it off, it can be entertaining and instructive at the same time.

CREATING DUELING CROSSWINDS

1. Start at Meigs Field, Chicago, or any other airport that supports the "Land Me" option.

2. Go to the World menu and choose Weather. Click the Winds tab.

3. Click on Add Layer and create a steady Surface Layer 20-knot wind 90° to the runway.

4. Click on Add Layer again and create a gusting Low Layer 20-knot wind 90° from the runway, with a base of 750 feet.

Figure 3-25 On a bad approach like this, or when you're pointed away from the runway at a low altitude, hit X and watch the instructor crank the plane around in an attempt to land it anyway.

Cessna Goes Zoom!

For the best view of airport activities, you have to turn on all of the detail options. On slower machines, this may cause the frame rate to drop quite a bit.

Slew mode is not just a very convenient way to position yourself in the *Flight Simulator* world. Slewing can also give you a real sensation of speed if you zoom along the ground in full-screen view. It's also a great way to show off your machine if you have a 3D graphics accelerator card installed. Simply start at any airport, and press Y to engage slew mode at any time. Your yoke then becomes a way to move your aircraft along the ground at tremendous speeds. Press Alt-Enter to enter full-screen mode, and press W to hide the instrument panel. In slew mode, you're invincible! Push forward on the yoke to zoom along the ground. It's also fun to turn on the smoke system in Aircraft Settings and pull back on the yoke. This causes you to slew backwards, and you can see your smoke trail out in front of you. It's an interesting perspective!

Front Row Seat

When I was a kid I used to like to go down to the airport and watch airplanes take off and land. Busy airports like Chicago O'Hare are a perfect place to watch large jets take off and land, and the very best place to watch (in *Flight Simulator*, of course) is from your very own seat, front row and center, right in the middle of the main runway!

1. Go to the World menu and choose "Scenery Complexity." Choose Very Dense from the Image Complexity pull-down menu and click OK.

2. Go to the World menu and choose "Dynamic Scenery." Turn on all the options, and choose Very Dense from the Scenery Frequency pull-down menu.

Figure 3-26 Hey, Just Like the Movies!

3. Go to the World menu and choose "Go to Airport."

4. Choose USA - Chicago from the Scenery Area pull-down menu. Choose O'Hare Intl - Rwy 27R from the Airport menu and click OK.

5. Go to the Aircraft menu and choose "Crash & Damage." Select "Ignore Crash" and click OK.

6. Congratulations—you're indestructible! Taxi around and look at the sights. Use the spot plane view and press W to get a wide-screen view.

If you taxi around and watch the flight operations, you will notice one particular runway where planes are landing and taking off. Station yourself on or near this runway for the best view.

Remote Control Plane

You can actually fly the Cessna from the spot plane view. This tests your knowledge of the instruments, as you no longer have a first-hand perspective. You do, however, have a nifty remote control plane, and a view that follows behind it constantly. If you can land the plane from the spot plane view, you have definitely mastered landings. See if you can buzz the Eiffel Tower!

Blowing Smoke

You can use the smoke system on the plane to leave a trail behind your aircraft. Although the smoke trail isn't long enough to write your name (unless it's one letter long), you can do loops and spins, and the smoke will mark the path of your plane. Once you are fairly high above the airport, use the Tower view for the best view (press S once), and press + to zoom in. You can turn the smoke system on in the Aircraft Settings box under the Aircraft menu.

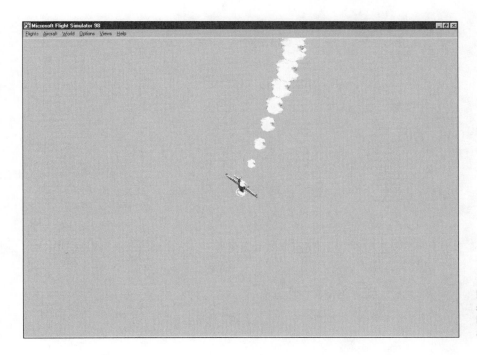

Figure 3-27 Use smoke to dramatically highlight your aerobatic feats.

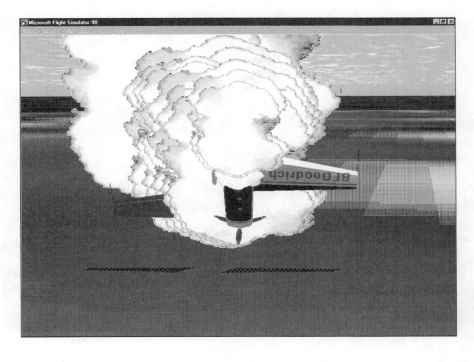

Figure 3-28 Smoke also makes it look pretty realistic when you crash.

CHAPTER
4

Commercial Pilot

So, now you're a Sierra Hotel pilot (you're hot!). You know your aircraft like the back of your hand. You've flown and landed in terrible weather and dueling crosswinds, just for the fun of it. You've buzzed the Grand Canyon and flown in reckless circles around the Eiffel Tower. What's next? Well, why not jump into a completely different plane and start flying commercial aircraft?

In this chapter, you will learn how radio communication works in *Flight Simulator 98.* You will also learn how to fly the largest, most powerful *Flight Simulator* aircraft, the Boeing 737-400.

HOW TO TALK TO THE TOWER

Mid-air collisions and near misses are fortunately extremely rare. It is even more unlikely that you would collide with another airplane while en route from, say, Tulsa to Oklahoma City. There is simply so much space out there to fly in that if you keep to customary altitudes, you won't run into anything. At a busy airport, however, where you might have dozens of planes all vying for the same airspace and runway clearance, you can imagine what a nightmare it would be if pilots just decided to land wherever and whenever they chose. To avoid problems, planes take off and land in an organized fashion, coordinated by air traffic controllers and preestablished rules of movement, called patterns. An example of these would be traffic patterns and holding patterns.

Video: Entering a Holding Pattern

Location: Flight School → Ground School → Navigation → Holding Patterns → Traffic Pattern

How to Keep from Getting Lonely

In *Flight Simulator* you have the freedom to land and depart in whatever fashion you choose. The air traffic controllers won't actually direct you into holding patterns or steer you clear of the flight paths of other airplanes, but the tower will talk to you, and after a while you may even find yourself responding. Here, then, is an explanation of how to talk to the tower and how to get the tower to talk back.

The Phonetic Alphabet

A	Alpha
B	Bravo
C	Charlie
D	Delta
E	Echo
F	Foxtrot
G	Golf
H	Hotel
I	India
J	Juliett
K	Kilo
L	Lima
M	Mike
N	November
O	Oscar
P	Papa
Q	Quebec
R	Romeo
S	Sierra
T	Tango
U	Uniform
V	Victor
W	Whiskey
X	Xray
Y	Yankee
Z	Zulu

How to Sound Like a Real Pilot

"Honolulu approach, *Microsoft Flight Simulator* niner five Whiskey, two zero miles south, inbound to Honolulu International with information Bravo." This is what you might say if you were 20 miles south of Honolulu International Airport, and the last ATIS message you received was Bravo. Notice how the numbers are always spoken one digit at a time to avoid miscommunications, like hearing "15" when the tower said "50."

In general, your messages to the tower can be broken down into the following parts:

1. Whom you are addressing
2. Who you are
3. What your location is
4. What you want to do

A Sample Dialogue

Communication in *Flight Simulator* is abbreviated but accurate. You can request clearances to take off and land and receive responses from the tower. The following dialogue is broken up into what a real dialogue might sound like, and then into what *Flight Simulator*'s communication sounds like, which is not quite the same. Your clearance requests will scroll across the top of the screen. But you can read the actual lines out loud as that happens, since it's more authentic and it sounds cool. Give it a try. Clear your throat, and announce in a deep, resounding voice: "Meigs ground, Cessna two one niner ready to take off runway three six." Don't you feel more authoritative already?

Getting Takeoff Clearance

Actual dialogue:

> YOU: Meigs Tower, Cessna two one niner ready for takeoff runway three six.
>
> ATC: Cessna two one niner, hold short of runway three six, landing traffic.

YOU: Hold short runway three six, Cessna two one niner.

Here, our Cessna requests takeoff clearance and is told to hold short, which means the runway isn't clear yet (in this case, due to other airplanes landing on that runway), so aircraft should wait in position at the end of the runway. Pilots are required to read back all hold short instructions and runway information, so here the Cessna repeats that information to the tower.

What to do in *Flight Simulator*:

Go to the Aircraft menu and choose "Communications."

Check the "Request to Take Off" option. Click OK. You will see the following:

"Microsoft Flight Simulator requesting takeoff clearance."

The controller will either give you clearance or ask you to hold short:

"Microsoft Flight Simulator, taxi to runway of your choice and hold short. Squawk 0272."

This means that the runway isn't clear yet, so you need to taxi to the runway and wait until it's clear. When you receive messages from ATC, you should repeat the instructions you have been given, so you would respond:

"Microsoft Flight Simulator, hold short runway three six."

Set your transponder to the requested code.

When it is clear to take off, you will see: *"Microsoft Flight Simulator* cleared for takeoff." It is now OK to throttle up and take off.

If "Crash When Hitting Dynamic Scenery" is checked in the Crash & Damage dialog box, taking off without the proper clearance may result in a mid-air collision!

Getting Landing Clearance

Actual dialogue:

YOU: Meigs Tower, Cessna two one niner, one five miles northwest, landing.

ATC: Cessna two one niner, you are cleared to land runway six.

This dialogue is pretty straightforward. The controller may, depending on conditions, order an incoming flight to enter a

holding pattern until it is clear to land or to hold short of a particular runway after landing on the cleared runway.

What to do in *Flight Simulator*:

> Go to the Aircraft menu and choose "Communications."
>
> Check the "Request to Land" option. Click OK. You will
> see the following: "*Microsoft Flight Simulator* requesting
> landing clearance."
>
> After a few seconds, the controller will respond: "*Microsoft
> Flight Simulator*, you are cleared to land."

Isn't that nice? You are always first priority for a landing.
Flight Simulator will never ask you to enter a holding pattern or to
perform a procedure turn, but you should keep your eyes open for
other planes taking off and landing in the vicinity. It's not unusual

Figure 4-1 Cessna
vs. 747: Why you
should get clearance
before
you take off.

to start a landing approach and see a Learjet taking off directly in front of you!

Other Stuff the Control Tower Tells You

For now, until actual air traffic control procedures are implemented in *Flight Simulator*, most of the messages you get from the control tower are "reading optional." Still, it's nice to know what they're trying to tell you. Following are translations of the tower's sometimes cryptic messages.

"Inform Controller On Initial Contact You Have Whiskey"

Note: This is not a request that you make a customs declaration! Keep quiet about the crate of Canadian whiskey in the back, and we won't tell anyone. Seriously, this is a message from ATIS to let you know how recent their update is. ATIS is the automatic terminal information service, and it's tuned in on your COM 1 radio. It provides regular updates on the weather, visibility conditions, and which runways are being used for landing and takeoff. It gives the air traffic controllers a break so they don't have to repeat all that information each time a new aircraft enters the pattern. Subsequent messages are tagged with a letter from the phonetic alphabet, so that when you first contact ATC, you can tell the air traffic controller how up-to-date you are.

"Squawk 0219"

Or, "squawk" any other four-digit number. This is actually a transponder code, and you need to enter it in the XPDR display on your instrument panel so that the air traffic controllers know who you are. They will check up on you to see if you have set it, so when you get this message you do need to actually change it.

THE BOEING 737-400

The Boeing 737-400 is the largest aircraft available to you in *Microsoft Flight Simulator 98*. The 737-400 is the largest of the 737 fleet, and it was first introduced in 1988. Flying this jet is like nothing else you've experienced. Large aircraft like the 737 handle very, very differently, requiring several flights before you really begin to get the "feel" of the aircraft and of just how far ahead you'll have to think.

Introductory Flight

Preflight

Although Meigs Field doesn't look like it has sufficient runway to handle a 737 (it probably doesn't), in this simulator it is possible, although unusual to take off from the airport on Lake Michigan. Take a minute to familiarize yourself with the cockpit of the 737,

Figure 4-2 The 737-400 is a completely different kind of animal compared to what you've been flying.

and if necessary, adjust the window size of the control panel in order to "see over the dash" a little better. You can also hit (Shift)-(Enter) to shift your view up. Hit (Shift)-(Del) to shift your view back down. For more information on the 737's checklists, go to the Aircraft Handbook of Help, Pilot's Help section of the main menu and select the Boeing 737-400. Here you will find checklists for every portion of flight from preflight to landing. While in the cockpit, you can press (Shift)-(C) to display abbreviated checklists in an easy-to-read spiral notebook format. You can do this for every aircraft, but it's particularly useful in a complicated aircraft like the Boeing 747-400. The (W) key is great for toggling the instrument panel on and off.

Takeoff

When you're ready, put your flaps down to 5° and smoothly increase the power. Keep on rolling down the runway until your speed is about 150 knots, then smoothly rotate slowly. Notice how

Figure 4-3
The 737-400
Instrument Panel

sloooooow it is to take off? This is no Extra. Raise your landing gear and continue your climb at a steep 15° until you reach 2,000 feet. Now, bank your jet (fairly tightly) to a heading of 110°, but be careful not to pull too much or you'll stall, and stalling a 737 isn't much fun. This course will take you away from downtown Chicago and out over Lake Michigan; this will give you a chance to familiarize yourself with the cockpit. Keep the 110° heading and stop your climb at around 5,000 feet. Reduce your throttle so that you don't exceed 250 knots.

Cruising

Once you're at or above 210 knots, gradually retract your flaps (if you haven't already) and take some time to experiment with the throttles. Reduce power to about 40 percent. Notice the power drop? The power curve in this jet is not linear, and setting the throttle to a low setting will eliminate more power than you might anticipate. Also note the delay while your engines "wind up" and "spin down."

Your power is certainly not on demand, so be sure to think ahead. Take the time to bank from left to right a little in order to get a feel for just how fast this slug of an aircraft responds. Try to keep basically on a heading of 110° (you'll notice you're heading away from the VOR signal).

Don't worry about where you're flying. Take time to experiment with minor changes in altitude and dipping your wings. Notice the sliding knob to the left of the throttles: This is your spoiler control, which helps control the speed of your aircraft. The spoiler is slow to deploy and retract, so again, think ahead when using it. As an example, deploy your spoiler and notice its effect on your overall speed.

Quick Turnaround?

Had enough cruising? OK, maintain an altitude of 5,000 feet, and prepare for a tight turn to your left. Increase the throttle to 80 percent and bank sharply to your left, coming to a heading of around 285°. This maneuver will give you a very good idea of how hard it is to manage difficult situations in the 737. If you are like most novice pilots, you will come out of your turn too late and will have to turn back to achieve a heading of 285°. Not to worry—you have plenty of time to get on course.

You are now heading back over downtown Chicago, and Meigs Field will be to your left; however, we are not going to land at Meigs Field. We are going to land at O'Hare International. As you approach Chicago, you'll need to descend to 2,500 feet in preparation for landing. This is a great opportunity for you to learn how to slow the aircraft while descending. Reducing power is the obvious choice, but you may also have to use your spoilers. Maintain an airspeed of 200 knots.

Maintain a heading of 285° (toward the river). After a short while you'll notice an airport toward your right-hand view; after it begins to pass out of your sight, make a right turn toward the airport and pick a runway to line up your approach. There are two runways that will be roughly in front of you from this approach; they both look a little short, and you may wonder if the 737 can land on them safely. Don't worry—they are both long enough to land without the use of reverse thrusters.

Landing

After you turn toward the airport, line up on one of the two runways ahead of you. Reduce the throttle to around 50 percent and lower your flaps to decrease your airspeed. If your approach is too fast, engage the spoiler as well. Landing the 737 is the same as landing any other aircraft, except you must think a bit farther ahead. Once you hit the tarmac there is the additional problem of stopping the 737 before it careens off the end of the runway. Transport aircraft do not maneuver easily at slow speeds and the momentum of a 130,000-pound aircraft does not change instantly. A stable approach is the key to a safe landing.

Once you hit the runway, hit the keypad ③ key then press the ⓪ keypad key several times. This will engage your reverse thrusters and help slow you down. Reverse thrusters don't actually "reverse" the engines; rather, they redirect the flow of air from the rear of the engine forward, thus thrusters in conjunction with your brakes should enable you to stop in plenty of time.

Figure 4-4 Be sure to line up on the runway far in advance, or you'll end up overshooting it.

The Differences

The main differences in the 737 are its vastly increased weight and its slower maneuverability and handling. But the 737 flies using the same basic principles of flight. This is done to prevent bending the airframe if full rudder deflection were applied at high speeds.

Larger aircraft like the 737 are designed to be flown with little changes to pitch and roll. Bank angles are usually limited to 25° or 30° and pitch angles of 10°–15°. Performance is the most important factor when considering safety, and stabilized approaches lead to successful landings.

The most important thing you need to remember when flying the 737 is to think ahead. This really cannot be stressed enough. The inherently slow response time of the controls on this aircraft will have you thinking that something is wrong the first time you take it up for a spin. However, after several flights you will begin

Loopy

If you like a challenge, take the 737 out for a spin with the realism set to medium, auto-coordination off, and make it so your plane can receive damage from stress. Then try to do a giant loop heading up and over. A properly flown loop imposes no unusual stress on the aircraft. It does, however, require a lot of altitude. Take it up to around 5,000 feet and get your speed up to at least 275 knots. Now pull back on the stick and begin the journey up and over. When you reach a vertical attitude things will begin to get tough, but you should have enough oomph to make it over the top, which is really the easy part. The hard part is diving back down the other side without your jet disintegrating under the stress. The best way to do this is to drop your throttle to zero the second you start to dive. It's also a good idea to extend the spoiler (this will also slow you). If you do things right, you'll never exceed 300 knots, and best of all, you'll still have a jet to land.

to get a feel for the 737, and you'll no doubt attempt some trick maneuvers.

The Instrument Panel and the HSI

Regardless of the size of the plane, the basic instruments are always there. The airspeed, attitude, altitude, HSI, and vertical speed is always present.

An HSI is really just a flat heading indicator with a course indicator tied to the VOR and ILS presentations. It provides all of the pilot's situational awareness for navigation.

The HSI gives you a top-down view of your airplane's position relative to a VOR signal. This top-down view means that your

Figure 4-5 Putting the 737 through a loop is very tricky (and dangerous), but it can be done.

aircraft is at the center of the HSI, with the magnetic heading at the top in green. The yellow arrow is the omnibearing selector, and it has a middle portion that moves back and forth to indicate any course deviation. The white triangle near the center of the indicator points toward the VOR station.

If you want to get a feel for the HSI, go up to the autopilot panel and click on the section marked "Course." Notice that as the course is adjusted, the yellow arrow on the HSI moves accordingly. To intercept the VOR, turn toward the offset middle yellow lines at about a 30° angle. These middle yellow lines will approach the center when you get on the VOR signal. Correct your course and voilá, you're on the VOR heading. It's really very simple, and handy as well.

Figure 4-6 The HSI is basically a VOR indicator overlayed on a heading indicator.

To use the HSI for ILS landings, tune the ILS frequency into the NAV radio. You can then intercept the landing approach just as you would a VOR signal. The glide slope indicator is a diamond that moves vertically on the right side of the HSI. Predictably, if it's below the middle, you're above the glide scope and vice versa.

ASK THE PILOT

I was very lucky to have Captain Ron Hunt of American Airlines at my disposal when writing this book. Ron is a twenty-year veteran of commercial piloting, and he currently flies Boeing 757s and 767s. We thought that since we were talking about large jets in this section, it would be interesting to throw a few "what ifs" at Ron to see how a seasoned pilot would respond.

What Are the "Basics" for Inflight Emergencies?

"Airline transport pilots go through a continuous training program during their careers. Captains typically go through training every six months in simulators, and first officers do this once a year. Along with this, a constant flow of information on the aircraft's systems and operations, as well as accident and incident reports, is provided throughout the year. Training not only involves aircraft systems and flying but also human factors. From all of this, the pilot is able to keep up with all the latest changes in the business and with the equipment. This also helps each pilot to develop a basic plan to any 'what if' question." That plan should always start with these basics:

1. Fly the airplane
2. Communicate—with each other and ATC
3. Assess the situation—run appropriate checklists
4. Land at the nearest suitable airport
5. Fly the airplane

"These seem very basic—just plain common sense—but accident investigations have shown that during a major malfunction it's easy for the entire crew to focus on the problem and neglect the fact that one person *must* stay in charge of the store—the aircraft must still be flown."

What Would You Do If You Had Engine Power but Lost the Hydraulics?

"This is a more common occurrence. However, all aircraft that use hydraulic-powered flight controls have backup systems. If they didn't, you would be nothing more than an unguided projectile. Generally, in this situation you will have limited control of the aircraft. Landing gear always have alternate extension systems, but the slats and flaps may not. The biggest problems you face will be very high landing speeds and limited braking. Brakes are always part of the hydraulic system. The plan in most cases would be to fly the aircraft down to minimum fuel, so you would be at the lowest possible landing weight. This translates to slowest possible

You can control the landing spotlight on the helicopter or on any of the aircraft by holding Ctrl and pressing the keypad keys. Ctrl-keypad 5 stops all movement.

landing speed. While doing this, you would want to plan landing on the longest possible runway into the wind. This is a serious situation but very manageable."

What Would You Do If You Lost One of Two Engines?

"This is also a more common occurrence. Fly the airplane. Communicate with ATC and the cabin crew. Land at the nearest airport. The worst place this can happen is during takeoff. You have little or no altitude cushion, and the aircraft has little flying speed. With the loss of an engine, the aircraft performance will be extremely degraded and a significant amount of yaw will create control problems. You want to get the aircraft cleaned up (gear and flaps retracted) and accelerate to the best single-engine climb speed. After this is accomplished, run the "Engine Failure" checklist, the "One Engine Approach and Landing" checklists, and any other checklist appropriate for the situation. Communicate with the cabin crew so they can prepare. Fly the aircraft to the nearest suitable airport and land."

In *Flight Simulator*, if the gear won't lower, you can try to pump the gear down by pressing Ctrl-G.

CHAPTER

5

Barnstormer

In this section you will learn about the engineless sailplane, the legendary Sopwith Camel, and the red-hot Extra 300S. All of these aircraft are on the higher end of the *Flight Simulator* learning curve, and as such they are considered barnstormer material. This chapter also includes handy breakdowns on how to defeat the challenges that *Microsoft Flight Simulator 98* has to offer.

THE SCHWEIZER 2-32 SAILPLANE

The moment you start flying in the sailplane, you will be struck by how quiet it is. By now, you have probably gotten used to hearing the drone of the Cessna's engine (a comforting sound given the alternative, of course). The sailplane has no throttle, no engine, no propeller. It is an unpowered glider that gets where it wants to go by soaring on columns of rising air. If you have ever looked up in

Figure 5-1 Get ready to learn some of the high-end tricks of the trade.

Figure 5-2 The sailplane's cockpit contains the bare necessities.

the sky and seen birds soaring on the wind, barely moving a feather, and wished you could be up there with them, then the sailplane is for you.

A Look at the Cockpit

The cockpit of the sailplane is very basic. You really only need the altimeter, an airspeed indicator, and a VSI to fly the sailplane. As luxuries, you will find a compass and radio. The most important instruments in the sailplane are your eyes and brain.

Some Good Places to Soar

The best places for sailplane activity are places that have a lot of columns of warm air rising vertically. You'll find great places to soar in Munich, Seattle, and San Francisco. If you have the desire to fly in Hawaii, there are some great places to fly on the Big

Island. If you go to the Flights menu and choose "Select Flight," you will find a number of sailplane situations.

How Is a Sailplane Like the Space Shuttle?

Sailplanes are towed into the air by an airplane, just as the space shuttle is lifted into the air by booster rockets. Sailplanes glide in for a landing, just like the space shuttle does. Okay, space shuttle pilots probably make more money than glider pilots, but hey, the sailplane is almost as much fun, I'd bet. Let's get into the air and try it out!

You don't have a tow cable on your sailplane, so to get into the air you need to activate slew mode by pressing Y. Press F4 to gain altitude quickly. When you get to about 4,000 feet, turn off slew by pressing Y. Congratulations—you're soaring!

In any airplane, altitude is airspeed. You can trade off altitude for airspeed by diving. Therefore, the more altitude you have, the more potential energy you have on your side. Think of it as an energy game: thermals provide energy that you store in the form of altitude, for those times when you are traveling between thermals or ridges.

Another way to get into the air is to take off in a different plane and switch to the sailplane when you are at altitude. There's a nifty trick you can't do in real life!

I have no engine! What do I do?

Important Tip #1: Keep a constant eye out for thermal areas or ridges to gain altitude.

Important Tip #2: Keep an eye on your altitude. If you run out of altitude, you crash.

Important Tip #3: Watch your airspeed. If it drops below 45 mph, you will stall (see Important Tip #2).

Thermal Soaring

Dark patches of ground absorb more heat than light patches. You can experience this yourself by walking barefoot on an asphalt parking lot in the hot sun—you'll quickly find the white lines are a lot cooler to walk on than the blacktop. Out in the countryside, desert areas and brown fields are heated by the sun and create thermal currents of air that rise constantly. Basically, brown fields will cause you to rise, and green areas won't. Head for dark patches of ground, get right above them, and watch your altimeter. If you start rising in the column of air, try to stay directly over the field by flying in circles and doubling back. You can get a lot of altitude this way.

Ridge Soaring

Another way to stay aloft is to look for ridges or cliffs that rise vertically from the ground. When wind hits the ridge, it travels upward. You can soar above a ridge as long as the wind lasts. One technique that works well is to fly along the edge of the ridge, then turn away from the ridge and head back in the other direction. When you get to that end, turn away from the ridge again and come back. In essence, you are flying in a figure-eight pattern, which is a good way to make use of the ridge lift. Be sure to stay parallel to the ridge line; it's easy to pass right over the ridge if your turns are too wide.

THE SOPWITH CAMEL

The Sopwith Camel is a great plane to play around with because it flies fairly slowly compared to the other planes and is highly maneuverable. This made the Sopwith Camel a great fighter plane in 1914. It makes the Sopwith Camel a great plane for buzzing metropolitan buildings in the present day. Try using the Sopwith Camel to take a low-altitude tour of Paris, or try to fly under all the bridges in New York City. To really feel the wind in your hair, try pressing $\boxed{S}$ to fly from the virtual cockpit.

When you're in a dive, use the spoilers by pressing $\boxed{/}$ to keep yourself from exceeding the sailplane's maximum airspeed of 150 mph.

Figure 5-3 The
Sopwith Camel
cockpit.

The Sopwith Camel
is a biplane, which
means it has an
extra set of wings
that generate
extra lift.

Take a Tour of the Cockpit

The Sopwith Camel does away with all those silly little frills that clutter the instrument panels of modern airplanes. Vertical speed indicator? Pshaw! In my day we threw blades of grass from the open cockpit. Artificial horizon? Harumph! That's what the real horizon's for! All you really need to fly the Sopwith Camel are the altimeter and the airspeed indicator. Keep an eye out for them German Aces.

The Camel Drags Its Tail

The Sopwith Camel is known as a tail-dragger, which means that the tail rests on a tail wheel. If you're used to taking off in a Cessna, you may be surprised to find that you have to apply a little forward pressure on the yoke as you accelerate for takeoff; this lifts the tail wheel off the ground slightly. As you gain airspeed, pull back smoothly on the stick, and you'll be in the air in no time.

Landing the Camel

Landing the Sopwith Camel is no mean feat; it takes even more practice than the other planes. You don't have a vertical speed indicator to monitor your rate of descent, so keep your eye on the altimeter to get an idea for how fast you're coming down.

THE EXTRA 300S

This is the hot rod of the pack in *Flight Simulator*. Manufactured in Germany, the Extra 300S is a pure performance machine designed specifically for aerobatics, and it's the aircraft of choice in many competitions. The composite-paneled, welded tube fuselage is capable of withstanding up to +/- 10 Gs, and it can roll at a rate of 400° per second. Sheesh, strap on your special flight suit and store some extra blood in your brain before you take this baby for a ride. It is not recommended that you go straight from flying the 737 to the Extra unless you are highly adaptive. The exaggerated

Figure 5-4 The Extra 300S cockpit.

gross movements required to coax the 737 into a turn will quickly send the Extra tumbling through the sky. You've been warned.

Taxi and Takeoff

The Extra's center of gravity is actually behind the landing gear, which makes for a mighty strange performance on the tarmac. Be sure to move around gingerly at first until you get a feel for it. If you are in the habit of increasing power before you release the brakes, you'll be in for a rather rude awakening. Simply put, the Extra will flip head over heels in a jiffy if you do this, so be careful. Remember, this is a light, nimble aircraft designed for precision aerobatics, so even a slight movement on the stick can translate into a major maneuver.

To begin, release the brakes and throttle up slowly to full power. You will quickly reach a speed of 70 knots, which is required speed for takeoff. Ease the Extra up—don't make drastic

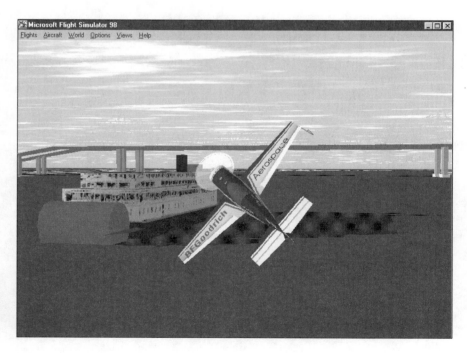

Figure 5-5 The Extra 300S is the fastest, most nimble aircraft available in *Flight Simulator*.

movements or you'll risk a stall. That's all there is to it! No flaps, no gear to retract, no muss, no fuss—just don't make any sudden moves and you won't have to cuss.

Cruising

The Extra wasn't made to fly cross country; there's usually only enough fuel for about 2.5 hours of flight when cruising at 150 knots. However, if you want to be able to do some sightseeing in tight and touchy locales, this is the aircraft to do it in. If you want to fly through the Arc de Triomphe, you'll have a fairly hard time in anything but the Extra. A decent cruising RPM is around 2,400.

Landing

Line yourself up on the runway, head in at 80 to 90 knots, and descend toward the ground. If you come in too fast, it'll be hard to

Figure 5-6 Learning to land the Extra can be tricky if you reach for the flaps.

Figure 5-7 Once you master inverted flight, you can try something like this.

set it down, and if you come in too slow, the Extra will drop like a rock. The key here is touch. You'll need to develop a feel for the aircraft. Fortunately, however, the Extra is roughly 180,000 times more forgiving than a 737, so there is considerably more room for error. As you land you'll find yourself making very slight throttle adjustments to coax this sprightly plane to the ground.

Aerobatics

The Extra is really known for its ability to do acrobatic maneuvers. Its forgiving nature, light weight, solid construction, and powerful engine make it the perfect aircraft for this purpose. All of the main acrobatic maneuvers are described in detail by ace pilot Patty Wagstaff in the Pilot Help section of *Flight Simulator*. Look here to access written descriptions as well as stunning videos and computer renderings of these maneuvers.

However, there is one area where the online tutorial falls short, and that is in inverted flight. The Extra can be easily flipped upside down, and it's relatively forgiving to fly in this manner. However, your brain will have to do somersaults when it comes to maneuvering upside down. Basically, the controls are reversed, and although it is easy enough to keep the nose level with the horizon, if you are aiming for a specific point and have to turn at all, the problems begin. Eventually you will develop a touch for this kind of flying, but you can aid the steering of the inverted Extra by turning off the auto-coordination and thus enabling the use of your rudders. If you do nothing else but keep the Extra level in inverted flight, the rudders can be successfully used for subtle course correction. Flying upside down under a bridge is a good example.

FLIGHT SIMULATOR SECRETS

This is an assortment of tips, tricks, and tweaks that can enhance your enjoyment of *Microsoft Flight Simulator 98*.

3D Acceleration

Undoubtedly the best new feature of *Flight Simulator 98* is its support for 3D accelerator cards. Adding a 3D accelerator card will greatly speed up the frame rate of the simulation, as well as smooth out the graphics and provide some really impressive transparent cloud effects. Here is some information about making the best use of *Flight Simulator*'s hardware acceleration features.

Enabling Hardware Acceleration

A good 3D accelerator card works with your existing video card to provide hardware acceleration in games that are specifically written to take advantage of it. The card I used while writing this book is the Monster 3D card by Diamond Multimedia (www.diamondmm.com). The card performed flawlessly and provided a real speed boost to every aspect of the game. The list price of the Monster 3D as this book went to press was $199. After you have

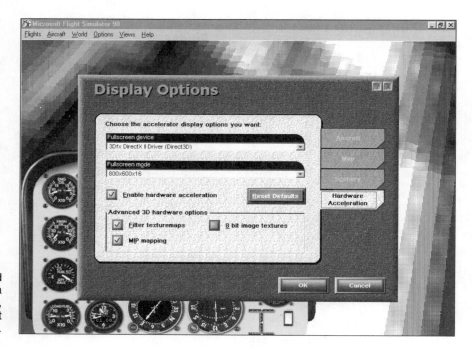

Figure 5-8 A good 3D card makes a world of difference, but you have to turn it on in here first.

purchased and installed a 3D accelerator card, you need to enable hardware acceleration in *Flight Simulator 98*. Here's how to maximize your visual enjoyment of *Flight Simulator:*

1. Go to the Options menu and choose "Preferences."
2. Click on the Display tab.
3. Click the Display Options button.
4. Click on the Scenery tab.
5. Make sure that "Cloud thickness effects" is not checked.
6. Click on the Hardware Acceleration tab.
7. Under the "Full Screen Device" menu, select your 3D accelerator card (in this case, "3Dfx DirectX II driver").
8. Under the "Full Screen Mode" menu, choose the highest resolution your card will support (in this case, 800x600x16 bit color).
9. Click the "Enable hardware acceleration" button.

10. If your card supports any Advanced 3D Hardware Options, you will see them enabled in the area below. Check 8-bit image textures only if you are having trouble with the 16-bit textures.

11. Click OK to close all the boxes.

12. Hit [Alt]-[Enter] to go into full-screen mode.

Note that cloud thickness effects must be de-selected in order to see some really spectacular transparent cloud effects. Also note that the 3Dfx card won't kick in until you hit [Alt]-[Enter] to run in a full screen. Once in a full screen, you won't have access to your menus, but you can hit the [Alt] key once to display the menu bar so you can choose a menu item without having to exit full-screen mode permanently.

> Note that with a monster 3D card, cloud thickness effects must be de-selected in order to see some really spectacular transparent cloud effects. Experiment with the settings to see which gives you the best results with your type of card.

Using Force Feedback

One of the exciting new features of *Flight Simulator 98* is the ability to actually feel the plane respond throughout the flight regime.

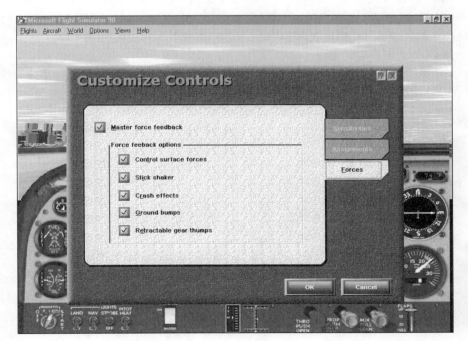

Figure 5-9
This is where you configure a force feedback joystick for use with *Flight Simulator 98*.

You can also feel the landing gear lock into place for a landing, or bump and shudder as you roll across the tarmac. Force feedback truly offers a new dimension to the Flight Simulator experience, but you need a force feedback-enabled joystick such as the Microsoft Sidewinder Force Feedback Pro or the CH Products Force FX to experience it. To turn on Force Feedback, select the Custom Controls dialog box from the Options menu and click on the Forces tab (this option will be greyed out until you have attached a Force Feedback joystick and have configured it in the Game Controllers control panel).

Put a check mark in the Master force feedback box to turn on force feedback. Place a check mark in each of the boxes described in this section to feel those effects as you fly. "Control surface forces" will cause trim force as you change your pitch with the elevator, or make a turn using your ailerons. "Stick shaker" will allow you to feel the stick shake as you approach a stall. This feature is enabled on real Boeing 737-400 and Learjet aircraft, to alert the pilot of an imminent stall. You will only feel these effects on these aircraft. Checking "Crash effects" will cause the stick to shake when you crash. "Ground bumps" will allow you to feel every bump and vibration as your aircraft rolls across the runway for takeoff. It will also allow you to feel the impact when the wheels touch down during a landing. Finally, checking "Retractable gear thumps" will let you feel the wheels as they lock into place when you extend or retract them. You will only feel this effect when you are flying an aircraft that has retractable gear, such as the Learjet 45, the Cessna 182 R6, or the Boeing 737-400.

It's best to fly the stick with a loose grip, since it will tend to move on its own during high speed maneuvers, or when approaching a runway under heavy turbulence. It's better to roll with the stick than to fight it all the way in. Many people find the stick feels a bit loose, since it doesn't center itself quite as much as other joysticks. You can adjust the Return to center setting in the Game Controllers control panel within Windows 95 to give the stick a tighter feel.

Stick an HSI in the Cessna

Anyone who has flown the Boeing 737-400 knows the value of having a good HSI (horizontal situation indicator) by your side. The HSI superimposes information from NAV 1 on a heading indicator to tell you exactly where you are in relation to a VOR signal. This little tweak shows you what a simple feat it is to customize the instrument panels, and it places this very handy instrument at your immediate disposal.

1. Go into the FS98/aircraft/c182/panel folder, and locate the "panel.cfg" file.

2. Make a duplicate of the file, and rename it "panel.old."

3. Open the panel.cfg file in Notepad, and change the line that reads "Gauge09=Cessna_182.Directional_Gyro, 238, 148" so that it reads "Gauge09=Bendix_King.HSI, 245, 131."

4. Save your changes, and restart *Flight Simulator*.

5. The Cessna now has an HSI in its panel.

Use Any Plane for the Challenges

You don't have to use the default plane in the challenges. If you feel more comfortable flying the Cessna, feel free to choose "Select Aircraft" from the Aircraft menu and change the aircraft to anything you want.

The Amazing Disappearing Instrument Panel

Because the view window and the instrument panel are resizeable, you can shrink the windows down to give you more of a view and to hide controls you don't use much anyway. On the sailplane, you can hide the entire right half of the panel by sliding it off the right edge of the screen. Pressing the [W] key toggles the panel on/off quickly. You can do without the VSI by watching the altimeter to see if you are gaining or losing altitude. You can also shrink down the entire panel to about one-quarter of its

Figure 5-10 You can resize the instrument panel to maximize your view.

normal size and still be able to read the dials, particularly at higher resolutions. With a multiple monitor setup, you can have one monitor display the cockpit view, and move all the dials and instruments windows to the other monitor.

Use the Auto-Throttle to Control the Jet

The *Flight Simulator 98* 737-400 has an exciting new feature built into the autopilot, called the auto-throttle. The auto-throttle manages your throttle settings to match the indicated airspeed that you have set in the autopilot control. The TOGA button (short for takeoff/go around) will help you to smoothly increase the throttle at takeoff so that all you have to do is pull back on the yoke at rotation speed. Here's how it works.

Toga! Toga!

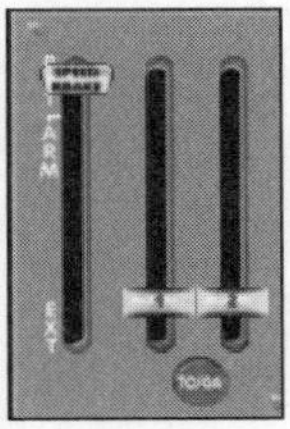

Taxi to your assigned runway and hold short. Arm the auto-throttle system by clicking on the red switch to the left of the autopilot. Once you receive takeoff clearance, hit the round TOGA button just under the throttle levers. The auto-throttle will spool up the engines smoothly, and when you reach 150 knots, all you need to do is pull back on the yoke to rotate.

Figure 5-11 The TOGA switch is located just under the throttle levers.

Using the Auto-Throttle to Maintain a Desired Speed

Once you are safely in the air and have retracted your landing gear, you can dial in a desired airspeed and altitude by clicking on the dials in the autopilot. If you want to climb to an altitude of 15,000 feet at 250 knots, you can set those numbers in the autopilot, then click on the ALT button to enable the Altitude Hold, and click on the SPD button to enable the Speed Hold. You will now see the throttle levers moving as the auto-throttle works to maintain the proper speed. Don't forget that on a big jet the engines can take a little while to respond, so you might see some deviation from your settings if you are climbing or descending rapidly. If you're using a joystick with a throttle control, make sure the joystick's throttle is set to zero before using the auto-throttle.

THE CHALLENGES SOLVED!

In this section I've picked out the most interesting and challenging challenges that *Flight Simulator* has to offer and provided some insight into how to complete them without having to adopt the nickname "Splat."

Beautiful Bay Area Night

It doesn't get any easier than this. You are flying a 737 in the San Francisco Bay Area at night, and you are perfectly lined up for a

Figure 5-12 Bay Area Night: It doesn't get any easier than this. Sit back and enjoy the view of San Francisco.

smooth landing. Don't change your course, just concentrate on speed, altitude, and lowering your landing gear, and everything should work out just fine. You won't even need to engage reverse thrusters once you land, but it might be a good idea to get in the practice.

Bell Carrier Ops (Basic)

This helicopter challenge is a piece of cake (see chapter 6 if you haven't yet tried flying the JetRanger). Just head straight through the opening in the aircraft carrier. Keep your nose pitched down a few degrees to maintain forward flight, and control your altitude with the collective. If you find yourself getting low, resist the temptation to pull back on the stick. Instead, smoothly increase the collective to maintain your altitude.

Figure 5-13 Bell Carrier: The aircraft carrier mid-deck is actually open on both sides.

Bell Carrier Ops (Challenging)

In this challenge, you start inside the aircraft carrier, on the mid-deck. You need to ferry the admiral to the flight deck, which means flying forward out of the carrier, then ascending to the level of the flight deck and landing. Here's a shortcut that will make your life much easier. When the challenge starts, increase collective to about 60 percent, then pitch the nose up slightly and fly backward out the other end of the flight deck, which is actually open on both sides. Then, all you need to do is come to a hover, add a little collective, and fly forward for a landing on the carrier deck, ready to receive your promotion.

The slogan "Prevent FOD" on the mid-deck of the U.S.S. Carl Vinson is a reminder to personnel not to leave spare parts, midshipmen, or other paraphernalia lying around that can get sucked into engines and cause FOD, or Foreign Object Damage.

Bell Carrier Ops (Difficult)

If you can master this challenge, you are a true chopper pilot. The trick here is to get from the flight deck back down below, and to taxi around on the mid-deck. Again, I found it easier to back up off the edge of the flight deck, then fly forward. You may need to add a little collective as the helicopter leaves the flight deck, since it does tend to sink toward the water at a disconcerting rate. Once you do get down below, keep your collective at about 55 percent and make small movements with the cyclic to move forward and backward. At low speeds, use the anit-torque pedals to turn.

Bell Carrier Ops (Mastery)

This one requires a lot of finesse and small, precise movements with the cyclic to maneuver the helicopter down the mid-deck, then out the right exit. Keep your collective as low as possible, pitch the nose forward just a small amount, and use the anti-torque pedals to squeak out the exit just before hitting the wall.

Bumpy Ride into Boston

Play misty for me. This is one of those hair-raising rides when you wish you could see through fog. You'll have to rely almost completely on your ILS for this landing. Keep your altitude above 400 feet. You have about twelve miles to the runway, and once you are within a mile, you'll be able to make out the strip. Be careful not to drift downward in the fog; keep your altitude.

Carrier Landing (Beginner)

Land your Cessna on the *Nimitz* aircraft carrier and come to a full stop without sliding into the ocean. Most navy carrier aircraft have an arresting hook, which snags one of four wires strung across the carrier deck and brings the aircraft to a stop. Because your Cessna doesn't have an arresting hook, you have to come in at a very low airspeed or you will run out of carrier before you come to a stop!

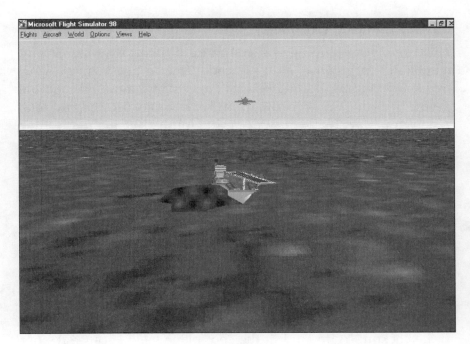

Figure 5-14 Carrier Landing: Landing this way on the carrier is not exactly standard operating procedure, but it makes the most of a very limited amount of landing space.

Practice flying at minimum controllable airspeed, then come in low and slow to the carrier. Just before you touch down, cut the throttle completely and hit the brakes as soon as you hear the wheels touch the deck. You can also ignore the landing strip and land on the longest part of the carrier to give yourself a little more room.

Carrier Landing (Challenging)

Land the Learjet on the *Nimitz*. Again, your biggest problem will be stopping in time. Try the landing at 100 knots or less. As soon as you touch down, hit F1 to cut the throttle completely, then hit 3 three times to engage your reverse thrusters, which should cut your stopping distance by a third. You'll still need every inch of runway, however, so if it looks as if you will overshoot, increase the throttle to full and take off again.

Carrier Landing (Difficult)

This time, your landing is made more difficult by some strong winds and turbulence, so it's a good time to brush up on your crosswind landing skills. This challenge is a lot more manageable if you turn off auto-coordination, so you can use the rudders. When you start out, you will be in clouds, but maintain your heading and watch the artificial horizon to make sure you don't end up in a dive and in danger of overspeed. Once you break through the clouds, line up on the carrier. You can make a pass over it and come around, or you can just land on it the way you are currently facing—you're backward, but no one's looking anyway, so go ahead and do it.

Carrier Landing (Mastery)

Attempt to land the Sopwith Camel on the deck of the *Nimitz* from the spot plane view. Although you can press [s] to place yourself in the cockpit, try to land in the spot plane view because it's not too difficult and it's a very cool viewing perspective. Because the speed of the transitions is set to slow, the view can take a bit of time to catch up with the movement of the plane. Make small adjustments, and wait for the view to catch up. Use the alignment of your wings with the horizon to judge your attitude, and watch the propeller to give you an idea of how high the throttle is set.

Cross-country (Basic)

This is a flight using VFR (visual flight rule) in the Chicago area. It helps to take a look at the map for this one. Depart Champaign and fly north toward Meigs Field. Set the autopilot to hold your heading, and speed up the simulation to reduce your flying time, if you wish. As you reach Lake Michigan, follow the shore north until you see Meigs Field. After landing at Meigs Field, take off again and land at Chicago O'Hare. Turn on "Very Dense" scenery and try to avoid all the air traffic.

Cross-country (Challenging)

This challenge involves VOR navigation. Take off from Paine Field and tune in to the Tatoosh VOR (112.20). After landing there, take off again and fly south to Hoquiam. Tune in to the VOR frequency at 117.70. From Hoquiam, you can tune in to the VOR at Astoria (114.40). Then, head northeast to Olympia (113.40), and finally, return to Paine Field. For a real challenge, try it at night.

Cross-country (Difficult)

Fly in Paris for a change! This one's pretty straightforward. Take off from Toussus-le-Noble and keep an eye on the OBI. NAV 1 is already tuned in, as is the ADF frequency for the next airport. Follow radial 51 to Paris, then center the ADF needle and fly to the Orly NDB. On the way to Orly, tune in the ILS on runway 26 (109.50) and make a nice night landing.

Cross-country (Mastery)

This is a long trip, but it's worth it, especially the little trip to Martha's Vineyard. Take off from Logan Airport in Boston. Fly south to Martha's Vineyard and land using ILS if you like (108.70), then take off again and fly southwest toward Long Island. Tune in the Hampton VOR when you get within range. Fly along Long Island, then land at JFK International Airport on runway 04L. If you want to make an ILS approach at JFK, the frequency is 110.9. Fly back to Logan Airport for the perfect end to a very full day.

Crosswind Landing (Basic)

This one's a piece of cake. You are landing a Cessna at Martha's Vineyard with a steady 10-knot crosswind. Auto-coordination is on, so you don't have to worry about the rudders. Just keep the nose of the aircraft pointed slightly to the right of the runway as you approach, just enough to keep your flight path aligned with

Figure 5-15
Crosswind Landing:
Don't go into external
view in this challenge
or you'll end up as
so much crumpled
metal.

the runway. You shouldn't even have to slip; just be ready to steer straight down the runway as you touch down.

Crosswind Landing (Challenging)

Land the Cessna at Van Nuys, California, in a steady 15-knot crosswind. This time, auto-coordination is off, so you need to correct with the rudders. You start this scenario with the gear already down, so don't inadvertently raise them! This is a good opportunity to practice the slip; bank the plane slightly to the left and add a little right rudder to keep yourself aligned with the runway. It is important to keep your wings level as you touch down or you will crash on contact. If you land hard, you might bounce back into the air, so be prepared to control the aircraft if necessary and prevent it from being blown to the side.

Crosswind Landing (Difficult)

Land the Cessna at JFK International in a steady 32-knot crosswind. This one isn't easy. You will need to crab as you approach the runway, and depending on your angle, you will have to slip in order to straighten out. Again, keep your wings level as you land. Don't forget to lower the landing gear!

Crosswind Landing (Mastery)

This is a tough landing at Chicago O'Hare in a steady 40-knot crosswind. Try to maintain a good crab angle, and cross your fingers. Winds this strong can be a little turbulent, so you will have to slip as you approach touchdown. You may also need to set the throttle a little higher than normal to maintain your course. If you have difficulty solving this one, try hitting X and let the instructor demonstrate how to land the plane.

Daredevil (Basic): LA Coliseum

This is a quick and easy stunt that should top any of the stunts they did at the opening ceremonies of the Olympics. You need to fly the Cessna into the Coliseum and make a quick landing right on the field. The hardest thing about this stunt is stopping in time, so immediately throttle down from full power, put on full flaps, and lower your landing gear. Just before you get inside the gate, throttle down to zero and pitch the nose up slightly. The floor drops down slightly inside the stadium.

Daredevil (Challenging): Golden Gate Bridge

The challenge here is to get the Cessna to make a loop all the way over the Golden Gate Bridge. I found that the easiest way to do this is to throttle down to about 50 RPM, then put the aircraft into a dive as you fly under the bridge. As soon as you clear the bridge, throttle back up to 100 RPM and pull back on the yoke to start the

Figure 5-16
Daredevil (Difficult):
Beware of high-flying
buildings!

first part of the loop. Keep the loop nice and tight, and watch the artificial horizon. When the ball flips over, keep back pressure on the yoke and watch for the bridge to come back into view. Wave to the pedestrians as you fly right under them again!

Daredevil (Difficult): World Trade Center

This a fun one. Fly inverted through New York City at night! You start out upside down, facing the Twin Towers of the World Trade Center. It is possible to fly between the towers, but you will have to time it just right. Don't forget that when you are upside down, the yoke works in the exact reverse direction as in level flight.

Daredevil (Mastery): Chicago

For real fun, turn off auto-coordination and practice your vertical flying as you fly between the buildings. You're making lots of steep banking turns downtown, so keep back pressure on the yoke as you make your turns and watch the VSI to ensure that you aren't losing altitude too quickly. You can also land the plane: hit W to expand the view, and have fun driving through the streets of Chicago.

Easter Island Roll

The key to rolling the 737 is to have enough altitude so that when you reach the sideways position you don't hit the ground. When you are sideways the aircraft has no lift, and since the 737 rolls so slowly, it will tend to lose a fair bit of altitude at that point. To complete this maneuver, raise the nose to about +150, get your speed up to 250 knots, get to at least 5,000 feet, make sure you have the use of your rudders, then bank hard right/rudder right. As soon as you begin to become inverted, push forward on the stick to compensate for any altitude you may be losing. Continue the roll. Apply smooth forward pressure as you bank greater than 90°. If all goes well, you should pull out at around 3,000 feet. The

Figure 5-17
Easter Island Roll: Keeping your speed down is important once you approach inverted position.

key to this challenge is not ending up in a nose dive once you invert. Watch your attitude!

Emergency Descent

You can follow what the pilot's handbook says, or you can do it this way. Drop your throttle to 10 percent, extend your spoilers, and fully extend your flaps, then make a 90° turn to the left and dive at around a 17° angle. The flaps, spoilers, and low throttle settings will ensure that you do not exceed 280 knots. The "rough" looking area to your left is around 7,000 feet, leaving you with plenty of room to bring in your 737 under 10,000 feet without ramming into a mountain. Nothing to it.

Follow the Leaders (Basic/Difficult/Mastery)

These challenges require you to play, quite literally, follow the leader. The best advice I can give is to make sure you stay within visual range of the aircraft you are following. To do this you need to be on your toes, especially while taxiing. If you find that it's getting a little too difficult to keep up, or conversely you are finding the taxiing tedious, then adjust the time to .5× or 2×, respectively.

The "Difficult" challenge is unique. You are required to do a touch-and-go landing at Meigs Field, then fly around without crashing into anyone else. The real challenge here is getting in a touch-and-go landing without smacking into another Cessna on the runway. Vary your speed to get ahead or stay behind the runway traffic as you approach.

IFR Cessna (Basic/Challenging/Difficult/Mastery)

These four challenges all have the exact same purpose; the differences lie in the conditions under which you must complete the maneuvers. You must take off and turn to a heading of 230° to intercept the localizer. Gain altitude to 5,000 feet and hang in until you have an approach to runway 32L (ILS).

The Challenging level introduces a fair bit of wind to deal with; Difficult adds a cloud ceiling you'll climb over; and Mastery adds pea soup and a pinch of salt. I recommend you turn auto-coordination off in order to better handle the elements in these challenges.

IFR Learjet (Basic/Challenging/Difficult/Mastery)

These challenges are basically the same as the IFR Cessna challenges. The goal is the same, with the details altered. First, you must taxi your Learjet down the tarmac, then handle a pair of 90° left turns to line yourself up on the runway. Once you're up in the air, head to 230°, climb to 5,000 feet, and be ready to be cleared for runway 32L (ILS) at O'Hare. The Challenging level adds a cloud ceiling of a thousand feet to the equation, while the Difficult factors in the night sky. And again, Mastery throws the whole enchilada at you, including very low visibility.

IFR San Francisco (Basic/Challenging/Difficult/Mastery)

Again, these four challenges have the same procedure, with increasingly difficult conditions—when you reach Mastery, visibility is one-sixteenth of a mile and there's plenty of turbulence. In all levels you must descend from over 20,000 feet to 4,000 feet, and then turn to 280° when you intercept the San Jose VOR. You are then to descend to 1,800 feet until you hit the airport. The Basic level should give you a good feel for these challenges, and this will ultimately help you to "feel" your way through the pea soup in Mastery.

Inverted Flight (Basic)

This is a breeze. You start out at around 700 feet with no engine (or gas) and . . . you're upside down. However, you do have over 100 knots of speed on your side, and the airport isn't that far away. All you have to do is a quick roll to get right side up, and then glide it into the runway. All too easy.

Inverted Flight (Challenging)

This time you have under 20 knots of speed and only 650 feet of altitude to help you out. You must flip the Cessna over quickly and set a straight glide for the airstrip. This can be easily accomplished, but there is much less room for error. Don't lower your gear until the last second; you don't want the gear to sap your speed with extra drag.

Inverted Flight (Difficult)

More of the same. The margin for error is again decreased, so you'll have to be really, really careful in your approach. The key here is to make it all the way to the runway. It's easy to land in the "rough" a couple hundred feet before the tarmac; the "real" pilots find a way to make it in.

Figure 5-18
Inverted Flight: Flip your ship in a hurry or you're dog meat! Then glide 'er in.

Inverted Flight (Mastery)

Same situation, but this time it's recommended that you fly inverted until you come under the cloud ceiling. Once you've got the runway clearly in front of you, flip over and glide that baby in!

Inverted Flight (Atlanta)

This is really rather difficult. You'll need to line up on the runway and flip as you approach. The goal is to fly inverted, 50 feet above the ground for the entire length of the runway. If you're finding that you're having difficulty maintaining direction when inverted, use your rudders to augment control. Good thing that this little trick isn't for real.

Landing Blind at Heathrow

This is a basic "zero visibility" landing from about fifteen miles out. You'll smack the ground at 400 feet, so maintain 1,00 feet until intercepting the glideslope. Although this long approach with no visual clues can be nerve-racking, keep the ILS lined up and everything will be just fine.

Lost in Rio

Here you are near Rio, the jewel of South America, in your Extra, but you've got a cloud ceiling of 600 feet and a visibility of only a couple miles. Worst of all, you've only got a finite amount of fuel at your disposal to help you find one of three airports to land at. These airports are all within a 20-mile range, but believe me, you can't see them. As if to add insult to injury, there are plenty of mountains nearby, and if you try to fly over them, you'll be in pea soup fog and looking for a mountain collision. Fortunately for you, I've found a quick and dirty way to an airport. From the starting point, just fly at a heading of 260° until you come to water, then follow the coastline to the right (staying a half mile off the coast) for a short while. You'll soon see an airport on your

Figure 5-19 Landing Blind: Looking good, feeling worse in pea soup at Heathrow.

left-hand side. The landing should be easy, and if you came straight in, you should have plenty of fuel.

Lost in the USA (Basic)

You are cleared to land at Martha's Vineyard on runway 24, where James Taylor is waiting to sing "Fire and Rain" for you. You are over the Providence VOR. It should be fairly basic to find Martha's Vineyard from here.

Lost in the USA (Challenging)

You must fly to the Oakland International runway 27R. The challenge is truly on. The game advises that you get your charts out. I concur. I also found that I endured the odd aircraft system malfunction in my Cessna.

Figure 5-20 Lost in Rio: When it comes to survival, it's not cheating to use the Map view (accessed by pressing [Shift]-[]]) to find this airfield on an island just offshore.

Lost in the USA (Difficult)

This time you'll be attempting to find Boeing Field in your Learjet. You must land on runway 13R. Head for Paine Field, then take a heading around 180° toward Boeing Field. You'll pass by Seattle's downtown en route. If you keep your altitude below around 7,000 feet, you should stay below the clouds and improve your visibility.

Lost in the USA (Mastery)

This time you need to set your VOR frequency and fly to it. The VOR is not on the runway, so once you find the VOR, turn to a heading of around 310° to 312° to find the strip. The clouds are almost to the ground, and you'll have to fly under 500 feet to see the ground at all. There is also a fair bit of turbulence to deal with in this challenge.

Manhattan Bridges Race

The idea here is to fly around Manhattan Island while keeping under 300 feet and flying under all the bridges. No problem. If you want to spice this one up a lot, then do it upside down. Trust me, it's much more fun.

Mountain Flying (Basic)

In this challenge you will be taking off from Livermore, California, and basically flying straight from the runway. The first airport you see will be where you want to go (Hayward Airport). If you follow a heading of around 250°, you should be okay, but you must keep your altitude around 500 feet because of a low ceiling. This is the most difficult portion of this challenge—any slight mental lapse in altitude maintenance can lead to pancakeville.

Figure 5-21
Manhattan Bridges
Race: The bridges of
Manhattan County.
Enjoy the sights.

Mountain Flying (Challenging)

As a newly recruited postal worker, it is your dubious responsibility to fly a Sopwith Camel through the mountains to Van Nuys. Keep your wits about you, and don't let your attention lapse for a second. It can be very difficult to find the Van Nuys Airport in the Camel.

Mountain Flying (Difficult)

This one can be a toughie. You are trying to make a landing on a road running along the left-hand side of the lake below you. Unfortunately, you must descend through thick patches of cloud that obscure the mountains below. Take your descent slowly, and keep an eye on your airspeed. It's easy to overspeed and fly your Cessna apart when you're trying to lose altitude.

Mountain Flying (Mastery)

You're in for one of the wildest rides in the wilderness with this one. Things will get very bouncy as you fly through the Cascade mountain range. It's best to just fly west and head for Seattle while observing the tried-and-true rule of mountain flight. Namely, don't fly into any mountains.

New York Movie Flight

This challenge is one of those things you've always wanted to do: fly among the skyscrapers of New York without risk of death. Start by buzzing Ms. Liberty, then head between the World Trade Center towers. Turn the scenery complexity up for this one (if your machine is fast enough). Enjoy.

Out of Gas (Basic)

This is what you might expect: You are either out of or low on fuel, and you must make a safe landing despite this. In this case you are in a Cessna and are already conveniently heading for the airport. The key is to squeeze the maximum amount of juice out of your evaporating gas fumes and reduce drag. Raise your landing gear right away, then make a choice as to whether you want to crank your engine and gain as much altitude as you can right away or lower the throttle and get a sustained low power for a little longer.

Out of Gas (Challenging)

In this case you are in a 737 and are in need of shedding around 40,000 feet in altitude. If you want to do it quickly, you'll need to use your spoilers and flaps to slow your descent; otherwise, make sure you have enough altitude on approach to keep your velocity up or you'll drop like a rock.

Out of Gas (Difficult)

Once you get control of the Cessna, turn to a heading near 290°. This will point you in the general direction of the airport. The rest will be up to you. You'll have to do some fancy moves to line up on the runway when you get there.

Out of Gas (Mastery)

You are in a Cessna at around 4,000 feet with no power and fairly severe turbulence. A heading of 115° will put you on a perpendicular path to the nearest runway. If you play your cards right, you might be able to swing around and make a successful landing, but it will take all your skill. Fortunately, your visibility is relatively high.

Partial Panel (Basic/Challenging/Difficult/Mastery)

Each of these challenges puts you on a landing approach with some, few, or none of your instrumentation. Learn to use back-up instruments when your primary instruments fail.

Figure 5-22 Partial Panel: As nice as your panel looks, it's useless in these challenges.

Perfect Pattern (Basic/Challenging/Difficult/Mastery)

As noted in the instructions, before trying these challenges, select "Flight Analysis" from the Options menu, then choose "Course Tracking," "Record Course," and "Display Course." You must then attempt to complete a perfect pattern at 1,000 feet. The only substantial differences between the levels are the differences in wind velocity.

Remote Control (Basic)

The remote control challenges require a different state of mind in order to complete them successfully. For the basic level, you need merely take off from Meigs Field in a Cessna and then land again;

however, this is easier said than done. It's best to take off, do a long turn, and just come right back in for a landing.

Remote Control (Challenging)

This time you have a Cessna lined straight up on the runway with only a few hundred feet to descend. If you keep the stick centered and just manage the descent, you will be able to land with minimal difficulties. Keep an eye on your speed as you descend.

Remote Control (Difficult)

In this challenge the Cessna will fly directly over you, thus causing a sudden change in control input. You'll want to bank a turn to the left, then turn right to come around for a landing. Watch your speed while you try to line up a landing at Meigs.

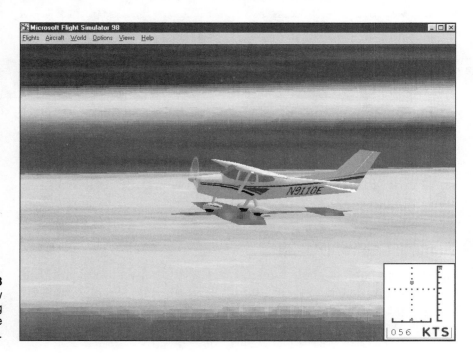

Figure 5-23
The point of view can be maddening in the Remote Control challenges.

Remote Control (Mastery)

This is a similar challenge to the previous three, with the exception that the viewpoint is a little different. And yes, for some reason this really is more difficult. Don't let your plane get too far away or it will be impossible to fly back for a landing. Stay calm—the previous remote control challenges have prepared you for this.

Sailplane (Basic)

Just as when you are flying the sailplane normally in *Microsoft Flight Simulator 98*, the sailplane challenges all have you groping for altitude and thermal currents in order to get you to a runway. In the basic challenge, keep on your course until you clear the ridge; there will be lift on the seaward side. It's probably best to head north to find the nearest runway.

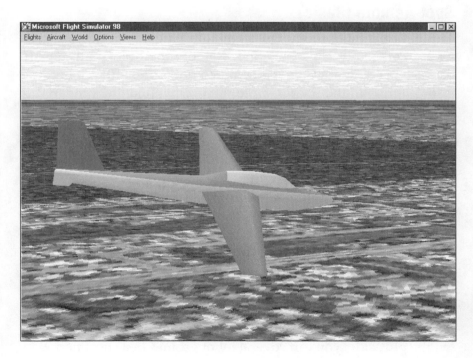

Figure 5-24 The Sailplane Challenges offer exciting sailplane scenarios.

Sailplane (Challenging)

Fly straight: a thermal awaits directly ahead. You'll have to do a tight turn to stay in the thermal in order to get some altitude. Get somewhere around 5,500 to 6,000 feet, then head to around 215° to 230°: there should be an airfield ahead.

Sailplane (Difficult)

Just like the description says, test the sailplane out. 'Nuff said.

Sailplane (Mastery)

Fly straight ahead, gain altitude, look for a runway to the right side of the city. Your heading should be roughly 350°. Enjoy the scenery.

Spot Remote (Basic)

This is your first chance to get a feel for flying a Spot Remote challenge. Personally I like this Spot Remote the best of all, mostly because the Sopwith Camel is so much fun to fly, but also because it looks great in the Spot Remote viewpoint. Take the time in this challenge to work on maneuvering the camera angle so that you can maximize your understanding of the plane's position. This usually means staying level (or slightly above) and behind the Camel. The Sopwith Camel is very, very forgiving, so use this to the extreme to explore the ins and outs of Spot Remote flight.

Spot Remote (Challenging)

Flying the Learjet in the Spot Remote mode means basically the same thing as when you are flying it in the cockpit view. You need to think far, far ahead. The Learjet is very powerful and moves very fast, so it can get out of control in a hurry, especially when you're trying to maneuver it from an unfamiliar viewing angle. On the plus side, you can cover a lot of ground in a short period of time with the power of the jet engines, so explore all the scenic areas nearby. Keep behind the Learjet when landing, and watch out for the Learjet's tendency to "nose-up" when your engines are running hard.

Spot Remote (Difficult)

In this challenge you must sail a Schweizer Sailplane over Sausalito, California. The sailplane is the most difficult to maneuver of all the aircraft in the Spot Remote challenges. If you make any mistakes with the sailplane, the results are magnified due to the obvious lack of a power source. Probably the best way to manage this scenario is to press the ⊡ key and go into the "fish-eye" view for most of the flight. This view will also give you an incredible set of scenery to enjoy while you glide around. It's also beneficial to stay behind the sailplane (and level with the horizon) so that you can prevent a stall.

Spot Remote (Mastery)

In this final chapter of the Spot Remote challenges, you are flying a Cessna at Van Nuys. You must take off, fly around, and land again (as in all Spot Remote challenges), but the catch is that you're doing it at night. This little wrinkle makes it even more difficult to judge the distance from your aircraft to the ground, so you'll have to stay frosty. You start out at 0200 hours, the cloud ceiling is 9,200 feet (but there are only scattered clouds) and the visibility is 40 miles. As with the Learjet, it's a good idea to use the ⊞ and ⊡ keys to gain perspective on your aircraft's position. If you're using a Sidewinder 3D Pro (or similar stick), you can use the hat switch to rotate your view around your aircraft. Keep your landing light off, as it can be more confusing than helpful when dealing with landings.

Under the Eiffel Tower

In this maneuver you are flying the Extra 300S. This nimble aircraft is fairly easy to fly under the Eiffel Tower—the important

Figure 5-25 Few things in life are better than flying through the legs of the Eiffel Tower.

part is making sure you line up square on the tower. You begin the challenge on a diagonal with the "legs" of the tower. If you maintained this flight path, you would have a difficult time indeed flying through the legs safely. However, if you swing to the left and then approach the tower through the park, you will have plenty of room to line up and ultimately fly under the tower while inverted. What could be better?

CHAPTER
6

Chopper Pilot

At low speeds or while in a hover, you can add some rudder to quickly pivot to any heading.

The helicopter is an entirely new beast to tame. It brings new challenges to master, and you will have to develop new skills in order to successfully pilot this inherently unstable craft. However, once you have become a successful chopper pilot, you will be able to perform some amazing aerial feats that would be impossible in a fixed-wing aircraft. This chapter will teach you the basics of helicopter flight, give you some pointers on the built-in lessons, and point out some fun things you can do with the helicopter in various locales.

Note that the helicopter's flight model is extremely realistic, making it the most difficult of the *Flight Simulator* aircraft. However, the challenge of mastering a totally new method of flight also makes the helicopter one of the most fun *Flight Simulator* aircraft. So, grab your propeller beanie, and let's fly!

Figure 6-1 The helicopter is fun but challenging to fly.

THE BELL 206B JETRANGER III

The Bell JetRanger is the most successful civilian helicopter ever built. Since their introduction, Bell JetRanger helicopters have served a crucial role in search-and-rescue missions, news and information gathering, military training, and the tourism and sightseeing industry. Flying in on a Bell JetRanger is also the height of style when you want to make a grand entrance at the next board meeting. Fortunately, you will find a convenient helipad on many of the skyscrapers in *Flight Simulator*'s Manhattan. With practice, you will be able to hop from building to building without your feet ever touching the ground.

Helicopter Controls

A helicopter uses three primary methods of control input: the collective, the cyclic, and the anti-torque pedals. In *Flight Simulator*, the joystick controls the cyclic. Pushing the cyclic backward and forward pitches the nose up and down. Pushing it to one side or

Figure 6-2 The pedals control the tail rotor, which counteracts torque generated by the main rotor.

The amount of lift a wing generates depends on two factors: airspeed and angle of attack. Helicopter rotor blades spin in a circular motion. If you compare a point near the hub of the rotor with a point at the end of the rotor, a point near the center actually has a shorter distance to travel than a point at the edge of the circle in the same amount of time. This means that the outside edges of a helicopter rotor actually spin *faster* than the inside edges! If the rotor blade had the same angle of attack throughout, the outer edges would generate much more lift than the inner edges, putting a tremendous amount of stress on the rotor. This is why rotor blades, propeller blades, and fan blades all are twisted toward the center to provide a greater angle of attack compensating for the reduced lift.

I highly recommend the use of a flight yoke with rudder pedals or, better yet, the Microsoft Sidewinder 3D Pro. Controlling the helicopter with the keyboard is quite difficult. Using a joystick that coordinates the cyclic, the rudder, and the collective will make your life much easier.

the other changes the bank angle of the main rotor, which causes the helicopter to bank to either side. The collective is your primary method of altitude control, and you control the amount of collective by using what is normally the throttle control. Changing the collective actually changes the angle of the rotor blades themselves, giving them a steeper angle of attack. Finally, the pedals control the force of the tail rotor. Pushing the pedals to the left causes the nose to yaw left, and vice versa. A helicopter pilot must simultaneously coordinate the cyclic, the collective, and the pedals to maintain stable flight.

The Pedals

A helicopter has what is essentially an enormous propeller mounted on its top, and as the rotor blades spin they generate a lot of torque, which makes the body of the helicopter want to rotate in the opposite direction. This means that as you increase the collective, you will have to compensate by using the pedals to counteract the helicopter's tendency to spin. At the same time, you will probably need to use some cyclic to keep the helicopter level.

The Collective

Increasing the collective changes the pitch of the rotor blades, which changes their angle of attack. Adding more collective causes more lift to be generated. The collective is therefore your primary method of altitude and power control. As you add collective, you will have to use the tail rotor to counteract the effects of torque.

The Cyclic

As a helicopter pitches its nose down, the rotor blades "bite" into the air, adding a horizontal component of lift similar to that generated by a propeller. Pitching the nose up causes a helicopter to slow down and even fly backward. The pitch of the helicopter controls its airspeed. Changing the helicopter's pitch can also change its altitude, so you may have to add some collective to compensate. You may also have to use the pedals to counteract the

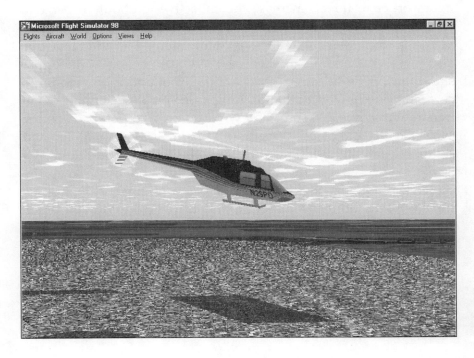

Figure 6-3
Helicopters move forward when the nose is pitched down.

torque created when you increase the collective, so get in the habit of using all three control inputs to maintain stability. Remember that small movements are the key to retaining control of the aircraft. Simply thinking about which direction to go is usually enough to get you there.

Basic Flight Maneuvers

In some ways, flying a helicopter is easier than a fixed-wing aircraft because of its unique abilities to hover and stop on a dime. These basic flight maneuvers are what you need to know to start practicing takeoffs and landings in your Bell 206B JetRanger helicopter.

The Hover

Just like an airplane, a helicopter uses wings to fly, only a helicopter's wings are the blades of the rotor. As air passes over the curved top surface of the rotor blade, it generates lift, and this causes the helicopter to lift off the ground into a hover.

In order to hover, increase the collective to about 60 percent. As the helicopter begins to move, you may hear a scraping noise as the landing skids leave the ground. Increasing the collective also makes the nose of the helicopter want to swing in the opposite direction, so be sure to add a little bit of anti-torque pedal to correct for this. Don't add too much, or you may send yourself into an unrecoverable spin. You will also need to pull back on the cyclic slightly if the nose starts to dip down, and use small left and right movements to keep yourself level. Pick a landmark on the horizon, such as a building or a mountain, and try to keep the same heading. If you find yourself spinning around, use some rudder in the opposite direction and try to stop yourself when you're facing the same heading.

Watch the airspeed indicator to see if you're still in a hover. If the nose is pitched down, you could start picking up some forward speed, and this may take you away from where you want to go. Raise the nose above the horizon to decrease your forward speed, and level it again when you approach zero (or you'll be flying backward!)

Figure 6-4 Use the virtual cockpit to line yourself up for a landing.

Forward Motion

Once you have gotten a feel for the hover, try pitching the nose down in order to fly forward. You will find that it is easier to maintain straight and level flight when you have a little bit of forward speed. Press ⒮ once to use the virtual cockpit view, and use the horizon as a reference to maintain straight and level flight. When you're moving forward, the helicopter acts much like an airplane. You can steer yourself left and right using the cyclic, and use your pitch to control your airspeed. Pitching up or down will also change your altitude, so watch your altimeter. If you overshoot your target, you don't need to go around. You can just level the helicopter to arrest your forward motion, then pitch the nose up about 5° above the horizon to back up and try again.

Landing the Helicopter

To land the helicopter, you will need to slow down and maintain a hover over the target. At an airport, you would fly a normal left hand traffic pattern with about a 10° descent angle at 55 knots. As

Figure 6-5 For a fun challenge, try to land in this stadium just outside of Meigs Field.

If you're having trouble controlling the helicopter during the Normal Takeoff lesson, go into the Weather settings and add a 10-knot headwind.

you approach the helipad, you need to transition to a hover by smoothly pulling back on the cyclic and increasing the collective to reduce your descent rate. This takes some practice! Your goal is to end up in a stable hover a few feet off the ground. Use the Virtual Cockpit view for better view of the landing site, or use the Views menu to add a small window with a view directly beneath you (Shift)-(5). You can then reduce the collective slowly to bring yourself down from the hover. Once you hear the skids scraping the ground, drop the collective the rest of the way and gently add some pressure to the pedals to make sure you are firmly on the ground.

Note that when you are in a hover close to the ground, you will have to deal with "ground effect." Ground effect is an increase in performance caused by the interaction of the rotor downwash and the ground. This can bounce you around and make the helicopter feel as if it is floating up. Reduce power when you are experiencing ground effect to maintain a hover.

Autorotation

One of the basic skills required of all chopper pilots is the ability to autorotate. Autorotation is an emergency procedure that can get you on the ground in one piece even if the helicopter loses its main engine. In brief, disengaging the rotor blades from the engine and pitching the nose down maintains rotor RPM, and when you approach the ground you "flare" by pitching the nose back up again. As long as the rotor blades are still spinning, they will create enough lift to land safely.

Autorotating in the Big Apple

Let's try a basic autorotation drill in New York City, which is a good choice because it has lots of helipads and its elevation is sea level, which means MSL and your altitude AGL are about the same. Wherever you are, however, the skills involved are the same, so you can practice autorotation anywhere, such as out in the Midwestern United States where there are lots of big, open fields.

Setting Up the Flight

1. Choose the Bell 206B JetRanger from the Select Aircraft dialog under the Aircraft menu.
2. Choose "Go to Airport" from the World menu.
3. Select "111 Wall Street" in New York City, New York, United States, North America and click OK.
4. If it isn't Day outside, choose Day from the Time & Season dialog box under the World menu.
5. You should find yourself ready for takeoff from a skyscraper on Wall Street.

Takeoff

Increase the collective to full, and take off as normal, avoiding the other buildings. You might find it easier to hover straight up until you are clear of all the buildings around you, ascending to 2,500 feet or so, and then start moving forward. This is a fun challenge in itself. If you're in a hurry, you can always use the "Go to Exact Location" dialog box to place yourself at 2,500 feet.

Figure 6-6
Engine out over
New York City!

Figure 6-7 Welcome
to 111 Wall Street.

Shutting Down the Engine

The Bell JetRanger has the highest safety rating of any helicopter, according to the National Transportation Safety Board (NTSB). We're about to change all that. Perhaps as a measure of added safety, the *Flight Simulator* helicopter doesn't allow you to shut off the single turbine engine entirely to simulate an engine-out scenario, but there is a way around this. You can manually dump all of the fuel from the center tank, and the engine will shut itself down on its own. When you're free and clear of all buildings, and ready to try an autorotation drill, hit P to pause the simulation. Choose "Aircraft Settings" from the Aircraft menu. Put a check in the box marked "Engine stops when out of fuel." Click on the Fuel tab. Enter a value of 0 percent in the Center Fuel tank and click OK to close this box. You can also just reduce power to flight idle— Ctrl F2

Step One: Reduce the Collective

The following step needs to be done quickly, so you may want to read ahead first. When you press P again to unpause the

If you ever want to idle the helicopter engine, hit Ctrl F1 to reduce the throttle to idle. Hit Ctrl F4 to spool it back up again. Idling the throttle this way also seems to kill your rotor RPM, so don't use this if you want to practice autorotation. This will only work if you don't lower collective.

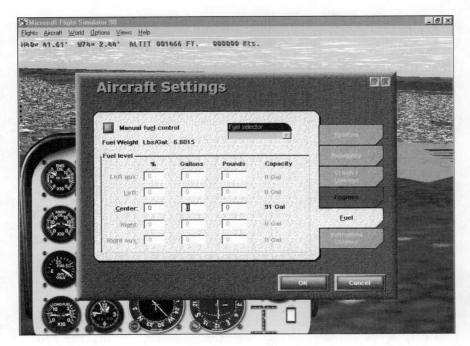

Figure 6-8 Giving yourself an empty fuel tank is a sure way to kill your engine.

In *Flight Simulator*, you will continue to hear the sound of the rotors even when they have stopped spinning and are no longer providing lift, so don't pay too much attention to the sound effects. Basically, when you can no longer pull the nose up to flare, your rotor has stopped spinning and it's time to get out the parachute.

simulation, you will hear your engine spin down. If this ever happens in normal flight, it's a sign that something is seriously wrong, so your first reflex should be to immediately reduce the collective by pressing F1 . If you don't reduce your collective quickly enough, the rotor blades will stop spinning, making it impossible for you to flare the aircraft for a safe landing.

Step Two: Pitch the Nose Down and Look for a Landing Spot

Pitch the nose down about 5° to build up some speed. As long as you keep the nose pitched down, the relative wind will keep your rotor blades spinning even though the engine is no longer running. You are, in effect, using the speed of your descent to keep the blades rotating automatically. This is important because you will need to conserve rotor RPM in order to have an effective flare near the ground. Start looking for flat places to land. The helicopter can glide in for a landing, much like a plane, but you will have to flare the helicopter by pulling back on the cyclic just before you touch the ground. If you really want an extra challenge, try making an emergency landing on top of a building.

Step Three: Add Collective and Pitch Up to Flare

When you're about 50 feet from the landing site, pull back gently on the cyclic to decrease your forward speed. Watch the VSI to get a sense of how fast your descent is. Just before touching the ground, add collective by pressing F3 . This changes the pitch angle of the rotor blades to lower your descent rate. Again, watch the VSI. You want to touch down as close to zero as possible. If you flare too early, you will decrease your descent rate to zero initially, then drop like a stone. If you flare too late, you won't cushion your landing at all—and even with the rotor blades spinning, the impact will probably cause you to crash. Timing is everything.

Virtual Cockpit View

Nowhere in *Flight Simulator* is the virtual cockpit view more useful than when you are flying the helicopter. Although the instruments aren't visible in this view, you can fly the helicopter by feel rather than by worrying about the attitude indicator. Flying the *Flight*

Figure 6-9 How I learned to stop worrying and love the helicopter.

Simulator helicopter is much more about cultivating that "feel" of instinctively balancing the cyclic, collective, and rudder in order to stay stable. The less you think about how to do what you're doing, the better you will become at doing it. You can access the virtual helicopter view, which simulates the view you would get while sitting in the seat, by pressing ⑤ or by choosing it from the Views menu. The virtual cockpit also gives you a much better view of your surroundings.

Succeeding at the Lessons

These lessons give you a guided narrative to hovering and landing in the Bell JetRanger helicopter, with the flight instructor at your side. Here are some tips on completing the built-in lessons, both of which take place at Meigs Field.

Normal Takeoff: Bell 206B Jet Ranger III

For most people, including me, it is so difficult at first to maintain a stable hover that you will probably crash and burn many times before you get the hang of things. You can greatly accelerate your learning curve if you hit Ⓟ right after the lesson starts and change the Aircraft settings to "Ignore Crashes." This will allow you to get a better feel for handling the helicopter without spending a lot of time waiting for the lesson to reload itself each time you spin out of control (and you will).

The lesson begins with a takeoff to a stable hover three feet off the ground. Smoothly increase collective to 60 percent. As the helicopter lifts off the ground, you will hear the landing skids scraping against the runway, and the nose will try to spin to the right. Counter this with a little left rudder, and use the cyclic to keep your nose level and centered on the horizon. If you pitch up or down, this will cause you to move out of the hover. It may be easier to add a little more collective, to give yourself more altitude to work with.

Try to anticipate which way the helicopter will lean, and correct for it gently. Simply reacting to the helicopter's movement will lock you into an ever-increasing series of oscillations that will quickly send you out of control. Break the helicopter's rhythm and control its movement. Use the attitude indicator to let you know if your nose is level and centered. Also keep an eye on the turn coordinator, and "step on the ball" to neutralize the turn. If the movements seem too wild, you might try going into the "Custom Controls" dialog box under the Options menu and decreasing the joystick sensitivity.

Normal Landing: Bell 206B Jet Ranger III

This lesson is a bit easier, since you start in the air, about two miles out of Meigs Field, with some forward speed. This lesson really is a piece of cake, as long as you keep your descent steady and smooth and avoid jerking motions with the cyclic. Use some right or left rudder to keep yourself aligned with the runway, and keep your approach speed slow, at less than 50 knots.

PREFLIGHT BRIEFINGS

Microsoft Flight Simulator 98 features twenty built-in Adventures that test your flying skill. As you listen to the rapid verbal instructions of your copilot and air traffic control, you will know the true meaning of sensory overload. These preflight briefings are reprinted from online help and contain all of the approach information you will need for each of these Adventures. There just is no substitute for having the preflight briefing right there in front of you as you fly.

To figure out your assigned altitude, multiply the flight level (FL) number by 100. For example, if you're told to cross Biggin above flight level 100, you would need to be above 10,000 feet.

Austrian Ski Trip: Learjet 45

The urge to schuss some slopes has hit hard. But you're in England, not exactly alpine country. No problem. Just head for London's Gatwick Airport, where you park your personal Learjet 45 and take a short hop to Innsbruck, where the powder is excellent.

Clearance

Here is your ATC clearance for this flight. (If you need information about the airports, VORs, or NDBs along your route, check the Airport/Facility directory on the World menu.)

> Learjet 45 Lima Juliett is cleared to the Innsbruck Airport via direct Biggin, UG1 Koksy, UG109 Karlsruhe, UL607 Kempten, direct, maintain flight level (FL) 370. Squawk 4245.

Specific Routing

> After takeoff from runway 8 right, fly runway heading. Intercept and track inbound on the Biggin (BIG) 040° radial.
>
> At BIG, intercept and track outbound on the 105° radial toward Dover (DVR). At DVR, intercept and track outbound on the 98° radial toward Koksy (KOK).
>
> At KOK, intercept and track outbound on the 120° radial toward Diekirch (DIK).
>
> At DIK, intercept and track outbound on the 1ZO° radial toward Karlsruhe (KRH).
>
> At KRH, intercept and track outbound on the 130° radial toward Tango (TGO).
>
> At TGO, intercept and track outbound on the 141° radial toward Kempten (KPT).

After KPT, expect vectors for the localizer DME east approach. Expect to land on runway 26.

Beat the Chunnel Train: Boeing 737-400

This flight from Orly Airport in Paris to Gatwick Airport near London tests jet technology against a fast ground (and underwater) route—the Chunnel Train. You're in command of a Bluesky 737, a Boeing 737-400.

Clearance

Here is your ATC clearance for this flight. (If you need information about the airports, VORs, or NDBs along your route, check the Airport/Facility directory on the World menu.)

> BLUESKY 737 is cleared to the Gatwick Airport via Abbeville 7P departure Abbeville, UA20 Biggin, direct, maintain flight level 200, squawk 3355.

Specific Routing

After takeoff on runway 25, fly runway heading and continue the climb to FL 200 (20,000 feet). At 7 DME turn left to heading 190 to intercept the Toussus (TSU) VOR 149° radial. As you cross the Orly VOR (OL) 217° radial (tuned in the radio magnetic indicator, or RMI), turn left to heading about 090° to intercept the Coulommiers (CLM) 243° radial inbound (inbound course 063°).

At 22 DME to CLM, turn left to heading 030° to intercept the Le Bourget (BT) VOR 168° radial inbound (inbound course 348). Cross BT at FL 200.

Fly outbound from the BT VOR on the 345° radial to Abbeville (ABB). At ABB, fly outbound on the 321° radial. Maintain FL 200.

At NASDA intersection (36 DME from ARE), the boundary between the Paris and London control centers, expect a clearance to the Mayfield (MAY) VOR. You'll turn left to heading

290° to intercept the MAY 132° radial inbound to MAY (inbound course 312°).

At 41 DME from MAY, expect a descent clearance to cross the MAY 30 DME fix at FL 140 (14,000 feet).

At 30 DME from MAY, expect a clearance to slow to 250 knots and cross TIMBA intersection, 7 DME from MAY, at FL 40 (4,000 feet).

At TIMBA intersection, expect a clearance to descend to cross MAY at 2,000 feet and to expect the ILS-DME runway 26 left approach at Gatwick.

As you cross the MAY VOR, slow to 200 knots and track outbound on the MAY 005° radial at 2,000 feet.

At 4 DME from MAY, expect a left turn to fly heading 330°. You'll also receive clearance to fly the ILS-DME runway 26 left approach. Report the Gulf Echo locator beacon to the tower for landing clearance.

ILS at Van Nuys, CA: Cessna Skylane RG

On this adventure you'll fly a long ILS approach in the Cessna Skylane RG into Van Nuys, California (VNY), one of the busiest general aviation airports in the world.

Preflight Checks

The lesson automatically configures your communication and navigation radios for the first part of the flight, but you should always make sure the aircraft is properly configured for the flight.

The VNY ILS (111.3) is tuned on the number 1 navigation radio and displayed on the VOR 1 indicator.

The VNY VOR/DME (113.1), located on the airport, is tuned on the number 2 navigation radio and displayed on the VOR 2 indicator to show your distance from the airport.

Auto-coordination is turned on to make flying a little easier. It's automatically turned off after landing so you can steer more easily on the ground.

The Clearance

This adventure starts in the air at 6,000 feet MSL 17 nautical miles (nm, or 31.5 km) northwest of the Van Nuys Airport. ATC will issue instructions to intercept the runway 16R ILS approximately 3 nm outside the outer marker. This approach has a long, 7.7 nm final segment with plenty of time to get stabilized.

Your initial clearance is to fly heading 070° and maintain 6,000 feet for vectors to the ILS.

Checkerboard Approach: Boeing 737-400

You're captain of a Bluesky 737, a Boeing 737-400, on a routine flight from Hong Kong. But nothing's ever routine at Hong Kong, an airport with an infamous twisting "checkerboard approach" to a short runway.

Clearance

Here is your ATC clearance for this flight. (If you need information about the airports, VORs, or NDBs along your route, check the Airport/Facility directory on the World menu.)

BLUESKY 737 is cleared to the Cheung Chau VOR ~ via direct WHISKEY intersection, direct. Maintain 6,000 feet and squawk 3337.

Specific Routing

After takeoff from runway 13, fly runway heading. Continue to the 23 DME fix from the Hong Kong ILS and then turn left to heading 330° to intercept the Cheung Chau (CH) O90° radial inbound to CH (inbound course 270).

At CH, expect instructions to slow to 200 knots and maintain 6,000. Expect lower altitude in 5 miles.

At 7 DME from CH, turn right heading 045° and descend to 4,500 feet. Expect a clearance to fly the IGS runway 13 approach. Report the Kilo Lima 9 DME fix to the tower for landing clearance.

Corporate Perks: Learjet 45

It's a tough job, but someone's got to do it. The company president and family want to spend a week on Martha's Vineyard, an island off Cape Cod, Massachusetts. You have to get them there in the corporate Learjet 45—and hang around if they need to make a quick hop back to Boston.

Clearance

Here is your ATC clearance for this flight. (If you need information about the airports, VORs, or NDBs along your route, check the Airport/Facility directory on the World menu.)

> Learjet 45 Lima Juliett is cleared to the Martha's Vineyard Airport via direct Marconi, V167 to PEAKE intersection, direct, maintain 17,000 feet and squawk 3212.

Specific Routing

> After takeoff, fly runway heading to the Boston VOR 4.0 DME fix, then turn right to heading 090. After the turn, expect another vector to fly heading 120 and intercept the 340° radial inbound (i.e., the inbound course is 160) to the Marconi (LFV) VOR. Climb and maintain 17,000 feet.

> After passing LFV, fly outbound on the 227° radial and expect a clearance to cross PEAKE intersection (31.4 DME from LFV) below 3,000 feet and maintain 1,500 feet.

> At PEAKE, expect a clearance to fly the ILS runway 24 approach at Martha's Vineyard.

Dallas to Denver: Boeing 737-400

On this adventure, you're the captain of Bluesky 737 on a flight from Dallas Ft. Worth International Airport (DFW) to the Denver International Airport (DEN). This is a daytime flight during the summer.

Clearance

Here is your ATC clearance for this flight. (If you need information about the airports, VORs, or NDBs along your route, check the Airport/Facility directory on the World menu.)

> BLUESKY 737 is cleared to the Denver International Airport via direct Wichita Falls, J168 Lamar, J20 Falcon, direct, maintain flight level 350. Squawk 3327.

Specific Routing

> After takeoff, climb to 2,000 feet then turn right to heading 240°. At 20 nm DME from DFW, turn right to heading 270 to intercept the Wichita Falls (SPS) VOR 140° radial inbound (i.e., the inbound course is 320°). Cross SPS above FL 310 (31,000 feet) and continue climbing to FL 350.

> As you cross SPS, join J168 (the 313° radial). Maintain FL 350.

> About 160 miles from SPS, switch to the Lamar (LAA) VOR and fly inbound on the 128° radial (inbound course 308). When you reach LAA, fly outbound on the 298° radial, which forms part of J20. Maintain FL 350.

> Continue on J20 toward the Hugo (HGO) VOR. You should be flying course 298°. When you're about 25 nm from HGO, expect a clearance to descend to 7,000 with the restriction that you must cross the Falcon (FQF) VOR below 9,000. ATC will advise that you should expect vectors for the runway 35 left ILS at Denver.

> At about 16 nm before you reach FQF, expect instructions to fly heading 300° to intercept the ILS.

Executive Charter: Boeing 737-400

On this flight, you're taking a group of business executives from San Jose, California, to a conference at Disneyland. You're in command of a Bluesky 737, a Boeing 737-400.

The busy airspace in the San Francisco Bay Area requires aircraft departing San Jose to fly a tight, climbing right turn immediately after takeoff. Follow ATC instructions to the letter—or you'll find yourself grounded.

Clearance

Here is your ATC clearance for this flight. (If you need information about the airports, VORs, or NDBs along your route, check the Airport/Facility directory on the World menu.)

> BLUESKY 737 is cleared to the John Wayne Airport via San Jose 8 departure, J1 LAX, V16 PRADO, direct, maintain flight level 230. Squawk 4523.

Specific Routing

> After takeoff on runway 30 left, fly runway heading to the SJC (San Jose) 1.8 DME fix then turn right to heading 110° within 4 nm of the SJC VOR. Climb and maintain 5,000 feet.

> After completing the turn, fly heading 110 until you intercept the Oakland (OAK) 121° radial outbound.

> At the OAK 30 DME fix expect a clearance to climb and maintain FL 230 (23,000 feet) with a restriction to cross MOONY intersection (47 DME from OAK on the 121° radial) above 12,000 feet.

> Proceed toward Avenal (AYE) VOR on a course of 124°. After passing AVE, fly outbound on the AVE 129° radial.

> You may receive a revised clearance to proceed to the Filmore (FIM) VOR and fly the 148° radial for the Tandy Two arrival. Fly inbound to FIM on a course of 130°. Cross FIM and fly outbound on the 148° radial.

> At 48 DME from FIM, expect vectors for the back course runway 1 left approach to the John Wayne Airport (SNA). Turn left to heading 100 and descend to 6,000 feet. Expect a further left turn to heading 060° and an approach clearance. Report NEWPO to the tower for landing clearance.

Executive Charter: Learjet 45

Once again, on this flight you're taking a group of business executives from San Jose, California, to a conference at Disneyland—this time in command of a Learjet 45. You'll be flying to the John Wayne Airport at Orange County (SNA).

The busy airspace in the San Francisco Bay Area requires aircraft departing San Jose to fly a tight, climbing right turn immediately after takeoff. During your arrival at SNA, be prepared for strong Santa Ana winds. And always follow ATC instructions to the letter—or you'll find yourself grounded.

Clearance

Here is your ATC clearance for this flight. (If you need information about the airports, VORs, or NDBs along your route, check the Airport/Facility directory on the World menu.)

> Learjet 45 is cleared to the John Wayne Airport via San Jose 8 departure, J1 LAX, V16 PRADO, direct, maintain flight level 230. Squawk 4523.

Specific Routing

> After takeoff on runway 30 left, fly runway heading to the SJC (San Jose) 1.8 DME fix then turn right to heading 110° within 4 nm of the SJC VOR. Climb and maintain 5,000 feet.

> After completing the turn, fly heading 110° until you intercept the Oakland (OAK) 121° radial outbound.

> At the OAK 30 DME fix expect a clearance to climb and maintain FL 230 (23,000 feet) with a restriction to cross MOONY intersection (47 DME from OAK on the 121° radial) above 12,000 feet.

> Proceed toward Avenal (AYE) VOR on a course of 124°. After passing AVE, fly outbound on the AVE 129° radial.

> You may receive a revised clearance to proceed to the Filmore (FIM) VOR and fly the 148° radial for the Tandy Two arrival. Fly inbound to FIM on a course of 130°. Cross FIM

and fly outbound on the 148° radial.

At 48 DME from FIM, expect vectors for the back course runway 1 left approach to the John Wayne Airport (SNA). Turn left to heading 100° and descend to 6,000 feet. Expect a further left turn to heading 060° and an approach clearance. Report NEWPO to the tower for landing clearance.

Hit the Slots: Learjet 45

This adventure takes you from the sandy beaches at Santa Monica (SMO) to the sandy streets of Las Vegas (LAS). High rollers travel in style, of course, so this is a job for the Learjet 45.

Clearance

Here is your ATC clearance for this flight. (If you need information about the airports, VORs, or NDBs along your route, check the Airport/Facility directory on the World menu.)

LearJet 45 Lima Juliett is cleared to the McCarran Airport via direct Los Angeles VOR J9 Las Vegas VOR, direct, maintain flight level 270 and squawk 4135.

Specific Routing

After takeoff from runway 21, fly runway heading to 7,000 feet and then turn left direct Los Angeles (LAX) VOR. You should track inbound on the 240° radial (inbound course 060).

At LAX, intercept and track outbound on the 041° radial toward Dagget (DAG). Climb and maintain flight level 270 (27,000 feet).

At DAG, intercept and track outbound on the 031° radial toward Las Vegas (LAS).

At LAS VOR, expect a vector to fly heading 110 for the ILS runway 25 right at McCarran.

Fly Before You Buy: Learjet 45

For this adventure, you're kicking the tires on business jets, trying to decide which one best suits your needs.

Before attempting this flight, you should be familiar with basic flight controls and understand the fundamentals of VOR navigation and flying an Instrument landing system ILS approach.

You'll also find it helpful to review the pilot's operating handbook for the Learjet 45 in the Aircraft Handbooks section of Help. You'll also want to have the chart of the Seattle area handy. It's in the back of the Pilot's Handbook

The Clearance

This quick VFR trip takes you south from Paine Field in Everett, WA over Puget Sound. It ends with an ILS approach to runway 13R at Seattle's King County International Airport (Boeing Field). Seattle Approach Control will provide vectors to the final approach course for the ILS.

The current owner of the Learjet is also along for the ride to provide flying tips as necessary.

Preflight Checks

The lesson automatically configures your communication and navigation radios for the first part of the flight.

The ILS is tuned in the number 1 navigation radio, and the EFIS display is activated to make intercepting and flying the ILS a little easier. You can make a visual approach if you choose.

Auto-coordination is turned on to make flying a little easier.

London Shopping Trip: Cessna Skylane RG

Here's an adventure that tests your flying skills in the crowded skies over Europe. Start at Le Havre, Octeville, for a pleasant trip across the English Channel to London City Airport.

Clearance

Here is your ATC clearance for this flight. (If you need information about the airports, VORs, or NDBs along your route, check the Airport/Facility directory on the World menu.)

> Cessna 2001 Zulu, after takeoff fly the Deauville 350° radial to DRAKE, the Seaford 196° radial to Seaford, the Seaford 003° radial to Mayfield and Mayfield 001° radial to London City. Maintain flight level 60 and squawk 1333.

Specific Routing

After takeoff from runway 05, fly runway heading to intercept the Deauville (DVL) 350° radial to DRAKE intersection (formed by the DVL 350° radial and the Seaford [SFD] 196° radial).

At DRAKE, call London Control. Expect a descent to FL 50 (5,000 feet). Intercept and fly inbound on the SFD 196° radial (inbound course 016). At SFD, intercept and fly outbound on the 003° radial to Mayfield (MAY).

At Mayfield, intercept and fly outbound on the 001° radial to London City.

At the MAY 18 DME fix contact City Tower and descend to 1,500 feet. Expect to enter a left-hand circuit on the base leg to land on runway 28.

Day Trip to Martha's Vineyard: Cessna Skylane RG

This adventure takes you to what promises to be a pleasant hop from Sikorsky Memorial Airport in Connecticut via Block Island to Martha's Vineyard, an island off Cape Cod, Massachusetts. But don't get complacent. Monitor the flight and engine instruments unless you want to practice your backstroke.

Clearance

Here is your ATC clearance for this flight. (If you need information about the airports, VORs, or NDBs along your route, check the Airport/Facility directory on the World menu.)

> Fly outbound on the Bridgeport 101° radial to CREAM intersection (13 DME east of Bridgeport). Proceed inbound on the 284° radial to the Sandy Point VOR on Block Island then

inbound on the Martha's Vineyard VOR 266° radial (i.e., the inbound course is 086). Maintain 3,500 feet and set the transponder to squawk code 2324.

Specific Routing

As you approach your destination, plan to cross the Martha's Vineyard VOR at 2,000 feet and expect to fly a right-hand traffic pattern to land on runway 6.

Medical Emergency: Learjet 45

This adventure starts at Boeing Field (BFI) in Seattle. Your mission is to fly vital medical supplies to San Francisco (SFO) to connect with flights that will take them to Christmas Island. Your aircraft is a Learjet 45 Lima Juliett.

It's critical that you get the supplies to SFO on time. If you miss the connection, the supplies will sit for two weeks waiting for the next available flight. So be prepared for a few surprises as you make your way south toward California.

Clearance

Here is your ATC clearance for this flight. (If you need information about the airports, VORs, or NDBs along your route, check the Airport/Facility directory on the World menu.)

Learjet 45 Lima Juliett is cleared to the San Francisco Airport via direct SEA VOR, Jet 1 OAK VOR, direct, maintain flight level 350. Squawk 3635.

Specific Routing

After takeoff from runway 31 left, fly runway heading until reaching 500 feet then turn right heading 030°. Climb and maintain 5,000 feet.

Expect a clearance direct to the Seattle (SEA) VOR and to climb and maintain FL 350 (35,000 feet). Cross SEA above 8,000.

Fly inbound to SEA on a course of 200°. At SEA, intercept the 165° radial outbound. Continue on a course of 165 to the Battle Ground (BTG) VOR. At BTG, fly outbound on the BTG 163° radial.

Your next checkpoint is the Rogue Valley (QED) VOR at Medford, Ore. About halfway between BTG and QED, start tracking the OED VOR and fly inbound on the 345° radial (inbound course 165).

As you pass QED, intercept and fly outbound on the 149° radial toward Red Bluff, Calif. (RBL). The inbound course to RBL is 150°.

At RBL, intercept and fly outbound on the 162° radial toward Oakland (OAK). At 70 DME north of OAK, expect a descent clearance to 8,000 feet with a restriction to cross OAK below 10,000 feet.

As you pass OAK, intercept and track the 219° radial outbound for vectors to the runway 28 right ILS. Expect a vector to heading 090 and a descent clearance to 5,000 feet. Slow to 200 knots.

Expect a further vector to heading 235 and a descent to 1,800 feet, where you'll be cleared for runway 28 right ILS approach. Report BRIJJ to the tower and expect clearance to land.

Movie Stunt Flying: Extra 300S

This adventure puts you in the seat of the Extra 300S to capture a chase scene through Las Vegas for a major motion picture. Try turning on the video recorder so you can play back the scenes.

Instructions

Here are your specific instructions for this adventure:

Extra 328PW, fly west to the airport boundary and then north over the Strip. Pass the Luxor (the pyramid-shaped hotel) below 2,300 feet, maintain less than 2,300 feet (below the building tops) until passing the Stratosphere (the tall tower at the north end of the Strip).

Night Transcontinental: Boeing 737-400

The airline's crew-scheduling computer crashed last week, and you suddenly find yourself assigned to fly a Bluesky 737, on the red-eye from Los Angeles (LAX) to New York's JFK Airport. Make sure there's plenty of coffee on board before you take off.

Clearance

Here is your ATC clearance for this flight. (If you need information about the airports, VORs, or NDBs along your route, check the Airport/Facility directory on the World menu.)

> BLUESKY 737 is cleared to JFK via direct Paradise, J64 Robbinsville, direct, maintain flight level 330. Squawk 5356.

Specific Routing

> After takeoff from runway 25 right, fly runway heading and climb to 3,000 feet. Then turn left to heading 140 to intercept the Paradise (PDZ) VOR 240° radial inbound (inbound course 060) and fly direct to PDZ. Make sure you cross PDZ above FL 180 (18,000 feet).

> At PDZ, intercept and track outbound on the 030° radial toward Hector (HEC).

> At HEC, intercept and track outbound on the 055° radial toward Peach Springs (PGS).

> At PGS, intercept and track outbound on the 059° radial toward Tuba City (TBC).

> At TBC, intercept and track outbound on the 060° radial toward Farmington (FMN)

> At FMN intercept and track outbound on the 047° radial toward Pueblo (PUB). Expect a climb clearance to flight level

370 (37,000 feet) with a restriction to cross PUB at FL 370.

At PUB, intercept and track outbound on the 059° radial toward Hill City (HLC).

At HLC, intercept and track outbound on the 064° radial toward Pawnee City (PWE).

At PWE, intercept and track outbound on the 071° radial toward Lamoni (LMN).

At LMN, intercept and track outbound on the 072° radial toward Bradford (BDF).

At BDF, intercept and track outbound on the 089° radial toward Fort Wayne (FWA).

At FWA, intercept and track outbound on the 091° radial toward Ellwood City (EWC)   At EWC, intercept and track outbound on the 102° radial toward Ravine (RAV).

At RAV, intercept and track outbound on the 102° radial toward Robbinsville (RBV). Expect a descent clearance of 8,000 feet with a restriction to cross RBV below 12,000 feet.

At RBV, intercept and track outbound on the 076° radial toward Colts Neck (COL).

At COL, expect radar vectors to the ILS runway 4 right approach at JFK. Fly heading 080 and maintain 8,000 feet.

Intercept the localizer and proceed inbound. At the 22 DME fix, expect a descent clearance to 3,000 feet. At NARRO intersection, the 15.5 DME fix on the ILS expect approach clearance. Contact the tower at EBBE for landing clearance.

Orlando Adventure: Cessna Skylane RG

The kids have finally worn you down, and it's time to pack them into the Cessna Skylane RG for a flight to Orlando, Florida. See if you can keep them from asking, "Are we there yet?" every five minutes on this flight from Charlotte, North Carolina.

Clearance

Here is your ATC clearance for this flight. (If you need information about the airports, VORs, or NDBs along your route, check the Airport/Facility directory on the World menu.)

> Cessna 2001 Zulu is cleared to Orlando Executive Airport via direct Charlotte, V37 Brunswick, V3 Ormond Beach, V51 OVIDO intersection, direct. Maintain 6,500 feet and squawk 3343.

Specific Routing

After takeoff from runway 23, turn left direct to the Charlotte (CLT) VOR. You will track inbound to Charlotte on the 001° radial (inbound course 181). Climb and maintain 6,500 feet.

At CLT, intercept and track outbound on the 189° radial toward Columbia (CAE).

At CAE, intercept and track outbound on the 195° radial toward Allendale (ALD).

At ALD, intercept and track outbound on the 171° radial toward Savannah (SAV).

At SAV, intercept and track outbound on the 196° radial toward Brunswick (SSI).

At SSi, intercept and track outbound on the 175° radial toward Ormond Beach (OMN).

At OMN, intercept and track outbound on the 183° radial toward OVIDO intersection (OMN 191° radial, 37 DME).

At OVIDO, expect radar vectors for the Orlando localizer back course approach to runway 25.

San Juan Island Tour: Cessna Skylane 182S

It's hard to beat the scenery in the Pacific Northwest—when you can see it. So when a sunny day comes along, it's time to fire up your new Cessna Skylane 182S and take a tour of the San Juan Islands northwest of Seattle. This adventure takes you from

Boeing Field (BFI) to Port Angeles (CLM), an airport on the Olympic Peninsula along the Strait of Juan de Fuca.

Clearance

Here is your ATC clearance for this flight. (If you need information about the airports, VORs, or NDBs along your route, check the Airport/Facility directory on the World menu.)

> Cessna 9110 Echo, after takeoff from runway 31 left, fly runway heading to intercept the Seattle 307° radial to JAWBN intersection, then fly the Tatoosh 080° radial. Maintain 6,500 feet and squawk 1221.

Specific Routing

> When you contact Seattle Departure control, expect a left turn to heading 290 to intercept the SEA 307° radial. Maintain 2,000 feet.

> At 17 DME from SEA, expect a clearance to climb to 6,500 feet and to contact Whidbey Approach.

> Expect a restriction to cross LOFAL intersection (29 DME from SEA) at 6,500 feet.

> At JAWBN intersection (43 DME from SEA), expect a left turn to heading 260 to intercept the Tatoosh (TOW) 080° radial outbound toward Port Angeles (CLM).

> Approaching CLM, descend and enter a left-hand traffic pattern to land on runway 8. The field elevation is 288 feet MSL.

Seafood Dinner: Learjet 45

The assistant undersecretary to the deputy director of a bureau in a large government agency is on a fact-finding mission. You don't need to know the details, only that he's in Washington, D.C., and there's an important meeting at an expensive seafood restaurant in Boston. Everything's on the q.t., and you've got to get him there before the filets get cold. That's a job for the Learjet 45.

Clearance

Here is your ATC clearance for this flight. (If you need information about the airports, VORs, or NDBs along your route, check the Airport/Facility directory on the World menu.)

Learjet 45 Lima Juliett is cleared to the Boston Logan Airport via direct Nottingham VOR, J42 Boston VOR, direct, maintain flight level 330 and squawk 3235.

Specific Routing

After takeoff from runway 18, fly runway heading and set reduced power for noise abatement to the Washington National (DCA) 10 DME.

Expect vectors from ATC to turn left to heading 120 to intercept the 270° radial inbound to Nottingham (OTT) VOR (inbound course 090). Cross OTT above 10,000 feet.

At OTT, intercept and track outbound on the 071° radial. Climb to FL 330 (33,000 feet).

You're now on J42. At GRACO intersection, 29 DME fix east of OTT, expect a turn to track inbound to Woodstown (OOD) VOR on the 235° radial (inbound course 055).

At OOD, intercept and track the 057° radial outbound toward Robbinsville (RBV). At RBV, intercept and track outbound on the 049° radial toward La Guardia (LGA).

At LGA, intercept and track the 054° radial outbound to the 37 DME fix. Intercept and track inbound on the Hartford (HFD) 229° radial (inbound course 069). At HFD, intercept and track the 072° radial outbound toward Putnam (PUT).

At PUT, intercept and track the 071° radial outbound toward Boston (BOS). Expect a descent clearance to cross the BOS VOR below 12,000 feet to maintain 9,000 feet.

Track inbound to Boston on the 234° radial (inbound course 074). Expect to contact Boston approach control at the BOS

VOR. ATC will issue vectors for the runway 22 left ILS approach at Boston Logan. Descend to 6,000 feet and fly heading 070.

At 11 DME from BOS, expect to slow to 200 knots and to turn left to heading 260. Descend to 3,000 feet.

As you're turning through 340°, expect an approach clearance. Contact the tower at the LYNDY outer marker for landing clearance.

Thanksgiving on Avalon: Cessna Skylane 182S

It's the start of the holiday season in southern California, and you're in charge of getting the family over the hills, across the strait, and to grandmother's house for Thanksgiving dinner on Catalina Island. This should be a pleasant VFR flight in your shiny new Cessna Skylane 182S, but remember that winter storms may bring high winds.

Clearance

Here is your ATC clearance for this flight. (If you need information about the airports, VORs, or NDBs along your route, check the Airport/Facility directory on the World menu.)

> Cessna 9110 Echo, after takeoff on runway 21 at Santa Monica, fly runway heading to 2,000 feet then turn left to heading 160°. Intercept the Santa Catalina VOR 340° radial to Avalon (inbound course 160). Maintain 3,500 feet and squawk 1217.

Specific Routing

> At 7 DME north of SXC descend to pattern altitude (2,600 feet MSL), which is 1,000 feet AGL. Catalina reports runway 4 in use and calm winds, so plan to fly a left-hand traffic pattern.

Tokyo Ferry Flight: Boeing 737-400

The previous crew landed the Boeing 737-400 at the wrong airport. While they're filling out paperwork and explaining their mistake to the chief pilot, you have to fly the plane from Narita to Haneda for the next outbound flight. And that's not as easy as it sounds. You'll have to be on your toes for this short, intense hop between airports. Your call sign is BLUESKY 737.

Clearance

Here is your ATC clearance for this flight. (If you need information about the airports, VORs, or NDBs along your route, check the Airport/Facility directory on the World menu.)

> BLUESKY 737, cleared to the Haneda Airport via Chiba Reversal Four departure, direct Kisarazu, direct, maintain 7,000 feet. Squawk 1514.

Specific Routing

> After takeoff from runway 34, fly the Narita (NRE) VOR 337° radial to the 7 DME fix. Make sure you cross the 7 DME fix above 2,800 feet.

> Within 10 DME, turn right to intercept the NRE 014° radial inbound (inbound course 194). Climb and maintain 7,000 feet.

> AT NRE, intercept and track outbound on the 337° radial direct to Kisarazu(KZE) VOR.

> At 25 DME before KZE, expect a right turn to heading 310° and a descent clearance to 3,000 feet. This is a vector for the runway 22 ILS at Haneda.

> At 18 nm from Haneda Airport, expect a left turn to heading 260 and a clearance for the runway 22 ILS approach. Report ARAKAWA (the 6 DME fix from the Haneda [HME] VOR) to the tower and expect landing clearance.

APPENDIX

A

A Pilot's Perspective

In preparation for this book, I got the chance to talk with Dan Koenig and Julian Black, pilots for a major commercial airline.

Which is your favorite aircraft to fly? What do you like about it?

I love flying the 767. It's the best aircraft I have ever flown. It's a newer aircraft, very powerful, with lots of features. If I could fly any aircraft I wanted, I would probably choose the 767 or the 777, the newest models in the fleet.

Which airports are the easiest to fly in and out of?

Well, that depends on a lot of factors. Some airports are great in good weather, but when the weather starts getting bad, things change quickly. Other airports are more difficult, but the challenge makes it worth it. Airports are airports, and it can get boring when things are always the same. As pilots we like to see our skills put to the test. The challenge is its own reward.

What is the most difffcult airport to fly out of?

Well, we flew out of Mexico City a few days ago. You have to plan your approach carefully. There are volcanoes that rise to 16,000 feet around the airport, so if something happened, if we lost an engine after takeoff for example, we would need to have planned a safe route to come back around. Here in Newark, of course, it's all flat—you can't run into anything—but there are noise abatement rules in effect, so you have to follow a particular course. John Wayne Airport in Santa Ana, California, is, without a doubt, the most challenging airport to take off from. They require you to fly out at a 22° nose-high attitude to reduce noise in the surrounding areas.

[In *Microsoft Flight Simulator 98*, you can use the horizontal marks on the vertical scale the AI to maintain a 20° angle. Go to full power at takeoff, and use full flaps.]

In *Microsoft Flight Simulator 98*, the EFIS/CFPD projects a series of rectangles on screen. On a real airplane, how does this system project the proper flight path?

It shows up right here on the ADI (attitude direction indicator) display. The display indicates the runway, your course deviation, and the proper glide slope for the approach.

[You can turn on EFIS/CFPD by choosing "Navigation" from the Aircraft menu. This will display a series of rectangles or bars that indicate the proper descent.]

The autopilot can't land the plane, can it?

Well, there are three autopilots on the 767, and three ILS displays, and yes, they can actually land the plane. In heavy weather, pilots will sometimes let the autopilot land the plane. We wouldn't even be able to turn the plane off the runway until the autopilot is disengaged. What the auto-land feature does is let you watch how the autopilot performs. If you are landing the plane yourself, you tend to be so focused in on what you're doing that it's hard to step back and watch from an overall perspective. When the autopilot is doing its thing, you can watch over it and be much more responsive to the situation as it changes.

[The 737-400 in *Microsoft Flight Simulator 98* supports an auto-throttle feature that will automatically manage the throttle settings to land the plane. Find a runway with an active ILS with glide slope, and start your final approach about 15 miles from the runway. Lock yourself onto the ILS, and engage the Autopilot "ILS Approach" and "Auto-throttle" when you hit the proper approach/land speed (hit [Shift]-[C] for the approach/land checklist). The 737 will manage the throttle during the descent and automatically cut the throttle over the runway. See Chapter 5 for more information on the auto-throttle.]

APPENDIX

B

See the World

O ne of the great things about *Microsoft Flight Simulator 98* is the incorporation of new cities and new 3D art for existing cities. Here's a tour of some of the new and newly enhanced cities this game has to offer. For each city, I'll give a quick and dirty explanation of how to get there and what to see, then you can just sit back and enjoy the scenery.

SYDNEY

Ever wanted to buzz by the famous Sydney Opera House, the one that has become the hallmark of this great city down under? Want to get a sneak preview of the Olympic city for the year 2000? Well, now's your chance! While you're there, can you pick me up a vegemite sandwich?

Setting Up the Flight

1. Go to the World menu and choose "Go to Airport."
2. Choose "Sydney, Australia" and "Kingsford Smith Intl." as the airport.
3. Also under the World menu, set the scenery complexity to "Very Dense" and the Time of Day to anything but "Night."

Take off from the Kingsford Smith Airport, gain around 2,500 feet of altitude, and turn to a heading of 360°. This course will take you directly over downtown Sydney, with the Sydney Opera House on your right and the Harbour Bridge straight ahead. It will take a few minutes to get over downtown if you're flying in the Cessna, so we suggest turning the speed up to 8X until the downtown area comes into view.

TORONTO

Toronto is one of Canada's largest cities, and it's home to several major sports franchises, including the NBA's Raptors and the NHL's Maple Leafs. The downtown core of Toronto provides an

Figure B-1 The Sydney Opera House in all its splendor, with downtown Sydney to the right and behind.

Figure B-2 If you're looking for some fun, why not take your aircraft right through the famous Harbour Bridge?

exciting and visually spectacular nighttime flight, while the CN Tower (the highest free-standing structure in the world) and the Skydome provide excellent daytime highlights.

Setting Up the Flight

1. Go to the World menu and choose "Go to Airport."

2. Choose "Toronto, Ontario, Canada" and "Toronto/City Center—Rwy 8" as the airport.

3. Also under the World menu, set the scenery complexity to "Very Dense" and the Time of Day to whatever you want. The Toronto skyline is impressive at night, but daytime flight allows for a better view of the city.

From this airport you are literally right beside the downtown core of Toronto. As you take off, have a look to your left to get a close-up view of the Skydome. This is what baseball's Toronto

Figure B-3 There are two world-class landmarks in Toronto: the CN Tower and the Skydome, where the Blue Jays and Argonauts play.

Figure B-4
The Skydome is immediately on your left after takeoff. Too bad the roof is closed today or you could take in a Jays game!

Blue Jays and the CFL's Toronto Argonauts call home. Just beside the Skydome is the CN Tower. If you fly the Cessna, you'll quickly get a good appreciation for just how tall this tower is—it takes a fair bit of climbing to fly over the tip of the needle.

WASHINGTON, D.C.

The capital of the United States holds almost mythical status worldwide. There are certainly plenty of landmarks to see in this city, from the Jefferson Memorial to Capitol Hill to the big guy's house—that would be the one painted white.

Setting Up the Flight

1. Go to the World menu and choose "Go to Airport."
2. Choose "Washington" as the city and "Andrews Air Force Base" as the airport.

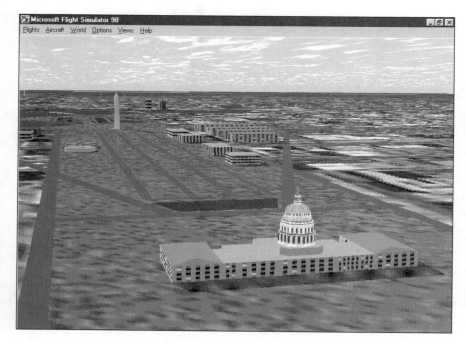

Figure B-5
The Capitol building is a great place to look across at the Washington Monument and the Lincoln Memorial beyond.

3. Also under the World menu, set the scenery complexity to "Very Dense" and the Time of Day to anything but nighttime.

Take off from Andrews Air Force Base, climb to the usual 2,500 feet or so, and turn to a heading of 320° to 325°. This course will take you almost straight to the back of Capitol Hill. Once you get there (you may want to increase the time compression to speed up your trip), turn to your left so that you are heading straight for the Washington Monument (that would be the tall obelisk). If you want to take a gander at the White House, hang a tight right at the monument. At this point, it's helpful to turn the time compression to 50 percent of normal or even lower, so that you can enjoy the scenery without having to panic over controlling your aircraft. The Lincoln Memorial lies behind the Washington Monument, and the Jefferson Memorial is to its left.

Figure B-6 Don't worry—the Secret Service won't shoot you down! In *Flight Simulator 98*, you're safe to buzz the White House all you want.

CHELAN, WASHINGTON

Although Chelan isn't a major city, the folks at Microsoft went to the trouble of including some fairly spectacular visuals for your enjoyment. This canyon is photorealistic and a real thrill to fly through. The wind currents are spectacular for gliding.

Setting Up the Flight

1. Go to the World menu and choose "Go to Airport."

2. Choose "Chelan, Washington" and "Chelan Muni—Rwy 20" as the airport.

3. Also under the World menu, set the scenery complexity to "Very Dense" and the Time of Day to anything but nighttime.

Figure B-7 This canyon just beyond the runway at Chelan showcases some of the great visual candy offered up by *Flight Simulator 98.*

Take off straight up the runway. You may want to take the Extra 300S on this jaunt, although the Cessna will do. This runway is a little too short to risk a 737, and the Learjet will be too fast for you to properly enjoy the scenery. Once you take off, head for the canyon; there's really not much more to say. For those who are flying at night, the heading you want is 190°.

ROME

Ah yes, Italy. There's nothing quite like buzzing over the Colosseum en route to a papal visit at the Vatican—which is good, since most of the detail in *Flight Simulator 98*'s Rome is centered around these two areas.

Figure B-8 The canyon near Chelan is a great place to switch to an external view.

Setting Up the Flight

1. Go to the World menu and choose "Go to Airport."

2. Choose "Rome, Italy" as the city and "Ciampino—Rwy 33" as the airport.

3. Also under the World menu, set the scenery complexity to "Very Dense" and the Time of Day to anything but night-time. Dawn or dusk are nice settings for Rome.

Once you take off and get your aircraft over 1,500 feet, turn to a heading of approximately 300°. This will take you directly over the Colosseum and then on to the Vatican. These are the only sections of Rome that have advanced buildings, so though you can go sight-seeing elsewhere, these are really the only areas worth visiting.

Figure B-9 There's nothing like Rome in the morning, with the sun casting long shadows off the city's ancient buildings.

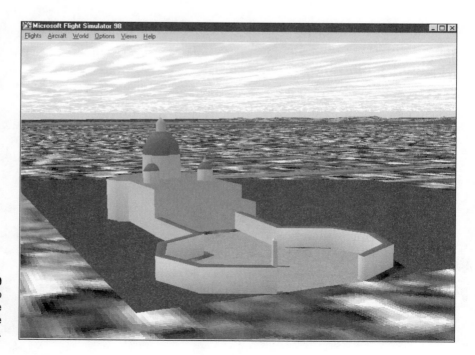

Figure B-10 Now's your chance to have an audience with the pope. The Vatican awaits.

ST. LOUIS

St. Louis, the Gateway to the West, is perhaps most famous for its arch, which signifies the passage from the East. The arch is also high on any barnstormer's list of must-fly-through structures, and it's a requirement for completing this simulation! The muddy Mississippi provides an appropriate foil for the downtown section of St. Louis. If you look closely, you can check out the baseball diamond in Busch Stadium.

Setting Up the Flight

1. Go to the World menu and choose "Go to Airport."
2. Choose "St. Louis, Missouri" as the city and "Lambert-St. Louis Intl." as the airport.
3. Also under the World menu, set the scenery complexity to "Very Dense" and the Time of Day to anything but nighttime.

Figure B-11 With the muddy Mississippi in the background, downtown St. Louis seems to stand out even more.

Once you take off from the St. Louis regional airport, climb to around 2,000 feet and set in a course for roughly 200° to 205°. This will eventually take you right over downtown St. Louis, and yes, the arch as well. Take the time to fly over the baseball stadium, where you can clearly see the diamond. You may want to increase time compression on your way out to the arch; in the Cessna it takes a few minutes. Then, do it. Building structures like this are really only invitations to pilots everywhere.

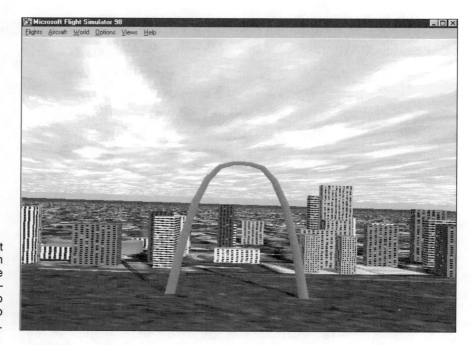

Figure B-12 Don't resist the temptation to fly through the arch in St. Louis— only in real life do you have to be so well disciplined.

APPENDIX
C
A Tour of the Hawaiian Islands

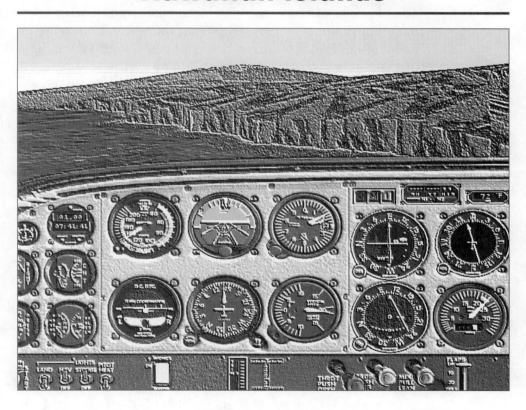

*M*icrosoft *Flight Simulator 98* contains enhanced scenery for Hawaii, the Caribbean, and Japan. With this book by your side, you will be able to experience a portion of this breathtaking scenery by taking a tour of the Hawaiian volcanoes at the height of a volcanic eruption. So without any further ado, spool up the engines and let's go!

HAWAIIAN VOLCANOES TOUR

The Hawaiian island chain is volcanic in origin. Each of the eight main Hawaiian islands rose up from the sea millions of years ago, and another island is currently forming just south of the Big Island of Hawaii, called Lo'ihi. Hawaii is one of the few places in the world where you can see an active volcano. Before we fly, we'll set the simulation date to 1983, the year of the big Kilauea eruption. We'll then take a tour of Hawaii's volcanoes, both active and extinct, and end the tour with a spectacular eruption on Kilauea's eastern slope.

Setting Up the Flight

1. Go to the Flights menu and choose "Create Flight."
2. Choose the Cessna Skylane 182S, and click OK.
3. Go to the "Scenery Complexity" dialog box under the World menu and turn on as much of the detail as you dare. The Hawaiian scenery is truly spectacular with all the options turned on.
4. Go to the World menu and choose "Go to Airport."
5. Select North America as the Global region, select United States as the country, and choose "Hawaii" from the list of states. Choose "Barbers Point NAS-Rwy 04R" and click OK to close this box.
6. Choose "Time & Season" from the World menu.
7. Click on the Set Time of Day button and choose Day from the pull-down menu.

8. Click on the Seasons tab and choose Set Exact Date. Enter 8 for the month, 5 for the day, and 1983 for the year. Click OK to close this box.

9. For this flight, I suggest turning off crashes in the Aircraft Settings dialog box. There are some places a Cessna just wasn't built to go.

10. Change any other settings you like, such as auto-coordination, wind conditions, or cloud cover. When you have finished, choose Save Flight from the Flights menu, and give it a title.

Takeoff

Barbers Point NAS is an old naval air station on Oahu's south shore. Request takeoff clearance, then release your parking brakes and go to full throttle. After take off, raise your landing gear and turn to a heading of 75°. Admire the scenery as you fly down the

Figure C-1 The reef runway is a distinctive feature of Honolulu International Airport.

Figure C-2 This is a view of Waikiki, with Diamond Head in the distance.

beach toward Pearl Harbor. As you draw closer to the mouth of Pearl Harbor, you will see the reef runway of Honolulu International Airport, a massive runway over two miles in length.

When this runway was first built it created a lot of controversy because residents were afraid it would spoil the beauty of the coastline. By moving the runway off shore, though, a lot of the noise from jetliner takeoffs and landings was minimized. The reef runway remains a unique and peculiar addition to Oahu's shoreline. If you would like to try a touch-and-go landing on the reef runway, you should be close to the proper heading already. Touch down, then throttle back up again and take off.

Waikiki Beach

Continue to follow the coastline until you see the hotels and buildings of Waikiki. If you look carefully, you can see the mouth of the Ala Wai Canal leading inland from the ocean. If your flying skills are up to it, you can shortcut through Waikiki and fly right up the

Figure C-3 This is a view of Ala Moana Center, a popular shopping mall with tourists and locals alike.

Ala Wai Canal. You can also land the plane and drive it along the canal, which, incidentally, is the only place to find free parking spaces when visiting Waikiki. The canal ends in a big green area called Kapiolani Park, at the base of Diamond Head.

You may also see a long, low building near Waikiki. This is actually one of the world's largest shopping centers. There was a well-known song in the sixties, "They Paved Paradise and Put Up a Parking Lot," which was written about the construction of Ala Moana Center in Honolulu.

Diamond Head

Continuing through Waikiki, you will soon see the unmistakable shape of Diamond Head, a peak that serves as the background for most Waikiki postcards and snapshots.

The story goes that the emerald-colored sparkling minerals found on the slopes of this ancient volcano were once thought to be diamonds, hence the name Diamond Head. Others contend the volcano got its name because of its diamond-shaped peak. In any case, the volcano is extinct now, and it's possible to hike around the inside of the crater and collect *olivine*, the green crystals that once caused so much excitement.

You can actually fly into the crater and take a look around. Along the beach at the base of Diamond Head is some of the most exclusive real estate in the world.

Hawaii Kai

Continue around the southern tip of Oahu and follow the coastline. In front of you, you will see the suburban oasis of Hawaii Kai, most parts of which are linked by many small canals. Just beyond Hawaii Kai, you will see another extinct volcano, called Koko Head. There is also a volcanic crater to the right, of which one side has broken apart and emptied out to the sea. This created Hanauma Bay, a beautiful coral refuge for multitudes of brilliantly

Figure C-4
Koko Head is the triangular peak; just ahead and to the right is Hanauma Bay, a beautiful marine preserve.

colored tropical fish and a spectacular place for diving or snorkeling. As you fly over Hanauma Bay, look for the different hues of blue; lighter areas denote parts of the coral reef.

On to Maui

As you pass Koko Head Crater, turn to a heading of 115° and head out to sea. We will now fly to Maui, home of the sun. If you like, you can tune NAV 1 to the Kahului VOR frequency, which is 114.3. On the way, you will pass over the islands of Molokai and Lanai. Both are used primarily for farming or hunting. Microsoft's Bill Gates once rented the entire island of Lanai for his wedding. Talk about deluxe accommodations!

Fly directly toward the Maui VOR station. Don't worry if your OBI doesn't register the signal right away. When you get within range, it should turn itself on. As you get closer to Maui, look for the brown peak of Mount Haleakala, which rises to 10,000 feet.

Figure C-5
Haleakala looms
in the distance.

Figure C-6 These observatories enjoy a view that is unparalleled.

You should also start a slow climb because our goal is to fly directly into Haleakala Crater.

The crater itself is over three miles in diameter. One of the most spectacular sights in the world is the view of the sunrise from Haleakala Crater. Because of the crater's size and high altitude, it looks as if the sun is rising right out of the crater. The Hawaiian name Haleakala means, literally, "House of the Sun." As you fly over the mountain, look carefully at the rim of the crater and you will actually see small observatory buildings, which house some of the world's most powerful telescopes. Remember that if the clouds obscure your view, you can always go to the Weather dialog box and remove that weather layer. When you have finished flying through the crater, turn to a heading of 120° and head straight for Upolu Point on the Big Island of Hawaii.

Figure C-7 If you look closely, you can see waterfalls along the Upolu coast.

The Big Island

The newest islands in the Hawaiian chain are still being formed by volcanic activity. The island of Hawaii, also known as the Big Island, is the southernmost island in the chain. Kilauea Crater is still active, and it erupts on a regular basis, sending floods of molten lava coursing down the sides of the ridge and into the sea. The Hawaiians believe in Pele, the fire goddess, and believe her face sometimes shows up in the silhouette of steam plumes rising from the point at which the molten lava meets the sea. Watch the eruption for yourself, and be on the lookout for this powerful goddess.

As you cross the coastline of the Big Island, you will see the volcanoes Mauna Kea and Mauna Loa. If you count the part beneath the sea, Mauna Kea is the tallest mountain in the world. As you continue toward the eastern tip of the Big Island, descend

Figure C-8 If the date in the Time & Seasons dialog box is set to 1983, you should see fiery plumes of lava shooting up from the ridgeline at Kilauea Crater.

to an altitude of 2,000 feet. As you do, look carefully for the erupting volcano near the shore. Fly low and slow over the lava flow and enjoy the view. If you really like to live dangerously, choose "Select Aircraft" from the Aircraft menu, and switch to the Schweizer sailplane. Come in low over the lava flow, and check out the lift you can get from a sea of molten lava. Well done!

When you've had enough fun for one day, tune NAV 1 to the VOR frequency at Hilo International, which is 116.9. Come in for a smooth landing, then relax with a mai tai and a round of golf.

APPENDIX
D

Multiplayer Flight

THE MULTIPLAYER EXPERIENCE

Flying with other people adds a whole new dimension to the *Flight Simulator* experience. *Flight Simulator 98* offers a number of multiplayer options that will allow you to fly with other people in your office, in another city, or around the world.

Configuring the Multiplayer Settings

There are a few settings that are useful to set up ahead of time. These are found in the Multiplayer Settings dialog box under the Flights menu. It is much easier to find the other player if you put check marks in the "ADF lock to aircraft" and the "DME lock to aircraft" boxes. The ADF indicator on your instrument panel will now display the other player's position relative to you, and the DME indicator will tell you how far away the other player is.

Setting up a multiplayer game is fairly straightforward no matter which way you decide to hook up. One of the players sets up a game and invites others to join in. All you need to do is decide

Figure D-1 The chat window offers you the opportunity to comment helpfully on your fellow player's progress.

Figure D-2 This is where you can change the multiplayer settings.

who will be the "host," specify the proper connection settings, and get ready to fly. Some of the different options are as follows.

Connecting Via the Internet

As long as you know the IP address of the person you are trying to connect with, you can fly over the internet. If you are hosting a game, make sure you E-mail your IP address to the other players or telephone them with the address. You can also find other players over the internet by connecting to Microsoft's Internet Gaming Zone web site (http://www.zone.com). Choose TCP/IP as your connection type. Lag times can vary widely over the internet, so for the smoothest connection you might want to connect during periods of light usage, such as late at night or early in the morning.

Connecting Via a Local Area Network

You can connect to other machines on a local area network by choosing TCP/IP or IPX as your connection type. This offers a fairly fast connection with a low latency rate.

If you are hosting a game and want to find out your IP address to send to other people, simply type "winipcfg" at a DOS prompt, hit return, and the computer will tell you.

Direct Connect

You can connect two computers by using a null modem cable. This option offers the fastest, most direct connection. Choose Serial connection as your method of connection. You can also direct connect using a modem, in which case you would choose Modem as your connection type.

Fun Things to Try with Other Players

Once you get over the initial thrill of seeing other players in midair, you might be looking for some other challenges. Here are just a few ideas for having fun in the air.

Follow the Leader

"Follow the Leader" is great for practicing your flying skills. Fly in a loose formation, just off the other player's wing. You will have to match your airspeed, so either use full throttle or agree on a com-

Figure D-3 Use different views and shrink the instrument panel by dragging its borders to give you a competitive edge.

Figure D-4 Astound and frighten other players with your feats of daring while in Multiplayer mode.

mon engine setting, such as 2400 RPM. Now, do your best to follow the other player's movements, barrel roll for barrel roll, Immelmann for Immelmann. The Extra 300S and the Sopwith Camel are great for this kind of pursuit, due to their maneuverability.

Alternately, you can play "Shoot the Leader" by starting out a given distance from each other, maneuvering to get on each other's tail, and hitting the (Print Screen) key to see who can take the closest picture.

High Speed Pass

Nothing adds more to that venerable old game of Chicken than dueling it out with $250,000 airplanes at 500 knots of closing speed. One famous airshow routine features two or four airplanes going vertical together, then each performs a split-S and the airplanes cross paths again at low altitude and high speeds. This maneuver takes precision and coordination, but looks very impressive to an observer.

Figure D-5 The helicopter is ideal for Multiplayer mode.

Fly from the Spot Plane View

Formation flying is probably most enjoyable when viewed from outside the cockpit. If you are accomplished enough to fly your aircraft from the spot plane view, you will reap the rewards by enjoying an unparalleled view of your plane and two or three others as you fly wingtip to wingtip. It's also much easier to find the other players this way.

Hide-and-Seek with Helicopters

The helicopter is, indisputably, king of Multiplayer mode. Its maneuverability and relatively slow speed make it ideal for flying with other players. At the same time, the challenge of maintaining stable flight makes formation flying a difficult but rewarding feat. The helicopter is also maneuverable enough to play hide-and-seek in dense urban areas. One player hides by hovering behind a building or landing in a park somewhere, and the other players try to locate the hidden helicopter using their ADF and DME

Figure D-6 Airplane CRW is probably best done at a higher altitude than this.

instruments. To make this more challenging, try to use only the DME reading to let you know if you are getting "hotter" or "colder." Make sure you turn off the "Display player names" option in the Multiplayer Settings dialog box, or your name will give you away!

Dirt Cheap CRW

Yes, it is actually possible to do relative work with multi-million-dollar airplanes, if you're flying a *Flight Simulator* aircraft. You will also want to turn on the "Ignore crash" setting under the Aircraft Settings. Make sure you match your heading and altitude, then glide forward smoothly to dock on the other aircraft.

Aerobatic Formation Flying

For performing aerobatics, there is just no substitute for the Extra 300S. For a real challenge, have one player fly inverted, then have the other plane come in smoothly, flying just above the other

Figure D-7
Successfully pull
off a stunt like this,
and you're ready to
fly in an airshow.

aircraft, so that the wheels are barely touching. It helps to have the spot plane view open in a window, so that you can judge your distance. Press P to pause the simulation when you have pulled this stunt off, and take a picture for posterity. An alternative to this stunt is to fly canopy to canopy.

APPENDIX

E

List of
Keyboard Commands

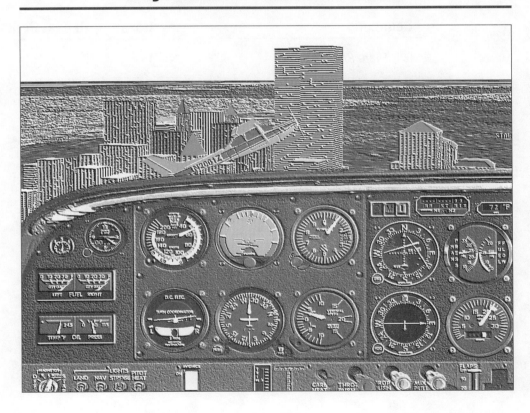

KEYBOARD SHORTCUTS

This table gives you a quick look at all the keyboard commands in *Microsoft Flight Simulator 98*. The column "Repeat Option?" simply lets you know whether you can set a key to repeat automatically when pressed and held (Y = yes, N =no). The "+" simply means "in addition to." For example, "CTRL + C" means you need to press the "Control" key along with the "C" key at the same time. An asterisk (*) under "Keystrokes" means that the key has not been assigned, but it *can* be assigned. You can assign keys in the "Customize Controls" dialogue in the Options menu.

Command	Keystrokes	Repeat Option?
Exit *Flight Simulator*	Ctrl + C	N
Exit *Flight Simulator* (immediately)	Ctrl + Break	N
Pause	P	N
Joystick on/off	K	N
Toggle sound	Q	N
Toggle slew mode	Y	N
Toggle mouse-as-yoke mode	Ctrl + Num Lock Del	N
Select time compression	R	N
Save flight	;	N
Reset current flight	Ctrl + ;	N
Decrease selection	−	Y
Increase selection	=	Y
Decrease selection slightly	Shift + −	N
Increase selection slightly	Shift + =	N
Select Item 1	1	N
Select Item 2	2	N
Select Item 3	3	N
Select Item 4	4	N

Command	Keystrokes	Repeat Option?
Left ailerons	Num Lock 4	N
Right ailerons	Num Lock 6	N
Left rudder	Num Lock 0	N
Right rudder	Num Lock Enter	N
Center ailerons and rudder	Num Lock 5	N
Up elevator	Num Lock 8	N
Down elevator	Num Lock 2	N
Decrease throttle	Num Lock 3	N
Increase throttle	Num Lock 9	N
Trim up	Num Lock 1	Y
Trim down	Num Lock 7	Y
Cut throttle	F1	N
Decrease throttle	F2	N
Increase throttle slightly	F3	N
Increase throttle	*	N
Full throttle	F4	N
Fully retract flaps	F5	N
Raise flaps	F6	Y
Lower flaps	F7	Y
Fully extend flaps	F8	N
Prop pitch low	Ctrl + F4	N
Increase prop pitch	*	N
Increase prop pitch slightly	Ctrl + F3	N
Decrease prop pitch	Ctrl + F2	N
Prop pitch high	Ctrl + F1	N
Fully rich mixture	Ctrl + Shift + F4	N

Command	Keystrokes	Repeat Option?
Enrich mixture	[*]	N
Enrich mixture slightly	[Ctrl] + [Shift] + [F3]	N
Lean mixture	[Ctrl] + [Shift] + [F2]	N
Fully lean mixture	[Ctrl] + [Shift] + [F1]	N
Toggle landing gear	[G]	N
Manually pump landing gear	[Ctrl] + [G]	N
Brakes	[.] (period)	Y
Brakes (left)	[F11]	N
Brakes (right)	[F12]	N
Set parking brake	[Ctrl] + [.] (period)	N
Toggle spoilers	[/]	N
Arm autospoilers	[Shift] + [/]	N
Toggle carb heat	[H]	N
Toggle pilot head	[Shift] + [H]	N
Select an engine	[E]	N
Select jet starter	[J]	N
Select magnetos	[M]	N
Toggle smoke system	[I]	N
Toggle all lights	[L]	N
Toggle strobe lights	[O]	N
Panel lights	[Shift] + [L]	N
Landing lights	[Ctrl] + [L]	N
Landing light up	[Ctrl] + [Num Lock] [8]	N
Landing light down	[Ctrl] + [Num Lock] [2]	N
Landing light left	[Ctrl] + [Num Lock] [4]	N
Landing light right	[Ctrl] + [Num Lock] [6]	N

Command	Keystrokes	Repeat Option?
Center landing light	Ctrl + Num Lock 5	N
Reset directional gyro	D	N
Reset altimeter	B	N
Land me	X	N
Autopilot master switch	Z	N
Autopilot attitude hold	Ctrl + T	N
Autopilot localizer hold	Ctrl + O	N
Autopilot approach mode	Ctrl + A	N
Autopilot heading hold	Ctrl + H	N
Autopilot altitude hold	Ctrl + Z	N
Autopilot wing leveler	Ctrl + V	N
Autopilot back course mode	Ctrl + B	N
Autopilot NAV1 hold	Ctrl + N	N
Toggle yaw damper	Ctrl + D	N
Toggle airspeed hold	Ctrl + R	N
Arm auto-throttle	Shift + R	N
Auto-throttle takeoff/go-around	Ctrl + Shift + R	N
Toggle mach hold	Ctrl + M	N
Autopilot vertical speed hold	*	N
Autopilot heading bug increment	*	N
Autopilot heading bug decrement	*	N
Select transponder	T	N
Select COM radio	C	N
Select NAV radio	N	N
Select an OBS indicator	V	N
Select a DME	F	N

Command	Keystrokes	Repeat Option?
Select ADF	`A`	N
Identify VOR1	`Ctrl` + `1`	N
Identify VOR2	`Ctrl` + `2`	N
Identify DME1	`Ctrl` + `3`	N
Identify DME2	`Ctrl` + `4`	N
Identify ADF	`Ctrl` + `5`	N
Send ATC text message	`Num Lock` + `*`	N
Cycle OBS,COM,NAV,ADF	`*`	Y
Cycle OBS,COM,NAV,ADF backward	`*`	N
Select EGT	`U`	N
View checklists	`Shift` + `C`	N
Close view window	`]`	N
Create new view window	`[`	N
Create new map window	`Shift` + `]`	N
Switch to next view	`Ctrl` + `Tab`	N
Switch to previous view	`Ctrl` + `Shift` + `Tab`	N
Cycle view modes	`S`	N
Cycle view modes backward	`Shift` + `S`	N
Cycle view types	`Ctrl` + `S`	N
Cycle view types backward	`Ctrl` + `Shift` + `S`	N
Full window view	`W`	N
Bring window to front	`'`	N
Toggle instrument panels	`Shift` + `[`	N
Toggle coordinates/frame rate	`Shift` + `Z`	N
Set zoom to 1X	`Backspace`	N
Select view direction	`Num Lock` `/`	N

Command	Keystrokes	Repeat Option?
Pan view left	`Ctrl` + `Shift` + `Backspace`	Y
Pan view right	`Ctrl` + `Shift` + `Enter`	Y
Pan view up	`Shift` + `Backspace`	Y
Pan view down	`Shift` + `Enter`	Y
Pan view left and up	`*`	Y
Pan view left and down	`*`	Y
Pan view right and up	`*`	Y
Pan view right and down	`*`	Y
Pan view tilt left	`*`	N
Pan view tilt right	`*`	N
Pan view reset	`Ctrl` + `Spacebar`	Y
Look ahead	`Shift` + `Num Lock` `8`	N
Look ahead/right	`Shift` + `Num Lock` `9`	N
Look right	`Shift` + `Num Lock` `6`	N
Look back/right	`Shift` + `Num Lock` `3`	N
Look back	`Shift` + `Num Lock` `2`	N
Look back/left	`Shift` + `Num Lock` `1`	N
Look left	`Shift` + `Num Lock` `4`	N
Look ahead/left	`Shift` + `Num Lock` `7`	N
Look down	`Shift` + `Num Lock` `5`	N
Stop video (replay or recording)	`Esc`	N
Add text to video	`,` (comma)	N
Stop analysis	`\`	N
Toggle panel window 1 on/off	`Shift` + `1`	N
Toggle panel window 2 on/off	`Shift` + `2`	N
Toggle panel window 3 on/off	`Shift` + `3`	N

Command	Keystrokes	Repeat Option?
Toggle panel window 4 on/off	Shift + 4	N
Toggle panel window 5 on/off	Shift + 5	N
Toggle panel window 6 on/off	Shift + 6	N
Toggle panel window 7 on/off	Shift + 7	N
Toggle panel window 8 on/off	Shift + 8	N
Toggle panel window 9 on/off	Shift + 9	N
Cycle through other players	Ctrl + Shift + T	N
Toggle track mode	Ctrl + Shift + D	N
Follow other player	Ctrl + Shift + F	N
Switch to observer mode	Ctrl + Shift + O	N
Toggle chat window on/off	Ctrl + Enter	N
Switch focus to chat window	Enter	N
Ailerons axis	*	N
Elevator axis	*	N
Rudder axis	*	N
Throttle axis	*	N
Elevator trim axis	*	N

APPENDIX
F

Airports, VORs, and NDBs

AFRICA

Airports

Gran Canaria, Canary Islands – Gran Canaria

Ident	LPA	ATIS	118.60
Elev	77	Rwy/Length/ILS/ID	03L/10171/109.90/ILP
Lat	N27°55'		21R/10171
Long	W15°23'		03R/10171
			21L/10171

Al Ismailiyah, Egypt – Al Ismailiyah AB

Ident	—	ATIS	—
Elev	39	Rwy/Length/ILS/ID	—
Lat	N30°42'		
Long	E32°14'		

Cairo, Egypt – Cairo Intl

Ident	CAI	ATIS	122.60
Elev	382	Rwy/Length/ILS/ID	05L/10827/110.90/CRL
Lat	N30°07'		23R/10827/110.30/CRR
Long	E31°24'		05R/13123/109.90/ROT
			23L/13123/109.50/LOT
			16/10279
			34/10279

Cairo, Egypt – Giza (Embada)

Ident	—	ATIS	—
Elev	58	Rwy/Length/ILS/ID	—
Lat	N30°04'		
Long	E31°11'		

Port Said, Egypt – Port Said

Ident	—	ATIS	—
Elev	11	Rwy/Length	—
Lat	N31°16'		
Long	E32°14'		

Abidjan, Ivory Coast – Port Bouet

Ident	ABJ	ATIS	118.10
Elev	20	Rwy/Length/ILS/ID	03/8858
Lat	N05°15'		21/8858/110.30/AN
Long	E03°55'		

Nairobi, Kenya – Jomo Kenyatta Intl

Ident	NBO	ATIS	118.70
Elev	5327	Rwy/Length/ILS/ID	06/13507/110.30/NL
Lat	S01°19'		24/13507
Long	E36°55'		

Antananarivo, Madagascar – Ivato

Ident	TNR	ATIS	118.10
Elev	4196	Rwy/Length/ILS/ID	11/10171/109.50/IO
Lat	S18°47'		29/10171
Long	E47°28'		

Casablanca, Morocco – Mohamed V

Ident	CMN	ATIS	118.50
Elev	656	Rwy/Length/ILS/ID	17/12205
Lat	N33°21'		35/12205/109.90/NR
Long	W07°34'		

Lagos, Nigeria – Murtala Muhammed

Ident	LOS	ATIS	123.80
Elev	135	Rwy/Length/ILS/ID	01R/9006/110.30/ILO
Lat	N06°34'		19L/9006
Long	E03°19'		01L/12795/109.30/ILC
			19R/12795/109.30/ILB

Seychelles, Seychelles Islands – Seychelles Intl

Ident	SEZ	ATIS	118.30
Elev	10	Rwy/Length/ILS/ID	13/9800
Lat	S04°40'		31/9800/110.30/SIA
Long	E55°31'		

Capetown, South Africa – D F Malan

Ident	CPT	ATIS	118.10
Elev	151	Rwy/Length/ILS/ID	01/10502/110.30/CT
Lat	S33°58'		19/10502/109.10/KS
Long	E18°36'		16/5581
			34/5581

Johannesburg, South Africa – Jan Smuts

Ident	JNB	ATIS	118.10
Elev	5558	Rwy/Length/ILS/ID	03L/14495/110.30/JS
Lat	S26°08'		21R/14495
Long	E28°14'		03R/11155/109.10/JN
			21L/11155/109.90/JA
			15/9285
			33/9285

Khartoum, Sudan – Khartoum

Ident	KRT	ATIS	119.20
Elev	1261	Rwy/Length/ILS/ID	18/9843/110.90/KIS
Lat	N15°36'		36/9843/110.30/KIN
Long	E32°33'		

Kinshasa, Zaire – N'Djili Intl

Ident	FIH	ATIS	118.10
Elev	1027	Rwy/Length/ILS/ID	06/11811
Lat	S04°23'		24/11811/110.30/KSA
Long	E15°27'		

VORs

Location/Name	Ident	Freq	Lat	Long
Canary Islands				
Fuerteventura	FTV	114.10	N28°26'	W13°51'
Gran Canaria	GDV	112.90	N28°04'	W15°25'
Lanzarote	LT	113.70	N28°56'	W13°36'
Lanzarote	LZR	115.20	N29°09'	W13°30'
Tenerife	TFN	112.50	N28°32'	W16°16'
Tenerife-South	TFS	116.40	N28°00'	W16°41'
Egypt				
Cairo	CAI	112.50	N30°09'	E31°25'
Cairo	CVO	115.20	N30°05'	E31°23'
Fayoum	FYM	117.30	N29°25'	E30°21'
Kenya				
Anthi River	TV	115.50	S01°30'	E37°01'
Lodwar	LOV	114.50	N03°07'	E35°37'
Nairobi	NI	113.10	S01°17'	E36°57'
Nakuru	NAK	115.10	S00°18'	E36°09'
Ngong	GV	115.90	S01°23'	E36°38'
Ivory Coast				
Abidjan	AD	114.30	N05°16'	W03°56'
Libya				
Djanet	DJA	114.10	N24°16'	E09°26'

Location/Name	Ident	Freq	Lat	Long
Madagascar				
Antananarivo	TVN	114.50	S18°48'	E47°31'
Toamasina	MT	113.10	S18°07'	E49°23'
Morocco				
Casablanca	CBA	116.90	N33°31'	W07°40'
Casablanca-Mohamed V	BRC	114.00	N33°17'	W07°33'
Rabat-Sale	RBT	116.50	N34°03'	W06°44'
Nigeria				
Cotonou	TYE	113.30	N06°21'	E02°23'
Ibadan	IB	112.10	N07°20'	E03°58'
Lagos	LG	113.70	N06°42'	E03°19'
Seychelles Islands				
Praslin	PRA	115.70	S04°18'	E55°42'
Seychelles	SEY	113.10	S04°40'	E55°32'
South Africa				
Cape Town	CTV	115.70	S33°58'	E18°36'
Grasmere	GAV	115.50	S26°30'	E27°40'
Hartebeespoortdam	HBV	112.10	S25°40'	E27°50'
Heidelberg	HGV	116.70	S26°41'	E28°17'
Jan Smuts	JSV	115.20	S26°09'	E28°13'
Lanseria	LAV	114.50	S25°56'	E27°55'
Witbank	WIV	113.30	S25°49'	E29°11'
Sudan				
Khartoum	KTM	112.10	N15°35'	E32°33'
Merowe	MRW	116.00	N18°24'	E31°49'
Zaire				
Brazzaville	BZ	113.10	S04°14'	E15°15'
Kinshasa	KSA	115.00	S04°24'	E15°25'
Zimbabwe				
Fydle	VFY	114.90	S18°10'	E29°59'
Harare	VSB	113.10	S17°54'	E31°07'

NDBs

Location/Name	Ident	Freq	Lat	Long
Canary Islands				
Gran Canaria	VR	365	N27°51'	W15°25'
Hierro	HR	376	N27°48'	W17°53'
Tenerife	FP	420	N28°29'	W16°22'
Egypt				
Cairo	OR	284	N30°02'	E31°19'
Cairo	OL	361	N30°09'	E31°28'
Moquattam	MKT	317	N30°02'	E31°16'
Nasar	NSR	340	N30°04'	E31°18'
Ivory Coast				
Abidijan	PB	294	N05°14'	W03°57'
Abidijan	AN	306	N05°20'	W03°53'
Afiendu	IVY	393	N05°24'	W02°55'
Kenya				
Athi River	TH	329.5	S01°30'	E37°01'
Embakasi	AL	379	S01°22'	E36°56'
Nairobi	NO	278	S01°21'	E36°51'
Nairobi	NI	283	S01°20'	E36°54'
Narok	NK	368	S01°06'	E35°51'
Ngong	GG	315	S01°23'	E36°38'
Libya				
Dijanet	DJA	274	N24°16'	E09°26'
Ghat	GHT	368	N25°11'	E10°08'
Madagascar				
Ankazobe	TN	385	S18°18'	E47°06'
Ivato	IO	305	S18°47'	E47°23'
Ivato	NT	340	S18°49'	E47°36'
Maromamy	MMY	267	S18°48'	E49°01'
Moramanga	TE	371	S18°57'	E48°13'
Morocco				
Ben Slimane	CAE	275	N33°37'	W07°07'
Casablanca	NSR	282	N33°17'	W07°33'
Casablanca	NUA	255	N33°25'	W07°36'
Daquartt	CSD	345	N32°56'	W08°03'

Location/Name	Ident	Freq	Lat	Long
Nigeria				
Ibadan	IB	400	N07°26'	E03°55'
Lagos	LB	368	N06°35'	E03°18'
Lagos	LA	336	N06°36'	E03°03'
Okitipupa	OK	345	N06°30'	E04°50'
Seychelles Islands				
Seychelles	SEY	373	S04°36'	E55°26'
South Africa				
Cape Town	CT	400	S34°02'	E18°37'
Cape Town	CB	462.5	S33°52'	E18°34'
Cape Town	CA	282.5	S33°59'	E18°36'
Clanwilliam	CW	372.5	S32°11'	E18°53'
Greyton	GE	270	S34°03'	E19°36'
Jan Smuts	JA	445	S26°04'	E28°15'
Jan Smuts	JS	220	S26°12'	E28°12'
Jan Smuts	JL	250	S26°09'	E28°13'
Jan Smuts	JN	420	S26°13'	E28°13'
Jan Smuts	JB	202	S26°02'	E28°15'
Meyerton	MT	385	S26°33'	E28°02'
New Largo	NL	367.5	S25°55'	E28°57'
Robben Island	ZUI	310.3	S33°48'	E18°22'
Sir Lowry's Pass	SP	222.5	S34°08'	E18°56'
Val	VAL	345	S26°47'	E28°55'
Wolseley	WY	247.5	S33°24'	E19°11'
Sudan				
Khartoum	KIS	358	N15°40'	E32°33'
Khartoum	KIN	335	N15°31'	E32°33'
Khartoum	KH	329	N15°38'	E32°33'
Zaire				
Brazzaville	BL	355	S04°18'	E15°11'
Kinshasa	OK	340	S04°20'	E15°31'
Zimbabwe				
Bromley	KU	363	S18°04'	E31°20'
Harare	OL	346	S17°59'	E31°01'
Makumbi	BZ	284	S17°31'	E31°15'
Norton	NZ	373	S17°53'	E30°41'
Zisco	RC	385	S19°00'	E29°42'

ASIA

Airports

Den Pasar, Bali – Bali Intl

Ident	DPS	ATIS	126.20
Elev	22	Rwy/Length/ILS/ID	09/9843/110.30/IDPS
Lat	S08°45'		27/9843/110.30/IDPS
Long	E115°10'		

Beijing, China – Capital

Ident	PEK	ATIS	127.6
Elev	118	Rwy/Length/ILS/ID	18L/12467/109.3/IOR
Lat	N40°04'		36R/12467/109.9/IQU
Long	E116°35'		18R/10499/110.3/ILG
			36L/10499/111.7/IDK

Shanghai, China – Hongqiao

Ident	SHA	ATIS	118.10
Elev	10	Rwy/Length/ILS/ID	18/10499/110.30/IPK
Lat	N31°12'		36/10499/110.30/IWB
Long	E121°20'		

Bombay, India – Bombay

Ident	BOM	ATIS	126.40
Elev	27	Rwy/Length/ILS/ID	9/11445
Lat	N19°05'		27/11445/110.30/SCZ
Long	E72°51'		14/8956
			32/8956

Calcutta, India – Calcutta

Ident	CCU	ATIS	126.40
Elev	17	Rwy/Length/ILS/ID	01L/7854
Lat	N22°39'		19R/7854
Long	E88°26'		01R/11900/109.90/CAL
			19L/11900/110.30/DUM

Ghat, India – Ghat

Ident	GHT	ATIS	—
Elev	2296	Rwy/Length	06/4921
Lat	N25°08'		24/4921
Long	E10°08'		17/11811
			35/11811

Atsugi, Japan – Atsugi Aero

Ident	—	ATIS	—
Elev	205	Rwy/Length/ILS/ID	01//111.3/IAG
Lat	N35°26'		
Long	E139°27'		

Camp Zama, Japan – Kastner AAF

Ident	—	ATIS	—
Elev	359	Rwy/Length	—
Lat	N35°30'		
Long	E139°24'		

Chofu, Japan – Chofu

Ident	—	ATIS	—
Elev	135	Rwy/Length	—
Lat	N35°40'		
Long	E139°32'		

Hyakuri, Japan – Hyakuri Aero

Ident	—	ATIS	—
Elev	105	Rwy/Length/ILS/ID	03//109.3/IHY
Lat	N36°10'		
Long	E140°25'		

Iruma, Japan – Iruma

Ident	—	ATIS	—
Elev	299	Rwy/Length	—
Lat	N35°50'		
Long	E139°24'		

Kasumigaura, Japan – Kasumigaura

Ident	—	ATIS	—
Elev	85	Rwy/Length	—
Lat	N36°01'		
Long	E140°11'		

Kisarazu, Japan – Kisarazu Aero

Ident	—	ATIS	—
Elev	10	Rwy/Length	—
Lat	N35°23'		
Long	E139°54'		

Kushiro, Japan – Kushiro

Ident	KUH	ATIS	118.05
Elev	311	Rwy/Length/ILS/ID	17/7546/108.90/IKS
Lat	N43°02'		35/7546
Long	E144°11'		

Matsudo, Japan – Shimofusa Aero

Ident	—	ATIS	—
Elev	98	Rwy/ILS/ID	18/109.1/ISH
Lat	N35°47'		
Long	E140°01'		

Matsumoto, Japan – Matsumoto

Ident	—	ATIS	—
Elev	2157	Rwy/Length	—
Lat	N36°09'		
Long	E137°55'		

Oshima, Japan – Oshima

Ident	—	ATIS	—
Elev	125	Rwy/Length	—
Lat	N34°46'		
Long	E139°21'		

Tachikawa, Japan – Tachikawa

Ident	—	ATIS	—
Elev	313	Rwy/Length	—
Lat	N35°42'		
Long	E139°24'		

Tateyama, Japan – Tateyama

Ident	—	ATIS	—
Elev	10	Rwy/Length	—
Lat	N34°59'		
Long	E139°53'		

Tokyo, Japan – Haneda

Ident	HND	ATIS	128.80
Elev	15	Rwy/Length/ILS/ID	4/8202
Lat	N35°32'		22/8202/111.70/IAD
Long	E139°46'		15/10335
			33/10335/110.90/IHM
			16/9843
			34/9843/110.10/IHA

Tokyo, Japan – New Tokyo Intl. Narita

Ident	—	ATIS	128.25
Elev	135	Rwy/Length/ILS/ID	16//111.5/IKF
Lat	N35°45'		34//111.9/IYQ
Long	E140°23'		

Tokyo, Japan – Yokota AB

Ident	—	ATIS	128.4
Elev	457	Rwy/Length/ILS/ID	36//109.7/IYOK
Lat	N35°44'		
Long	E139°21'		

Yaizu, Japan – Shizuhama Aero

Ident	—	ATIS	—
Elev	23	Rwy/Length	—
Lat	N34°48'		
Long	E138°18'		

Hong Kong, Hong Kong – Intl

Ident	HKG	ATIS	128.20
Elev	15	Rwy/Length/ILS/ID	13/10930/111.90/KL
Lat	N22°18'		31/10930/109.90/IHK
Long	E114°12'		

Male, Maldives – Male Intl

Ident	MLE	ATIS	118.10
Elev	4	Rwy/Length/ILS/ID	18/10499
Lat	N04°11'		36/10499/108.70/IML
Long	E73°32'		

Ulaanbaatar, Mongolia – Buyant-Ukhaa

Ident	ULN	ATIS	—
Elev	4314	Rwy/Length	14/10170
Lat	N47°50'		32/10170
Long	E106°46'		01/5905 Grass
			19/5905 Grass
			14/7217 Grass
			32/7217 Grass
			15/6561 Grass
			33/6561 Grass

Karachi, Pakistan – Quaid-E-Azam Intl

Ident	KHI	ATIS	126.70
Elev	100	Rwy/Length/ILS/ID	07L/10500/
Lat	N24°54'		25R/10500/109.70/ICZ
Long	E67°09'		07R/7500
			25L/7500

Manila, Philippines – Ninoy Aquino Intl

Ident	MNL	ATIS	126.40
Elev	75	Rwy/Length/ILS/ID	6/11004/109.10/IML
Lat	N14°30'		24/11004/109.90/IMA
Long	E121°01'		13/7959
			31/7959

Bratsk, Russia – Bratsk

Ident	BTK	ATIS	—
Elev	1609	Rwy/Length/ILS/ID	12/10335/110.30/IBS
Lat	N56°22'		30/10335/110.30/IBS
Long	E101°41'		12/6562 Grass
			30/6562 Grass

Moscow, Russia – Domodedovo

Ident	—	ATIS	128.3
Elev	587	Rwy/Length/ILS/ID	32R//111.9/IDE
Lat	N55°24'		14L//108.5/IDW
Long	E37°54'		32L//109.3/IDO
			14R//110.1/IDM

Moscow, Russia – Sheremetyevo

Ident	SVO	ATIS	126.37
Elev	627	Rwy/Length/ILS/ID	07R/12139/109.10/INL
Lat	N55°58'		25L/12139/110.50/IBW
Long	E37°24'		

Moscow, Russia – Vnukovo

Ident	—	ATIS	125.87
Elev	686	Rwy/Length/ILS/ID	02//111.7/IWM
Lat	N55°35'		24//111.1/IOB
Long	E37°16'		06//108.9/IGG
			20//111.5/ITQ

Novosibirsk, Russia – Tolmachevo

Ident	OVB	ATIS	—
Elev	364	Rwy/Length/ILS/ID	03/3281
Lat	N55°01'		21/3281
Long	E82°40'		06/3281 Grass
			24/3281 Grass
			07/11808/110.10/IRO
			25/11808/108.50/IKT
			07/9843 Grass
			25/9843 Grass
			17/3281
			35/3281

Orenburg, Russia – Orenburg Central

Ident	REN	ATIS	128.00
Elev	387	Rwy/Length/ILS/ID	08/8202/109.90/IWP
Lat	N51°47'		26/8202/109.30/ILM
Long	E55°27'		08/8202 Grass
			26/8202 Grass
			04/2297
			22/2297
			17/2133
			35/2133

Petropavlovsk-Kamchatsky, Russia – Yelizovo

Ident	PKC	ATIS	—
Elev	131	Rwy/Length/ILS/ID	16L/11155/110.30/IPR
Lat	N53°10'		34R/11155/110.30/IPR
Long	E158°27'		16R/8202
			34L/8202

Changi, Singapore – Changi

Ident	SIN	ATIS	128.60
Elev	22	Rwy/Length/ILS/ID	02L/13123/110.90/ICW
Lat	N01°21'		20R/13123/108.90/ICH
Long	E103°59'		02R/13123/108.30/ICE
			20L/13123/109.70/ICC

Seoul, South Korea – Kimpo Intl

Ident	SEL	ATIS	126.40
Elev	58	Rwy/Length/ILS/ID	14R/10499/110.10/IOFR
Lat	N37°33'		32L/10499
Long	E126°47'		14L/11811/109.90/ISEL
			32R/11811/110.70/ISKP

Columbo, Sri Lanka – Katunayake

Ident	CMB	ATIS	118.70
Elev	29	Rwy/Length/ILS/ID	4/10991/110.30/IKA
Lat	N07°10'		22/10991
Long	E79°53'		

Kaohsiung, Taiwan – Kaohsiung Intl

Ident	KHH	ATIS	127.80
Elev	31	Rwy/Length/ILS/ID	09R/10007
Lat	N22°34'		27L/10007
Long	E120°20'		09L/10335/108.30/IKHG
			27R/10335

Bangkok, Thailand – Bangkok Intl

Ident	BKK	ATIS	126.40
Elev	9	Rwy/Length/ILS/ID	03R/11483
Lat	N13°54'		21L/11483/110.30/IDMG
Long	E100°36'		03L/12139
			21R/12139/109.30/IBKK

VORs

Location/Name	Ident	Freq	Lat	Long
Hong Kong				
Cheung Chau	CH	112.30	N22°13'	E114°01'
Tathong Point	TH	115.50	N22°14'	E114°17'
Tung Lung	TD	116.10	N22°15'	E114°17'
India				
Aurangabad	AAU	116.30	N19°51'	E75°23'
Bombay	BBB	116.60	N19°05'	E72°52'
Calcutta	CEA	112.50	N22°38'	E88°27'
Daman	DMN	113.30	N20°26'	E72°51'
Jamshedpur	JJS	115.40	N22°48'	E86°10'
Rajshahi	RAJ	114.60	N24°26'	E88°37'
Japan				
Ami	TLE	116.00	N36°01'	E140°12'
Choshi	CVC	113.60	N35°43'	E140°48'
Hammatsu	LHE	110.00	N34°44'	E137°41'
Haneda	HME	109.40	N35°32'	E139°46'

Location/Name	Ident	Freq	Lat	Long
Japan (continued)				
Kisarazu	KZE	114.50	N35°23'	E139°54'
Kohtoh	KWE	115.00	N35°36'	E139°49'
Kushiro	KSE	112.50	N43°01'	E144°12'
Memanbetsu	TBE	110.85	N43°52'	E144°10'
Monbetsu	MVE	110.00	N44°15'	E143°31'
Moriya	SNE	114.00	N35°55'	E139°59'
Nakashibetsu	NSE	115.60	N43°34'	E144°57'
Obihiro	OBE	109.65	N42°43'	E143°13'
Onjuku	OJC	115.70	N35°10'	E140°22'
Sakuri	TYE	112.70	N35°46'	E140°16'
Sekiyado	SYE	117.00	N36°00'	E139°50'
Tateyama	PQE	112.50	N34°56'	E139°53'
Yokosuka	HYE	116.20	N35°15'	E139°35'
Korea				
Anyang	SEL	115.10	N37°24'	E126°55'
Kimpo	KIP	113.60	N37°33'	E126°47'
Osan	OSN	114.70	N37°05'	E127°01'
Pyongtaek	PTK	108.20	N36°58'	E127°01'
Seoul	KSM	113.00	N37°26'	E127°06'
Indonesia				
Bali	BLI	116.20	S08°45'	E115°09'
Maldives				
Male	MLE	114.70	N04°11'	E73°32'
Pakistan				
Karachi	KC	112.10	N24°54'	E67°10'
Nawabshah	NH	112.90	N26°13'	E68°23'
Phillipines				
Cabanatuan	CAB	112.70	N15°27'	E120°58'
Jomalig	JOM	116.70	N14°43'	E122°24'
Lipa	LIP	115.10	N13°57'	E121°07'
Manila	MIA	113.80	N14°30'	E121°01'
Russia				
Bratsk	BRT	113.60	N56°22'	E101°41'
Sheremetyevo	MR	114.60	N55°57'	E37°20'

Location/Name	Ident	Freq	Lat	Long
Singapore				
Batum	BTM	116.00	N01°08'	E104°07'
Johor Bahru	VJR	112.70	N01°43'	E103°37'
Papa Uniform	PU	115.10	N01°25'	E103°56'
Sinjon	SJ	113.50	N01°13'	E103°51'
Tekong	VTK	116.50	N01°24'	E104°01'
Sri Lanka				
Batticaloa	BAT	114.60	N07°42'	E81°40'
Columbo Katunayake	KAT	112.70	N07°09'	E79°52'
Columbo Ratmalana	RML	116.70	N06°49'	E79°53'
Taiwan				
Green I	GID	116.90	N22°40'	E121°28'
Hengchun	HCN	113.70	N21°55'	E120°50'
Shikang	TNN	113.30	N23°08'	E120°11'
Thailand				
Bangkok	BKK	115.90	N13°59'	E100°39'
Korat	KRT	113.70	N14°55'	E102°07'
U-Taphao	BUT	110.80	N12°39'	E101°00'

NDBs

Location/Name	Ident	Freq	Lat	Long
China				
Shanghi	PK	369	—	—
Shanghi	CU	280	—	—
Shanghi	BF	528	—	—
Shanghi	WB	240	—	—
Hong Kong				
Cape D'anguilar	HKG	338	N22°13'	E114°14'
Cheung Chau	CC	360	N22°12'	E114°01'
Hong Kong Intl	RW	337	N22°12'	E114°11'
Sha Lo Wan	SL	286	N22°17'	E113°54'
Sheremetyevo	NL	380	N55°57'	E037°19'
Stonecutters	SC	236	N22°19'	E114°07'
Tathong Point	TH	280	N22°14'	E114°17'

Location/Name	Ident	Freq	Lat	Long
India				
Berachampa	BC	220	N22°42'	E88°42'
Bombay	BB	265	N19°07'	E72°00'
Indonesia				
Den Pasar	OR	230	S08°44'	E115°10'
Mataram	GA	330	S08°33'	E116°05'
Japan				
Akan	KQ	221	N43°08'	E144°08'
Arakawa	AD	385	N35°38'	E139°50'
Haneda	HME	337	N35°33'	E139°45'
Kisarazu	CL	200	N35°23'	E139°54'
Kushiro	KS	194	N43°02'	E144°12'
Kuzumi	KF	342	N35°49'	E140°19'
Tateyama	PQ	373	N34°59'	E139°52'
Tokachi	OH	239	N42°52'	E143°09'
Yokoshiba	YQ	256	N35°40'	E140°26'
Korea				
Anyang	SL	336	N37°24'	E126°55'
Korea	OF	246	N37°36'	E126°43'
Korea	SE	219	N37°36'	E126°43'
Seoul	CP	388	N37°26'	E127°05'
Pakistan				
Cape Manze	KA	244	N24°50'	E66°40'
Gharo	KF	296	N24°46'	E67°34'
Hyderabad	KD	223	N25°18'	E68°23'
Karachi	MR	354	N24°56'	E66°56'
Karachi	KC	271	N24°53'	E67°10'
Philippines				
Alabat	AL	247	N14°14'	E121°55'
Manila	MIA	389	N14°30'	E121°01'
Manila	OL	375	N14°32'	E121°05'
Rizal	RZL	327	N14°28'	E121°11'
Rosario	RS	285	N14°25'	E120°51'

Location/Name	Ident	Freq	Lat	Long
Russia				
Borovoye	JK	816	N54°40'	E82°37'
Buzharovo	AR	1080	N55°59'	E36°48'
Kolyvan	GV	660	N55°19'	E82°43'
Kostino	KN	642	N56°18'	E37°43'
Legostayevo	OC	320	N54°38'	E83°49'
Malka	MK	345	N53°19'	E157°32'
Matveyevsky	EB	1170	N54°56'	E83°05'
Novosibirsk	KT	310	N55°01'	E82°44'
Novosibirsk	RO	310	N55°00'	E82°33'
Novotryshkino	KD	715	N55°17'	E82°24'
Opalikha	KS	565	N55°50'	E37°16'
Orenburg	LM	415	N51°47'	E55°32'
Orenburg	WP	415	N51°47'	E55°22'
Petropavlovsk -Kamchatsky	Q	1040	N53°11'	E158°26'
Petropavlovsk-Kamchatsky	PR	535	N53°06'	E158°29'
Pretoriia	PO	730	N52°15'	E54°19'
Savelovo	SW	1285	N56°22'	E37°26'
Sheremetyevo	NL	380	N55°57'	E37°19'
Sheremetyevo	MR	700	N55°57'	E37°19'
Sheremetyevo	BW	380	N55°59'	E37°30'
Sheremetyevo	AD	700	N55°59'	E37°30'
Talmenka	TM	988	N53°48'	E83°32'
Ust-Bolsheretsk	UB	907	N52°49'	E156°16'
Zaeltsovsky	PG	860	N55°05'	E82°54'
Zheltoie	VL	1005	N51°38'	E56°36'
Singapore				
Bedok	BED	232	N01°19'	E103°57'
Jaybee	JB	400	N01°29'	E103°43'
Kong Kong	KK	286	N01°31'	E103°59'
Tanjung Pinang	TI	385	N00°55'	E104°32'
Tekong	TEK	259	N01°25'	E104°01'
Sri Lanka				
Katunayake	CNL	315	N07°16'	E79°56'
Katunayake	ASL	330	N07°07'	E79°50'
Ratmalana	RM	350	N06°50'	E79°53'
Taiwan				
Hengchun	KW	415	N21°56'	E120°49'
Kaohsiung	CO	220	N22°34'	E120°17'

Location/Name	Ident	Freq	Lat	Long
Thailand				
Bangkok	BK	293	N13°59'	E100°39'
Prachin Buri	PB	201	N14°06'	E101°22'

CANADA

Airports

Calgary, Canada – Calgary Intl

Ident	YYC	ATIS	—
Elev	3557	Rwy/Length/ILS/ID	7/6200
Lat	N51°06'		25/6200
Long	W114°01'		10/8000/110.90/IAQ
			28/8000/110.90/IAQ
			16/12675/109.30/IEM
			34/12675/111.50/NC

Edmonton, Canada – Edmonton Intl

Ident	YEG	ATIS	128.00
Elev	2373	Rwy/Length/ILS/ID	2/11000/110.30/IEG
Lat	N53°18'		20/11000
Long	W113°34'		12/10200/109.90/IFP
			30/10200/109.10/IKB

Gander, Canada – Gander Intl

Ident	YQX	ATIS	124.80
Elev	496	Rwy/Length/ILS/ID	04/10500/109.50/IQX
Lat	N48°56'		22/10500/109.90/IGN
Long	W54°34'		13/8900
			311/8900

Goose Bay, Canada – Goose Bay

Ident	YYR	ATIS	128.10
Elev	160	Rwy/Length/ILS/ID	8/11046/110.30/IVR
Lat	N53°19'		26/11046
Long	W60°25'		16/9580
			34/9580

Toronto, Canada – Buttonville Muni

Ident	—	ATIS	127.1
Elev	650	Rwy/Length/ILS/ID	15//111.1/IKZ
Lat	N43°51'		
Long	W79°22'		

Toronto, Canada – Toronto/City Center

Ident	—	ATIS	133.6
Elev	251	Rwy/Length	—
Lat	N43°37'		
Long	W79°23'		

Toronto, Canada – Pearson Intl

Ident	YYZ	ATIS	120.82
Elev	569	Rwy/Length/ILS/ID	06R/9500/109.10/IJS
Lat	N43°40'		24L/9500/109.30/INV
Long	W79°37'		06L/10500/109.70/ITX
			24R/10500/111.50/IYZ
			15/11050/110.50/IRW
			33/11050/110.30/ILE

Vancouver, Canada – Coal Harbour / Intl

Ident	YVR	ATIS	124.60
Elev	9	Rwy/Length/ILS/ID	8/11000/109.50/IVR
Lat	N49°11'		26/11000/110.70/IFZ
Long	W123°11'		12/7300/111.10/IMK
			30/7300
			26A/3500

Godthab, Greenland – Godthab

Ident	GOH	ATIS	119.10
Elev	283	Rwy/Length	06/3117
Lat	N64°11'		
Long	W51°41'		

VORs

Location/Name	Ident	Freq	Lat	Long
Alberta				
Calgary	YYC	116.70	N51°06'	W113°52'
Edmonton	VEG	117.60	N53°11'	W113°52'
Empress	YEA	115.90	N50°55'	W109°59'

Location/Name	Ident	Freq	Lat	Long
Alberta (continued)				
Grande Prairie	YQU	113.10	N55°10'	W119°01'
High Level	YOJ	113.30	N58°33'	W117°05'
Lethbridge	YQL	115.70	N49°38'	W112°40'
Medicine Hat	YXH	116.50	N49°57'	W110°48'
Peace River	YPE	117.20	N56°12'	W117°30'
Rocky Mountain	YRM	114.30	N52°30'	W115°19'
Spring Bank	YBW	108.60	N51°06'	W114°22'
Wainwright	YWV	114.50	N52°58'	W110°50'
Whitecourt	YZU	112.50	N54°08'	W115°47'
British Columbia				
Cranbrook	YXC	112.10	N49°33'	W116°05'
Enderby	YNY	115.20	N50°40'	W118°56'
Fort Nelson	YYE	112.90	N58°53'	W123°00'
Fort Saint John	YXJ	114.20	N56°17'	W120°53'
Port Hardy	YZT	112.00	N50°41'	W127°21'
Prince George	YXS	112.30	N53°53'	W122°27'
Princeton	YDC	113.90	N49°22'	W120°22'
Sandspit	YZP	114.10	N53°15'	W131°48'
Vancouver	YVR	115.90	N49°04'	W123°09'
Victoria	YYJ	113.70	N48°43'	W123°29'
Williams Lake	YWL	113.60	N52°14'	W122°10'
Manitoba				
Brandon	YBR	113.80	N49°54'	W99°56'
Churchill	YYQ	114.10	N58°44'	W94°08'
Dauphin	YDN	116.10	N51°06'	W100°03'
Langruth	VLR	112.20	N50°25'	W98°43'
Lynn Lake	YYL	112.60	N56°51'	W101°04'
Portage	YPG	114.60	N49°53'	W98°16'
The Pas	YQD	113.60	N53°58'	W101°06'
Winnipeg	YWG	115.50	N49°55'	W97°14'
Northwest Territories				
Baker Lake	YBK	114.50	N64°19'	W96°06'
Cambridge Bay	YCB	112.70	N69°07'	W105°10'
Fort Good Hope	YGH	112.30	N66°14'	W128°37'
Fort Simpson	YFS	117.90	N61°46'	W121°17'
Hall Beach	YUX	117.30	N68°46'	W81°14'
Norman Wells	YVQ	112.70	N65°15'	W126°43'
Wrigley	YWY	113.10	N63°11'	W123°21'
Yellowknife	YZF	115.50	N62°27'	W114°26'

Location/Name	Ident	Freq	Lat	Long
New Bruswick				
Fredericton	YFC	113.00	N45°53'	W66°25'
Moncton	YQM	117.30	N46°11'	W64°34'
Saint John	YSJ	113.50	N45°24'	W65°52'
Newfoundland				
Deer Lake	YDF	113.30	N49°14'	W57°12'
Gander	YQX	112.70	N48°54'	W54°32'
Goose	YYR	117.30	N53°19'	W60°17'
St Johns	UYT	108.60	N47°37'	W52°44'
Stephenville	YJT	113.10	N48°34'	W58°40'
Torbay	YYT	113.50	N47°29'	W52°51'
Nova Scotia				
Halifax	YHZ	115.10	N44°55'	W63°24'
Sydney	YQY	114.90	N46°09'	W60°03'
Ontario				
Ameson	YAN	112.40	N49°46'	W84°35'
Coehill	VIE	115.10	N44°39'	W77°53'
Geraldton	YGQ	114.20	N49°46'	W86°59'
Killaloe	YXI	115.60	N45°39'	W77°36'
London	YXU	117.20	N43°02'	W81°08'
Mans	YMS	114.50	N44°08'	W80°08'
Marathon	YSP	115.90	N48°44'	W86°19'
Midland	YEE	112.80	N44°34'	W79°47'
Moosenee	YMO	112.90	N51°17'	W80°36'
North Bay	YYB	115.40	N46°21'	W79°26'
Ottawa	YOW	114.60	N45°26'	W75°53'
Red Lake	YRL	114.00	N51°04'	W93°45'
Simcoe	YSO	117.35	N44°14'	W79°10'
Sioux Narrows	VBI	115.20	N49°28'	W94°02'
Stirling	VQC	113.50	N44°23'	W77°43'
Sudbury	YSB	112.30	N46°37'	W80°47'
Thunder Bay	YQT	114.10	N48°15'	W89°26'
Timmins	YTS	113.00	N48°34'	W81°22'
Toronto	YYZ	113.30	N43°40'	W79°38'
Waterloo	YWT	115.00	N43°27'	W80°22'
Wawa	YXZ	112.70	N47°57'	W84°49'
Wiarton	YVV	117.70	N44°44'	W81°06'
Windsor	YQG	113.80	N42°14'	W82°49'

Location/Name	Ident	Freq	Lat	Long
Prince Edward Island				
Charlottetown	YYG	114.10	N46°12'	W62°58'
Quebec				
Bagotville	XBG	111.80	N48°19'	W70°59'
Baie-Comeau	YBC	117.70	N49°08'	W68°13'
Beauce	VLV	117.20	N45°55'	W70°50'
Gaspe	YGP	115.40	N48°45'	W64°24'
Grindstone	YGR	112.00	N47°25'	W61°46'
Mirabel	YMX	116.70	N45°53'	W74°22'
Mont Joli	YYY	115.90	N48°36'	W68°12'
Montreal	YUL	116.30	N45°36'	W73°58'
Quebec	YQB	112.80	N46°42'	W71°37'
Riviere Du Loup	YRI	113.90	N47°45'	W69°35'
Saguenay	VBS	114.20	N48°01'	W71°15'
Sept-Iles	YZV	114.50	N50°13'	W66°16'
Sherbrooke	YSC	113.20	N45°18'	W71°47'
St Jean	YJN	115.80	N45°15'	W73°19'
Val-D'or	YVO	113.70	N48°10'	W77°49'
Saskatchewan				
Broadview	YDR	117.50	N50°21'	W102°32'
Lumsden	VLN	114.20	N50°40'	W104°53'
Prince Albert	YPA	113.00	N53°12'	W105°39'
Saskatoon	YXE	116.20	N52°10'	W106°43'
Swift Current	YYN	117.40	N50°17'	W107°41'
Yorkton	YQV	115.80	N51°15'	W102°28'
Yukon Territory				
Watson Lake	YQH	114.90	N60°05'	W128°51'
Whitehorse	YXY	116.60	N60°37'	W135°08'

NDBs

Location/Name	Ident	Freq	Lat	Long
Alberta				
Calgary	YC	344	N51°04'	W113°54'
Echo	E	254		
Echo	E	308	N53°15'	W113°39'
Edmonton	XD	266	N53°38'	W113°30'

Location/Name	Ident	Freq	Lat	Long
Alberta (continued)				
Foxtrot	F	292	N53°21'	W113°40'
Golf	G	379	N53°23'	W113°29'
Kilo	K	215	N53°14'	W113°29'
Lethbridge	QL	248	N49°36'	W112°53'
Medicine Hat	XH	332	N50°00'	W110°47'
Rainbow Lake	YOP	344	N58°27'	W119°15'
Shell	B2	352	N57°22'	W119°47'
Turner Valley	TV	295	N50°45'	W114°22'
Vulcan	Z5	274	N50°24'	W113°16'
Xray	X	201	—	—
Yankee	Y	233	N51°02'	W114°01'
British Columbia				
Abbotsford	XX	344	N49°00'	W122°29'
Active Pass	AP	378	N48°52'	W123°17'
Anahim Lake	UAB	200	N52°22'	W125°10'
Atlin	YSQ	260	N59°37'	W133°40'
Bella Bella	YJQ	325	N52°11'	W128°06'
Campbell River	YBL	203	N50°00'	W125°21'
Cape Scott	ZES	353	N50°46'	W128°25'
Carmi	YXO	335	N49°29'	W119°05'
Castlegar	CG	227	N49°26'	W117°34'
Chetwynd	F6	210	N55°41'	W121°32'
Comox	QQ	400	N49°45'	W124°57'
Cranbrook	XC	242	N49°40'	W115°46'
Cultus	LU	241	N49°01'	W122°02'
Dawson Creek	DQ	394	N55°43'	W120°04'
Egg Island	UEM	207	N51°14'	W127°50'
Enderby	NY	350	N50°38'	W118°55'
Estevan Point	EP	373	N49°23'	W126°32'
Fairmont	D6	261	N50°19'	W115°52'
Fort Nelson	YE	382	N58°47'	W122°43'
Fort St John	XJ	326	N56°17'	W120°50'
Hope	HE	245	N49°23'	W121°25'
Kelowna	LW	257	N50°03'	W119°24'
Kitimat	ZKI	203	N54°03'	W128°40'
Liard River	ZL	263	N59°28'	W126°08'
Mackenzie	2U	284	N55°18'	W123°08'
Masset	1U	278	N54°01'	W132°07'
Mcinnes Island	MS	388	N52°15'	W128°43'
Mill Bay	MB	293	N48°40'	W123°32'
Naniamo	YCD	251	N49°07'	W123°52'
Naramata	UNT	312	N49°35'	W119°36'
Papa	P	350	N54°18'	W130°27'

Location/Name	Ident	Freq	Lat	Long
British Columbia (continued)				
Pitt Meadows	PK	227	N49°12'	W122°42'
Sandspit	ZP	368	N53°11'	W131°46'
Skeena	TB	254	N54°28'	W128°35'
Skookum	SX	368	N49°57'	W115°47'
Smithers	YD	230	N54°44'	W127°06'
Telkwa (Smithers)	TK	391	N54°40'	W126°59'
Terrace	XT	332	N54°22'	W128°34'
Tofino	YAZ	359	N49°02'	W125°42'
Vancouver	VR	266	N49°10'	W123°03'
Victor	V	368	N49°11'	W123°13'
Victoria	YJ	200	N48°38'	W123°23'
White Rock	WC	332	N49°00'	W122°45'
Greenland				
Godthab	NK	273	N64°40'	W51°22'
Godthab	QT	258	N64°20'	W51°35'
Godthab	GH	314	N64°10'	W51°45'
Manitoba				
Berens River	YBV	370	N52°21'	W97°01'
Brandon	BR	233	N49°54'	W100°04'
Delta	UDE	269	N50°09'	W98°18'
Winnipeg	WG	248	N49°53'	W97°20'
New Brunswick				
Bathurst	2F	382	N47°35'	W65°50'
Charlo	CL	207	N48°00'	W66°26'
Chatham	F9	530	N47°00'	W65°25'
Fredericton	FC	326	N45°55'	W66°35'
Juliet	J	397	N45°13'	W65°57'
Lima	L	281	N47°58'	W66°13'
Moncton	QM	224	N46°06'	W64°34'
St Leonard	YSL	404	N47°12'	W67°52'
Newfoundland				
Channel Head	CM	379	N47°34'	W59°09'
Gander	QX	280	N48°57'	W54°40'
Goose	Y	212	N53°16'	W60°31'
Goose	YR	257	N53°20'	W60°31'
Rigolet	JC	396	N54°10'	W58°26'
Stephenville	JT	390	N48°32'	W58°45'
Torbay	YT	260	N47°40'	W52°48'

Location/Name	Ident	Freq	Lat	Long
Northwest Territories				
Aklavik	YKD	208	N68°13'	W135°00'
Fort Liard	YJF	368	N60°14'	W123°27'
Fort Mcpherson	ZFM	373	N67°24'	W134°52'
Ft Simpson	FS	375	N61°47'	W121°15'
Inuvik	EV	254	N68°19'	W133°35'
Norman Wells	VQ	326	N65°15'	W126°40'
Trout Lake	7I	258	N60°26'	W121°14'
Tuktoyaktuk	UB	380	N69°26'	W133°01'
Wrigley	WY	222	N63°12'	W123°25'
Nova Scotia				
Alfa	A	201	N44°41'	W63°34'
Debert	8F	239	N45°25'	W63°27'
Digby	Y9	220	N44°32'	W65°47'
Golf	G	364	N44°48'	W63°35'
Greenwood	YZX	266	N44°55'	W65°06'
Isle Madame	W	304	N45°33'	W60°55'
Liverpool	A9	330	N44°13'	W64°51'
Sable Island	SA	374	N43°55'	W60°01'
Shearwater	YAW	353	N44°36'	W63°26'
Sydney	QY	263	N46°12'	W59°58'
Trenton	5Y	338	N45°36'	W62°37'
Yarmouth	QI	206	N43°47'	W66°07'
Ontario				
Armstrong	YYW	223	N50°18'	W89°01'
Atikokan	IB	209	N48°49'	W91°34'
Brantford	FD	207	N43°04'	W80°24'
Buttonville	KZ	248	N43°56'	W79°19'
Chapleau	YLD	335	N47°45'	W83°24'
Charlottetown	YG	347	N46°11'	W63°08'
Downsview	YZD	356	N43°45'	W79°28'
Dryden	YHD	413	N49°51'	W92°50'
Earlton	YXR	257	N47°42'	W79°47'
Elliot Lake	YEL	276	N46°22'	W82°37'
Fort Frances	YAG	376	N48°41'	W93°32'
Gibraltar Point	TZ	257	N43°36'	W79°23'
Goderich	GD	286	N43°44'	W81°43'
Golf	G	398	N42°14'	W83°02'
Gore Bay	YZE	245	N45°55'	W82°36'
Gros Cap	A	286	N46°30'	W84°36'
Hamilton	HM	221	N43°07'	W80°00'
Hanover	S7	268	N44°09'	W81°03'

Location/Name	Ident	Freq	Lat	Long
Ontario (continued)				
Juliett	J	236	N43°37'	W79°41'
Kasing	YYU	341	N49°27'	W82°30'
Kenora	YQK	326	N49°47'	W94°25'
Kincardine	D7	350	N44°12'	W81°36'
Kingston	YGK	263	N44°17'	W76°36'
Kirkland	YKX	201	N48°13'	W79°52'
Lima	L	368	N43°37'	W79°32'
London	XU	383	N43°05'	W81°13'
Manitouwadge	YMG	219	N49°02'	W85°54'
Moosonee	MO	224	N51°16'	W80°37'
Muskoka	YQA	272	N45°02'	W79°16'
Nakina	QN	233	N50°10'	W86°37'
North Bay	YB	394	N46°23'	W79°28'
November	N	347	N43°43'	W79°31'
Oscar	O	344	N45°16'	W75°44'
Oshawa	OO	391	N43°55'	W78°54'
Ottawa	OW	236	N45°21'	W75°33'
Pembroke	YTA	409	N45°48'	W77°13'
Red Lake	RL	218	N51°03'	W93°47'
Romeo	R	403	N43°44'	W79°42'
Romeo	R	317	N44°03'	W77°37'
Sandspit	ZP	368	N53°11'	W131°46'
Sierra	S	344	N46°41'	W80°44'
Sioux Lookout	YXL	346	N50°07'	W91°53'
Smith Falls	YSH	334	N44°54'	W76°00'
St Catherines	SN	408	N43°08'	W79°15'
St Thomas	7B	375	N42°46'	W81°06'
Sudbury	SB	362	N46°38'	W80°55'
Tango	T	341	N43°37'	W79°43'
Tango	T	263	N48°23'	W89°13'
Terrace Bay	YTJ	250	N48°47'	W87°09'
Thunder Bay	QT	332	N48°20'	W89°26'
Timmins	TS	212	N48°33'	W81°27'
Trenton	YTR	215	N44°11'	W77°24'
Uplands	YUP	352	N45°13'	W75°29'
Wapisk	YAT	260	N52°55'	W82°26'
Waterloo	K	335	N43°29'	W80°17'
Xray	X	385	N43°44'	W79°34'
Yankee	Y	404	N46°19'	W79°31'
Prince Edward Island				
Charlottetown	YG	347	N46°11'	W63°08'

Location/Name	Ident	Freq	Lat	Long
Quebec				
Amos	9Q	291	N48°33'	W78°14'
Bagotville	YBG	356	N48°20'	W71°08'
Baie-Comeau	BC	414	N49°07'	W68°19'
Bromont	6R	343	N45°14'	W72°47'
Champlain	BV	336	N46°52'	W71°16'
Charlevoix	ML	392	N47°37'	W70°19'
Chiboo	MT	209	N49°47'	W74°29'
Chute-Des-Passes	DG	244	N49°53'	W71°15'
Drummondville	Y8	401	N45°50'	W72°23'
Eastmain	ZEM	338	N52°13'	W78°31'
Forestville	FE	239	N48°44'	W69°06'
Gaspe	GP	232	N48°46'	W64°23'
Grindstone	GR	370	N47°22'	W61°54'
Havre St-Pierre	YGV	344	N50°15'	W63°39'
Heath Point	HP	335	N49°05'	W61°42'
Hotel	H	407	N45°33'	W73°20'
La Tuque	YLQ	289	N47°24'	W72°47'
Lg-4	YFM	332	N53°42'	W73°42'
Lima	L	284	N45°32'	W73°39'
Maniwaki	YMW	366	N46°12'	W75°57'
Mars	URX	269	N48°00'	W70°49'
Matagami	NM	218	N49°43'	W77°44'
Matane	ME	216	N48°50'	W67°32'
Mike	M	348	N45°31'	W73°39'
Mont-Joli	YY	340	N48°34'	W68°15'
Montreal	UL	248	N45°27'	W73°50'
Nemiscau	K8	214	N51°41'	W76°08'
Parent	YPP	303	N47°53'	W74°40'
Rimouski	YXK	373	N48°28'	W68°30'
Riviere Ouelle	Z8	347	N47°26'	W69°58'
Riviere-Du-Loup	RI	201	N47°45'	W69°34'
Ruoyn	YUY	218	N48°10'	W78°56'
Sept-Iles	Z	248	N53°21'	W131°56'
Sept-Iles	ZV	273	N50°12'	W66°09'
Sherbrooke	SC	362	N45°28'	W71°47'
St Bruno De Guigu	YBM	230	N47°27'	W79°25'
Ste-Foy	OU	329	N46°46'	W71°17'
St-Felix-De-Valoi	UFX	260	N46°11'	W73°25'
St-Honore	YRC	213	N48°32'	W71°09'
Thetford Mines	R1	275	N46°02'	W71°16'
Trois-Rivieres	YRQ	205	N46°22'	W72°39'
Uniform	U	201	N45°27'	W73°46'
Val-D'or	VO	239	N48°03'	W77°47'
Victoriaville	F8	384	N46°06'	W71°55'

Location/Name	Ident	Freq	Lat	Long
Quebec (continued)				
Waki	G8	327	N46°16'	W75°59'
Waskaganish	YKQ	351	N51°29'	W78°44'
Saskatchewan				
Beechy	BY	266	N50°50'	W107°27'
Dafoe	VX	368	N51°52'	W104°34'
Estevan	L7	395	N49°12'	W102°51'
Moose Jaw	YMJ	375	N50°17'	W105°26'
Regina	QR	290	N50°22'	W104°34'
Saskatoon	XE	257	N52°11'	W106°48'
Yarmouth	QI	206	N43°47'	W66°07'
Yukon Territory				
Beaver Creek	YXQ	239	N62°24'	W140°51'
Burwash	DB	341	N61°20'	W138°59'
Dawson	DA	214	N64°01'	W139°10'
Faro	ZFA	378	N62°12'	W133°23'
Laberge	JB	236	N60°56'	W135°08'
Lac La Martre	Z3	304	N63°08'	W117°15'
Lakeshore	XG	338	N60°06'	W128°47'
Mayo	MA	365	N63°37'	W135°53'
Old Crow	YOC	284	N67°34'	W139°50'
Robinson	PJ	329	N60°26'	W134°51'
Ross River	YDM	218	N61°58'	W132°25'
Shell	B2	352	N57°22'	W119°47'
Teslin	ZW	269	N60°10'	W132°44'
Watson Lake	QH	248	N60°10'	W128°50'
Whitehorse	XY	302	N60°46'	W135°06'
Xray	X	353	N60°38'	W135°00'

CENTRAL AMERICA

Airports

Belize City, Belize – Philip SW Goldson Intl

Ident	BZE	ATIS	118.00
Elev	15	Rwy/Length	07/7100
Lat	N17°32'		25/7100
Long	W88°18'		

Bermuda, Bermuda – Bermuda

Ident	BDA	ATIS	—
Elev	12	Rwy/Length	12/9660
Lat	N32°21'		30/9660
Long	W64°40'		

Guantanamo, Cuba – Guantanamo Bay NAS

Ident	NBW	ATIS	126.20
Elev	56	Rwy/Length	10/8000
Lat	N19°54'		28/8000
Long	W75°12'		

San Salvador, El Salvador – Ilopango Intl

Ident	SAL	ATIS	118.30
Elev	2021	Rwy/Length	15/7347
Lat	N13°41'		33/7347
Long	W89°07'		

Guatemala City, Guatemala – La Aurora Intl

Ident	GUA	ATIS	—
Elev	4952	Rwy/Length	01/9800
Lat	N14°34'		19/9800
Long	W90°31'		

Montego Bay, Jamaica – Sangster Intl

Ident	MBJ	ATIS	127.90
Elev	4	Rwy/Length	07/8705
Lat	N18°30'		25/8705
Long	W77°55'		

Ixtapa, Mexico – Ixtapa / Zihuatanejo

Ident	ZIH	ATIS	118.30
Elev	20	Rwy/Length	08/8202
Lat	N17°36'		26/8202
Long	W101°27'		

Mexico City, Mexico – Benito Juarez Intl

Ident	MEX	ATIS	127.70
Elev	7341	Rwy/Length/ILS/ID	05R/12795/109.10/IMWX
Lat	N19°26'		23L/12795/109.70/IMEX
Long	W99°04'		05L/12618
			23R/12618

San Jose, Mexico – Juan Santa Maria Intl

Ident	SJO	ATIS	—
Elev	3021	Rwy/Length/ILS/ID	07/9882/109.50/IOCO
Lat	N09°59'		25/9882
Long	W84°12'		

San Juan, Puerto Rico – Luis Munoz Marin Intl

Ident	SJU	ATIS	—
Elev	10	Rwy/Length/ILS/ID	08/10002/110.30/ISJU
Lat	N18°26'		26/10002
Long	W66°00'		10/8016/109.70/ICLA
			28/8016

VORs

Location/Name	Ident	Freq	Lat	Long
Antigua				
V C Bird	ANU	114.50	N17°07'	W61°47'
Aruba				
Aruba	ABA	112.50	N12°30'	W69°56'
Bahamas				
Bimini	ZBV	116.70	N25°42'	W79°17'
Eleuthera I	ZGV	112.50	N25°15'	W76°18'
Nassau	ZQA	112.70	N25°01'	W77°27'
Treasure Cay	ZTC	112.90	N26°44'	W77°22'
Barbados				
Adams	BGI	112.70	N13°04'	W59°29'
Belize				
Belize	BZE	114.30	N17°32'	W08°18'
Bermuda				
Bermuda	BDA	113.90	N32°21'	W64°41'
Cayman Islands				
France	FTD	109.00	N09°21'	W79°51'

Location/Name	Ident	Freq	Lat	Long
Cuba				
Manzanillo	UMZ	116.00	N20°18'	W77°06'
Navy Guantanamo Bay	NBW	114.60	N19°54'	W75°11'
Nuevas	UNV	116.30	N21°23'	W77°13'
Santiago De Cuba	UCU	113.30	N20°04'	W75°09'
Costa Rica				
El Coco	TIO	115.70	N09°59'	W84°14'
Liberia	LIB	112.80	N10°35'	W85°32'
Limon	LIO	116.30	N09°57'	W83°01'
Dominican Republic				
Cabo Rojo	CRO	114.30	N17°56'	W71°38'
Puerto Plata	PTA	115.10	N19°45'	W70°34'
Punta Cana	PNA	112.70	N18°33'	W68°21'
Punta Caucedo	CDO	114.70	N18°25'	W69°40'
El Salvador				
El Salvador	CAT	117.50	N13°26'	W89°02'
Ilopango	YSV	114.70	N13°41'	W89°07'
La Aurora	AUR	114.50	N14°35'	W90°31'
La Mesa	LMS	113.10	N15°28'	W87°54'
Guadeloupe				
Pointe A Pitre	PPR	115.10	N16°16'	W61°30'
Guatemala				
La Aurora	AUR	114.50	N14°35'	W90°31'
Rabinal	RAB	116.10	N15°00'	W90°28'
San Jose	SJO	114.10	N13°56'	W90°51'
Haiti				
Cap Haitien	HCN	113.90	N19°43'	W72°11'
Obleon	OBN	113.20	N18°26'	W72°16'
Port Au Prince	PAP	115.30	N18°34'	W72°18'
Jamacia				
Kingston	KIN	115.90	N17°58'	W16°53'
Montego Bay	MBJ	115.70	N18°29'	W77°55'
Martinique				
Fort De France	FOF	113.30	N14°35'	W60°59'

Location/Name	Ident	Freq	Lat	Long
Mexico				
Apan	APN	114.80	N19°38'	W98°23'
Chihuahua	CUU	114.10	N28°48'	W105°57'
Ciudad Juarez	CJS	116.70	N31°38'	W106°25'
Colima	COL	117.70	N19°16'	W103°34'
Cozumel	CZM	112.60	N20°28'	W86°57'
Cuautla	CUA	116.30	N18°47'	W98°54'
Del Norte	ADN	115.40	N25°51'	W100°14'
Del Norte	ADN	115.40	N25°51'	W100°14'
Guadalajara	GDL	117.30	N20°31'	W103°18'
Hermosillo	HMO	112.80	N29°05'	W111°02'
Lucia	SLM	116.60	N19°44'	W99°01'
Manzanillo	ZLO	116.80	N19°09'	W104°34'
Matamoros	MAM	114.30	N25°46'	W97°31'
Mateo	SMO	112.10	N19°33'	W99°13'
Merida	MID	117.70	N20°54'	W89°38'
Mexico City	MEX	115.60	N19°26'	W99°04'
Monterrey	MTY	114.70	N25°46'	W100°06'
Nautla	NAU	112.30	N20°11'	W96°44'
Nuevo Laredo	NLD	112.60	N27°26'	W99°33'
Otumba	OTU	115.00	N19°41'	W98°46'
Pachuca	PCA	112.70	N20°07'	W98°41'
Pasteje	PTJ	114.50	N19°38'	W99°47'
Poza Rica	PAZ	111.50	N20°36'	W97°28'
Puebla	PBC	115.20	N19°09'	W98°22'
Reynosa	REX	112.40	N26°00'	W98°13'
Tampico	TAM	117.50	N22°17'	W97°51'
Tequis	TEQ	113.10	N18°41'	W99°15'
Tijuana	TIJ	116.50	N32°32'	W116°57'
Toluca	TLC	114.30	N19°21'	W99°34'
Uruapan	UPN	114.20	N19°23'	W102°02'
Zihuatanejo	ZIH	113.80	N17°36'	W101°28'
Neth Antilles				
Curacao	PJG	116.70	N12°12'	W69°00'
St Maarten	PJM	113.00	N18°02'	W63°07'
Panama				
David	DAV	114.30	N08°23'	W82°26'
France	FTD	109.00	N09°21'	W79°51'
Santiago	STG	114.50	N08°05'	W80°56'
Taboga Island	TBG	110.00	N08°47'	W79°33'
Tocumen	TUM	117.10	N09°03'	W79°24'

Location/Name	Ident	Freq	Lat	Long
Puerto Rico				
Borinquen	BQN	113.50	N18°29'	W67°06'
Mayaguez	MAZ	110.60	N18°15'	W67°09'
Ponce	PSE	109.00	N17°59'	W66°31'
San Juan	SJU	114.00	N18°26'	W65°59'
Trinidad				
Piarco	POS	116.90	N10°27'	W61°23'
Turks Islands				
Grand Turk	GTK	114.20	N21°26'	W71°08'
Virgin Islands				
St Croix	COY	108.20	N17°44'	W64°42'
St Thomas	STT	108.60	N18°21'	W65°01'

NDBs

Location/Name	Ident	Freq	Lat	Long
Antigua				
V C Bird	ANU	351	N17°07'	W61°48'
V C Bird	ZDX	369	N17°09'	W61°46'
Belize				
Belize	BZE	392	N17°32'	W88°18'
Bahamas				
Bimini	ZBB	396	N25°42'	W79°16'
Freeport	ZFP	209	N26°31'	W78°46'
Freeport	BHF	326	N26°34'	W78°39'
Great Inagua	ZIN	376	N20°57'	W73°40'
Marsh Harbour	ZMH	361	N26°30'	W77°04'
Nassau	ZQA	251	N25°02'	W77°28'
Rock Sound	RSD	348	N24°53'	W76°10'
Stella Maris	ZLS	526	N23°34'	W75°15'
Treasure Cay	ZTC	233	N26°44'	W77°17'
West End	ZWE	317	N26°41'	W78°58'
Bermuda				
St Davids Head	BSD	323	N32°22'	W64°38'

Location/Name	Ident	Freq	Lat	Long
Caicos Islands				
Providenciales	PV	387	N21°46'	W72°15'
Cayman Islands				
Cayman Brac	CBC	415	N19°41'	W79°51'
Grand Cayman	ZIY	344	N19°17'	W81°22'
Costa Rica				
Barra Del Colorado	COL	380	N10°46'	W83°35'
Horcones	HOR	260	N09°57'	W84°17'
Limon	LIO	380	N09°58'	W83°01'
Parrita	PAR	395	N09°31'	W84°20'
Cuba				
Alegre	UPA	382	N22°22'	W78°46'
Baracoa	UBA	278	N20°22'	W71°34'
Gerona	UNG	412	N21°45'	W82°52'
Guantanamo	UGT	300	N20°04'	W74°57'
Manzanillo	UMZ	232	N20°16'	W77°10'
Mao	UMO	212	N20°38'	W74°31'
Nuevas	UNV	256	N21°24'	W77°13'
Simones	USR	315	N21°44'	W78°48'
Varder	UVR	272	N23°05'	W81°22'
Dominica				
Melville Hall	DOM	273	N15°32'	W61°17'
El Salvador				
Amate Campo	LAN	331	N13°24'	W89°08'
Ilopango	YSX	215	N13°42'	W89°07'
Guadeloupe				
Pointe A Pitre	AR	402	N16°17'	W61°37'
Pointe A Pitre	PPR	300	N16°15'	W61°31'
Guatemala				
Guatemala	TGE	375	N14°35'	W90°31'
Iztapa	IZP	400	N13°56'	W90°44'
Rabinal	RBN	313	N15°00'	W90°28'
Haiti				
Cap Haitien	HTN	288	N19°44'	W72°11'
Port Au Prince	HHP	270	N18°34'	W72°17'

Location/Name	Ident	Freq	Lat	Long
Honduras				
Tegucigalpa	TGU	355	N13°56'	W87°14'
Toncontin	TNT	405	N14°03'	W87°13'
Jamaica				
Kingston	KIN	360	N18°57'	W76°52'
Montego Bay	MBJ	248	N18°30'	W77°55'
Martinique				
Fort De France	FXF	314	N14°35'	W61°05'
Mexico				
Cozumel	CZM	330	N20°31'	W99°09'
Nautla	NAU	392	N20°12'	W86°55'
Plaza	MW	370	N19°23'	W96°44'
Santa Elena	SNE	260	N26°43'	W98°34'
Tepexpan	TPX	359	N19°36'	W98°57'
Tizayuca	TIZ	341	N19°52'	W98°59'
Tulancingo	TCG	308	N20°05'	W98°21'
Neth Antilles				
St Maarten	PJM	308	N18°02'	W63°07'
Puerto Rico				
Mayaguez	MAZ	254	N18°15'	W67°09'
Patty (Lom/Ndb)	SJ	330	N18°24'	W66°05'
Saint Croix				
Peste (Lom)	SX	241	N17°41'	W64°53'
Saint Vincent Islands				
E T Joshua	SV	403	N13°08'	W61°13'
San Andres				
San Andres	SPP	387	N12°34'	W81°41'
Trinidad				
Piarco	POS	382	N10°35'	W61°25'
Turks Islands				
Grand Turk	GT	232	N21°26'	W71°08'

EUROPE

Airports

Innsbruck, Austria – Innsbruck

Ident	LOWI	ATIS	—
Elev	1900	Rwy/Length	08/6562
Lat	N47°15'		26/6562
Long	E11°20'		

Saint Johann, Austria – Saint Johann

Ident	LOIJ	ATIS	—
Elev	2201	Rwy	13
Lat	N47°31'		31
Long	E12°27'		

Salsburg, Austria – Salsburg

Ident	LOWS	ATIS	—
Elev	1411	Rwy/Length	16/8366
Lat	N47°47'		34/8366
Long	E13°00'		

Scharding, Austria – Scharding

Ident	LOXX	ATIS	—
Elev	1073	Rwy	08
Lat	N48°24'		26
Long	E13°27'		

Vienna, Austria – Schwechat

Ident	VIE	ATIS	118.72
Elev	600	Rwy/Length/ILS/ID	12/9843/110.30/OEW
Lat	N48°07'		30/9843/109.70/OEX
Long	E16°34'		16/11811/108.50/OEZ
			34/11811/108.10/OEN

Zell Am See, Austria – Zell Am See

Ident	LOWZ	ATIS	—
Elev	2470	Rwy/Length	05/1873
Lat	N47°17'		23/1873
Long	E12°47'		

Santa Maria, Azores Islands – Santa Maria

Ident	SMA	ATIS	123.45	
Elev	308	Rwy/Length/ILS/ID	18/10000/110.30/MA	
Lat	N36°58'		36/10000/110.30/MA	
Long	W25°10'			

Brussels, Belgium – Brussels National

Ident	BRU	ATIS	132.47
Elev	184	Rwy/Length/ILS/ID	02/9790/109.90/IBX
Lat	N50°54'		20/9790
Long	E4°29'		17L/11936
			25R/11936/108.90/IBR
			17R/10535
			25L/10535/110.30/IBL

Prague, Czech Republic – Ruzyne

Ident	PRG	ATIS	122.15
Elev	1247	Rwy/Length/ILS/ID	04/6955
Lat	N50°06'		22/6955
Long	E14°15'		06/12188
			24/12188/109.10/PR
			13/10663
			31/10663/109.50/PG

Copenhagen, Denmark – Kastrup

Ident	CPH	ATIS	122.85
Elev	17	Rwy/Length/ILS/ID	04L/9843/110.50/CH
Lat	N55°37'		22R/9843/110.90/IGLK
Long	E12°39'		04R/10827/109.30/NE
			22L/10827/109.50/OXS
			12/7759/109.90/KA
			30/7759/108.90/OY

Helsinki, Finland – Helsinki-Vantaa

Ident	HEL	ATIS	—
Elev	167	Rwy/Length/ILS/ID	04/11286/111.30/HG
Lat	N60°19'		22/11286/110.30/HK
Long	E24°58'		15/9514/109.10/HL
			33/9514

Amiens, France – Glisy

Ident	LFAY	ATIS	—
Elev	197	Rwy/Length	12/4134
Lat	N49°52'		30/4134
Long	E2°23'		12/2953 Grass
			30/2953 Grass

Beauvais, France – Tille

Ident	LFOB	ATIS	—
Elev	358	Rwy/Length	13/7972
Lat	N49°27'		31/7972
Long	E2°06'		05/3625
			23/3625
			13/2838 Grass
			31/2838 Grass

Bretigny-sur-Orge, France – Bretigny-sur-Orge

Ident	—	ATIS	—
Elev	269	Rwy/Length/ILS/ID	05//108.9/BY
Lat	N48°35'		
Long	E02°19'		

Cambrai, France – Niergnies

Ident	LFYG	ATIS	—
Elev	312	Rwy/Length	02/2231 Grass
Lat	N50°08'		20/2231 Grass
Long	E3°15'		08/2953
			26/2953
			15/7874
			33/7874

Chateaudun, France – Chateaudun

Ident	LFOC	ATIS	
Elev	433	Rwy/Length	10/7546
Lat	N48°03'		28/7546
Long	E1°22'		

Deauville, France – St Gatien

Ident	LFRG	ATIS	—
Elev	479	Rwy/Length	12/8366
Lat	N49°21'		30/8366
Long	E00°09'		12/2297 Grass
			30/2297 Grass

Joigny, France – Joigny

Ident	LFGK	ATIS	—
Elev	728	Rwy/Length	08/3510
Lat	N47°59'		26/3510
Long	E3°23'		08/2297 Grass
			26/2297 Grass

Le Havre, France – Octeville

Ident	LFOH	ATIS	—
Elev	312	Rwy/Length	05/7546
Lat	N49°32'		23/7546
Long	E00°05'		11/2461 Grass
			29/2461 Grass

Le Mans, France – Arnage

Ident	LFRM	ATIS	—
Elev	194	Rwy/Length	02/4626
Lat	N47°57'		20/4626
Long	E00°12'		

Melun, France – Villaroche

Ident	—	ATIS	128.17
Elev	302	Rwy/Length/ILS/ID	29//110.5/MV
Lat	N48°36'		
Long	E02°40'		

Paris, France – Les Mureaux

Ident	—	ATIS	—
Elev	89	Rwy/Length	—
Lat	N48°59'		
Long	E01°56'		

Paris, France – Orly

Ident	LFPO	ATIS	126.50
Elev	292	Rwy/Length/ILS/ID	02L/7874/110.30/OLN
Lat	N48°43'		20R/7875
Long	E02°22'		07/11975/108.50/ORE
			25/11975/110.90/OLO
			08/10892/108.15/OLE
			26/10892/109.50/OLW
			06/1640 Grass
			24/1640 Grass

Paris, France – Charles DeGaulle

Ident	LFPG	ATIS	128.0
Elev	387	Rwy/Length/ILS/ID	09/11811/110.10/CGE
Lat	N49°01'		27/11811/110.70/CGW
Long	E02°32'		10/11860/108.70/GLE
			28/11860/109.10/GAU

Paris, France – Le Bourget

Ident	LFPB	ATIS	120.0
Elev	217	Rwy/Length/ILS/ID	03/8743
Lat	N48°58'		21/8743
Long	E02°26'		07/9843/109.90/LBE
			25/9843/111.10/LBW
			27//110.55/RGE

Peroone-St Quentin, France – Peroone-St Quentin

Ident	LFAG	ATIS	—
Elev	292	Rwy/Length	09/8005
Lat	N49°52'		27/8005
Long	E3°01'		

Persan-Beaumont, France – Persan-Beaumont

Ident	LFPA	ATIS	—
Elev	148	Rwy/Length	10L/2723
Lat	N49°10'		28R/2723
Long	E02°18'		10R/2887
			28L/2887

Pontoise, France – Cormeilles-en-Vexin

Ident	LFPT	ATIS	121.2
Elev	325	Rwy/Length/ILS/ID	05/5545/108.1/CVN
Lat	N49°05'		23/5545
Long	E02°02'		12/5413
			30/5413

Reims, France – Champagne

Ident	LFST	ATIS	—
Elev	312	Rwy/Length	07/8143
Lat	N49°18'		25/8143
Long	E4°03'		

Rouen, France – Boox

Ident	LFOP	ATIS	—
Elev	512	Rwy/Length	04/5577
Lat	N49°23'		22/5577
Long	E1°11'		

St Andre De L'Eure, France – St Andre De L'Eure

Ident	LFFD	ATIS	—
Elev	492	Rwy	06
Lat	N48°54'		24
Long	E1°15'		

Toussus-Le-Nouble, France – Toussus-Le-Nouble

Ident	LFPN	ATIS	127.47
Elev	538	Rwy/Length	07L/3609
Lat	N48°45'		25R/3609/109.3/TNO
Long	E02°06'		07R/3445
			25L/3445

Troyes, France – Barberey

Ident	LFQB	ATIS	—
Elev	394	Rwy/Length/ILS/ID	05/2854
Lat	N48°19'		23/2854
Long	E04°01'		18/5413/111.9/TY
			36/5413

Villacoublay, France – Velizy AB

Ident	—	ATIS	—
Elev	581	Rwy/Length	—
Lat	N48°46'		
Long	E02°12'		

Aalen-Heidenhaim, Germany – Elchingen

Ident	EDTA	ATIS	—
Elev	1916	Rwy/Length	09L/3281
Lat	N48°46'		27R/3281
Long	E10°16'		09R/2625 Grass
			27L/2625 Grass

Arnbruck, Germany – Arnbruck

Ident	EDYB	ATIS	—
Elev	1716	Rwy/Length	17/2001
Lat	N49°07'		35/2001
Long	E12°59'		

Augsburg, Germany – Augsburg

Ident	EDMA	ATIS	118.22
Elev	1515	Rwy/Length	07/4199
Lat	N48°25'		25/4199
Long	E10°56'		

Berlin, Germany – Tegel

Ident	—	ATIS	125.9
Elev	121	Rwy/Length/ILS/ID	26R//110.1/ITLW
Lat	N52°33'		26L//109.3/ITGW
Long	E13°17'		08L//109.1/ITLE
			08R//108.5/ITGE

Berlin, Germany – Tempelhof

Ident	—	ATIS	126.02
Elev	164	Rwy/Length/ILS/ID	09R//109.7/IDBR
Lat	N52°28'		27L//109.5/IDLB
Long	E13°24'		

Deggendorf, Germany – Deggendorf

Ident	EDMW	ATIS	—
Elev	1030	Rwy/Length	09/1903
Lat	N48°49'		27/1903
Long	E12°52'		

Donauwoerth, Germany – Donauwoerth-Genderkingen

Ident	EDMQ	ATIS	—
Elev	1312	Rwy/Length	09/1739
Lat	N48°42'		27/1739
Long	E10°51'		

Eggenfelden, Germany – Eggenfelden

Ident	EDME	ATIS	—
Elev	1342	Rwy/Length	09/2920
Lat	N48°23'		27/2920
Long	E12°43'		

Giengen/Brenz, Germany – Giengen/Brenz

Ident	EDGI	ATIS	—
Elev	1695	Rwy/Length	17/1804
Lat	N48°38'		35/1804
Long	E10°13'		

Gunzenhausen, Germany – Reutberg

Ident	EDMH	ATIS	—
Elev	1591	Rwy/Length	06/2379
Lat	N49°06'		24/2379
Long	E10°47'		

Hamburg, Germany – Hamburg

Ident	EHAM	ATIS	—
Elev	53	Rwy/Length/ILS/ID	05/10663/110.50/IHB
Lat	N53°37'		23/10663/111.50/DLH
Long	E9°59'		15/12028/111.10/IAM
			33/12028

Jesenwang, Germany – Jesenwang

Ident	EDMJ	ATIS	—
Elev	1861	Rwy/Length	07/1460
Lat	N48°10'		25/1460
Long	E11°07'		

Landshut, Germany – Landshut

Ident	EDML	ATIS	—
Elev	1312	Rwy/Length	07/2953
Lat	N48°30'		25/2953
Long	E12°02'		

Leutkirch, Germany – Unterzeil

Ident	EDYL	ATIS	—
Elev	2099	Rwy/Length	06/3346
Lat	N47°51'		24/3346
Long	E10°00'		

Mindelheim, Germany – Mattsies

Ident	EDMN	ATIS	—
Elev	1857	Rwy/Length	15/2067
Lat	N48°06'		33/2067
Long	E10°31'		

Muhldorf, Germany – Muhldorf

Ident	EDMY	ATIS	—
Elev	1325	Rwy/Length	08/1969
Lat	N48°16'		26/1969
Long	E12°30'		

Munich, Germany – Munich

Ident	EDDM	ATIS	118.37
Elev	1486	Rwy/Length/ILS/ID	08L/13123/110.30/IMNE
Lat	N48°21'		26R/13123/108.70/IMNW
Long	E11°47'		08R/13123/110.90/IMSE
			26L/13123/108.30/IMSW

Nordlingen, Germany – Nordlingen

Ident	EDNO	ATIS	—
Elev	1384	Rwy/Length	04/1640
Lat	N48°52'		22/1640
Long	E10°30'		

Oberpfaffenhofen, Germany – Oberpfaffenhofen

Ident	EDMO	ATIS	—
Elev	1946	Rwy/Length	04/7500
Lat	N48°04'		22/7500
Long	E11°17'		

Regensburg, Germany – Oberhub

Ident	EDYR	ATIS	—
Elev	1298	Rwy/Length	10/2234
Lat	N49°08'		28/2234
Long	E12°05'		

Straubing, Germany – Wallmuhle

Ident	EDMS	ATIS	—
Elev	1046	Rwy/Length	10/3478
Lat	N48°54'		28/3478
Long	E12°31'		

Vilshofen, Germany – Vilshoven

Ident	EDMV	ATIS	—
Elev	991	Rwy/Length	12/3281
Lat	N48°38'		30/3281
Long	E13°11'		

Vogtareuth, Germany – Vogtareuth

Ident	EDYV	ATIS	—
Elev	1535	Rwy/Length	06/1535
Lat	N47°56'		24/1535
Long	E12°12'		

Athens, Greece – Athens

Ident	ATH	ATIS	123.40
Elev	68	Rwy/Length/ILS/ID	15L/11483
Lat	N37°53'		33R/11483/110.30/IATH
Long	E23°43'		15R/10335
			33L/10335

Keflavik, Iceland – Keflavik

Ident	KEF	ATIS	118.30
Elev	171	Rwy/Length/ILS/ID	02/10000
Lat	N63°59'		20/10000/110.30/IKO
Long	W22°36'		07/6942
			25/6942
			11/10013/109.50/IKF
			29/10013

Dublin, Ireland – Dublin

Ident	DUB	ATIS	124.52
Elev	242	Rwy/Length/ILS/ID	10/8652/108.90/IDE
Lat	N53°25'		28/8652/108.90/IDW
Long	W6°15'		11/4450
			29/4450
			16/6800/111.50/IAC
			34/6800

Rome, Italy – Ciampino

Ident	—	ATIS	—
Elev	426	Rwy/Length/ILS/ID	15//109.9/CIA
Lat	N47°54'		
Long	E12°35'		

Rome, Italy – Fiumicino

Ident	FCO	ATIS	121.7
Elev	14	Rwy/Length/ILS/ID	07/10810
Lat	N41°48'		25/10810/109.70/FEE
Long	E12°15'		16L/12795/108.10/FLL
			34R/12795/109.30/FSS
			16R/12795/110.30/FRR
			34L/12795/108.90/ISW

Rome, Italy – Urbe

Ident	—	ATIS	—
Elev	55	Rwy/Length	—
Lat	N41°57'		
Long	E12°30'		

Bergen, Norway – Flesland

Ident	BGO	ATIS	125.25
Elev	165	Rwy/Length/ILS/ID	18/8038/109.90/BR
Lat	N60°17'		36/8038/110.50/BG
Long	E5°13'		

Warsaw, Poland – Okecie

Ident	WAW	ATIS	118.30
Elev	362	Rwy/Length/ILS/ID	11/9186
Lat	N52°10'		29/9186
Long	E20°58'		15/12106
			33/12106/110.30/WA

Lisbon, Portugal – Lisbon

Ident	LIS	ATIS	118.10
Elev	374	Rwy/Length/ILS/ID	03/12484/109.10/LI
Lat	N38°46'		21/12484/109.50/LB
Long	W9°08'		17/7874
			35/7874

Glasgow, Scotland – Glasgow

Ident	GLA	ATIS	118.80
Elev	26	Rwy/Length/ILS/ID	05/8720/110.10/IUU
Lat	N55°52'		23/8720/110.10/IOO
Long	E4°25'		10/3570
			26/3570

Barcelona, Spain – Barcelona

Ident	BCN	ATIS	118.65
Elev	10	Rwy/Length/ILS/ID	02/8924
Lat	N41°17'		20/8924
Long	E2°04'		07/10197/110.30/QAA
			25/10197/109.50/BCA

Madrid, Spain – Barajas

Ident	MAD	ATIS	118.25
Elev	1998	Rwy/Length/ILS/ID	18/12139
Lat	N40°28'		36/12139/110.30/BJS
Long	E3°33'		15/13451
			33/13451/109.90/MAA

Stockholm, Sweden – Skavsta

Ident	SKN	ATIS	127.70
Elev	140	Rwy/Length/ILS/ID	09/7802/111.30/WEK
Lat	N58°47'		27/7802/111.90/EKN
Long	E16°54'		16/6637
			34/6637

Geneva, Switzerland – Cointrin

Ident	GUA	ATIS	125.72
Elev	1411	Rwy/Length/ILS/ID	05/12795/110.90/INE
Lat	N46°14'		23/12795/109.90/ISW
Long	W6°06'		05/2700 Grass
			23/2700 Grass

Andrewsfield, UK. – Andrewsfield

Ident	—	ATIS	127.17
Elev	286	Rwy	09
Lat	N51°53'		27
Long	E00°27'		

Biggin Hill, UK. – Biggin Hill

Ident	EGKB	ATIS	—
Elev	600	Rwy/Length/ILS/ID	03/5932
Lat	N51°19'		21/5932/109.35/IBGH
Long	E00°02'		11/2677
			29/2677

Blackbushe, UK. – Blackbushe

Ident	EGLK	ATIS	—
Elev	329	Rwy/Length	08/4403
Lat	N51°19'		26/4403
Long	W00°50'		08/1640 Grass
			26/1640 Grass

Denham, UK. – Denham

Ident		ATIS	133.07
Elev	249	Rwy/Length	6/2556
Lat	N51°35'		24/2556
Long	W00°30'		12/1850 Grass
			30/1850 Grass

Dunsfold, UK. – Dunsfold

Ident	—	ATIS	128.47
Elev	172	Rwy/Length	7/6221
Lat	N51°07'		25/6221
Long	W00°32'		

Elstree, UK. – Elstree

Ident	EGTR	ATIS	—
Elev	334	Rwy/Length	08/2152
Lat	N51°39'		26/2152
Long	W00°19'		

Fairoaks, UK. – Fairoaks

Ident	EGTF	ATIS	—
Elev	80	Rwy/Length	06/2625
Lat	N51°20'		24/2625
Long	W00°33'		

Farnborough, UK. – Farnborough

Ident	EGLF	ATIS	—
Elev	237	Rwy/Length	07/7874
Lat	N51°16'		25/7874
Long	W00°46'		11/4494
			29/4494
			18/4205
			36/4205

Halton AB, UK. – Halton AB

Ident	—	ATIS	120.57
Elev	370	Rwy/Length	02/3707 Grass
Lat	N51°47'		20/3707 Grass
Long	W00°44'		08/2710 Grass
			26/2710 Grass

Hatfield, UK. -(CLOSED)

Ident	—	ATIS	120.57
Elev	254	Rwy	24
Lat	N51°45'		
Long	W00°15'		

Leavesden, UK. – (CLOSED)

Ident	—	ATIS	133.07
Elev	335	Rwy	24
Lat	N51°41'		
Long	W00°25'		

London, UK. – Gatwick

Ident	EGKK	ATIS	128.47
Elev	196	Rwy/Length/ILS/ID	08R/10364/110.90/IGG
Lat	N51°09'		26L/10364/110.90/IWW
Long	W00°11'		08L/8415
			26R/8415

London, UK. – Heathrow

Ident	EGLL	ATIS	123.9
Elev	80	Rwy/Length/ILS/ID	09R/12000/109.50/IBB
Lat	N51°28'		27L/12000/109.50/ILL
Long	W00°27'		09L/12802/110.30/IAA
			27R/12802/110.30/IRR
			23/6450

London, UK. – London City

Ident	EGLC	ATIS	—
Elev	17	Rwy/Length/ILS/ID	10/3934/111.15/LST
Lat	N51°30'		28/3934/111.15/LSR
Long	E00°03'		

London, UK. – Luton

Ident	—	ATIS	120.57
Elev	526	Rwy/ILS/ID	08//109.15/ILTN
Lat	N51°52'		26//109.15/ILJ
Long	E00°22'		

London, UK. – Stansted

Ident	EGSS	ATIS	127.17
Elev	347	Rwy/Length/ILS/ID	05/10000/110.50/ISED
Lat	N51°53'		23/10000/110.50/ISX
Long	E00°14'		08/7087/109.15/ILTN
			26/7087/109.15/ILJ

Northolt, UK. – Northolt AB

Ident	EGWU	ATIS	—
Elev	124	Rwy/Length	07/5525
Lat	N51°33'		25/5525
Long	W00°25'		

North Weald, UK. – North Weald

Ident	—	ATIS	127.17
Elev	321	Rwy/Length	2/6332
Lat	N51°43'		20/6332
Long	E00°09'		13/3005
			31/3005

Panshanger, UK. – Panshanger

Ident	—	ATIS	120.57
Elev	250	Rwy/Length	11/2362 Grass
Lat	N51°48'		29/2362 Grass
Long	W00°09'		

Redhill, UK. – Redhill

Ident	—	ATIS	128.47
Elev	221	Rwy/Length	8R/2943 Grass
Lat	N51°12'		26L/2943 Grass
Long	W00°08'		8L/2224 Grass
			26R/2224 Grass
			01/2789 Grass
			19/2789 Grass

Stapleford, UK. – Stapleford

Ident	EGSG	ATIS	—
Elev	185	Rwy/Length	04/3533 Grass
Lat	N51°39'		22/3533 Grass
Long	E00°09'		10/2346 Grass
			28/2346 Grass

White Waltham, UK. – White Waltham

Ident	—	ATIS	133.07
Elev	130	Rwy/Length	07/3642 Grass
Lat	N51°30'		25/3642 Grass
Long	W00°46'		03/3363 Grass
			21/3363 Grass
			11/3051 Grass
			29/3051 Grass

Wycombe Air Park (Booker), UK. – Wycombe Air Park

Ident	—	ATIS	133.07
Elev	520	Rwy/Length	07/2411
Lat	N51°36'		25/2411
Long	W00°48'		07/2001 Grass
			25/2001 Grass
			17/2582 Grass
			35/2582 Grass

VORs

Location/Name	Ident	Freq	Lat	Long
Austria				
Eurach	EUR	115.20	N47°44'	E11°15'
Fischamend	FMD	110.40	N48°06'	E16°37'
Kempten	KPT	109.60	N47°44'	E10°21'
Linz	LNZ	116.60	N48°13'	E14°06'
Munich	MUN	112.30	N48°10'	E11°49'
Roding	RDG	114.70	N49°02'	E12°31'
Salzburg	SBG	113.80	N48°00'	E12°53'
Souenau	SNU	115.50	N47°52'	E16°17'
Stockerau	STO	113.00	N48°25'	E16°01'
Villach	VIW	112.90	N46°41'	E13°54'
Wagram	WGM	112.20	N48°19'	E16°29'
Belgium				
Affligem	AFI	114.90	N50°54'	E4°08'
Bruno	BUN	110.60	N51°04'	E4°46'
Brussels	BUB	114.60	N50°54'	E4°32'
Chievers	CIV	113.20	N50°34'	E3°50'
Chievers	CIV	113.20	N50°34'	E3°49'
Costa	COA	111.80	N51°20'	E3°21'
Diekirch	DIK	114.40	N49°51'	E6°07'

Location/Name	Ident	Freq	Lat	Long
Belgium (continued)				
Haamstede	HSD	115.50	N51°43'	E3°51'
Huldenberg	HUL	117.55	N50°45'	E4°38'
Koksy	KOK	114.50	N51°05'	E2°39'
Koksy	KOK	114.50	N51°06'	E2°39'
Luxembourg	DIK	114.40	N49°51'	E6°07'
Nicky	NIK	117.40	N51°10'	E4°11'
Olno	LNO	112.80	N50°35'	E5°42'
Spirmont	SPI	113.10	N50°30'	E5°37'
Czech Republic				
Cheb	OKG	115.70	N50°03'	E12°24'
Hermsdorf	HDO	115.00	N50°55'	E14°22'
Neratovice	NER	108.60	N50°18'	E14°23'
Prague	OKL	112.60	N50°06'	E14°13'
Roudnice	RCE	117.60	N50°27'	E14°12'
Vlasim	VLM	114.30	N49°42'	E15°04'
Vozice	VOZ	116.30	N49°32'	E14°52'
Denmark				
Alma	ALM	116.40	N55°24'	E13°33'
Astor	AOR	113.90	N56°07'	E12°57'
Codan	CDA	114.90	N55°00'	E12°22'
Kastrup	KAS	112.50	N55°35'	E12°36'
Korsa	KOR	112.80	N55°26'	E11°38'
Nora	NOA	112.60	N56°06'	E12°14'
Odin	ODN	115.50	N55°34'	E10°39'
Sevda	SVD	116.20	N56°10'	E12°34'
Sturup	SUP	113.00	N55°32'	E13°22'
Trano	TNO	117.40	N55°46'	E11°26'
Finland				
Anton	ANT	113.70	N60°51'	E25°07'
Helsinki	HEL	114.20	N60°20'	E24°57'
Utti	UTT	114.60	N60°53'	E26°56'
Vihti	VTI	117.00	N60°27'	E24°14'
France				
Abberville	ABB	116.60	N50°08'	E1°51'
Amboise	AMB	113.70	N47°25'	E1°03'
Angers	ANG	113.00	N47°32'	W00°51'
Beauvais	BVS	115.90	N49°26'	E2°09'

Location/Name	Ident	Freq	Lat	Long
France (continued)				
Boursonne	BSN	112.50	N49°11'	E3°03'
Bray	BRY	114.10	N48°24'	E3°17'
Caen	CAN	115.40	N49°10'	W00°27'
Cambrai	CMB	112.60	N50°13'	E3°09'
Charles-De-Gaulle (Paris)	CGN	115.35	N49°01'	E2°30'
Charles-De-Gaulle (Paris)	PGS	117.05	N49°00'	E2°37'
Chartres	CHW	115.20	N48°28'	E00°59'
Chateaudun	CDN	116.10	N48°03'	E1°23'
Chatillon	CTL	117.60	N49°08'	E3°34'
Coulommiers	CLM	112.90	N48°50'	E3°00'
Creil	CRL	109.20	N49°15'	E2°31'
Deauville	DVL	110.20	N49°18'	E00°18'
Dieppe	DPE	115.80	N49°55'	E1°10'
Dijion	DIJ	113.50	N47°16'	E5°05'
Dijion	DIJ	113.50	N47°16'	E5°05'
Epernon	EPR	115.65	N48°37'	E1°39'
Evreux	EVX	112.40	N49°01'	E1°13'
L'aigle	LGL	115.00	N48°47'	E00°32'
Le Bourget (Paris)	BT	108.80	N48°58'	E2°27'
Melun	MEL	109.80	N48°27'	E2°48'
Montdidier	MTD	113.65	N49°33'	E2°29'
Moulins	MOU	116.70	N46°42'	E3°38'
Nevers	NEV	113.40	N47°09'	E2°55'
Orly (Paris)	OL	111.20	N48°43'	E2°23'
Pithiviers	PTV	116.50	N48°09'	E2°15'
Pontoise	PON	111.60	N49°05'	E2°02'
Rambouillet	RBT	114.70	N48°39'	E1°59'
Reims	REM	112.30	N49°18'	E4°02'
Rolampont	RLP	117.30	N47°54'	E5°15'
Rouen	ROU	116.80	N49°27'	E1°16'
Toussus	TSU	108.25	N48°45'	E2°06'
Troyes	TRO	116.00	N48°15'	E3°57'
Germany				
Allersberg	ALB	111.20	N49°12'	E11°13'
Alsie	ALS	114.70	N54°54'	E9°59'
Alster	ALF	115.80	N53°38'	E9°59'
Ausburg	AUG	115.90	N48°25'	E10°56'
Brunkendorf	BKD	117.70	N53°02'	E11°32'
Dinkelsbuhl	DKB	117.80	N49°08'	E10°14'
Elbe	LBE	115.10	N52°39'	E9°35'
Erding	ERD	113.60	N48°19'	E11°57'
Erlangen	ERL	114.90	N49°39'	E11°09'

Location/Name	Ident	Freq	Lat	Long
Germany (continued)				
Eurach	EUR	115.20	N47°44'	E11°15'
Hamburg	HAM	113.10	N53°41'	E10°12'
Hehlingen	HLZ	117.30	N52°21'	E10°47'
Helgoland	DHE	116.30	N54°11'	E7°54'
Karlspuhe	KRH	115.95	N48°59'	E8°35'
Kempten	KPT	109.60	N47°44'	E10°21'
Klagenfurt	KFT	113.10	N46°35'	E14°33'
Leine	DLE	115.20	N52°15'	E9°53'
Lubeck	LUB	110.60	N53°56'	E10°40'
Luburg	LBU	109.20	N48°54'	E9°20'
Maisach	MAH	108.40	N48°15'	E11°18'
Michaelsdorf	MIC	112.10	N54°18'	E11°00'
Milldorf	MDF	117.00	N48°14'	E12°20'
Moosburg	MBG	117.15	N48°34'	E12°15'
Munich	MUN	112.30	N48°10'	E11°49'
Munich	DMN	116.00	N48°22'	E11°47'
Munich	DMS	108.60	N48°20'	E11°46'
Nienburg	NIE	116.50	N52°37'	E9°22'
Roding	RDG	114.70	N49°02'	E12°31'
Tango	TGO	112.50	N48°37'	E9°15'
Transdingen	TRA	114.30	N47°41'	E8°26'
Villach	VIW	112.90	N46°41'	E13°54'
Walda	WLD	112.80	N48°34'	E11°07'
Warburg	WRB	113.70	N51°30'	E9°06'
Weser	WSR	112.90	N53°21'	E8°52'
Wurzburg	WUR	116.35	N49°43'	E9°56'
Zurich	ZUE	110.50	N47°35'	E8°49'
Greece				
Athens	ATH	114.40	N37°54'	E23°43'
Didimon	DDM	117.20	N37°28'	E23°13'
Kea	KEA	115.00	N37°33'	E24°18'
Milos	MIL	113.50	N36°44'	E24°31'
Tripolis	TRL	116.20	N37°24'	E22°20'
Hungary				
Gyor	GYR	115.10	N47°39'	E17°43'
Iceland				
Ingo	ING	112.40	N63°48'	W16°38'
Keflavik	KEF	112.00	N63°59'	W2°36'

Location/Name	Ident	Freq	Lat	Long
Ireland				
Baldonnel	BAL	115.80	N53°18'	W6°26'
Connaught	CON	117.40	N53°54'	W8°49'
Dublin	DUB	114.90	N53°30'	W6°18'
Isle Of Man	IOM	112.20	N54°04'	W4°45'
Shannon	SHA	113.30	N52°43'	W8°53'
Italy				
Ajaccio	AJO	114.80	N41°46'	E8°46'
Alghero	ALG	113.80	N40°27'	E8°14'
Bastia	BTA	114.15	N42°34'	E9°28'
Bolsena	BOL	114.40	N42°37'	E12°02'
Campagnano	CMP	111.40	N42°07'	E12°22'
Carbonara	CAR	115.10	N39°06'	E9°30'
Elba	ELB	114.70	N42°43'	E10°23'
Ostia	OST	114.90	N41°48'	E12°14'
Pescara	PES	115.90	N42°26'	E14°11'
Pisa	PIS	112.10	N43°40'	E10°23'
Ponza	PNZ	114.60	N40°54'	E12°57'
Sorrento	SOR	112.20	N40°34'	E14°20'
Tarquinia	TAQ	111.80	N42°12'	E11°44'
Teano	TEA	112.90	N41°17'	E13°58'
Norway				
Flesland	FLE	114.50	N60°18'	E5°12'
Vollo	VOO	114.85	N60°32'	E5°07'
Poland				
Karnice	KRN	117.80	N51°56'	E20°26'
Lodz	LDZ	112.40	N51°48'	E19°39'
Piaseczno	PNO	112.90	N52°03'	E21°03'
Siedlce	SIE	114.70	N52°09'	E22°12'
Warsaw	OKE	113.40	N52°10'	E20°57'
Zaborowek	WAR	114.90	N52°15'	E20°39'
Portugal				
Beja	BEJ	115.80	N38°07'	W7°55'
Espichel	ESP	112.50	N38°25'	W9°11'
Fatima	FTM	113.50	N39°39'	W8°29'
Lisbon	LIS	114.80	N38°53'	W9°09'
Sintra	SRA	112.10	N38°49'	W9°20'

Location/Name	Ident	Freq	Lat	Long
Spain				
Bagur	BGR	112.20	N41°56'	E3°12'
Barahona	BAN	112.80	N41°19'	W2°37'
Barcelona	QUV	114.30	N41°17'	E2°05'
Campo Real	CPL	114.50	N40°19'	W3°22'
Castejon	CJN	115.60	N40°22'	W2°32'
Colmenar Viejo	CNR	117.30	N40°38'	W3°44'
Domingo	DGO	112.60	N42°27'	W2°52'
Maella	MLA	112.10	N41°07'	E00°10'
Reus	RES	114.20	N41°09'	E1°10'
Toledo	TLD	113.20	N39°58'	W4°20'
Torrejon	TJZ	115.10	N40°28'	W3°28'
Villatobas	VTB	112.70	N39°46'	W3°27'
Sweden				
Mantor	MNT	114.00	N58°23'	E15°17'
Trosa	TRS	114.30	N58°56'	E17°30'
Switzerland				
Chambery	CBY	115.40	N45°53'	E5°45'
Epinal	EPL	113.00	N48°19'	E6°03'
Fribourg	FRI	110.85	N46°46'	E7°13'
Geneva	GVA	114.60	N46°15'	E6°08'
Hochwald	HOC	113.20	N47°28'	E7°40'
Martigues	MTG	117.30	N43°23'	E5°05'
Nice	NIZ	112.40	N43°46'	E7°15'
Passeiry	PAS	116.60	N46°09'	E6°00'
Rolampont	RLP	117.30	N47°54'	E5°15'
Saronno	SRN	113.70	N45°38'	E9°01'
Satolas	LSA	114.75	N45°43'	E5°05'
St Prex	SPR	113.90	N46°28'	E6°26'
Tour Du Pin	TDP	110.60	N45°29'	E5°26'
United Kingdom				
Barkway	BKY	116.25	N51°59'	E00°03'
Biggin	BIG	115.10	N51°19'	E00°02'
Blackbushe	BLC	116.20	N51°19'	W00°50'
Boulogne	BNE	113.80	N50°37'	E1°54'
Bovingdon	BNN	113.75	N51°43'	W00°32'
Brookmans Park	BPK	117.50	N51°44'	W00°06'
Burnham	BUR	117.10	N51°31'	W00°40'
Clacton	CLN	114.55	N51°50'	E1°09'
Compton	CPT	114.35	N51°29'	W1°13'

Location/Name	Ident	Freq	Lat	Long
United Kingdom (continued)				
Daventry	DTY	116.40	N52°10'	W1°06'
Deancross	DCS	115.20	N54°43'	W3°20'
Fairoaks	FRK	109.85	N51°20'	W00°33'
Glasgow	GOW	115.40	N55°52'	W4°26'
Lambourne	LAM	115.60	N51°38'	E00°09'
London	LON	113.60	N51°29'	W00°27'
Lydd	LYD	114.05	N50°59'	E00°52'
Manchester	MCT	113.55	N53°21'	W2°15'
Mayfield	MAY	117.90	N51°00'	E00°07'
Midhurst	MID	114.00	N51°03'	W00°37'
Ockham	OCK	115.30	N51°18'	W00°26'
Odiham	ODH	109.60	N51°13'	W00°56'
Perth	PTH	110.40	N56°26'	W3°22'
Pole Hill	POL	112.10	N53°44'	W2°06'
Saint Abbs	SAB	112.50	N55°54'	W2°12'
Seaford	SFD	117.00	N50°45'	E00°07'
Southampton	SAM	113.35	N50°57'	W1°20'
Talla	TLA	113.80	N55°30'	W3°21'
Turnberry	TRN	117.50	N55°18'	W4°47'

NDBs

Location/Name	Ident	Freq	Lat	Long
Austria				
Absam	AB	313	N47°17'	E11°30'
Bruck	BRK	408	N48°03'	E16°43'
Innsbruck	INN	420	N47°13'	E11°24'
Kuhtai	KTI	413	N47°10'	E11°01'
Rattenberg	RTT	303	N47°25'	E11°56'
Salzburg	SBG	382	N47°58'	E12°53'
Salzburg	SI	410	N47°49'	E12°59'
Salzburg	SU	356	N47°52'	E12°57'
Steinhof	STE	293	N48°12'	E16°14'
Vienna	WO	303	N48°08'	E16°27'
Belgium				
Bressy	BUS	283.5	N50°41'	E4°08'
Bruno	BUN	341.5	N51°04'	E4°46'
Brussels	OB	293	N50°55'	E4°37'
Brussels	OP	402	N50°56'	E4°35'
Brussels	OZ	314	N50°49'	E4°28'

Location/Name	Ident	Freq	Lat	Long
Belgium (continued)				
Dender	DEN	393	N50°52'	E4°01'
Diekirch	DIK	307	N49°51'	E6°07'
Klien Brogel	ONT	431	N51°12'	E5°33'
Nicky	NIK	336	N51°09'	E4°11'
Czech Republic				
Rakovnik	RAK	386	N50°05'	E13°41'
Ruzyne Middle	PG	307	N50°02'	E14°22'
Ruzyne North	PR	356	N50°08'	E14°22'
Finland				
Espoo	ESP	381	N60°14'	E24°48'
Foxtrot	F	408	N60°16'	E25°02'
Heka	HEK	344	N60°15'	E25°29'
Hyvinkaa	HYV	396	N60°33'	E24°43'
Korso	KOR	322	N60°22'	E25°04'
Pakka	PAK	368	N60°42'	E25°32'
France				
Alencon	AL	380	N48°27'	E00°06'
Amiens	GI	339	N49°50'	E2°29'
Beauvais	BV	391	N49°29'	E2°01'
Bray	BRY	277	N48°24'	E3°17'
Charles-De-Gaulle (Paris)	CGO	343	N48°59'	E2°24'
Charles-De-Gaulle (Paris)	CGZ	370	N49°00'	E2°44'
Charles-De-Gaulle (Paris)	RSO	364	N49°00'	E2°21'
Charles-De-Gaulle (Paris)	RSY	356	N49°01'	E2°42'
Chateaudun	CDN	359.5	N48°03'	E1°21'
Compiegne	CO	553.5	N49°26'	E2°48'
Etampes	EM	295.5	N48°22'	E2°04'
Le Bourget (Paris)	BGW	334	N48°56'	E2°16'
Le Havre	LHO	346	N49°35'	E00°11'
Le Mans	LM	326	N47°53'	E00°10'
Melun	MV	434	N48°33'	E2°58'
Orleans	OAN	385	N48°00'	E1°46'
Orly (Paris)	OLS	328	N48°38'	E2°20'
Orly (Paris)	ORW	402	N48°40'	E2°11'
Orly (Paris)	OYE	349	N48°45'	E2°32'
Peronne-St. Quentin	PM	382	N49°52'	E3°08'
Troyes	TY	320	N48°24'	E4°00'
Villacoublay	TA	286.5	N48°46'	E2°05'
Villacoublay	TH	302	N48°46'	E2°22'
Villacoublay	HOL	315	N48°43'	E1°49'

Location/Name	Ident	Freq	Lat	Long
Germany				
Ansbach	ANS	452	N49°18'	E10°37'
Augsburg	AGB	318	N48°25'	E10°56'
Gluckstadt	GLX	365	N53°51'	E9°27'
Hamburg	FU	350.5	N53°34'	E9°52'
Hamburg	HAM	339	N53°40'	E10°05'
Hamburg	GT	323	N53°40'	E10°05'
Hofenfels	HFX	286	N49°13'	E11°51'
Ingolstadt	IGL	345	N48°44'	E11°38'
Landsberg	LQ	448	N48°05'	E11°02'
Mengen	MEG	401	N48°03'	E9°22'
Mike	MIQ	426.5	N48°34'	E11°36'
Munich	MNE	358	N48°21'	E11°40'
Munich	MNW	338	N48°22'	E11°54'
Munich	MSE	385	N48°20'	E11°39'
Munich	MSW	400	N48°21'	E11°54'
Nordlingen	NDG	375	N48°49'	E10°25'
Oberpfaffenhofen	OBI	429	N48°04'	E11°17'
Greece				
Aigina	EGN	382	N37°45'	E23°25'
Athens	HN	294	N37°52'	E23°44'
Athens	HK	275	N37°49'	E23°46'
Elefsis	ELF	418	N38°04'	E23°46'
Karistos	KRS	285	N38°00'	E24°25'
Kavouri	KVR	357	N37°48'	E23°45'
Korinthos	KOR	392	N37°56'	E22°56'
Sounion	SUN	319	N37°40'	E24°02'
Tangra	TNG	303	N38°20'	E23°43'
Hungary				
Pusztasabolcs	PTB	386	N47°08'	E18°45'
Gyor	GYR	354	N47°39'	E17°43'
Iceland				
Ellidavain	EL	335	N64°04'	W21°46'
Keflavik	KF	392	N63°59'	W22°36'
Kilo	OK	364	N64°03'	W22°36'
Reyjavik	RK	355	N64°09'	W22°01'
Skagi	SA	379	N64°18'	W21°58'
Skardsfjara	SR	312.6	N63°31'	W17°58'
Vestmannaey Jar	VM	375	N63°24'	W20°17'

Location/Name	Ident	Freq	Lat	Long
Ireland				
Clonmel	CML	387	N52°27'	W7°28'
Dublin	OE	316	N53°25'	W6°25'
Dublin	OP	397	N53°24'	W6°08'
Garristown	GAR	407	N53°31'	W6°26'
Killiney	KLY	378	N53°16'	W6°06'
Rush	RSH	326	N53°30'	W6°06'
Italy				
Alghero	ALG	382	N40°35'	E8°15'
Ciampino	CMP	412	N41°51'	E12°33'
Fiumicino	FN	421	N41°54'	E12°14'
Fiumicino	FW	345	N41°52'	E12°11'
Fiumicino	FE	354	N41°49'	E12°21'
Frosinone	FRS	371	N41°38'	E13°17'
Ostia	OST	321	N41°48'	E12°14'
Pratica Di Mara	PRA	339	N41°40'	E12°27'
Urbe	URB	285	N41°56'	E12°29'
Norway				
Omastrand	OMA	326	N60°13'	E5°59'
Vollo	VOL	391	N60°32'	E5°06'
Poland				
Przysucha	TMS	488	N51°21'	E22°38'
Warsaw	WAG	336	N52°12'	E20°48'
Warsaw	W	361	N52°08'	E20°59'
Warsaw	WAO	412	N52°05'	E21°01'
Warsaw	WAG	375	N52°10'	E20°56'
Spain				
Alcobendas	ACD	417	N40°35'	W3°40'
Arbacon	ARN	291	N40°57'	W3°07'
Barajas	MA	390	N40°24'	W3°29'
Barajas	BJ	308	N40°26'	W3°33'
Barajas	RS	326	N40°23'	W3°33'
Barajas	MD	369	N40°33'	W3°33'
Barcelona	QA	338	N41°16'	E1°59'
Getafe	GE	421	N40°12'	W3°50'
Lerida	LRD	404	N41°33'	E00°39'
Navas Del Rey	NVS	432	N40°22'	W4°14'

Location/Name	Ident	Freq	Lat	Long
Spain (continued)				
Sabadell	SBD	367	N41°31'	E2°06'
Somosierra	SMA	350	N41°08'	W3°34'
Torralba De Aragon	TRL	335	N41°56'	W00°30'
Villanueva	VNV	380	N41°12'	E1°42'
Sweden				
Skavasta	PEO	398	N58°47'	E17°02'
Skavasta	NW	364	N58°47'	E16°47'
Switzerland				
Gland	GLA	320	N46°24'	E6°14'
United Kingdom				
Blackbushe	BLK	328	N51°19'	W00°50'
Chiltern	CHT	277	N51°37'	W00°31'
Cumbernauld	CBN	374	N55°58'	W3°58'
Epsom	EPM	316	N51°19'	W00°22'
Fairoaks	FOS	348	N51°20'	W00°33'
Gatwick (London)	GY	365	N51°07'	W00°18'
Gatwick (London)	GE	338	N51°09'	W00°04'
Glasgow	AC	325	N55°48'	W4°32'
Glasgow	GLG	350	N55°55'	W4°20'
Heathrow (London)	OW	389	N51°27'	W00°34'
Heathrow (London)	OE	389	N51°27'	W00°20'
Henton	HEN	395	N51°45'	W00°47'
London City	LCY	322	N51°30'	E00°04'
Luton	LUT	345	N51°53'	W00°14'
Redhill	RDL	343	N51°12'	W00°08'
Stansted (London)	SAN	359	N51°56'	E00°18'
Westcott	WCO	335	N51°51'	W00°57'
Woodley	WOD	352	N51°27'	W00°52'

MIDDLE EAST

Airports

Jerusalem, Israel – Jerusalem

Ident	—	ATIS	—
Elev	2485	Rwy/Length/ILS/ID	30//111.9/IR
Lat	N31°51'		
Long	E35°13'		

Tel Aviv, Israel – Ben Gurion Intl

Ident	TLV	ATIS	132.50
Elev	135	Rwy/Length/ILS/ID	03/5840
Lat	N32°00'		21/5840
Long	E34°52'		08/11998
			26/11998/108.70/BA
			12/10210/110.30/BG
			30/10210

Amman, Jordan – Queen Alia Intl

Ident	—	ATIS	127.6
Elev	2395	Rwy/Length/ILS/ID	26L//110.9/IQA
Lat	N31°43'		08L//109.3/IQAN
Long	E35°59'		

Kuwait, Kuwait – Kuwait Intl

Ident	KWI	ATIS	118.30
Elev	210	Rwy/Length/ILS/ID	15L/11483/110.10/IKIC
Lat	N29°13'		33R/11483/110.50/IKID
Long	E47°58'		15R/11155
			33L/11155/109.50/IKIA

Riyadh, Saudi Arabia – King Khalid Intl

Ident	RUH	ATIS	118.60
Elev	2082	Rwy/Length/ILS/ID	15L/13780/109.5/IELF
Lat	N24°57'		33R/13780/109.10/IKIA
Long	E46°42'		15R/13780/110.50/ITIH
			33L/13780/110.10/IFAT

Istanbul, Turkey – Ataturk

Ident	IST	ATIS	128.20
Elev	158	Rwy/Length/ILS/ID	06/7546/110.30/IIST
Lat	N40°58'		24/7546/110.30/IIST
Long	E28°49'		18/9843/111.10/IISB
			36/9843/108.10/IYES

Aden, Yemen – Aden International

Ident	ADE	ATIS	118..70
Elev	12	Rwy/Length	8/10171
Lat	N12°49'		26/10171
Long	E45°01'		

VORs

Location/Name	Ident	Freq	Lat	Long
Israel				
Bengurion	BGN	115.40	N32°00'	E34°52'
Metzada	MZD	115.00	N31°19'	E35°23'
Natania	NAT	112.40	N32°20'	E34°58'
Kuwait				
Kuwait	KUA	115.50	N29°13'	E47°58'
Ras Al Mishab	RAS	116.40	N28°04'	E48°36'
Wafra	KFR	112.00	N28°37'	E47°57'
Saudi Arabia				
Al Ahsa	HSA	116.60	N25°16'	E49°29'
Al Kharj	AKJ	117.30	N24°04'	E47°24'
King Khalid	KIA	113.30	N24°53'	E46°45'
Magala	MGA	116.30	N26°13'	E47°16'
Riyadh	RIY	114.50	N24°43'	E46°43'
Thumamah	TIH	113.80	N25°09'	E46°33'
Turkey				
Beykoz	BKZ	117.30	N41°07'	E29°08'
Istanbul	IST	112.50	N40°58'	E28°48'
Tekirdag	EKI	116.30	N40°57'	E27°25'
Yalova	YAA	117.70	N40°34'	E29°22'

Location/Name	Ident	Freq	Lat	Long
Yemen				
Aden	KRA	112.50	N12°49'	E45°01'
Taiz	TAZ	113.60	N13°42'	E44°08'

NDBs

Location/Name	Ident	Freq	Lat	Long
Israel				
Jerusalem	IRM	366	N31°51'	E35°12'
Tel Aviv	LL	331	N32°03'	E34°46'
Kuwait				
Kuwait	WR	368	N29°18'	E47°55'
Turkey				
Cekmece	CEK	328	N41°00'	E28°31'
Istanbul	ST	340	N41°03'	E28°48'
Istanbul	IS	396	N41°03'	E28°48'
Toakapi	TOP	370	N41°00'	E28°59'
Yemen				
Aden	KRY	400	N12°49'	E45°°02'
Aden	AD	361	N12°52'	E45°°00'

PACIFIC OCEAN

Airports

Alice Springs, Australia – Alice Springs

Ident	ASP	ATIS	118.30
Elev	1789	Rwy/Length/ILS/ID	06/3376
Lat	S23°48'		24/3376
Long	E133°53'		12/7999/109.90/IAS
			30/7999
			17/3717
			35/3717

Brisbane, Australia – Brisbane

Ident	BNE	ATIS	125.50
Elev	13	Rwy/Length/ILS/ID	01/11680/109.50/IBA
Lat	S27°25'		19/11680/110.10/IBS
Long	E153°05'		14/5577
			32/5577

Darwin, Australia – Darwin

Ident	DRW	ATIS	133.10
Elev	103	Rwy/Length/ILS/ID	11/10906
Lat	S12°25'		29/10906/109.70/IDN
Long	E130°52'		18/5000
			36/5000

Melbourne, Australia – International

Ident	MEB	ATIS	114.10/132.70
Elev	434	Rwy/Length/ILS/ID	16/11998/109.70
Lat			34/11998
Long			09/7500
			27/7500/109.30/IMW

Perth, Australia – Perth Intl

Ident	PER	ATIS	123.80
Elev	67	Rwy/Length/ILS/ID	03/11299
Lat	S31°56'		21/11299/109.50/IGD
Long	E115°58'		06/7096
			24/7096
			11/5233
			29/5233

Sydney, Australia – Kingsford Smith

Ident	SYD	ATIS	127.60
Elev	21	Rwy/Length/ILS/ID	07/8301/109.90/ISY
Lat	S33°56'		25/8301
Long	E151°10'		16R/12999/109.50/IKS
			34L/12999/110.10/ISN
			16L/12999/110.9/ISS
			34R/12999/109.3/IKN

Christmas Island, Christmas Island – Christmas Island

Ident	XCH	ATIS	—
Elev	916	Rwy/Length	18/6900
Lat	S10°27'		36/6900
Long	E105°41'		

Nadi, Fiji – Nadi Intl

Ident	NAN	ATIS	119.10
Elev	57	Rwy/Length/ILS/ID	02/10499/109.90/INN
Lat	S17°45'		20/10499
Long	E177°26'		09/6998
			27/6998

Guam, Guam – Agana NAS

Ident	NGM	ATIS	118.10
Elev	297	Rwy/Length/ILS/ID	06R/8001
Lat	N13°28'		24L/8001
Long	E144°47'		06L/10014/110.30/IGUM
			24R/10014

Johnston Atoll, Johnston Atoll – Johnston Atoll

Ident	JON	ATIS	122.80
Elev	7	Rwy/Length	05/9000
Lat	N16°43'		23/9000
Long	W169°32'		

Midway Island, Midway Island – Midway NAF

Ident	MDY	ATIS	126.20
Elev	13	Rwy/Length	06/7900
Lat	N28°11'		24/7900
Long	W177°23'		

Auckland, New Zealand – Auckland Intl

Ident	AKL	ATIS	127.80
Elev	23	Rwy/Length/ILS/ID	05/11926/110.30/IAA
Lat	S37°00'		23/11926/109.90/IMG
Long	E174°47'		

Queenstown, New Zealand – Queenstown

Ident	ZQN	ATIS	118.10
Elev	1171	Rwy/Length	05/4000
Lat	S45°01'		23/4000
Long	E168°44'		14/3097 Grass
			32/3097 Grass

Wellington, New Zealand – Wellington Intl

Ident	WLG	ATIS	126.90
Elev	40	Rwy/Length/ILS/ID	16/6348/110.30/IEB
Lat	S41°19'		34/6348/109.90/IMP
Long	E174°48'		

Port Moresby, Papua New Guinea – Jackson's Intl

Ident	POM	ATIS	128.00
Elev	126	Rwy/Length/ILS/ID	14R/6798
Lat	S09°26'		32L/6798
Long	E147°13'		14L/9022/110.10/IWG
			32R/9022/109.50/IBB

Wake Island, Wake Island – Wake Island

Ident	AWK	ATIS	128.00
Elev	14	Rwy/Length	10/9859
Lat	N19°16'		28/9859
Long	E166°38'		

VORs

Location/Name	Ident	Freq	Lat	Long
Australia				
Alice Springs	AS	115.90	S23°47'	E133°52'
Avalon	AV	116.10	S38°03'	E144°27'
Ballidu	BIU	114.30	S30°35'	E116°46'
Bindook	BIK	116.80	S34°10'	E150°06'
Brisbane	BN	113.20	S27°22'	E153°08'
Christmas Island	XMX	112.40	S10°25'	E105°41'
Coolangatta	CG	112.30	S28°10'	E153°30'
Cowes	CWS	117.60	S38°30'	E145°12'
Darwin	DN	112.40	S12°24'	E130°51'
Darwin	DAR	113.70	S12°24'	E130°52'
Eildon Weir	ELW	112.30	S37°12'	E145°50'

Location/Name	Ident	Freq	Lat	Long
Australia (continued)				
Fentons Hill	FTH	115.30	S37°30'	E144°48'
Jacobs Well	JCW	116.50	S27°45'	E153°20'
Laravale	LAV	117.80	S28°05'	E152°55'
Maroochydore	MC	114.20	S26°36'	E153°05'
Melbourne	ML	114.10	S37°39'	E144°50'
Mt Mcquoid	MQD	117.30	S33°06'	E151°08'
Perth	PH	113.70	S31°56'	E115°57'
Sydney	SY	115.40	S33°56'	E151°10'
Tennant Creek	TNK	112.90	S19°38'	E134°10'
West Maitland	WMD	114.60	S32°45'	E151°31'
Wonthaggi	WON	115.90	S38°28'	E145°37'
Yarrowee	YWE	114.30	S37°44'	E143°45'
Fiji Island				
Nadi	NN	112.50	S17°39'	E177°23'
Nausori	NA	112.20	S18°02'	E178°33'
Guam				
Nimitz	UNZ	115.30	N13°27'	E144°43'
Johnston Island				
Johnston Island	JON	111.80	N16°44'	W169°32'
New Zealand				
Auckland	AA	114.80	S37°00'	E174°48'
Hamilton	HN	113.30	S37°51'	E175°19'
Invercargill	NV	112.90	S46°24'	E168°19'
Palmerston North	PM	113.40	S40°19'	E175°36'
Slope Hill	SH	113.60	S44°59'	E168°47'
Tory	TR	114.60	S41°11'	E174°21'
Wellington	WN	112.30	S41°20'	E174°49'
Whenuapai	WP	108.80	S36°47'	E174°37'
Papua New Guinea				
Girua	GUA	116.50	S08°44'	E148°15'
Port Moresby	PY	117.00	S09°27'	E147°12'
Wake Island				
Wake Island	AWK	113.50	N19°17'	E166°37'

NDBs

Location/Name	Ident	Freq	Lat	Long
Australia				
Alice Springs	AS	335	S23°47'	E133°52'
Amberley	AMB	359	S27°39'	E152°43'
Archerfield	AF	419	S27°34'	E153°00'
Bagot	BGT	308	S12°24'	E130°51'
Bolinda	BOL	362	S37°27'	E144°47'
Brisbane	BN	302	S27°24'	E153°05'
Calga	CAA	392	S33°24'	E151°10'
Caversham	CVM	329	S31°52'	E115°58'
Christmas Island	XMX	341	S10°25'	E105°41'
Cuderdin	CUN	293	S31°37'	E117°13'
Darwin	DN	344	S12°26'	E130°57'
East Lakes	ETL	218	S33°56'	E151°12'
Epping	EPP	377	S37°40'	E145°01'
Essendon	EN	356	S37°43'	E144°54'
Glenfield	GLF	317	S33°59'	E150°58'
Guildford	GFD	272	S31°56'	E115°56'
Howard Springs	HWS	257	S12°26'	E131°02'
Kilcoy	KCY	392	S26°55'	E152°34'
Meadow	MEA	230	S37°39'	E144°53'
Parkerville	PRL	352	S31°51'	E116°06'
Pearce	PEA	340	S31°39'	E116°01'
Perth	PH	400	S32°01'	E115°48'
Pingeuy	PIY	233	S32°32'	E117°04'
Plenty	PLE	218	S37°43'	E145°06'
Redland Bay	RLB	218	S27°37'	E153°18'
Rockdale	ROC	338	S37°35'	E144°49'
Simpsons Gap	SPG	362	S23°43'	E133°44'
Singleton	SGT	290	S32°33'	E151°15'
Temple Bar	TPB	352	S23°44'	E133°47'
Wallaby	WAY	372	S23°52'	E134°01'
West Pymble	WPB	254	S33°46'	E151°07'

Fiji Island

Location/Name	Ident	Freq	Lat	Long
Malolo	AL	385	S17°49'	E177°23'
Momi	MI	364	S17°54'	E177°19'
Nadi	NN	290	S17°47'	E177°25'
Navakai	VK	405	S17°47'	E177°25'
Navua	NV	281	S18°14'	E178°10'

Location/Name	Ident	Freq	Lat	Long
Guam				
Mt Macajna	AJA	385	N13°27'	E144°44'
Saipan	SN	312	N15°06'	E145°42'

Johnston Island

Location/Name	Ident	Freq	Lat	Long
Apollo	APO	388	N16°43'	W169°32'

New Zealand

Location/Name	Ident	Freq	Lat	Long
Alexandra	LX	386	S45°10'	E169°28'
Auckland	AA	374	S37°01'	E174°45'
Cape Campbell	CC	286	S41°44'	E174°16'
Newlands	NL	358	S41°13'	E174°49'
Queenstown	QN	362	S45°01'	E168°44'
Surrey	SY	350	S37°14'	E175°10'
Titahi Bay	TY	234	S41°07'	E174°49'
Waiuku	WI	254	S37°16'	E174°48'
Wellington	WN	298	S41°20'	E174°48'
Westpoint	OT	398	S37°03'	E174°36'
Whitford	HD	334	S36°57'	E175°00'

Papua New Guinea

Location/Name	Ident	Freq	Lat	Long
Girua	GUA	224	S08°44'	E148°15'
Jackson	JSN	380	S09°22'	E147°10'
Kubuna	KUB	1662	S08°41'	E146°45'
Parer	PRE	395	S09°19'	E147°08'
Port Moresby	PY	368	S09°27'	E147°13'
Tavai	TVI	350	S09°43'	E147°28'

SOUTH AMERICA

Airports

Buenos Aires, Argentina – Ezeiza Intl

Ident	EZE	ATIS	119.10
Elev	66	Rwy/Length/ILS/ID	11/10827/110.10/PC
Lat	S34°49'		29/10827
Long	W58°32'		17/9203
			35/9203/108.70/EZ
			05/7215
			23/7215

Ascension Island, Ascension Island – Ascension Aux AB

Ident	ASI	ATIS	—
Elev	273	Rwy/Length	14/10000
Lat	S07°58'		32/10000
Long	W14°23'		

La Paz, Bolivia – Kennedy Intl

Ident	LPB	ATIS	118.30
Elev	13313	Rwy/Length/ILS/ID	09R/13124/110.30/ILP
Lat	S16°30'		27L/13124
Long	W68°10'		09L/7480
			27R/7480
			04/6365
			22/6365

Brasilia, Brazil – Brasilia Intl

Ident	BSB	ATIS	127.80
Elev	3473	Rwy/Length/ILS/ID	11/10499/110.30/IBR
Lat	S15°51'		29/10499
Long	W47°54'		

Natal, Brazil – August Severo

Ident	NAT	ATIS	118.70
Elev	169	Rwy/Length	12/5988
Lat	S05°54'		30/5988
Long	W35°14'		16R/5906
			34L/5906
			16L/7448
			34R/7448

Rio De Janeiro, Brazil – Rio De Janeiro Intl. Galeao

Ident	GIG	ATIS	127.60
Elev	30	Rwy/Length/ILS/ID	10/13123/109.30/ITB
Lat	S22°48'		28/13123/111.50/ILM
Long	W43°15'		15/10433/110.30/IGL
			33/10433

Rio De Janeiro, Brazil – Santa Cruz AB

Ident	—	ATIS	—
Elev	10	Rwy/Length	—
Lat	S22°55'		
Long	W43°43'		

Rio De Janeiro, Brazil – Santos Dumont

Ident	—	ATIS	127.6
Elev	11	Rwy/Length/ILS/ID	20L//111.1/IRJ
Lat	S22°54'		
Long	W43°09'		

Isla De Pascua, Chile – Mateveri Intl.

Ident	—	ATIS	—
Elev	227	Rwy/Length/ILS/ID	10//110.3/IIPA
Lat	S27°09'		
Long	W109°25'		

Santiago, Chile – Arthur Merino Benite

Ident	SCL	ATIS	132.10
Elev	1554	Rwy/Length/ILS/ID	17/10499/110.30/IUEL
Lat	S33°23'		35/10499
Long	W70°47'		

Santafe De Bogata, Columbia – Eldorado Intl

Ident	BOG	ATIS	118.10
Elev	8355	Rwy/Length/ILS/ID	12/12467/109.90/IEDR
Lat	N04°42'		30/12467
Long	W74°08'		12/3423
			30/3423

Quito, Ecuador – Mariscal Sucre Intl

Ident	UIO	ATIS	118.10
Elev	9223	Rwy/Length/ILS/ID	17/10236/110.50
Lat	S00°08'		35/10236/110.50/IQO
Long	W78°29'		

Cayenne, French Guiana – Rochambeau

Ident	CAY	ATIS	118.10
Elev	26	Rwy/Length/ILS/ID	08/10499/110.30/CA
Lat	N04°49'		26/10499
Long	W52°21'		

Asuncion, Paraguay – Silvio Pettirossi

Ident	ASU	ATIS	118.10
Elev	292	Rwy/Length/ILS/ID	2/11001
Lat	S25°14'		20/11001/109.50/IPST
Long	W57°31'		

Lima, Peru – Jorge Chavez Intl

Ident	LIM	ATIS	118.10
Elev	112	Rwy/Length/ILS/ID	15/11506/109.70/IJCH
Lat	S12°01'		33/11506
Long	W77°07'		

VORs

Location/Name	Ident	Freq	Lat	Long
Argentina				
Ezeiza	EZE	116.50	S34°49'	W58°32'
General Belgrando	GBE	115.60	S35°45'	W58°27'
La Plata	PTA	113.70	S34°58'	W57°53'
Lobos	BOS	114.60	S35°12'	W59°08'
Moriano Moreno	ENO	112.90	S34°33'	W58°47'
San Fernando	FDO	114.40	S34°27'	W58°35'
Ascension Island				
Ascension Aux	ASI	112.20	S07°58'	W14°23'
Azores				
Lajes	LM	112.30	N38°47'	W27°06'
Lajes	LAJ	110.80	N38°42'	W27°07'
Santa Maria	VSM	113.70	N36°57'	W25°10'
Bolivia				
Arica	ARI	116.50	S18°21'	W70°20'
Cochabamba	CBA	112.10	S17°25'	W66°10'
La Paz	PAZ	115.70	S16°30'	W68°13'
San Borja	BOR	117.50	S14°55'	W66°44'
Brazil				
Anapolis	ANP	115.40	S16°15'	W48°59'
Brasilia	BRS	115.90	S15°52'	W48°01'
Caxias	CAX	113.00	S22°46'	W43°20'
Goiania	GOI	112.70	S16°37'	W49°12'
Marica	MRC	114.00	S22°58'	W42°53'
Mossoro	MSS	112.40	S05°11'	W37°21'
Natal	NTL	114.30	S05°54'	W35°14'

Location/Name	Ident	Freq	Lat	Long
Brazil (continued)				
Pirai	PAI	115.00	S22°27'	W43°50'
Porto	PCX	114.60	S22°42'	W42°51'
Santa Cruz	SCR	113.60	S22°57'	W43°43'
Chile				
Los Cerrillos	SCL	112.30	S33°29'	W70°42'
Quintero	ERO	113.30	S32°47'	W71°30'
Santiago	AMB	116.10	S33°25'	W70°47'
Santo Domingo	SNO	113.70	S33°39'	W71°36'
Tabon	TBN	113.90	S32°55'	W70°50'
Columbia				
Bogota	BOG	114.70	N04°50'	W74°19'
Girardot	GIR	117.30	N04°11'	W74°52'
Mariquita	MQU	116.10	N05°12'	W74°55'
Villavicencio	VVC	116.70	N04°04'	W73°23'
Ecuador				
Ambato	AMV	112.70	S01°16'	W78°32'
Condorcocha	QIT	115.30	S00°02'	W78°30'
Ipiales	IPI	113.60	N00°51'	W77°40'
Monjas Sur	QMS	115.00	S00°13'	W78°28'
French Guiana				
Rochambeau	CYR	115.10	N04°48'	W52°22'
Parauay				
Asuncion	VAS	115.90	S25°08'	W57°29'
Formosa	FSA	115.60	S26°12'	W58°13'
Peru				
Asia	ASI	115.00	S12°45'	W76°36'
Chimbote	BTE	112.50	S09°08'	W78°31'
Lima	LIM	114.50	S12°00'	W77°07'
Pisco	SCO	114.10	S13°44'	W76°12'
Salinas	SLS	114.70	S11°17'	W77°34'

NDBs

Location/Name	Ident	Freq	Lat	Long
Argentina				
Ezeiza	OC	330	S34°48'	W58°37'
Ezeiza	OA	270	S34°53'	W58°30'
Ascension Island				
Ascension Island	ASN	360	S07°56'	W14°24'
Azores				
Ponta Delgada	MGL	371	N37°44'	W25°35'
Ponta Delgada	PD	351	N37°44'	W25°40'
Santa Maria	SMA	323	N36°59'	W25°10'
Santa Maria	STA	240	N36°56'	W25°10'
Boliva				
Charana	CHA	310	S17°35'	W69°26'
Coroico	CRC	305	S16°11'	W67°43'
La Paz	R	330	S16°30'	W68°13'
La Paz	LPZ	350	S16°29'	W68°11'
Brazil				
Afonsos	AFS	270	S22°52'	W43°22'
Brasilia	BRS	340	S15°52'	W48°01'
Campina Grande	CPG	230	S07°16'	W35°53'
Caxias	CAX	400	S22°45'	W43°20'
Cocho	CH	240	S15°51'	W47°53'
Formosa	FRM	210	S15°33'	W47°21'
Ilha	YLA	330	S22°47'	W43°10'
Joao Pessoa	JPS	320	S07°08'	W34°57'
Luziania	LUZ	400	S16°15'	W47°57'
Meriti	IT	290	S22°49'	W43°21'
Mossoro	MSS	275	S05°11'	W37°21'
Natal	NTL	400	S05°54'	W35°14'
Nova	NOA	215	S22°43'	W43°28'
Oiapoque	OIA	340	N03°51'	W51°48'
Paiol	PP	415	S22°52'	W43°09'
Rasa	IH	315	S23°03'	W43°08'

Location/Name	Ident	Freq	Lat	Long
Chile				
Casablanca	CAS	328	S33°18'	W71°23'
Huechun	HUN	250	S33°02'	W70°48'
Lo Castro	CAS	220	S33°18'	W70°47'
Quintero	ERO	384	S32°44'	W71°29'
Tabon	TBN	288	S32°55'	W70°48'
Columbia				
Ambalema	ABL	300	N04°47'	W74°46'
Bogota	BOG	388	N04°50'	W74°19'
Bogota	ED	244	N04°46'	W74°13'
El Paso	EPO	225	N04°30'	N075°30'
Romeo	R	274	N04°40'	W74°06'
Techo	TEH	284	N04°38'	W74°09'
Zipaquira	ZIP	294	N05°01'	W74°01'
Equador				
Ascazubi	ZUI	290	S00°04'	W78°17'
Olmedo	OLM	400	N00°10'	W78°03'
Quito	UIO	350	S00°10'	W78°28'
French Guiana				
Rochambeau	FXC	327	N04°49'	W52°21'
St Laurent Du Maroni	CW	283	N05°28'	W54°01'
Paraguay				
Asuncion	ASU	360	S25°14'	W57°30'
Asuncion	VB	350	S25°16'	W57°31'
Asuncion	ST	340	S25°08'	W57°29'
Paraguari	PRI	350	S25°36'	W57°08'
Peru				
Las Palmas	LP	300	S12°13'	W77°01'
Lima-Callao	CH	248	S11°59'	W77°07'
Oyon	YON	360	S10°39'	W76°46'
Ventanilla	JC	375	S11°55'	W77°08'

UNITED STATES

Alabama

Airports

Huntsville, AL – Madison County

Ident	HSV	ATIS	121.25
Elev	630	Rwy/Length/ILS/ID	18R/8000/109.30/IHSV
Lat	N34°38'		36L/8000/108.50/IELL
Long	W86°46'		18L/10000/111.90/ITVN
			36R/10000

Montgomery, AL – Dannelly Field

Ident	MGM	ATIS	124.42
Elev	221	Rwy/Length/ILS/ID	03/4010
Lat	N32°17'		21/4010
Long	W86°23'		10/9001/109.90/IMGM
			28/9001/108.50/IDLV

VORs

Location/Name	Type	Ident	Freq	Lat	Long	Elev
Andalusia	VOR	UIA	110.20	N31°18'	W86°23'	0
Brookley	VORTAC	BFM	112.80	N30°36'	W88°03'	10
Brookwood	VORTAC	OKW	111.00	N33°14'	W87°15'	649
Cahaba	VOR	CAQ	114.90	N32°20'	W86°59'	160
Cairns	VOR	OZR	111.20	N31°16'	W85°43'	300
Decatur	VOR-DME	DCU	112.80	N34°38'	W86°56'	590
Enterprise	VOR	EDN	116.60	N31°17'	W85°54'	369
Eufaula	VORTAC	EUF	109.20	N31°57'	W85°07'	280
Gadsden	VOR-DME	GAD	112.30	N33°58'	W86°05'	586
Hamilton	VORTAC	HAB	110.40	N34°11'	W88°00'	810
Hanchey	VOR	HEY	110.60	N31°22'	W85°39'	300
Monroeville	VORTAC	MVC	116.80	N31°27'	W87°21'	417
Montgomery	VORTAC	MGM	112.10	N32°13'	W86°19'	270
Muscle Shoals	VORTAC	MSL	116.50	N34°42'	W87°29'	580
Rocket	VORTAC	RQZ	112.20	N34°47'	W86°38'	1200
Semmes	VORTAC	SJI	115.30	N30°43'	W88°21'	190
Talladega	VOR-DME	TDG	108.80	N33°34'	W86°02'	530
Troy	VOR	TOI	110.00	N31°51'	W86°00'	400
Tuscaloosa	VORTAC	TCL	117.80	N33°15'	W87°32'	370
Tuskegee	VOR-DME	TGE	117.30	N32°29'	W85°40'	490
Vulcan	VORTAC	VUZ	114.40	N33°40'	W86°53'	750
Wiregrass	VORTAC	RRS	111.60	N31°17'	W85°25'	360

NDBs

Location/Name	Ident	Freq	Lat	Long	Elev
Alexander City	DER	382	N32°52'	W85°57'	641
Bessemer	BEQ	368	N33°18'	W86°55'	660
Blood (LOM/NDB)	TO	365	N31°49'	W86°06'	500
Bogga (LOM)	AN	211	N33°32'	W85°55'	579
Boll Weevil	BVG	308	N31°20'	W85°58'	—
Brantley	XBR	410	N31°33'	W86°17'	—
Calera	AOA	215	N33°07'	W86°46'	610
Capshaw	CWH	350	N34°46'	W86°46'	—
Choctaw	BCZ	228	N32°06'	W88°07'	115
Cole Spring	CPP	230	N34°22'	W86°49'	830
Fayette	FDF	204	N33°42'	W87°48'	359
Fort Payne	FTP	426	N34°31'	W85°40'	900
Gragg-Wade	GGY	338	N32°51'	W86°36'	590
Greensboro	EOG	417	N32°36'	W87°39'	160
Hanchey	HYE	221	N31°22'	W85°38'	300
Judd	JUY	264	N31°18'	W86°23'	330
Lowe	LOR	269	N31°21'	W85°44'	—
Marengo	RZO	391	N32°24'	W88°00'	109
Marra (LOM)	MG	245	N32°18'	W86°30'	—
Opole (LOM)	AU	423	N32°30'	W85°26'	515
Persimmon	PRN	359	N31°51'	W86°36'	625
Pollk (LOM/NDB)	SE	344	N32°16'	W86°55'	225
Redstone	HUA	287	N34°41'	W86°41'	—
Roeby (LOM)	RO	394	N33°36'	W86°40'	838
Ruckr (LOM/NDB)	OZ	212	N31°13'	W85°48'	—
Saratoga	ARF	296	N34°15'	W86°13'	1049
Spring Hill	XNE	281	N31°41'	W85°58'	495
Summerdale	ESU	204	N30°29'	W87°43'	60
Sylacauga	SCD	284	N33°10'	W86°19'	670
Tuske (LOM)	TC	362	N33°09'	W87°40'	—
Wilcox Co	IWE	350	N31°58'	W87°20'	141
Wisle (LOM/NDB)	MO	248	N30°45'	W88°18'	—

Alaska

Airports

Anchorage, AK – Anchorage Intl

Ident	ANC	ATIS	118.40
Elev	144	Rwy/Length/ILS/ID	14/10496
Lat	N61°10'		32/10496
Long	W149°59'		6L/10600/109.90/ITGN
			24R/10600
			6R/10897/111.30/IANC
			24L/10897

Barrow, AK – Wiley Post-Will Rodgers Mem

Ident	PBI	ATIS	123.60
Elev	44	Rwy/Length/ILS/ID	06/6500/109.10/IBRW
Lat	N71°17'		24/6500
Long	W156°45'		

Fairbanks, AK – Fairbanks Intl

Ident	FAI	ATIS	124.40
Elev	434	Rwy/Length/ILS/ID	1L/10300/109.10/ICNA
Lat	N64°48'		19R/10300/110.30/IFAI
Long	W147°51'		1R/3200
			19L/3200
			18/3980 Gravel
			36/3980 Gravel

Adak Island, AK – Adak Island

Ident	NUD	ATIS	—
Elev	18	Rwy/Length	05/7790
Lat	N51°52'		23/7790
Long	W176°38'		18/7606
			36/7606

Unalaska, AK – Unalaska

Ident	DUT	ATIS	122.60
Elev	22	Rwy/Length	12/3900
Lat	N53°53'		30/3900
Long	W166°32'		

VORs

Location/Name	Type	Ident	Freq	Lat	Long	Elev
Adak	DME	NUD	113.00	N51°52'	W176°40'	—
Amchitka	VORTAC	NIA	113.20	N51°22'	E179°16'	—
Anchorage	VOR-DME	ANC	114.30	N61°09'	W150°12'	280
Annette Island	VORTAC	ANN	117.10	N55°03'	W131°34'	174
Barrow	VORTAC	BRW	116.20	N71°16'	W156°47'	40
Bethel	VORTAC	BET	114.10	N60°47'	W161°49'	130
Bettles	VORTAC	BTT	116.00	N66°54'	W151°32'	645
Big Delta	VORTAC	BIG	114.90	N64°00'	W145°43'	1230
Big Lake	VORTAC	BGQ	112.50	N61°34'	W149°58'	160
Biorka Island	VORTAC	BKA	113.80	N56°51'	W135°33'	240
Cold Bay	VORTAC	CDB	112.60	N55°16'	W162°46'	97
Deadhorse	VORTAC	SCC	113.90	N70°11'	W148°24'	50
Dillingham	VOR-DME	DLG	116.40	N58°59'	W158°33'	130
Dutch Harbor	DME	DUT	113.90	N53°54'	W166°32'	278
Emmonak	VOR-DME	ENM	117.80	N62°47'	W164°29'	14
Fairbanks	VORTAC	FAI	108.20	N64°48'	W148°00'	1493
Fort Yukon	VORTAC	FYU	114.40	N66°34'	W145°16'	425

Location/Name	Type	Ident	Freq	Lat	Long	Elev
Galena	VORTAC	GAL	114.80	N64°44'	W156°46'	130
Gulkana	VORTAC	GKN	115.60	N62°09'	W145°27'	1544
Homer	VORTAC	HOM	114.60	N59°42'	W151°27'	694
Hooper Bay	VOR-DME	HPB	115.20	N61°30'	W166°08'	176
Huslia	VOR-DME	HSL	117.40	N65°42'	W156°22'	122
Inuvik	VOR-DME	YEV	112.50	N68°18'	W133°32'	538
Johnstone Point	VORTAC	JOH	116.70	N60°28'	W146°35'	47
Kenai	VOR-DME	ENA	117.60	N60°36'	W151°11'	109
King Salmon	VORTAC	AKN	112.80	N58°43'	W156°45'	80
Kipnuk	VOR-DME	IIK	115.90	N59°56'	W164°02'	1
Kodiak	VORTAC	ODK	117.10	N57°46'	W152°20'	130
Kotzebue	VOR-DME	OTZ	115.70	N66°53'	W162°32'	120
Kukuliak	VOR-DME	ULL	117.30	N63°41'	W170°28'	830
Level Island	VOR-DME	LVD	116.50	N56°28'	W133°04'	100
Mc Grath	VORTAC	MCG	115.50	N62°57'	W155°36'	340
Middleton Island	VOR-DME	MDO	115.30	N59°25'	W146°21'	121
Moses Point	VOR-DME	MOS	116.30	N64°41'	W162°04'	14
Nenana	VORTAC	ENN	115.80	N64°35'	W149°04'	1600
Nome	VORTAC	OME	115.00	N64°29'	W165°15'	100
Northway	VORTAC	ORT	116.30	N62°56'	W141°54'	1178
Selawik	VOR-DME	WLK	114.20	N66°35'	W159°59'	11
Shemya	VORTAC	SYA	109.00	N52°43'	E174°03'	68
Sisters Island	VORTAC	SSR	114.00	N58°10'	W135°15'	50
Sparrevohn	VOR-DME	SQA	117.20	N61°05'	W155°38'	2501
Talkeetna	VOR-DME	TKA	116.20	N62°17'	W150°06'	360
Tanana	VOR-DME	TAL	116.60	N65°10'	W152°10'	390
Unalakleet	VORTAC	UNK	116.90	N63°53'	W160°41'	430
Yakutat	VORTAC	YAK	113.30	N59°30'	W139°38'	35

NDBs

Location/Name	Ident	Freq	Lat	Long	Elev
Adak	NUD	347	N51°55'	W176°34'	—
Ambler	AMF	403	N67°06'	W157°51'	—
Aniak	ANI	359	N61°35'	W159°35'	—
Anvik	ANV	365	N62°38'	W160°11'	—
Attu	ATU	375	N52°49'	E173°10'	—
Barter Island	BTI	308	N70°07'	W143°38'	—
Bear Creek	BCC	212	N65°10'	W152°12'	—
Bethel (LMM)	ET	344	N60°47'	W161°49'	—
Bishop	BZP	331	N64°44'	W156°48'	—
Borland	HBT	390	N55°18'	W160°31'	—
Browerville	VIR	281	N71°16'	W156°47'	—
Bruck (LOM)	AN	387	N61°10'	W150°10'	—
Buckland	BVK	325	N65°58'	W161°08'	26
Cairn Mountain	CRN	281	N61°05'	W155°33'	—
Campbell Lake	CMQ	338	N61°10'	W150°02'	—
Cape Lisburne	LUR	385	N68°51'	W166°04'	—
Cape Newenham	EHM	385	N58°39'	W162°04'	—

Location/Name	Ident	Freq	Lat	Long	Elev
Cape Romanzof	CZF	275	N61°47'	W165°58'	—
Chena	CUN	257	N64°50'	W147°29'	—
Clam Cove	CMJ	396	N55°20'	W131°41'	—
Coghlan Island	CGL	212	N58°21'	W134°41'	—
Delta Junction	DJN	347	N64°01'	W145°41'	—
Dutch Harbor	DUT	283	N53°54'	W166°32'	—
Eagle	EAA	519	N64°46'	W141°08'	—
Elephant	EEF	391	N58°10'	W135°15'	—
Elfee (LOM/NDB)	CD	341	N55°17'	W162°47'	—
Evansville	EAV	391	N66°53'	W151°33'	—
Farewell Lake	FXW	412	N62°32'	W153°37'	—
Fort Davis	FDV	529	N64°29'	W165°18'	—
Fort Richardson	FRN	196	N61°16'	W149°38'	—
Fox	FOX	356	N64°58'	W147°34'	—
Fredericks Point	FPN	372	N56°47'	W132°49'	—
Galbraith Lake	GBH	417	N68°28'	W149°29'	—
Gambell	GAM	369	N63°46'	W171°44'	—
Glacier River	GCR	404	N60°29'	W145°28'	—
Glennallen	GLA	248	N62°11'	W145°28'	—
Gold	OYN	208	N64°30'	W165°26'	—
Gustavus	GAV	219	N58°25'	W135°42'	—
Haines	HNS	245	N59°12'	W135°25'	—
Hinchinbrook	HBK	362	N60°23'	W146°05'	—
Ice Pool	ICW	525	N64°32'	W149°04'	—
Iliamna	ILI	328	N59°44'	W154°54'	209
Kachemak	ACE	277	N59°38'	W151°30'	—
Koyuk	KKA	299	N64°55'	W161°08'	1026
Kulik Lake	HCP	334	N59°01'	W155°36'	—
Mendenhall	MND	332	N58°21'	W134°38'	—
Minchumina	MHM	227	N63°53'	W152°18'	—
Mineral Creek	MNL	524	N61°07'	W146°21'	—
Mt Edgecumbe	IME	414	N57°02'	W135°22'	—
Nabesna	AES	390	N62°57'	W141°53'	—
Nanwak	AIX	323	N60°23'	W166°12'	—
Noatak	OQK	414	N67°34'	W162°58'	—
Norton Bay	OAY	263	N64°41'	W162°03'	—
Oliktok	OLI	329	N70°29'	W149°53'	—
Oscarville	OSE	251	N60°47'	W161°52'	—
Peters Creek	PEE	305	N62°19'	W150°05'	—
Pitsand	PYC	290	N70°19'	W149°38'	—
Point Hope	PHO	221	N68°20'	W166°47'	—
Point Lay	PIZ	347	N69°44'	W163°00'	—
Port Heiden	PDN	371	N56°57'	W158°38'	—
Priblof	SRI	399	N56°34'	W169°38'	—
Prospect	PPC	340	N66°49'	W150°38'	—
Prudhoe Bay	PUO	368	N70°14'	W148°23'	—
Puntilla Lake	PTI	397	N62°04'	W152°43'	—
Put River	PVQ	234	N70°13'	W148°25'	—
Saldo (LOM/NDB)	SALDO	400	N58°44'	W156°46'	—

Location/Name	Ident	Freq	Lat	Long	Elev
Shemya	SYA	221	N52°43'	E174°03'	—
Shishmaref	SHH	365	N66°15'	W166°03'	—
Sitka	SIT	358	N56°51'	W135°32'	—
Skwentna	SKW	269	N61°57'	W151°12'	—
Soldotna	OLT	346	N60°28'	W150°52'	—
Summit	UMM	326	N63°19'	W149°07'	—
Sumner Strait	SQM	529	N56°27'	W133°05'	—
Takotna River	VTR	350	N62°56'	W155°33'	—
Tin City	TNC	347	N65°33'	W167°54'	—
Togiak	TOG	393	N59°03'	W160°22'	—
Umiat	UMT	360	N69°22'	W152°08'	—
Wearr (LOM)	FA	230	N64°53'	W147°42'	—
Wessels	ESS	260	N59°25'	W146°20'	—
Wildwood	IWW	379	N60°35'	W151°12'	—
Wiley	IEY	248	N71°17'	W156°48'	—
Wood River	BTS	429	N58°59'	W158°32'	—
Woody Island	RWO	394	N57°46'	W152°19'	—
Wrangell	RGL	206	N56°29'	W132°23'	—
Yakataga	CYT	209	N60°05'	W142°29'	—
Yukon River	FTO	242	N66°34'	W145°12'	—

Arizona

Airports

Grand Canyon, AZ – Grand Canyon Ntnl Pk

Ident	GCN	ATIS	124.30
Elev	6606	Rwy/Length/ILS/ID	03/8999/108.90/IGCN
Lat	N35°57'		21/8999
Long	W112°08'		

Phoenix, AZ – Sky Harbor Intl

Ident	PHX	ATIS	124.30
Elev	1133	Rwy/Length/ILS/ID	8R/10300/108.30/IPHX
Lat	N33°26'		26L/10300/111.75/IPZZ
Long	W112°00'		8L/110001
			26R/110001

Tucson, AZ – Avra Valley

Ident	E14	ATIS	—
Elev	2031	Rwy/Length	03/4200
Lat	N32°24'		21/4200
Long	W111°13'		

VORs

Location/Name	Type	Ident	Freq	Lat	Long	Elev
Bard	VORTAC	BZA	116.80	N32°46'	W114°36'	130
Buckeye	VORTAC	BXK	110.60	N33°27'	W112°49'	1060
Cochise	VORTAC	CIE	115.80	N32°02'	W109°45'	4230
Douglas	VORTAC	DUG	108.80	N31°28'	W109°36'	4160
Drake	VORTAC	DRK	114.10	N34°42'	W112°28'	4960
Flagstaff	VOR-DME	FLG	108.20	N35°08'	W111°40'	7020
Gila Bend	VORTAC	GBN	116.60	N32°57'	W112°40'	790
Grand Canyon	VOR-DME	GCN	113.10	N35°57'	W112°08'	6670
Kingman	VOR-DME	IGM	108.80	N35°15'	W113°56'	3410
Libby	VOR	FHU	111.60	N31°35'	W110°20'	4625
Nogales	VOR-DME	OLS	108.20	N31°24'	W110°50'	3870
Page	VOR-DME	PGA	117.60	N36°55'	W111°27'	4245
Peach Springs	VORTAC	PGS	112.00	N35°37'	W113°32'	4760
Phoenix	VORTAC	PXR	115.60	N33°25'	W111°58'	1180
Pine Bluff	VORTAC	PBF	116.00	N34°14'	W91°55'	210
Saint Johns	VORTAC	SJN	112.30	N34°25'	W109°08'	6840
San Simon	VORTAC	SSO	115.40	N32°16'	W109°15'	3600
Stanfield	VORTAC	TFD	114.80	N32°53'	W111°54'	1316
Tuba City	VORTAC	TBC	113.50	N36°07'	W111°16'	5060
Tucson	VORTAC	TUS	116.00	N32°05'	W110°54'	2670
Willie	VORTAC	IWA	113.30	N33°18'	W111°39'	1370
Winslow	VORTAC	INW	112.60	N35°03'	W110°47'	4910

NDBs

Location/Name	Ident	Freq	Lat	Long	Elev
Dragoo	DAO	410	N31°35'	W110°20'	4646
Falcon Field	FFZ	281	N33°27'	W111°43'	1392
Glendale	GEU	215	N33°31'	W112°17'	1083
Globe	GAZ	255	N33°21'	W110°39'	3195
Golden Eagle	OEG	413	N32°51'	W114°26'	200
Nogales	ENZ	394	N31°25'	W110°50'	3915
Pulliam	PUU	379	N35°08'	W111°40'	6994
Robles	RBJ	220	N32°04'	W111°21'	2607
Ryan	RYN	338	N32°08'	W111°09'	2415
Scottsdale	SDL	224	N33°37'	W111°54'	1542
Sedona	SEZ	334	N34°49'	W111°48'	—
Show Low	SOW	206	N34°16'	W110°00'	6411
Window Rock	AWR	254	N35°39'	W109°04'	—

Arkansas

Airports

Little Rock, AR – Adams Field

Ident	LIT	ATIS	125.65
Elev	260	Rwy/Length/ILS/ID	4L/6870/110.30/ILIT
Lat	N34°43'		22R/6870/110.30/IAAY
Long	W92°13'		4R/6155
			22L/6155/110.70/IBWY
			18/5084
			36/5084

VORs

Location/Name	Type	Ident	Freq	Lat	Long	Elev
Drake	VOR-DME	DAK	108.80	N36°02'	W94°11'	1530
El Dorado	VORTAC	ELD	115.50	N33°15'	W92°44'	230
Flippin	VOR-DME	FLP	112.80	N36°17'	W92°27'	780
Fort Smith	VORTAC	FSM	110.40	N35°23'	W94°16'	430
Gilmore	VOR-DME	GQE	113.00	N35°20'	W90°28'	211
Gosnell	VOR	GOJ	111.80	N35°57'	W89°56'	255
Harrison	VOR-DME	HRO	112.50	N36°19'	W93°12'	1400
Hot Springs	VOR-DME	HOT	110.00	N34°28'	W93°05'	530
Jonesboro	VOR-DME	JBR	108.60	N35°52'	W90°35'	250
Little Rock	VORTAC	LIT	113.90	N34°40'	W92°10'	240
Monticello	VORTAC	MON	111.60	N33°33'	W91°42'	280
Razorback	VORTAC	RZC	116.40	N36°14'	W94°07'	1330
Texarkana	VORTAC	TXK	116.30	N33°30'	W94°04'	270
Walnut Ridge	VORTAC	ARG	114.50	N36°06'	W90°57'	260

NDBs

Location/Name	Ident	Freq	Lat	Long	Elev
Arkadelphia	ADF	275	N34°03'	W93°06'	—
Ash Flat	AJX	344	N36°10'	W91°36'	815
Bakky (LOM)	HR	233	N36°11'	W93°09'	—
Bridge	BDQ	208	N35°08'	W92°42'	320
Brinkley	BKZ	242	N34°52'	W91°10'	—
Camden	CDH	335	N33°36'	W92°46'	—
Carter	CJD	263	N36°27'	W94°04'	—
Clarksville	CZE	201	N35°28'	W93°25'	450
Conway	CWS	302	N35°05'	W92°25'	317
Crossett	CRT	396	N33°10'	W91°53'	181
De Queen	DEQ	281	N34°02'	W94°23'	—

Location/Name	Ident	Freq	Lat	Long	Elev
Dumas	DZM	305	N33°53'	W91°31'	163
Forrest City	FCY	332	N34°56'	W90°46'	—
Heber Springs	HBZ	296	N35°30'	W92°00'	625
Hicks	IUI	299	N35°56'	W89°50'	254
Hope	HPC	362	N33°43'	W93°38'	340
Hossy (LOM/NDB)	HO	385	N34°25'	W93°11'	471
Independence Co	INY	317	N35°41'	W91°47'	470
Lados (LOM)	EL	418	N33°17'	W92°43'	140
Lasky (LOM/NDB)	LI	353	N34°40'	W92°18'	—
Lawrence Co	TNZ	227	N36°12'	W90°55'	316
Magnolia	AGO	266	N33°13'	W93°12'	311
Malvern	MVQ	215	N34°20'	W92°45'	535
Mena	MEZ	242	N34°32'	W94°12'	1055
Morrilton	MPJ	410	N35°07'	W92°55'	—
Newport	EWP	400	N35°38'	W91°10'	237
Ozark	OZZ	329	N35°30'	W93°50'	—
Peno Bottoms	AFT	311	N35°19'	W94°28'	—
Russellville	RUE	379	N35°15'	W93°05'	385
Searcy	SRC	323	N35°12'	W91°43'	260
Siloam Springs	SLG	284	N36°11'	W94°29'	1625
Stuttgart	SGT	269	N34°39'	W91°35'	226
Tecco (LOM)	TX	247	N33°31'	W93°54'	260
Thompson-Robbins	HEE	251	N34°34'	W90°40'	240
Toneyville	TYV	290	N34°57'	W92°01'	—
Walcott	PZX	221	N36°01'	W90°35'	471
Warren	REN	226	N33°32'	W92°05'	180
West Memphis	AWM	362	N35°08'	W90°13'	212
Wilcox	VLX	348	N35°52'	W92°05'	783
Wizer (LOM/NDB)	FS	223	N35°21'	W94°13'	—

California

Airports

Alameda, CA – Alameda NAS/Nimitz Field

Ident	NGZ	ATIS	—
Elev	14	Rwy	07
Lat	N37°47'		25
Long	W122°19'		13
			31

Angwin,CA – Parrett

Ident	203	ATIS	—
Elev	1848	Rwy/Length	—
Lat	N38°34'		
Long	W122°26'		

Auburn, CA – Auburn

Ident	AUN	ATIS	—
Elev	1520	Rwy/Length	—
Lat	N38°57'		
Long	W121°04'		

Avalon,CA – Catalina Island

Ident	AVX	ATIS	—
Elev	1602	Rwy/Length	04/3240
Lat	N33°24'		22/3240
Long	W118°24'		

Beckwourth, CA – Nervino

Ident	O02	ATIS	—
Elev	4894	Rwy/Length	—
Lat	N39°49'		
Long	W120°21'		

Burbank, CA – Glendale-Pasadena

Ident	BUR	ATIS	134.5
Elev	775	Rwy/Length	—
Lat	N34°12'		
Long	W118°21'		

Byron, CA – Byron

Ident	C83	ATIS	—
Elev	76	Rwy/Length	—
Lat	N37°49'		
Long	W121°37'		

Cameron, CA – Cameron Park

Ident	O61	ATIS	—
Elev	1286	Rwy/Length	—
Lat	N38°41'		
Long	W120°59'		

Carlsbad, CA – McClellan-Palomar

Ident	CRQ	ATIS	120.15
Elev	328	Rwy/Length	06/4700
Lat	N33°71'		24/4700
Long	W117°16'		

Carmel Valley, CA – Carmel Valley

Ident	O62	ATIS	—
Elev	450	Rwy/Length	—
Lat	N36°28'		
Long	W121°43'		

Chico, CA – Chico Muni

Ident	CIC	ATIS	—
Elev	238	Rwy/Length	13L/6724
Lat	N39°47'		31R/6724
Long	W121°51'		13R/3005
			31L/3005

Chino, CA – Chino

Ident	CNO	ATIS	121.15
Elev	650	Rwy/Length	03/6032
Lat	N33°58'		21/6032
Long	W117°38'		08/4856
			26/4856

Clarksburg, CA – Borges

Ident	C14	ATIS	—
Elev	12	Rwy/Length	—
Lat	N38°26'		
Long	W121°30'		

Columbia, CA – Columbia

Ident	O22	ATIS	—
Elev	2118	Rwy/Length	17/4670
Lat	N38°01'		35/4670
Long	W120°24'		11/2600 Grass
			28/2600 Grass

Compton, CA – Compton

Ident	CPM	ATIS	—
Elev	97	Rwy/Length	7R/3670
Lat	N33°53'		25L/3670
Long	W118°14'		7L/3670
			25R/3670

Concord, CA – Buchanan Field

Ident	CCR	ATIS	124.7
Elev	23	Rwy/Length/ILS/ID	1R/2768
Lat	N37°59'		19L/2768
Long	W122°03'		1L/4400
			19R/4400/108.5/ICCR
			14R/2800
			32L/2800
			14L/4601
			32R/4601

Corona, CA – Corona Muni

Ident	L66	ATIS	—
Elev	533	Rwy/Length	07/3200
Lat	N33°53'		25/3200
Long	W117°36'		

Crows Landing, CA – Crows Landing NALF

Ident	NRC	ATIS	—
Elev	165	Rwy	12
Lat	N37°24'		30
Long	W121°06'		17
			35

Davis, CA – University

Ident	00S	ATIS	—
Elev	68	Rwy/Length	—
Lat	N38°31'		
Long	W121°47'		

Davis Woodland Winters, CA – Yolo Co.

Ident	2Q3	ATIS	—
Elev	98	Rwy/Length	—
Lat	N38°34'		
Long	W121°51'		

El Monte, CA – El Monte

Ident	EMT	ATIS	118.75
Elev	296	Rwy/Length	01/3995
Lat	N34°05'		19/3995
Long	W118°02'		

Elk Grove, CA – Sunset Skyranch

Ident	Q40	ATIS	—
Elev	54	Rwy/Length	—
Lat	N38°23'		
Long	W121°19'		

Emigrant Gap, CA – Blue Canyon/Nyack

Ident	BLU	ATIS	—
Elev	5284	Rwy/Length	—
Lat	N39°16'		
Long	W120°42'		

Fallbrook, CA – Fallbrook Community Airpark

Ident	L18	ATIS	—
Elev	708	Rwy/Length	18/2160
Lat	N33°21'		36/2160
Long	W117°14'		

Fairfield, CA – Travis AFB

Ident	SUU	ATIS	116.4
Elev	62	Rwy/Length/ILS/ID	03L//110.1/ITXV
Lat	N38°15'		21L//110.1/ISUU
Long	W121°55'		

Franklin, CA – Franklin

Ident	Q53	ATIS	—
Elev	21	Rwy/Length	—
Lat	N38°18'		
Long	W121°25'		

Fresno, CA – Chandler Downtown

Ident	FCH	ATIS	—
Elev	278	Rwy/Length	12R/3202
Lat	N36°43'		30L/3202
Long	W119°49'		12L/3006
			30R/3006

Fresno, CA – Fresno Air Terminal

Ident	FAT	ATIS	121.35
Elev	333	Rwy/Length	11R/7206
Lat	N36°46'		29L/7206
Long	W119°42'		11L/9222
			29R/9222

Ft Ord, CA – Fritzsche

Ident		ATIS	124.6
Elev	134	Rwy/Length	—
Lat	N36°40'		
Long	W121°45'		

Garberville, CA – Garberville

Ident	O16	ATIS	—
Elev	545	Rwy/Length	18/3050
Lat	N40°05'		36/3050
Long	W123°48'		

Georgetown, CA – Georgetown

Ident	Q61	ATIS	—
Elev	2588	Rwy/Length	—
Lat	N38°55'		
Long	W120°51'		

Gualala, CA – Gualala

Ident	Q69	ATIS	—
Elev	940	Rwy/Length	—
Lat	N38°48'		
Long	W123°31'		

Gustine, CA – Gustine

Ident	3O1	ATIS	—
Elev	75	Rwy/Length	—
Lat	N37°15'		
Long	W120°57'		

Half Moon Bay, CA – Half Moon Bay

Ident	HAF	ATIS	—
Elev	67	Rwy/Length	12/5000
Lat	N37°30'		30/5000
Long	W122°30'		

Hawthorne, CA – Hawthorne Muni

Ident	HHR	ATIS	118.4
Elev	63	Rwy/Length	07/4956
Lat	N33°55'		25/4956
Long	W118°20'		

Hayward, CA – Hayward Air Terminal

Ident	HWD	ATIS	126.7
Elev	47	Rwy/Length/ILS/ID	10R/5024
Lat	N37°39'		28L/5024/111.5/IHWD
Long	W122°07'		10L/3107
			28R/3107

Healdsburg, CA – Healdsburg

Ident	O31	ATIS	—
Elev	278	Rwy/Length	—
Lat	N38°39'		
Long	W122°54'		

Hollister, CA – Frazier Lake

Ident	1C9	ATIS	—
Elev	151	Rwy/Length	—
Lat	N36°57'		
Long	W121°27'		

Hollister, CA – Hollister Muni

Ident	307	ATIS	—
Elev	230	Rwy/Length	—
Lat	N36°53'		
Long	W121°24'		

Jackson, CA – Westover/Amador Co.

Ident	O70	ATIS	—
Elev	1690	Rwy/Length	—
Lat	N38°22'		
Long	W120°47'		

King City, CA – Mesa Del Rey

Ident	KIC	ATIS	—
Elev	370	Rwy/Length	—
Lat	N36°13'		
Long	W121°07'		

La Verne, CA – Brackett Field

Ident	POC	ATIS	—
Elev	1011	Rwy/Length	08R/4839
Lat	N34°05'		26L/4839
Long	W117°46'		08L/3661
			26R/3661

Lakeport, CA – Lampson

Ident	102	ATIS	—
Elev	1378	Rwy/Length	—
Lat	N38°59'		
Long	W122°54'		

Lincoln, CA – Lincoln Regl.

Ident	O51	ATIS	—
Elev	119	Rwy/Length	—
Lat	N38°54'		
Long	W121°21'		

Little River, CA – Little River

Ident	O48	ATIS	—
Elev	572	Rwy/Length	11/5250
Lat	N39°15'		29/5250
Long	W123°45'		

Livermore, CA – Livermore Muni

Ident	LVK	ATIS	119.65
Elev	397	Rwy/Length/ILS/ID	07L/5255
Lat	N37°41'		25R/5255/110.5/ILVK
Long	W121°49'		07R/2699
			25L/2699

Loch Lomond, CA – Loch Lomond

Ident	Q79	ATIS	—
Elev	2080	Rwy/Length	—
Lat	N38°52'		
Long	W122°40'		

Lodi, CA – Kingdon Airpark

Ident	O20	ATIS	—
Elev	15	Rwy/Length	12/4000
Lat	N38°05'		30/4000
Long	W121°21'		

Lodi, CA – Lodi

Ident	103	ATIS	—
Elev	58	Rwy/Length	08/3085
Lat	N38°12'		26/3085
Long	W121°16'		12/2070
			30/2070

Lodi, CA – Lodi Airpark

Ident	Q80	ATIS	—
Elev	25	Rwy/Length	—
Lat	N38°05'		
Long	W121°19'		

Long Beach, CA – Long Beach

Ident	LGB	ATIS	127.75
Elev	57	Rwy/Length/ILS/ID	30//110.3/ILGB
Lat	N33°49'		
Long	W118°09'		

Los Angeles, CA – Los Angeles Intl

Ident	LAX	ATIS	135.65
Elev	126	Rwy/Length/ILS/ID	06R/10285/111.70/IGPE
Lat	N33°57'		24L/10285/111.70/IHQB
Long	W118° 24'		06L/8925/108.50/IUWU
			24R/8925/108.50/IOSS
			07R/11096/109.90/IMKZ
			25L/11096/109.90/ILAX
			07L/12091/111.10/IIAS
			25R/12091/111.10/ICFN

Markleeville, CA – Alpine Co.

Ident	Q82	ATIS	—
Elev	5867	Rwy/Length	—
Lat	N38°44'		
Long	W119°45'		

Marysville, CA – Yuba County

Ident	MYV	ATIS	—
Elev	62	Rwy/Length	05/3281
Lat	N39°05'		23/3281
Long	W121°24'		14/6006
			32/6006

Merced, CA – Merced Muni – Macready Field

Ident	MCE	ATIS	—
Elev	153	Rwy/Length	12/5903
Lat	N37°17'		30/5903
Long	W120°30'		

Modesto, CA – Modesto City

Ident	MOD	ATIS	127.7
Elev	97	Rwy/Length/ILS/ID	10R/3459
Lat	N37°37'		28L/3459
Long	W120°57'		10L/5911
			28R/5911/111.9/IMOD

Monterey, CA – Monterey Peninsula

Ident	MRY	ATIS	119.25
Elev	254	Rwy/Length/ILS/ID	10R/7598/110.7/IMRY
Lat	N36°35'		28L/7298/110.7/IMTB
Long	W121°50'		10L/9501
			28R/9501

Mountain View, CA – Moffett Field NAS

Ident	NUQ	ATIS	—
Elev	34	Rwy	14R
Lat	N37°24'		32L
Long	W122°02'		14L
			32R

Napa, CA – Napa Co.

Ident	APC	ATIS	124.05
Elev	33	Rwy/Length/ILS/ID	36L//111.3/IAPC
Lat	N38°12'		
Long	W122°16'		

Novato, CA – Gnoss

Ident	O56	ATIS	—
Elev	2	Rwy	—
Lat	N38°08'		
Long	W122°33'		

Novato, CA – Hamilton (AFB)

Ident	NZZ	ATIS	—
Elev	2	Rwy	12
Lat	N38°03'		30
Long	W122°30'		

Oakland, CA – Metro Oakland Intl

Ident	OAK	ATIS	128.50
Elev	6	Rwy/Length/ILS/ID	09R/6212
Lat	N37°43'		27L/6212
Long	W122°13'		09L/5453
			27R/5453/109.90/IOAK
			11/10000/111.90/IAAZ
			29/10000/108.70/IINB
			15/3366
			33/3366

Oceanside, CA – Oceanside Muni

Ident	L32	ATIS	—
Elev	28	Rwy/Length	06/3061
Lat	N33°13'		24/3061
Long	W117°21'		

Ontario, CA – Ontario Intl

Ident	ONT	ATIS	124.25
Elev	943	Rwy/Length/ILS/ID	08L/12200/109.70/IAOD
Lat	N34°03'		26R/12200/109.70/IONT
Long	W117°36'		08R/10200
			26L/10200/109.70/ITWO

Oroville, CA – Oroville Muni

Ident	OVE	ATIS	—
Elev	190	Rwy/Length	01/4528
Lat	N39°29'		19/4528
Long	W121°37'		12/3280
			30/3280

Palo Alto, CA – Palo Alto

Ident	PAO	ATIS	120.6
Elev	5	Rwy/Length	12/2500
Lat	N37°27'		30/2500
Long	W122°06'		

Petaluma, CA – Petaluma Muni

Ident	O69	ATIS	—
Elev	87	Rwy/Length	—
Lat	N38°15'		
Long	W122°36'		

Placerville, CA – Placerville

Ident	PVF	ATIS	—
Elev	2583	Rwy/Length	05/4200
Lat	N38°43'		23/4200
Long	W120°45'		

Porterville, CA – Porterville

Ident	PTV	ATIS	—
Elev	442	Rwy/Length	12/5908
Lat	N36°01'		30/5908
Long	W119°03'		

Rancho Murieta, CA – Rancho Murieta

Ident	RIU	ATIS	—
Elev	142	Rwy/Length	—
Lat	N38°29'		
Long	W121°06'		

Red Bluff, CA – Red Bluff Muni

Ident	RBL	ATIS	—
Elev	349	Rwy/Length	15/5984
Lat	N40°09'		33/5984
Long	W122°15'		

Rio Linda, CA – Rio Linda

Ident	Q94	ATIS	—
Elev	45	Rwy/Length	—
Lat	N38°40'		
Long	W121°26'		

Rio Vista, CA – Rio Vista Muni

Ident	O88	ATIS	—
Elev	20	Rwy/Length	—
Lat	N38°11'		
Long	W121°42'		

Riverside, CA – Riverside Muni

Ident	RAL	ATIS	128.8
Elev	816	Rwy/Length	09/5400
Lat	N33°57'		27/5400
Long	W117°26'		16/2850
			34/2850

Sacramento, CA – Mather AFB

Ident	MHR	ATIS	119.15
Elev	96	Rwy/Length/ILS/ID	22L/110.7/IMHR
Lat	N38°33'		04R/110.7/IPOK
Long	W121°17'		

Sacramento, CA – McClellan AFB

Ident	MCC	ATIS	109.2
Elev	75	Rwy/ILS/ID	16/109.7/IMCC
Lat	N38°40'		34/109.7/IFKZ
Long	W121°24'		

Sacramento, CA – Natomas

Ident	Q96	ATIS	—
Elev	22	Rwy/Length	—
Lat	N38°18'		
Long	W121°30'		

Sacramento, CA – Sacramento Metro

Ident	SMF	ATIS	126.75
Elev	25	Rwy/Length/ILS/ID	16R/8600/111.1/ISMF
Lat	N38°41'		34L/8600/111.1/IHUX
Long	W121°35'		16L/8600/111.75/IMDK
			34R/8600

Sacramento, CA – Sacramento Executive

Ident	SAC	ATIS	125.5
Elev	21	Rwy/Length/ILS/ID	02/5503/110.3/ISAC
Lat	N38°30'		20/5503
Long	W121°29'		12/3836
			30/3836
			16/3485
			34/3485

Salinas, CA – Salinas Muni

Ident	SNS	ATIS	124.85
Elev	84	Rwy/Length/ILS/ID	08/5005
Lat	N36°39'		26/5005
Long	W121°36'		13/4825
			31/4825/108.5/ISNS
			14
			32

San Andreas, CA – Calaveras Co.-Rasmussen

Ident	O03	ATIS	—
Elev	1325	Rwy/Length	—
Lat	N38°08'		
Long	W120°38'		

San Carlos, CA – San Carlos

Ident	SQL	ATIS	125.9
Elev	2	Rwy/Length	12/2600
Lat	N37°30'		30/2600
Long	W122°15'		

San Diego, CA – San Diego Intl-Lindbergh Field

Ident	SAN	ATIS	134.80
Elev	14	Rwy/Length/ILS/ID	09/9400/110.90/ISAN
Lat	N32°44'		27/9400
Long	W117°11'		13/4439
			31/4439

San Francisco, CA – San Francisco Intl

Ident	SFO	ATIS	118.85
Elev	11	Rwy/Length/ILS/ID	1R/8901
Lat	N37°37'		19L/8901/108.90/ISIA
Long	W122°22'		1L/7001
			19R/7001
			10R/10600
			28L/10600/109.55/ISFO
			10L/11870
			28R/11870/111.70/IGWQ

San Jose, CA – Reid-Hillview

Ident	RHV	ATIS	125.2
Elev	133	Rwy/Length	13L/3101
Lat	N37°20'		31R/3101
Long	W121°49'		13R/3099
			31L/3099

San Jose, CA – San Jose Intl

Ident	SJC	ATIS	126.95
Elev	58	Rwy/Length/ILS/ID	11/4599
Lat	N37°21'		29/4599
Long	W121°55'		12R/10200/110.9/ISLV
			30L/10200/110.9/ISJC
			12L/4419
			30R/4419

San Martin, CA – South Co. of Santa Clara

Ident	Q99	ATIS	—
Elev	281	Rwy/Length	—
Lat	N37°04'		
Long	W121°35'		

San Rafael, CA – Hamilton

Ident	CA35	ATIS	—
Elev	3	Rwy/Length	—
Lat	N38°03'		
Long	W122°3'0		

Santa Ana, CA – John Wayne Apt/Orange County

Ident	SNA	ATIS	126.00
Elev	54	Rwy/Length/ILS/ID	01R/2887
Lat	N33°40'		19L/2887
Long	W117°52'		01L/5700
			19R/5700/111.75/ISNA
			19R/5700/108.3/IOJW

Santa Barbara, CA – Santa Barbara Muni

Ident	SBA	ATIS	—
Elev	10	Rwy/Length/ILS/ID	07/6052/110.30/ISBA
Lat	N34°25'		25/6052
Long	W119°50'		15R/4183
			33L/4183
			15L/4179
			33R/4179

Santa Monica, CA – Santa Monica Muni

Ident	SMO	ATIS	119.15
Elev	175	Rwy/Length	03/4987
Lat	N34°00'		21/4987
Long	W118°27'		

Santa Rosa, CA – Sonama County

Ident	STS	ATIS	120.55
Elev	125	Rwy/Length/ILS/ID	14/5115
Lat	N38°30'		32/5115/109.3/ISTS
Long	W122°48'		01/5002
			19/5002

Schellville-Sonoma, CA – Sonama Valley

Ident	0Q3	ATIS	—
Elev	10	Rwy/Length	—
Lat	N38°13'		
Long	W122°27'		

Sierraville, CA – Dearwater

Ident	O79	ATIS	—
Elev	4984	Rwy/Length	—
Lat	N39°34'		
Long	W120°21'		

Sonoma, CA – Sonoma Skypark

Ident	0Q9	ATIS	—
Elev	20	Rwy/Length	—
Lat	N38°15'		
Long	W122°26'		

South Lake Tahoe, CA – Lake Tahoe

Ident	TVL	ATIS	—
Elev	6264	Rwy/Length/ILS/ID	18/8544/108.9/ITVL
Lat	N38°53'		36/8544
Long	W119°59'		

Stockton, CA – Sharpe Army Depot

Ident	LRO	ATIS	—
Elev	18	Rwy/Length	—
Lat	N37°50'		
Long	W121°16'		

Stockton, CA – Stockton Metro

Ident	SCK	ATIS	—
Elev	30	Rwy/Length/ILS/ID	11L/8650
Lat	N37°53'		29R/8650/109.1/ISCK
Long	W121°14'		11R/2996
			29L/2996

Torrance, CA – Zamperini Field

Ident	TOA	ATIS	125.6
Elev	101	Rwy/Length	11R/3000
Lat	N33°48'		29L/3000
Long	W118°20'		11L/5000
			29R/5000

Tracy, CA – Tracy Muni

Ident	TCY	ATIS	—
Elev	192	Rwy/Length	—
Lat	N37°41'		
Long	W121°26'		

Truckee, CA – Truckee-Tahoe

Ident	TRK	ATIS	—
Elev	5900	Rwy/Length	01/4650
Lat	N39°19'		19/4650
Long	W120°08'		10/7000
			28/7000

Vacaville, CA – Nut Tree

Ident	O45	ATIS	—
Elev	114	Rwy/Length	—
Lat	N38°22'		
Long	W121°57'		

Van Nuys, CA – Van Nuys

Ident	VNY	ATIS	118.45
Elev	799	Rwy/Length/ILS/ID	16R/8001/111.30/IVNY
Lat	N34°12'		34L/8001
Long	W118°29'		16L/4000
			34R/4000

Visalia, CA – Visalia Muni

Ident	VIS	ATIS	—
Elev	292	Rwy/Length	12/6556
Lat	N36°19'		30/6556
Long	W119°23'		

Watsonville, CA – Watsonville Muni

Ident	WVI	ATIS	—
Elev	160	Rwy/Length/ILS/ID	02/4501/108.3/IAYN
Lat	N36°56'		20/4501
Long	W121°47'		08/3999
			26/3999

Willows, CA – Willows-Glenn County

Ident	WLW	ATIS	—
Elev	139	Rwy/Length	16/7506
Lat	N39°30'		34/7506
Long	W122°12'		13/4210
			31/4210

Woodland, CA – Watts-Woodland

Ident	O41	ATIS	—
Elev	125	Rwy/Length	—
Lat	N38°40'		
Long	W121°52'		

VORs

Location/Name	Type	Ident	Freq	Lat	Long	Elev
Amedee	VOR-DME	AHC	109.00	N40°16'	W120°09'	4008
Arcata	VOR-DME	ACV	110.20	N40°58'	W124°06'	191
Avenal	VORTAC	AVE	117.10	N35°38'	W119°58'	710
Beale	VOR	BAB	108.60	N39°08'	W121°26'	165
Big Sur	VORTAC	BSR	114.00	N36°10'	W121°38'	4080
Bishop	VOR-DME	BIH	109.60	N37°22'	W118°21'	4110
Blythe	VORTAC	BLH	117.40	N33°35'	W114°45'	410
Camarillo	VOR-DME	CMA	115.80	N34°12'	W119°05'	60
Camp Pendleton	VOR	NFG	111.80	N33°18'	W117°21'	75
Chico	VOR-DME	CIC	109.80	N39°47'	W121°50'	220
China Lake	VORTAC	NID	111.60	N35°41'	W117°41'	2272
Clovis	VORTAC	CZQ	112.90	N36°53'	W119°48'	360
Concord	VOR-DME	CCR	117.00	N38°02'	W122°02'	5
Crescent City	VORTAC	CEC	109.00	N41°46'	W124°14'	50
Daggett	VORTAC	DAG	113.20	N34°57'	W116°34'	1760
Edwards	VORTAC	EDW	116.40	N34°58'	W117°43'	2354
El Nido	VOR-DME	HYP	114.20	N37°13'	W120°24'	180
Fellows	VORTAC	FLW	117.50	N35°05'	W119°51'	3870
Fillmore	VORTAC	FIM	112.50	N34°21'	W118°52'	2200
Fort Jones	VORTAC	FJS	109.60	N41°26'	W122°48'	4900
Fortuna	VORTAC	FOT	114.00	N40°40'	W124°14'	400
Friant	VORTAC	FRA	115.60	N37°06'	W119°35'	2380
Gaviota	VORTAC	GVO	113.80	N34°31'	W120°05'	2620
Goffs	VORTAC	GFS	114.40	N35°07'	W115°10'	4000
Gorman	VORTAC	GMN	116.10	N34°48'	W118°51'	4920
Guadalupe	VOR	GLJ	111.00	N34°57'	W120°31'	140
Hangtown	VOR-DME	HNW	115.50	N38°43'	W120°44'	2600
Hector	VORTAC	HEC	112.70	N34°47'	W116°27'	1850
Homeland	VOR	HDF	113.40	N33°46'	W117°11'	1414
Imperial	VORTAC	IPL	115.90	N32°44'	W115°30'	-20
Julian	VORTAC	JLI	114.00	N33°08'	W116°35'	5560
Lake Hughes	VORTAC	LHS	108.40	N34°40'	W118°34'	5790
Linden	VORTAC	LIN	114.80	N38°04'	W121°00'	260
Los Angeles	VORTAC	LAX	113.60	N33°55'	W118°25'	180
Manteca	VORTAC	ECA	116.00	N37°50'	W121°10'	40
Marine El Toro	VORTAC	NZJ	117.20	N33°40'	W117°43'	357
Marysville	VOR-DME	MYV	110.80	N39°05'	W121°34'	60
Maxwell	VORTAC	MXW	110.00	N39°19'	W122°13'	110
Mc Clellan	VORTAC	MCC	109.20	N38°40'	W121°24'	72
Mendocino	VORTAC	ENI	112.30	N39°03'	W123°16'	2980
Mission Bay	VORTAC	MZB	117.80	N32°46'	W117°13'	10
Modesto	VOR-DME	MOD	114.60	N37°37'	W120°57'	90
Morro Bay	VORTAC	MQO	112.40	N35°15'	W120°45'	1462
Needles	VORTAC	EED	115.20	N34°45'	W114°28'	620
Oakland	VORTAC	OAK	116.80	N37°43'	W122°13'	10
Oceanside	VORTAC	OCN	115.30	N33°14'	W117°25'	90
Palm Springs	VORTAC	PSP	115.50	N33°52'	W116°25'	1600
Palmdale	VORTAC	PMD	114.50	N34°37'	W118°03'	2500
Panoche	VORTAC	PXN	112.60	N36°42'	W120°46'	2060
Paradise	VORTAC	PDZ	112.20	N33°55'	W117°31'	1430
Parker	VORTAC	PKE	117.90	N34°06'	W114°40'	1000

Location/Name	Type	Ident	Freq	Lat	Long	Elev
Paso Robles	VORTAC	PRB	114.30	N35°40'	W120°37'	820
Poggi	VORTAC	PGY	109.80	N32°36'	W116°58'	580
Point Reyes	VORTAC	PYE	113.70	N38°04'	W122°52'	1340
Pomona	VORTAC	POM	110.40	N34°04'	W117°47'	1260
Porterville	VOR-DME	PTV	109.20	N35°54'	W119°01'	580
Priest	VOR	ROM	110.00	N36°08'	W120°39'	3880
Red Bluff	VORTAC	RBL	115.70	N40°05'	W122°14'	320
Redding	VOR-DME	RDD	108.40	N40°30'	W122°17'	490
Riverside	VOR	RAL	112.40	N33°57'	W117°26'	780
Sacramento	VORTAC	SAC	115.20	N38°26'	W121°33'	10
Salinas	VORTAC	SNS	117.30	N36°39'	W121°36'	80
San Francisco	VOR-DME	SFO	115.80	N37°37'	W122°22'	10
San Jose	VOR-DME	SJC	114.10	N37°22'	W121°56'	40
San Marcus	VORTAC	RZS	114.90	N34°30'	W119°46'	3620
Santa Catalina	VORTAC	SXC	111.40	N33°22'	W118°25'	2090
Santa Monica	VOR-DME	SMO	110.80	N34°00'	W118°27'	120
Santa Rosa	VOR-DME	STS	113.00	N38°30'	W122°48'	140
Sausalito	VORTAC	SAU	116.20	N37°51'	W122°31'	1040
Scaggs Island	VORTAC	SGD	112.10	N38°10'	W122°22'	10
Seal Beach	VORTAC	SLI	115.70	N33°46'	W118°03'	20
Shafter	VORTAC	EHF	115.40	N35°29'	W119°05'	550
Squaw Valley	VOR-DME	SWR	113.20	N39°10'	W120°16'	8850
Thermal	VORTAC	TRM	116.20	N33°37'	W116°09'	-110
Travis	VOR	TZZ	116.40	N38°20'	W121°48'	30
Twentynine Palms	VORTAC	TNP	114.2	N34°06'	W115°46'	1350
Van Nuys	VOR-DME	VNY	113.10	N34°13'	W118°29'	810
Ventura	VOR-DME	VTU	108.20	N34°06'	W119°02'	1560
Visalia	VOR-DME	VIS	109.40	N36°22'	W119°28'	260
Williams	VORTAC	ILA	114.40	N39°04'	W122°01'	50
Woodside	VORTAC	OSI	113.90	N37°23'	W122°16'	2170

Location/Name	Ident	Freq	Lat	Long	Elevv
Hunter Liggett	HGT	209	N35°56'	W121°09'	—
Jorge (LMM)	JC	249	N37°20'	W121°54'	—
Jotly (LOM)	SC	271	N37°49'	W121°08'	52
Kanan (LOM)	CC	335	N38°02'	W122°02'	5
Kearn (LOM)	UK	371	N39°16'	W123°14'	871
Lampson	LOP	217	N38°59'	W122°53'	1355
Lanee (LOM)	HU	400	N38°37'	W121°36'	15
Lassn (LOM)	RD	367	N40°23'	W122°17'	—
Lompoc	LPC	223	N34°39'	W120°27'	74
Maagg (LMM)	NA	337	N33°41'	W117°51'	53
Metre (LOM)	SM	230	N38°47'	W121°35'	15
Montague	MOG	382	N41°43'	W122°28'	2620
Munso (LOM)	MR	385	N36°37'	W121°56'	—
Niley (LOM)	BF	385	N35°21'	W118°58'	398
Norde (LOM)	CI	327	N39°53'	W121°55'	248
Oroville	OVE	212	N39°29'	W121°37'	199
Pacoima	PAI	370	N34°15'	W118°24'	—
Pajar (LOM/NDB)	AY	327	N36°54'	W121°48'	93
Petis (LOM/NDB)	SB	397	N34°03'	W117°21'	—
Proberta	PBT	338	N40°06'	W122°14'	400
Reiga (LOM/NDB)	LV	374	N37°41'	W121°41'	683
Romen (LOM)	OS	278	N33°57'	W118°16'	136
Roray (LMM)	AK	341	N37°43'	W122°11'	10
Salyer Farms	COR	205	N36°05'	W119°32'	—
San Clemente	NUC	350	N33°01'	W118°34'	180
San Jacinto	SJY	227	N33°47'	W116°59'	1498
San Nicolas Navy	NSI	203	N33°14'	W119°26'	—
Santa Ynez	IZA	394	N34°36'	W120°04'	656
Sharpe	LRO	282	N37°49'	W121°16'	—
Swan Lake (LOM/NDB)	LKA	257	N33°58'	W117°33'	666
Vilia (LOM)	VI	220	N36°15'	W119°18'	306
Vinee (LMM)	UR	253	N34°11'	W118°22'	727
Wowar (LOM)	MO	367	N37°34'	W120°51'	115

NDBs

Location/Name	Ident	Freq	Lat	Long	Elev
Abeta (LMM)	CV	233	N40°57'	W124°05'	159
Alturas	ARU	215	N41°28'	W120°33'	—
Becca (LOM)	LG	233	N33°45'	W118°04'	—
Boing (LMM)	AN	245	N32°44'	W117°12'	—
Brijj (LOM)	SF	379	N37°34'	W122°15'	—
Chandler	FCH	344	N36°43'	W119°50'	—
China Lake (Navy)	NID	348	N35°41'	W117°41'	2272
Chualar	UAD	263	N36°29'	W121°28'	105
Columbia	CUF	404	N38°01'	W120°24'	2112
Compton	CPM	378	N33°53'	W118°14'	—
Deoro (LOM)	MY	210	N32°46'	W117°02'	537
El Monte	EMT	359	N34°05'	W118°01'	—
Execc (LOM)	SA	356	N38°26'	W121°32'	5
General Fox	GWF	282	N34°44'	W118°13'	—
Halow (LOM/NDB)	MY	222	N39°10'	W121°36'	64
Hilan (LOM)	FA	266	N36°43'	W119°38'	340

Colorado

Airports

Denver, CO – Denver Intl

Ident	DIA	ATIS	125.60
Elev	5431	Rwy/Length/ILS/ID	07/12000/111.55/IDZG
Lat	N39°51'		25/12000/111.55/IERP
Long	W104°40'		08/12000/108.90/IFUI
			26/12000/108.90/IJOY
			16/12000/111.10/ILTT
			34/12000/111.10/IOUF
			17L/12000/110.15/IBXP
			35R/12000/110.15/IDPP
			17R/12000/108.50/IACX
			35L/12000/108.50/IAQD

Denver, CO – Stapleton Intl

Ident	DEN	ATIS	124.45
Elev	5333	Rwy/Length/ILS/ID	07/4871
Lat	N39°46'		25/4871
Long	W104°52'		8R/10004/110.30/IGQW
			26L/10004/110.30/IDEN
			8L/8599
			26R/8599
			17R/11500
			35L/11500/110.70/ISPO
			17L/12000/109.30/IHMX
			35R/12000/109.30/IRRV
			18/7750/111.90/IUGT
			36/7750/111.90/IEBC

Telluride, CO – Telluride

Ident	TEX	ATIS	—
Elev	9078	Rwy/Length	09/6870
Lat	N37°57'		27/6870
Long	W107°54'		

VORs

Location/Name	Type	Ident	Freq	Lat	Long	Elev
Akron	VORTAC	AKO	114.40	N40°09'	W103°10'	4620
Alamosa	VORTAC	ALS	113.90	N37°20'	W105°48'	7530
Blue Mesa	VORTAC	HBU	114.90	N38°27'	W107°02'	8730
Buckley	VOR	BKF	109.60	N39°42'	W104°45'	5580
Butts	VOR	FCS	108.80	N38°40'	W104°45'	5829
Byers	VOR/DME	BVR	113.50	N39°46'	W103°55'	5252
Colorado Springs	VORTAC	COS	112.50	N38°56'	W104°38'	6930
Cones	VOR-DME	ETL	110.20	N38°02'	W108°15'	8460
Cortez	VOR-DME	CEZ	108.40	N37°23'	W108°33'	6220
Denver	VORTAC	DEN	117.00	N39°48'	W104°53'	5334
Denver	VOR-DME	DEN	117.90	N39°48'	W104°39'	5440
Dove Creek	VORTAC	DVC	114.60	N37°48'	W108°55'	6990
Durango	VOR-DME	DRO	108.20	N37°09'	W107°44'	6660
Falcon	VORTAC	FQF	116.30	N39°41'	W104°37'	5789
Fruita	VOR	RHU	109.00	N39°11'	W108°38'	4710
Gill	VORTAC	GLL	114.20	N40°30'	W104°33'	4910
Grand Junction	VORTAC	JNC	112.40	N39°03'	W108°47'	7100
Hayden	VOR-DME	CHE	115.60	N40°31'	W107°18'	7230
Hugo	VORTAC	HGO	112.10	N38°48'	W103°37'	5233
Jeffco	VOR-DME	BJC	115.40	N39°54'	W105°08'	5734
Kremmling	VORTAC	RLG	113.80	N40°00'	W106°26'	9370
Lamar	VORTAC	LAA	116.90	N38°11'	W102°41'	3950
Meeker	VORTAC	EKR	115.20	N40°04'	W107°55'	7620
Mile High	VORTAC	DVV	114.70	N39°53'	W104°37'	5270
Montrose	VOR-DME	MTJ	117.10	N38°30'	W107°53'	5710
Pueblo	VORTAC	PUB	116.70	N38°17'	W104°25'	4760
Red Table	VOR-DME	DBL	113.00	N39°26'	W106°53'	11758

Location/Name	Type	Ident	Freq	Lat	Long	Elev
Rifle	VOR-DME	RIL	110.60	N39°31'	W107°42'	5529
Robert	VOR-DME	BQZ	112.20	N40°27'	W106°52'	8251
Snow	VOR-DME	SXW	109.20	N39°37'	W106°59'	8060
Thurman	VORTAC	TXC	112.90	N39°41'	W103°12'	4890
Tobe	VORTAC	TBE	115.80	N37°15'	W103°36'	5730

NDBs

Location/Name	Ident	Freq	Lat	Long	Elev
Aruba (LOM/NDB)	TF	373	N38°17'	W104°21'	4671
Batten	BAJ	392	N40°31'	W103°13'	4025
Betee(LMM/NDB)	PO	308	N39°45'	W104°52'	5311
Carbondale	CQL	344	N39°24'	W107°09'	—
Casse (LOM/NDB)	AP	260	N39°27'	W104°50'	6412
Colln (LOM)	FN	400	N40°21'	W104°58'	4957
Eagle	EGE	357	N39°38'	W106°54'	—
Greey (LOM)	GS	348	N40°27'	W104°46'	4076
Heginbotham	HEQ	404	N40°34'	W102°16'	3717
Ironhorse	IHS	335	N38°40'	W104°45'	—
Kit Carson	ITR	209	N39°14'	W102°17'	4200
La Junta	LHX	239	N38°02'	W103°37'	—
Laporte	LQP	387	N40°34'	W105°02'	—
Leadville	LXV	236	N39°13'	W106°18'	9958
Mertz (LOM)	PU	302	N38°17'	W104°38'	—
Monte Vista	MVI	311	N37°31'	W106°02'	7605
Petey (LOM/NDB)	CO	407	N38°41'	W104°42'	5570
Skipi (LOM)	FT	321	N39°47'	W104°26'	5407
Trinidad	TAD	329	N37°18'	W104°20'	—

Connecticut

Airports

Bridgeport, CT – Igor Sikorsky Memorial

Ident	BDR	ATIS	119.15
Elev	10	Rwy/Length/ILS/ID	06/4677/110.7/IBDR
Lat	N41°09'		24/4677
Long	W73°07'		11/4761
			29/4761

Chester, CT – Chester

Ident	3B9	ATIS	—
Elev	416	Rwy/Length	17/2566
Lat	N41°23'		35/2566
Long	W72°30'		

Danbury, CT – Danbury Muni

Ident	DXR	ATIS	—
Elev	457	Rwy/Length	08/4422
Lat	N41°22'		26/4422
Long	W73°28'		17/3135
			35/3135

Danielson, CT – Danielson

Ident	5B3	ATIS	—
Elev	238	Rwy/Length	13/2700
Lat	N41°49'		31/2700
Long	W71°54'		

Hartford, CT – Hartford-Brainard

Ident	HFD	ATIS	126.45
Elev	19	Rwy/Length/ILS/ID	02/4418/109.7/IFHD
Lat	N41°44'		20/4418
Long	W72°39'		11/2315
			29/2315
			NE/2350 Grass
			SW/2350 Grass

Meriden, CT – Meriden Markham Muni

Ident	MMK	ATIS	—
Elev	103	Rwy/Length	18/3100
Lat	N41°30'		36/3100
Long	W72°49'		

New Haven, CT – Tweed-New Haven

Ident	HVN	ATIS	133.65
Elev	13	Rwy/Length/ILS/ID	02/5600/109.1/IHVN
Lat	N41°15'		20/5600
Long	W72°53'		14/3634
			32/3634

Oxford, CT – Waterbury-Oxford

Ident	OXC	ATIS	—
Elev	727	Rwy/Length	13/1999
Lat	N41°28'		31/1999
Long	W73°08'		18/5000
			36/5000

Willimantic, CT – Windham

Ident	IJD	ATIS	—
Elev	247	Rwy/Length	09/4278
Lat	N41°44'		27/4278
Long	W72°10'		18/2797
			36/2797

Windsor Locks, CT – Bradley Intl

Ident	BDL	ATIS	118.15
Elev	174	Rwy/Length/ILS/ID	01/5145
Lat	N41°56'		19/5145
Long	W72°41'		06/9502/111.1/IBDL
			24/9502/111.1/IMYQ
			15/6846
			33/6846/108.55/IKX

VORs

Location/Name	Type	Ident	Freq	Lat	Long	Elev
Bradley	VORTAC	BDL	109.00	N41°56'	W72°41'	160
Bridgeport	VOR	BDR	108.80	N41°09'	W73°07'	10
Groton	VOR	TMU	111.80	N41°19'	W72°03'	10
Hartford	VORTAC	HFD	114.90	N41°38'	W72°32'	850
Madison	VOR-DME	MAD	110.40	N41°18'	W72°41'	230
New Haven	VOR-DME	HVN	109.80	N41°15'	W72°53'	10
Norwich	VORTAC	ORW	110.00	N41°33'	W71°59'	310
Putnam	VOR-DME	PUT	117.40	N41°57'	W71°50'	650

NDBs

Location/Name	Ident	Freq	Lat	Long	Elev
Chupp (LOM)	BD	388	N41°52'	W72°45'	—
Clera (LOM)	OX	362	N41°24'	W73°07'	—
Lomis (LOM/NDB)	HF	244	N41°38'	W72°37'	45
Meriden	MMK	238	N41°30'	W72°49'	—
Waterbury	TBY	257	N41°31'	W73°08'	—

Deleware

Airports

Wilmington, DE – New Castle County

Ident	ILG	ATIS	123.95
Elev	80	Rwy/Length/ILS/ID	01/7002/110.30/IILG
Lat	N39°40'		19/7002
Long	W75°36'		09/7165
			27/7165
			14/4594
			32/4594

VORs

Location/Name	Type	Ident	Freq	Lat	Long	Elev
Dupont	VORTAC	DQO	114.00	N39°40'	W75°36'	71
Smyrna	VORTAC	ENO	111.40	N39°13'	W75°30'	10
Waterloo	VOR-DME	ATR	112.60	N38°48'	W75°12'	10

NDBs

Location/Name	Ident	Freq	Lat	Long	Elev
Hadin (LOM)	IL	248	N39°34'	W75°36'	—

Florida

Airports

Cape Canaveral, FL – Cape Canaveral AFS Skip Strip

Ident	XMR	ATIS	—
Elev	10	Rwy/Length/ILS/ID	—
Lat	N28°28'		
Long	W80°34'		

Cocoa Beach, FL – Patrick AFB

Ident	COF	ATIS	119.17
Elev	9	Rwy/Length/ILS/ID	02//109.1/ICOF
Lat	N28°14'		20//110.9/IPKC
Long	W80°36'		

Everglades, FL – Everglades

Ident	X01	ATIS	—
Elev	5	Rwy/Length/ILS/ID	—
Lat	N25°50'		
Long	W81°23'		

Homestead, FL – Homestead AFB

Ident	HST	ATIS	—
Elev	7	Rwy/Length	—
Lat	N25°29'		
Long	W80°23'		

Homestead, FL – Homestead General (CLOSED)

Ident	X51	ATIS	—
Elev	9	Rwy/Length	—
Lat	N25°29'		
Long	W80°33'		

Jacksonville, FL – Jacksonville Intl

Ident	JAX	ATIS	125.85
Elev	30	Rwy/Length/ILS/ID	07/8000/110.70/IJAX
Lat	N30°29'		25/8000/109.10/IPEK
Long	W81°41'		13/7700/108.90/ICZH
			31/7700

Key West, FL – Key West NAS

Ident	NQX	ATIS	—
Elev	6	Rwy/Length	—
Lat	N24°34'		
Long	W81°41'		

Key West, FL – Key West Intl.

Ident	EYW	ATIS	—
Elev	4	Rwy/Length	—
Lat	N24°33'		
Long	W81°45'		

Marathon, FL – Marathon

Ident	MTH	ATIS	—
Elev	7	Rwy/Length	—
Lat	N24°43'		
Long	W81°03'		

Miami, FL – Dade-Collier

Ident	TNT	ATIS	—
Elev	14	Rwy/Length/ILS/ID	09//108.3/ITNT
Lat	N25°51'		
Long	W80°53'		

Miami, FL – Miami Intl

Ident	MIA	ATIS	119.15
Elev	11	Rwy/Length/ILS/ID	9R/13000/110.90/IBUL
Lat	N25°47'		27L/13000/109.50/IMIA
Long	W80°17'		9L/10502/110.30/IMFA
			27R/10502/109.10/IVIN
			12/9355/108.90/IGEM
			30/9355/111.70/IDCX

Miami, FL – Opa Locka

Ident	OPF	ATIS	125.9
Elev	10	Rwy/Length/ILS/ID	09L//110.5/IOPF
Lat	N25°54'		
Long	W80°17'		

Orlando, FL – Orlando Intl

Ident	MCO	ATIS	121.25
Elev	96	Rwy/Length/ILS/ID	17/10000/111.75/IDIZ
Lat	N28°25'		35/10000/110.50/IDDO
Long	W81°19'		18R/12004/111.90/ITFE
			36L/12004
			18L/12004
			36R/12004/110.70/IOJP

Titusville, FL – Dunn

Ident	X21	ATIS	—
Elev	28	Rwy/Length	—
Lat	N28°37'		
Long	W80°50'		

Titusville, FL – NASA Shuttle Landing Facility

Ident	X68	ATIS	—
Elev	9	Rwy/Length	—
Lat	N28°36'		
Long	W80°41'		

Titusville, FL – Space Center Executive

Ident	TIX	ATIS	—
Elev	35	Rwy/Length/ILS/ID	36//108.7/ITIX
Lat	N28°30'		
Long	W80°48'		

Tallahassee, FL – Tallahassee Muni

Ident	TLH	ATIS	119.45
Elev	81	Rwy/Length/ILS/ID	09/8000
Lat	N30°23'		27/8000/111.90/IPLQ
Long	W84°20'		18/6065
			36/6065/110.30/ITLH

VORs

Location/Name	Type	Ident	Freq	Lat	Long	Elev
Cecil	VOR	VQQ	117.90	N30°12'	W81°53'	70
Craig	VORTAC	CRG	114.50	N30°20'	W81°30'	40
Crestview	VORTAC	CEW	115.90	N30°49'	W86°40'	255
Cross City	VORTAC	CTY	112.00	N29°35'	W83°02'	30
Cypress	VOR-DME	CYY	108.60	N26°09'	W81°46'	10

Location/Name	Type	Ident	Freq	Lat	Long	Elev
Dolphin	VORTAC	DHP	113.90	N25°48'	W80°20'	8
Eglin	VOR	VPS	109.80	N30°23'	W86°32'	90
Fort Lauderdale	VOR-DME	FLL	114.40	N26°04'	W80°09'	10
Gainesville	VORTAC	GNV	116.20	N29°34'	W82°21'	60
Greenville	VORTAC	GEF	109.00	N30°33'	W83°46'	220
Key West	VORTAC	EYW	113.50	N24°35'	W81°48'	10
La Belle	VORTAC	LBV	110.40	N26°49'	W81°23'	30
Lakeland	VORTAC	LAL	116.00	N27°59'	W82°00'	130
Lee Co	VORTAC	RSW	111.80	N26°31'	W81°46'	20
Marianna	VORTAC	MAI	114.00	N30°47'	W85°07'	120
Melbourne	VOR-DME	MLB	110.00	N28°06'	W80°38'	30
Miami	VORTAC	MIA	115.90	N25°57'	W80°27'	—
Ocala	VORTAC	OCF	113.70	N29°10'	W82°13'	80
Orlando	VORTAC	ORL	112.20	N28°32'	W81°20'	110
Ormond Beach	VORTAC	OMN	112.60	N29°18'	W81°06'	20
Pahokee	VORTAC	PHK	115.40	N26°46'	W80°41'	20
Palm Beach	VORTAC	PBI	115.70	N26°40'	W80°05'	20
Panama City	VORTAC	PFN	114.30	N30°12'	W85°40'	10
Pompano Beach	VOR	PMP	108.80	N26°14'	W80°06'	20
Punta Gorda	VOR	PGD	110.20	N26°55'	W81°59'	23
Saint Augustine	VOR-DME	SGJ	109.40	N29°57'	W81°20'	10
Saint Petersburg	VORTAC	PIE	116.40	N27°54'	W82°41'	10
Sarasota	VORTAC	SRQ	115.20	N27°23'	W82°33'	20
Saufley	VOR	NUN	108.80	N30°28'	W87°20'	80
Tallahassee	VORTAC	TLH	117.50	N30°33'	W84°22'	180
Taylor	VORTAC	TAY	112.90	N30°30'	W82°33'	140
Vero Beach	VORTAC	VRB	117.30	N27°40'	W80°29'	20
Virginia Key	VOR-DME	VKZ	117.10	N25°45'	W80°09'	92

NDBs

Location/Name	Ident	Freq	Lat	Long	Elev
Allentown (Navy)	NVK	368	N30°46'	W87°04'	—
Brooksville	BKV	278	N28°28'	W82°26'	—
Caloo (LOM)	FM	341	N26°30'	W81°56'	5
Capok (LOM)	PI	360	N27°59'	W82°42'	39
Cook	CKK	365	N25°47'	W80°20'	7
Cosme (LOM)	TP	368	N28°05'	W82°31'	—
Deland	DED	201	N29°04'	W81°16'	—
Dinns (LOM/NDB)	JA	344	N30°27'	W81°48'	19
Eastport	EYA	357	N30°25'	W81°36'	15
Fish Hook	FIS	332	N24°32'	W81°47'	—
Foley	FPY	254	N29°59'	W83°35'	—
Fort Pierce	FPR	275	N27°29'	W80°22'	24
Geiger Lake	GGL	375	N28°35'	W80°48'	—
Greenville	GRE	233	N38°50'	W89°22'	220
Herlong	HEG	332	N30°16'	W81°48'	—
Herny (LOM)	OR	221	N28°30'	W81°26'	—
Jumpi (LOM)	OC	423	N29°03'	W82°13'	75
Keyes (LOM)	MI	248	N25°47'	W80°11'	—

Location/Name	Ident	Freq	Lat	Long	Elev
Kissimmee	ISM	329	N28°17'	W81°26'	82
Knight	TPF	270	N27°54'	W82°27'	7
Kobra (LOM)	CE	201	N30°51'	W86°32'	255
Lake City	LCQ	204	N30°11'	W82°34'	200
Lakeland	LQL	263	N41°40'	W81°22'	130
Lynne (LOM)	PF	278	N30°19'	W85°46'	—
Marathon	MTH	260	N24°42'	W81°05'	—
Marco	MKY	375	N25°59'	W81°40'	152
Monry (LOM)	TN	227	N25°51'	W81°00'	—
Muffe (LOM)	RS	336	N26°29'	W81°50'	—
Naples	APF	201	N26°09'	W81°46'	—
New Smyrna Beach	EVB	417	N29°03'	W80°56'	12
Palatka	IAK	243	N29°39'	W81°48'	90
Pickens	PKZ	326	N30°26'	W87°10'	—
Picny (LOM/NDB)	AM	388	N27°51'	W82°32'	—
Plant City	PCM	346	N28°00'	W82°09'	134
Plantation	PJN	242	N26°07'	W80°13'	—
Praiz (LOM/NDB)	FX	221	N26°11'	W80°17'	15
Qeezy (LOM)	TM	266	N25°38'	W80°30'	8
Ringy (LOM)	SRI	245	N27°19'	W82°28'	—
Rubin (LOM/NDB)	PB	356	N26°41'	W80°12'	—
Sanford	SFB	408	N28°47'	W81°14'	—
Satellite	SQT	257	N28°05'	W80°42'	—
Sebring	SEF	382	N27°27'	W81°20'	119
Soyya	SMY	329	N30°52'	W85°13'	—
Tomok (LOM)	DA	263	N29°08'	W81°08'	47
Tri Co	BKK	275	N30°51'	W85°36'	—
Venice	VNC	206	N27°03'	W82°25'	19
Vero Beach	VEP	392	N27°39'	W80°25'	20
Wakul (LOM/NDB)	TL	379	N30°19'	W84°21'	—
Wirey (LOM)	LA	227	N27°56'	W82°04'	100
Wynds (LOM/NDB)	GN	269	N29°40'	W82°10'	—
Zephyrhills	RHZ	253	N28°13'	W82°09'	80

Georgia

Airports

Atlanta, GA – Hartsfield Intl

Ident	ATL	ATIS	125.55
Elev	1026	Rwy/Length/ILS/ID	8R/10000/109.90/IATL
Lat	N33°38'		26L/10000/108.70/IBRU
Long	W84°25'		8L/9000/109.30/IHFW
			26R/9000/110.10/IGXZ
			9R/9000/108.90/IFUN
			27L/9000/108.50/IFSQ
			9L/11889/110.50/IHZK
			27R/11889/111.30/IAFA

Atlanta, GA – Peachtree City-Falcon

Ident	FFC	ATIS	—
Elev	808	Rwy/Length/ILS/ID	31//111.95/IFFC
Lat	N33°21'		
Long	W84°34'		

Atlanta/Dekalb, GA – Peachtree

Ident	PDK	ATIS	128.4
Elev	1002	Rwy/Length/ILS/ID	20L/111.1/IPDK
Lat	N33°52'		
Long	W84°18'		

Atlanta/Fulton Co., GA – Brown

Ident	FTY	ATIS	120.17
Elev	841	Rwy/Length/ILS/ID	08//109.1/IFTY
Lat	N33°46'		
Long	W84°31'		

VORs

Location/Name	Type	Ident	Freq	Lat	Long	Elev
Alma	VORTAC	AMG	115.10	N31°32'	W82°30'	200
Athens	VORTAC	AHN	109.60	N33°56'	W83°19'	790
Atlanta	VORTAC	ATL	116.90	N33°37'	W84°26'	1000
Brunswick	VORTAC	SSI	109.80	N31°03'	W81°26'	10
Columbus	VORTAC	CSG	117.10	N32°36'	W85°01'	630
Dublin	VORTAC	DBN	113.10	N32°33'	W82°49'	300
Foothills	VORTAC	ODF	113.40	N34°41'	W83°17'	1700
Harris	VORTAC	HRS	109.80	N34°56'	W83°54'	3660
Hunter	VOR	SVN	111.60	N32°00'	W81°08'	40
La Grange	VORTAC	LGC	115.60	N33°02'	W85°12'	790
Lawson	VOR	LSF	111.40	N32°19'	W84°59'	260
Macon	VORTAC	MCN	114.20	N32°41'	W83°38'	350
Moultrie	VOR-DME	MGR	108.80	N31°04'	W83°48'	291
Peachtree	VOR-DME	PDK	116.60	N33°52'	W84°17'	970
Pecan	VORTAC	PZD	116.10	N31°39'	W84°17'	280
Rome	VORTAC	RMG	115.40	N34°09'	W85°07'	1150
Savannah	VORTAC	SAV	112.70	N32°09'	W81°06'	10
Tift Myers	VOR	IFM	112.50	N31°25'	W83°29'	351
Valdosta	VOR-DME	OTK	114.80	N30°46'	W83°16'	200
Vienna	VORTAC	VNA	116.50	N32°12'	W83°29'	300
Waycross	VORTAC	AYS	110.20	N31°16'	W82°33'	150

NDBs

Location/Name	Ident	Freq	Lat	Long	Elev
Alcovy	VOF	370	N33°37'	W83°46'	658
Barrow Co	BMW	404	N33°56'	W83°35'	810
Bay Creek	BEP	350	N32°27'	W83°45'	60
Bulldog	BJT	221	N33°57'	W83°13'	738
Bullock Co	IBU	407	N32°24'	W81°39'	125
Burke Co	BXG	356	N33°02'	W82°00'	295
Bushe (LOM)	AG	233	N33°17'	W81°56'	300
Caidy	CYR	338	N30°53'	W84°09'	245
Calhoun	OUK	323	N34°24'	W84°55'	695
Camilla	CXU	369	N31°12'	W84°14'	—
Canton	DJD	415	N34°15'	W84°29'	1100
Carrollton	GPQ	239	N33°33'	W85°07'	1000
Cartersville	EVZ	308	N34°11'	W84°50'	773
Catta (LOM)	AT	375	N33°38'	W84°32'	956
Coffee Co	OWC	390	N31°24'	W82°55'	260
Commerce	DDA	244	N34°03'	W83°31'	880
Coney	OHY	400	N31°59'	W83°51'	340
Coweta Co	EQQ	234	N33°15'	W84°42'	—
Culvr	ML	380	N33°09'	W83°09'	385
Donaldsonville	ONG	352	N31°00'	W84°52'	146
Eastman	EZM	270	N32°12'	W83°07'	300
Emanuel Co	EEX	309	N32°40'	W82°27'	256
Emory	EMR	385	N33°27'	W81°59'	424
Fenix (LOM)	CS	355	N32°27'	W85°02'	368
Fitzgerald	SUR	362	N31°36'	W83°17'	385
Flanc (LOM/NDB)	FT	344	N33°45'	W84°38'	900
Flowery Branch	FKV	365	N34°12'	W83°54'	1135
Floyd	OYD	388	N34°17'	W85°09'	—
Greensboro	EJK	397	N33°35'	W83°08'	662
Gwnet (LOM/NDB)	TX	419	N34°01'	W83°51'	984
Habersham	AJR	347	N34°30'	W83°32'	—
Hazlehurst	AZE	414	N31°52'	W82°38'	240
Homerville	HOE	209	N31°03'	W82°46'	180
Jeffi (LOM)	BQ	275	N31°13'	W81°32'	10
Kaolin	OKZ	212	N32°57'	W82°50'	430
Lawson	AWS	335	N32°17'	W85°01'	—
Lindbergh	LKG	242	N32°10'	W84°06'	475
Louvale	XLE	407	N32°09'	W84°50'	—
Mavis (LOM)	SA	368	N32°07'	W81°19'	—
Mc Duffie	THG	341	N33°31'	W82°26'	490
Mc Intosh	MOQ	263	N31°49'	W81°30'	—
Mc Rae	MQW	280	N32°05'	W82°53'	205
Metter	MHP	432	N32°22'	W82°05'	193
Monroe	JNM	429	N33°44'	W83°43'	820
Montezuma	IZS	426	N32°22'	W84°00'	435
Onyun	UQN	372	N32°13'	W82°17'	152
Patten	GTP	245	N30°57'	W83°49'	245
Pecat (LOM/NDB)	FF	316	N33°18'	W84°29'	850
Pickens Co	JZP	285	N34°27'	W84°27'	1535

Location/Name	Ident	Freq	Lat	Long	Elev
Pine Mountain	PIM	272	N32°50'	W84°52'	—
Prison	RVJ	424	N32°03'	W82°09'	—
Putny (LOM/NDB)	AB	227	N31°27'	W84°16'	—
Redan (LOM/NDB)	BR	266	N33°38'	W84°18'	834
Slover	JES	340	N31°33'	W81°53'	95
Sofke (LOM)	MC	290	N32°38'	W83°42'	—
Sylvania	JYL	245	N32°38'	W81°35'	181
Tifto (LOM)	TM	409	N31°21'	W83°26'	293
Turkey Creek	UPK	251	N32°29'	W83°00'	275
Washington-Wilkes Co.	IIY	435	N33°46'	W82°48'	651
Wassa (LOM)	SV	335	N32°00'	W80°59'	—
Whitfield	UWI	400	N34°47'	W84°56'	705
Willis	LYZ	359	N30°58'	W84°31'	130

Hawaii

Airports

Honolulu, HI – Honolulu Intl

Ident	HNL	ATIS	127.90
Elev	13	Rwy/Length/ILS/ID	08L/12357/109.50/IHNL
Lat	N21°19'		26R/12357
Long	W157°54'		08R/12000
			26L/12000/109.10/IEPC
			4L/6952
			22R/6952
			4R/9000/110.50/IIUM
			22L/9000

VORs

Location/Name	Type	Ident	Freq	Lat	Long	Elev
Hilo	VORTAC	ITO	116.90	N19°43'	W155°00'	23
Honolulu	VORTAC	HNL	114.80	N21°18'	W157°55'	10
Kamuela	VOR-DME	MUE	113.30	N19°59'	W155°40'	2670
Koko Head	VORTAC	CKH	113.90	N21°15'	W157°42'	640
Kona	VORTAC	IAI	115.70	N19°39'	W156°01'	50
Lanai City	VORTAC	LNY	117.70	N20°45'	W156°58'	1250
Lihue	VORTAC	LIH	113.50	N21°57'	W159°20'	110
Maui	VORTAC	OGG	114.30	N20°53'	W156°25'	30
Midway	TACAN	NQM	114.60	N28°12'	W177°22'	16
Molokai	VORTAC	MKK	116.10	N21°08'	W157°10'	1421
South Kauai	VORTAC	SOK	115.40	N21°54'	W159°31'	630
Upolu Point	VORTAC	UPP	112.30	N20°12'	W155°50'	1760

NDBs

Location/Name	Ident	Freq	Lat	Long	Elev
Bradshaw	BSF	339	N19°45'	W155°35'	—
Ewabe (LOM/NDB)	HN	242	N21°19'	W158°02'	—
Kaneohe Bay	NGF	265	N21°27'	W157°45'	47
Lanai	LLD	353	N20°46'	W156°57'	—
Valley Island	VYI	327	N20°52'	W156°26'	—

Idaho

Airports

Boise, ID – Boise Air Terminal – Gowen

Ident	BOI	**ATIS**	123.90
Elev	2858	**Rwy/Length/ILS/ID**	10R/9763/108.50/IBOI
Lat	N43°33'		28L/9763
Long	W116°13'		10L/7400
			28R/7400

VORs

Location/Name	Type	Ident	Freq	Lat	Long	Elev
Boise	VORTAC	BOI	113.30	N43°33'	W116°11'	2870
Burley	VORTAC	BYI	114.10	N42°34'	W113°51'	4230
Coeur D' Alene	VOR-DME	COE	108.80	N47°46'	W116°49'	2290
Donnelly	VORTAC	DNJ	116.20	N44°46'	W116°12'	7300
Dubois	VORTAC	DBS	116.90	N44°05'	W112°12'	4920
Idaho Falls	VOR-DME	IDA	109.00	N43°31'	W112°03'	4720
Malad City	VOR-DME	MLD	117.40	N42°11'	W112°27'	7330
Mountain Home	VOR	MUO	114.90	N42°58'	W115°46'	2990
Mullan Pass	VOR-DME	MLP	117.80	N47°27'	W115°38'	6100
Nez Perce	VOR-DME	MQG	108.20	N46°22'	W116°52'	1720
Pocatello	VORTAC	PIH	112.60	N42°52'	W112°39'	4430
Salmon	VOR-DME	LKT	113.50	N45°01'	W114°05'	9258
Twin Falls	VORTAC	TWF	115.80	N42°28'	W114°29'	4140

NDBs

Location/Name	Ident	Freq	Lat	Long	Elev
Bear Lake	BBH	233	N42°15'	W111°20'	—
Challis	LLJ	397	N44°31'	W114°12'	5030

Location/Name	Ident	Freq	Lat	Long	Elev
Council	CQI	274	N44°45'	W116°26'	2945
Grain	GVV	280	N45°56'	W116°13'	—
Hailey	HLE	220	N43°19'	W114°14'	4950
Leeny (LOM)	CO	347	N47°44'	W116°57'	2153
Mc Call	IOM	363	N44°48'	W116°06'	4912
Sandpoe	SZT	264	N48°17'	W116°33'	—
Steelhead	HDG	211	N42°54'	W114°40'	3622
Strik (LOM)	TW	389	N42°28'	W114°21'	4065
Sturgeon	STI	333	N43°06'	W115°40'	3130
Sweden	SWU	350	N43°25'	W112°09'	—
Tyhee (LOM)	PI	383	N42°57'	W112°30'	—
Uconn (LOM)	ID	324	N43°35'	W111°58'	4794
Ustik (LOM/NDB)	BO	359	N43°35'	W116°18'	2700

Illinois

Airports

Alton/St. Louis, IL – St. Louis Regl.

Ident	ALN	**ATIS**	128.0
Elev	544	**Rwy/Length/ILS/ID**	29//108.5/IALN
Lat	N38°53'		
Long	W90°02'		

Bloomington/Normal, IL – Bloomington/Normal

Ident	BMI	**ATIS**	135.35
Elev	875	**Rwy/Length/ILS/ID**	03/3723
Lat	N40°28'		21/3723
Long	W88°55'		11/6500
			29/6500/108.3/IBMI

Champaign/Urbana, IL – Univ of IL-Willard

Ident	CMI	**ATIS**	124.85
Elev	754	**Rwy/Length/ILS/ID**	04L/6500
Lat	N40°02'		22R/6500
Long	W88°16'		14R/8100
			32L/8100/109.10/ICMI
			18/5299
			36/5299

Chicago/Aurora – Aurora Muni

Ident	ARR	**ATIS**	—
Elev	707	**Rwy/Length/ILS/ID**	09/6500/108.9/IARR
Lat	N41°46'		27/6500
Long	W88°28'		18/3199
			36/3199

Chicago,IL – Chicago Midway

Ident	MDW	ATIS	132.75
Elev	619	Rwy/Length/ILS/ID	4R/6446/111.5/IHKH
Lat	N41°47'		22L/6446
Long	W87°45'		4L/5509
			22R/5509
			13R/3859
			31L/3859
			13C/6521/109.9/IMDW
			31C/6521/109.9/IMXT
			13L/5141
			31R/5141

Chicago, IL – Chicago O'Hare Intl

Ident	ORD	ATIS	135.40
Elev	668	Rwy/Length/ILS/ID	4R/8071/110.10/IFJU
Lat	N41°59'		22L//110.10/ILQQ
Long	W87°54'		4L/7500/111.30/IHNA
			22R/7500/111.30/IRXZ
			9R//111.10/IMED
			27L/10141/111.10/ITSL
			9L//110.50/IJAV
			27R/7966/110.50/IIAC
			14R/13000/109.75/IORD
			32L/13000/108.95/IRVG
			14L/10003/110.90/IOHA
			32R/10003/110.75/IIDN
			18/5341
			36/5341

Chicago, IL – Lansing Muni

Ident	3HA	ATIS	—
Elev	616	Rwy/Length	09/3658
Lat	N41°32'		27/3658
Long	W87°31'		18/2322 Grass
			36/2322 Grass

Chicago/Schaumburg – Schaumburg Air Park

Ident	O6C	ATIS	—
Elev	797	Rwy/Length	10/3000
Lat	N41°59'		28/3000
Long	W88°06'		

Chicago, IL – Dupage

Ident	DPA	ATIS	124.8
Elev	758	Rwy/Length/ILS/ID	1L/5100/111.7/IGVK
Lat	N41°54'		19R/5100
Long	W88°15'		1R/3300
			19L/3300
			10/4750/109.5/IDPA
			28/4750
			15/3401
			33/3401

Chicago, IL – Meigs

Ident	CGX	ATIS	127.35
Elev	593	Rwy/Length	18/3947
Lat	N51°31'		36/3947
Long	W87°36'		

Chicago/Prospect Heights/Wheeling – Palwaukee Municipal

Ident	PWK	ATIS	124.2
Elev	647	Rwy/Length/ILS/ID	16//111.9/IPWK
Lat	N42°06'		
Long	W87°54'		

Chicago/Romeoville, IL – Lewis Univ

Ident	LOT	ATIS	—
Elev	668	Rwy/Length	09/4000
Lat	N41°36'		27/4000
Long	W88°05'		06/2400 Grass
			24/2400 Grass

Chicago/Waukegan, IL – Waukegan Regional

Ident	UGN	ATIS	132.4
Elev	727	Rwy/Length/ILS/ID	23//110.7/IUGN
Lat	N42°25'		
Long	W87°52'		

Danville, IL – Vermilion County

Ident	DNV	ATIS	—
Elev	696	Rwy/Length/ILS/ID	03/5399
Lat	N40°12'		21/5399/108.5/IDNV
Long	W87°35'		16/3999
			34/3999
			12/2500 Grass
			30/2500 Grass

Dwight, IL – Dwight

Ident	DTG	ATIS	—
Elev	632	Rwy/Length	09/2368 Grass
Lat	N41°07'		27/2368 Grass
Long	W88°26'		18/2000 Grass
			36/2000 Grass

Frankfort, IL – Frankfort

Ident	C18	ATIS	—
Elev	778	Rwy/Length	—
Lat	N41°28'		
Long	W87°50'		

Gibson City, IL – Gibson City Muni

Ident	C34	ATIS	—
Elev	758	Rwy/Length	09/2400 Grass
Lat	N40°29'		27/2400 Grass
Long	W88°16'		18/3400
			36/3400

Glenview, IL – Glenview NAS

Ident		ATIS	—
Elev	653	Rwy/Length	—
Lat	N42°05'		
Long	W87°49'		

Grayslake, IL – Campbell

Ident	C81	ATIS	—
Elev	788	Rwy/Length	—
Lat	N42°19'		
Long	W88°04'		

Greenwood/Wonder Lake, IL – Galt

Ident	10C	ATIS	—
Elev	875	Rwy/Length	—
Lat	N42°24'		
Long	W88°22'		

Joliet, IL – Joliet Park District

Ident	JOT	ATIS	—
Elev	582	Rwy/Length	12/2970
Lat	N41°31 '		30/2970
Long	W88°10'		04/3452 Grass
			22/3452 Grass

Kankakee, IL – Greater Kankakee

Ident	IKK	ATIS	—
Elev	630	Rwy/Length/ILS/ID	04/5985/108.7/IIKK
Lat	N41°04'		22/5985
Long	W87°50'		16/4400
			34/4400

Lake in the Hills, IL – Lake in the Hills

Ident	3CK	ATIS	—
Elev	886	Rwy/Length	—
Lat	N42°12'		
Long	W88°19'		

Monee, IL – Sanger

Ident	C56	ATIS	—
Elev	790	Rwy/Length	05/2313
Lat	N41°22'		23/2313
Long	W87°40'		09/2412
			27/2412

Morris, IL – Morris Muni-James R. Washburn

Ident	C09	ATIS	—
Elev	584	Rwy/Length	18/4000
Lat	N41°25'		36/4000
Long	W88°25'		

New Lenox, IL – Howell-New Lenox

Ident	1C2	ATIS	—
Elev	753	Rwy/Length	05/2103
Lat	N41°28'		23/2103
Long	W87°55'		13/2857
			31/2857

Paxton, IL – Paxton

Ident	1C1	ATIS	—
Elev	779	Rwy/Length	18/3409
Lat	N40°26'		36/3409
Long	W88°07'		

Plainfield, IL – Clow Intl

Ident	1C5	ATIS	—
Elev	670	Rwy/Length	18/3370
Lat	N41°41'		36/3370
Long	W88°07'		

Urbana, IL – Frasca Field

Ident	C16	ATIS	—
Elev	735	Rwy/Length	09/4000
Lat	N40°08'		27/4000
Long	W88°12'		

VORs

Location/Name	Type	Ident	Freq	Lat	Long	Elev
Bible Grove	VORTAC	BIB	109.00	N38°55'	W88°28'	540
Bloomington	VOR-DME	BMI	108.20	N40°28'	W88°55'	880
Bradford	VORTAC	BDF	114.70	N41°09'	W89°35'	810
Capital	VORTAC	CAP	112.70	N39°53'	W89°37'	590
Centralia	VORTAC	ENL	115.00	N38°25'	W89°09'	550
Champaign	VORTAC	CMI	110.00	N40°02'	W88°16'	750
Chicago Heights	VORTAC	CGT	114.20	N41°30'	W87°34'	630
Chicago-Ohare	VOR-DME	ORD	113.90	N41°59'	W87°54'	650
Danville	VORTAC	DNV	111.00	N40°17'	W87°33'	700
Decatur	VORTAC	DEC	117.20	N39°44'	W88°51'	700
Dupage	VOR-DME	DPA	108.40	N41°53'	W88°21'	800
Galesburg	VOR-DME	GBG	109.80	N40°56'	W90°26'	760
Jacksonville	VOR-DME	IJX	108.60	N39°46'	W90°14'	615
Joliet	VORTAC	JOT	112.30	N41°32'	W88°19'	590
Kankakee	VOR	IKK	111.60	N41°04'	W87°50'	618

Location/Name	Type	Ident	Freq	Lat	Long	Elev
Lawrenceville	VOR-DME	LWV	113.50	N38°46'	W87°35'	429
Marion	VOR-DME	MWA	110.40	N37°45'	W89°00'	490
Mattoon	VOR-DME	MTO	109.40	N39°28'	W88°17'	720
Moline	VORTAC	MZV	114.40	N41°19'	W90°38'	820
Mount Vernon	VOR-DME	VNN	113.80	N38°21'	W88°48'	555
Northbrook	VORTAC	OBK	113.00	N42°13'	W87°57'	710
Peoria	VORTAC	PIA	115.20	N40°40'	W89°47'	730
Peotone	VORTAC	EON	113.20	N41°16'	W87°47'	690
Polo	VORTAC	PLL	111.20	N41°57'	W89°31'	840
Pontiac	VORTAC	PNT	109.60	N40°49'	W88°44'	680
Quincy	VORTAC	UIN	113.60	N39°50'	W91°16'	710
Roberts	VORTAC	RBS	116.80	N40°34'	W88°09'	780
Rockford	VORTAC	RFD	110.80	N42°13'	W89°11'	860
Samsville	VOR-DME	SAM	116.60	N38°29'	W88°05'	540
Troy	VORTAC	TOY	116.00	N38°44'	W89°55'	570
Vandalia	VORTAC	VLA	114.30	N39°05'	W89°09'	610

NDBs

Location/Name	Ident	Freq	Lat	Long	Elev
Abraham	AAA	329	N40°09'	W89°20'	592
Alpos (LOM)	AL	218	N38°51'	W89°56'	—
Belleville	BL	362	N38°27'	W89°45'	419
Bellgrade	BDD	254	N37°08'	W88°40'	388
Benton	BEE	414	N38°00'	W88°55'	445
Cabbi (LOM)	MD	388	N37°52'	W89°14'	411
Cahokia	CPS	375	N38°34'	W90°09'	413
Cairo	CIR	397	N37°03'	W89°13'	318
Canton	CTK	236	N40°33'	W90°04'	715
Carmi	CUL	332	N38°05'	W88°07'	384
Casey	CZB	359	N39°18'	W88°00'	643
Civic Memorial	CVM	263	N38°53'	W90°03'	—
Deana (LOM/NDB)	ME	350	N41°58'	W88°01'	—
Dekalb	DKB	209	N41°55'	W88°42'	911
Dwight	DTG	344	N41°08'	W88°26'	624
Elm River	FOA	353	N38°40'	W88°27'	—
Elwin (LOM)	DE	275	N39°47'	W88°57'	—
Ermin (LOM/NDB)	HK	332	N41°43'	W87°50'	691
Freeport	FEP	335	N42°14'	W89°35'	—
Gilmy (LOM)	RF	275	N42°06'	W89°05'	—
Harrisburg/Raleigh	HSB	230	N37°48'	W88°32'	397
Homer	HMJ	281	N40°01'	W87°57'	—
Huskk (LOM/NDB)	SP	382	N39°46'	W89°45'	—
Jocky (LOM)	RV	257	N41°53'	W87°49'	—
Jonny (LOM)	MW	382	N37°50'	W88°58'	390
Kedzi (LOM/NDB)	MX	248	N41°44'	W87°41'	623
Kewanee	EZI	245	N41°12'	W89°57'	856
Leama (LOM)	OH	368	N42°04'	W87°59'	—
Macomb	JZY	251	N40°31'	W90°33'	622

Location/Name	Ident	Freq	Lat	Long	Elev
Metropolis	MIX	281	N37°11'	W88°45'	—
Molli (LOM)	ML	215	N41°26'	W90°37'	578
Mount Carmel	AJG	524	N38°36'	W87°43'	—
Olney	OLY	272	N38°43'	W88°10'	470
Ottawa	OIX	266	N41°21'	W88°51'	—
Palestine	PLX	391	N39°00'	W87°38'	—
Paris	PRG	341	N39°41'	W87°40'	655
Pittsfield	PPQ	344	N39°38'	W90°46'	702
Quincy (LOM/NDB)	UI	293	N39°53'	W91°15'	—
Roamy (LOM)	OR	394	N42°03'	W88°00'	693
Salem	SLO	400	N38°38'	W88°58'	—
Shelbyville	SYZ	365	N39°24'	W88°50'	810
Sparta	SAR	239	N38°08'	W89°42'	532
Taffs (LOM)	IA	414	N41°59'	W87°47'	—
Taylorville	TAZ	395	N39°32'	W89°19'	613
Tungg (LOM/NDB)	PI	356	N40°36'	W89°35'	—
Valley	VYS	230	N41°21'	W89°08'	652
Veals (LOM)	CM	407	N39°57'	W88°10'	—
Wauke (LOM)	UG	379	N42°27'	W87°48'	—
Wayne Co	FWC	257	N38°22'	W88°24'	421
Whiteside	BOZ	254	N41°42'	W89°47'	934
Zebre (LOM/NDB)	MT	347	N39°26'	W88°10'	575

Indiana

Airports

Gary, IN – Gary Regional

Ident	GYY	ATIS	125.6
Elev	591	Rwy/Length/ILS/ID	30//108.3/IGYY
Lat	N41°00'		
Long	W87°24'		

Griffith, IN – Merrillville

Ident	05C	ATIS	—
Elev	634	Rwy/Length	—
Lat	N41°31'		
Long	W87°24'		

Indianapolis, IN – Indianapolis Intl

Ident	IND	ATIS	124.4
Elev	797	Rwy/Length/ILS/ID	5L/10005/109.30/IIND
Lat	N39°43'		23R/10005/110.90/IUZK
Long	W86°17'		5R/10000/111.15/IOQV
			23L/10000/111.75/IFVJ
			14/7604/110.50/IBJP
			32/7604/110.50/ICOA

Lowell, IN – Lowell

Ident	C97	ATIS	—
Elev	675	Rwy/Length	—
Lat	N41°13'		
Long	W87°30'		

VORs

Location/Name	Type	Ident	Freq	Lat	Long	Elev
Boiler	VORTAC	BVT	115.10	N40°33'	W87°04'	750
Fort Wayne	VORTAC	FWA	117.80	N40°58'	W85°11'	800
Goshen	VORTAC	GSH	113.70	N41°31'	W86°01'	850
Grissom	VORTAC	GUS	116.50	N40°38'	W86°09'	810
Hoosier	VORTAC	OOM	110.20	N39°08'	W86°36'	850
Huntingburg	VOR-DME	HNB	109.20	N38°15'	W86°57'	530
Indianapolis	VORTAC	VHP	116.30	N39°48'	W86°22'	870
Knox	VORTAC	OXI	115.60	N41°19'	W86°38'	690
Kokomo	VORTAC	OKK	109.80	N40°31'	W86°03'	830
Marion	VOR-DME	MZZ	108.60	N40°29'	W85°40'	850
Muncie	VOR-DME	MIE	114.40	N40°14'	W85°23'	940
Nabb	VORTAC	ABB	112.40	N38°35'	W85°38'	710
Pocket City	VORTAC	PXV	113.30	N37°55'	W87°45'	430
Richmond	VORTAC	RID	110.60	N39°45'	W84°50'	1135
Shelbyville	VORTAC	SHB	112.00	N39°37'	W85°49'	810
Terre Haute	VORTAC	TTH	115.30	N39°29'	W87°14'	610
Wolf Lake	VOR	OLK	110.40	N41°14'	W85°29'	970

NDBs

Location/Name	Ident	Freq	Lat	Long	Elev
Airpa (LOM)	EY	209	N39°55'	W86°14'	882
Angola	ANQ	347	N41°38'	W85°05'	—
Balll (LOM)	JN	365	N40°10'	W85°19'	980
Bedford	BFR	344	N38°50'	W86°26'	720
Brinn (LOM)	OQ	219	N39°37'	W86°24'	710
Captain	EQZ	308	N38°52'	W85°58'	592
Claye (LOM/NDB)	BM	382	N39°03'	W86°35'	761
Clifs (LOM/NDB)	BA	410	N39°19'	W85°49'	700
Colfa (LOM)	CO	232	N39°39'	W86°11'	—
Crawfordsville	CFJ	388	N39°58'	W86°54'	803
Culver	CPB	391	N41°13'	W86°23'	—
Earle (LOM)	LA	401	N40°25'	W87°03'	670
Evansville	PDW	284	N38°02'	W87°31'	382
Ferdinand	FNZ	239	N38°14'	W86°50'	550
Garie (LOM)	GY	236	N41°34'	W87°19'	—
Greencastle	TVX	521	N39°42'	W86°48'	825
Greenwood	HFY	318	N39°37'	W86°05'	818
Happs (LOM)	JV	331	N38°28'	W85°44'	525

Location/Name	Ident	Freq	Lat	Long	Elev
Hoagy (LOM)	FW	251	N40°55'	W85°07'	—
Huntington	HHG	417	N40°51'	W85°27'	808
Larez (LOM)	FV	349	N39°47'	W86°11'	710
Logansport	GGP	263	N40°42'	W86°22'	732
Madison	IMS	404	N38°45'	W85°27'	874
Metropolitan	UMP	338	N39°56'	W86°03'	788
Michigan City	MGC	203	N41°42'	W86°48'	—
Misha (LOM)	SB	341	N41°42'	W86°13'	—
New Castle	UWL	385	N39°52'	W85°19'	—
North Vernon	OVO	374	N39°02'	W85°36'	—
Oranj	RRJ	368	N38°31'	W86°31'	615
Portland	PLD	257	N40°27'	W84°59'	—
Pully (LOM/NDB)	IN	266	N39°38'	W86°23'	682
Rensselaer	RZL	362	N40°56'	W87°11'	—
Rochester	RCR	216	N41°03'	W86°11'	786
Sedly (LOM/NDB)	VP	212	N41°27'	W86°52'	—
Sullivan	SIV	326	N39°06'	W87°26'	—
Tell City	TEL	206	N38°00'	W86°41'	663
Vicci (LOM)	EV	219	N38°07'	W87°26'	440
Video (LOM/NDB)	AI	371	N40°04'	W85°30'	970
Vincennes	OEA	251	N38°41'	W87°33'	414
Wabash	IWH	329	N40°45'	W85°47'	—
Washington	DCY	212	N38°41'	W87°07'	471
White Co	MCX	377	N40°42'	W86°45'	676
Winamac	RWN	335	N41°05'	W86°36'	707
Winchester	AWW	212	N40°10'	W84°55'	1110
Yinno (LOM/NDB)	HU	245	N39°23'	W87°23'	—
Zionsville	HZP	248	N39°56'	W86°14'	885

Iowa

Airports

Sioux City, IA – Sioux Gateway

Ident	SUX	ATIS	119.45
Elev	1098	Rwy/Length/ILS/ID	13/8999/111.30/IOIQ
Lat	N42°24'		31/8999/109.30/ISUX
Long	W96 23		17/6599
			35/6599

VORs

Location/Name	Type	Ident	Freq	Lat	Long	Elev
Cedar Rapids	VORTAC	CID	114.10	N41°53'	W91°47'	870
Davenport	VORTAC	CVA	113.80	N41°42'	W90°29'	760

Location/Name	Type	Ident	Freq	Lat	Long	Elev
Des Moines	VORTAC	DSM	117.50	N41°26'	W93°38'	940
Dubuque	VORTAC	DBQ	115.80	N42°24'	W90°42'	1060
Elmwood	VOR	EMD	111.00	N42°06'	W92°54'	992
Estherville	VOR	EST	110.40	N43°24'	W94°44'	1320
Fort Dodge	VORTAC	FOD	113.50	N42°36'	W94°17'	1150
Iowa City	VORTAC	IOW	116.20	N41°31'	W91°36'	770
Lamoni	VORTAC	LMN	116.70	N40°35'	W93°58'	1140
Mason City	VORTAC	MCW	114.90	N43°05'	W93°19'	1210
Newton	VOR-DME	TNU	112.50	N41°47'	W93°06'	980
Ottumwa	VORTAC	OTM	111.60	N41°01'	W92°19'	820
Port City	VOR-DME	RTY	108.80	N41°22'	W91°08'	538
Sheldon	VOR-DME	DDL	108.60	N43°12'	W95°50'	1420
Sioux City	VORTAC	SUX	116.50	N42°20'	W96°19'	1080
Spencer	VOR-DME	SPW	110.00	N43°09'	W95°12'	1330
Waterloo	VORTAC	ALO	112.20	N42°33'	W92°23'	865
Waukon	VORTAC	UKN	116.60	N43°16'	W91°32'	1300

NDBs

Location/Name	Ident	Freq	Lat	Long	Elev
Algona	AXA	403	N43°04'	W94°16'	1210
Ames	AMW	275	N41°59'	W93°37'	929
Atlantic	AIO	365	N41°24'	W95°02'	1153
Audubon	ADU	266	N41°41'	W94°54'	1320
Auney (LOM)	DV	353	N41°41'	W90°39'	748
Barro (LOM)	FO	341	N42°30'	W94°18'	1149
Bloomfield	BEX	269	N40°44'	W92°25'	850
Boone	BNW	407	N42°03'	W93°51'	1143
Burns (LOM)	BR	390	N40°39'	W91°07'	575
Carroll	CIN	397	N42°02'	W94°47'	1202
Centerville	TVK	290	N40°41'	W92°53'	1020
Chariton	CNC	209	N41°01'	W93°21'	1050
Charles City	CCY	375	N43°04'	W92°36'	1130
Chukk	IY	417	N43°08'	W92°43'	1063
Cindy (LOM)	CI	326	N41°53'	W91°48'	—
Clarinda	ICL	353	N40°43'	W95°01'	988
Clarion	CAV	387	N42°44'	W93°45'	1152
Clinton	CWI	377	N41°49'	W90°19'	710
Corning	CRZ	296	N40°59'	W94°45'	1245
Cresco	CJJ	293	N43°21'	W92°07'	1265
Decorah	DEH	347	N43°16'	W91°44'	1137
Denison	DNS	350	N41°59'	W95°22'	1290
Eagle Grove	EAG	302	N42°42'	W93°54'	1128
Emmetsburg	EGQ	410	N43°06'	W94°42'	1200
Fairfield	FFL	332	N41°00'	W91°59'	778
Forem (LOM)	DS	344	N41°28'	W93°34'	—

Location/Name	Ident	Freq	Lat	Long	Elev
Forest City	FXY	359	N43°14'	W93°37'	1197
Garrison	VTI	338	N42°13'	W92°01'	825
Greenfield	GFZ	338	N41°19'	W94°26'	1359
Grinnell	GGI	248	N41°42'	W92°43'	995
Guthrie Center	GCT	518	N41°40'	W94°25'	1277
Hampton	HPT	230	N42°43'	W93°13'	1164
Harlan	HNR	272	N41°34'	W95°20'	1200
Hawkeye	UOC	524	N41°37'	W91°32'	648
Hillz (LOM)	FN	517	N41°45'	W90°23'	631
Iowa Falls	IFA	368	N42°28'	W93°15'	1132
Jefferson	EFW	391	N42°00'	W94°20'	1041
Keokuk	EOK	366	N40°27'	W91°26'	671
Knoxville	OXV	284	N41°17'	W93°06'	920
Le Mars	LRJ	382	N42°46'	W96°11'	1190
Little Sioux	LTU	326	N43°07'	W95°07'	1312
Mapleton	MEY	335	N42°10'	W95°47'	1250
Maquoketa	OQW	386	N42°03'	W90°44'	765
Marshalltown	MIW	239	N42°06'	W92°55'	974
Merle (LOM)	IA	362	N41°54'	W93°39'	1022
Monticello	MXO	397	N42°12'	W91°08'	—
Mount Pleasant	MPZ	212	N40°56'	W91°30'	—
Muscatine	MUT	272	N41°21'	W91°08'	547
Oelwein	OLZ	260	N42°41'	W91°58'	—
Orange City	ORC	521	N42°59'	W96°03'	1414
Oskaloosa	OOA	414	N41°13'	W92°29'	—
Pella	PEA	257	N41°24'	W92°56'	—
Perry	PRO	251	N41°49'	W94°09'	1014
Pilot Rock	CKP	423	N42°43'	W95°33'	1220
Pocahontas	POH	314	N42°44'	W94°38'	—
Price (LOM)	AL	382	N42°37'	W92°30'	921
Puff	PUF	345	N43°21'	W94°44'	1300
Red Oak	RDK	230	N41°00'	W95°15'	1040
Rock Rapids	RRQ	515	N43°27'	W96°10'	1360
Sac City	SKI	356	N42°22'	W94°58'	1245
Salix (LOM/NDB)	SU	414	N42°19'	W96°17'	1080
Sheldon	SHL	338	N43°12'	W95°50'	1419
Shenandoah	SDA	411	N40°45'	W95°24'	968
Sibley	ISB	269	N43°22'	W95°45'	1531
Sioux Center	SOY	368	N43°07'	W96°11'	1435
Snore (LOM)	SP	394	N43°13'	W95°19'	1430
Storm Lake	SLB	227	N42°36'	W95°14'	1485
Surff (LOM)	MC	308	N43°03'	W93°19'	—
Tommi (LOM/NDB)	OI	305	N42°27'	W96°27'	—
Union Co	UNE	379	N40°57'	W94°20'	1268
Wapsie	IIB	206	N42°27'	W91°57'	960
Washington	AWG	219	N41°16'	W91°40'	752
Webster City	EBS	323	N42°26'	W93°52'	1100
West Union	XWY	278	N42°56'	W91°46'	1250
Zilom (LOM)	DB	341	N42°19'	W90°35'	980

Kansas

Airports

Great Bend, KS – Great Bend Muni

Ident	GBD	**ATIS**	122.80	
Elev	1887	**Rwy/Length/ILS/ID**	11/4698	
Lat	N38°20'		29/4698	
Long	W98°51'		17/7999	
			35/7999/111.90/IGBD	

Topeka, KS – Philip Billard

Ident	TOP	**ATIS**	118.70	
Elev	1080	**Rwy/Length/ILS/ID**	03/8002	
Lat	N39°04'		21/8002	
Long	W95°37'		13/12819/110.70/ITOP	
			31/12819	

VORs

Location/Name	Type	Ident	Freq	Lat	Long	Elev
Anthony	VORTAC	ANY	112.90	N37°09'	W98°10'	1390
Chanute	VOR-DME	CNU	109.20	N37°37'	W95°35'	1080
Dodge City	VORTAC	DDC	108.20	N37°51'	W100°00'	2565
Emporia	VORTAC	EMP	112.80	N38°17'	W96°08'	1220
Fort Riley	VOR	FRI	109.40	N38°58'	W96°51'	1240
Garden City	VORTAC	GCK	113.30	N37°55'	W100°43'	2880
Goodland	VORTAC	GLD	115.10	N39°23'	W101°41'	3650
Hays	VORTAC	HYS	110.40	N38°50'	W99°16'	2020
Hill City	VORTAC	HLC	113.70	N39°15'	W100°13'	2690
Hutchinson	VORTAC	HUT	116.80	N37°59'	W97°56'	1530
Johnson Co	VOR-DME	OJC	113.00	N38°50'	W94°44'	1030
Liberal	VORTAC	LBL	112.30	N37°02'	W100°58'	2890
Manhattan	VOR-DME	MHK	110.20	N39°08'	W96°40'	1060
Mankato	VORTAC	TKO	109.80	N39°48'	W98°15'	1880
Oswego	VORTAC	OSW	117.60	N37°09'	W95°12'	930
Salina	VORTAC	SLN	117.10	N38°55'	W97°37'	1315
Strother	VOR	SOR	109.60	N37°10'	W97°02'	1160
Topeka	VORTAC	TOP	117.80	N39°08'	W95°32'	1070
Wichita	VORTAC	ICT	113.80	N37°44'	W97°35'	1470

NDBs

Location/Name	Ident	Freq	Lat	Long	Elev
Atwood	ADT	365	N39°50'	W101°02'	2936
Babsy (LOM)	GB	419	N38°15'	W98°51'	1932
Bear Creek	JHN	341	N37°38'	W101°44'	3324
Biloy (LOM/NDB)	TO	521	N39°07'	W95°41'	913
Boyd	UKL	245	N38°17'	W95°43'	1171
Cavalry	CVY	314	N39°01'	W96°47'	1060
Clay Center	CYW	362	N39°22'	W97°09'	1205
Coffeyville	CFV	212	N37°05'	W95°34'	754
Concordia	CNK	335	N39°33'	W97°39'	1459
Dustt (LOM)	IX	368	N38°44'	W94°53'	1040
El Dorado	EQA	383	N37°46'	W96°48'	1370
Elkhart	EHA	377	N37°00'	W101°53'	3617
Flory (LOM)	SL	344	N38°40'	W97°38'	1315
Fort Scott	FSK	379	N37°47'	W94°45'	900
Furor (LOM)	OJ	526	N38°56'	W94°44'	1028
Harvs (LOM)	CA	395	N38°08'	W97°16'	1530
Herington	HRU	407	N38°41'	W96°48'	1485
Hilyn	HIL	308	N38°21'	W98°54'	1900
Hugoton	HQG	365	N37°09'	W101°22'	3129
Independence	IDP	400	N37°09'	W95°46'	826
Larned	LQR	296	N38°12'	W99°05'	2010
Lyons	LYO	386	N38°20'	W98°13'	—
Marysville	MYZ	341	N39°51'	W96°38'	997
Mc Dowell Creek	MQD	391	N39°07'	W96°37'	1060
Mc Pherson	MPR	227	N38°20'	W97°41'	1490
Meade	MEJ	389	N37°17'	W100°21'	—
Monarch	MSB	410	N37°47'	W95°24'	972
Morrison	DBX	212	N39°45'	W97°02'	1380
Nette (LOM)	HY	374	N38°46'	W99°15'	1978
Newton	EWK	281	N38°03'	W97°16'	—
Norton	NRN	230	N39°51'	W99°53'	2343
Oakley	OEL	380	N39°06'	W100°48'	3042
Oberlin	OIN	341	N39°49'	W100°32'	2655
Ottawa	OWI	251	N38°32'	W95°15'	959
Panck (LOM)	LB	383	N36°57'	W100°57'	2845
Parsons	PPF	293	N37°20'	W95°30'	887
Phillipsburg	PHG	368	N39°42'	W99°17'	1855
Piche (LOM/NDB)	IC	332	N37°34'	W97°27'	—
Pieve (LOM/NDB)	GC	347	N37°49'	W100°43'	2824
Pittsburg	PTS	365	N37°26'	W94°43'	918
Pratt	PTT	356	N37°43'	W98°44'	1951
Republican	RPB	414	N39°48'	W97°39'	—
Riply (LOM)	FO	326	N38°53'	W95°34'	1048
Saint Francis	SYF	386	N39°43'	W101°45'	3454
Saltt (LOM)	HU	404	N38°07'	W97°55'	—
Sawcy (LOM)	SO	353	N37°05'	W97°02'	1169
Scott City	TQK	256	N38°28'	W100°53'	2962
Shugr (LOM/NDB)	GL	414	N39°17'	W101°36'	3597
Ulysses	ULS	395	N37°35'	W101°22'	—
Wellington	EGT	414	N37°19'	W97°23'	1270
Wheatfield	JDM	408	N39°30'	W101°02'	3153

Kentucky

Airports

Louisville, KY – Standiford Field

Ident	SDF	**ATIS**	118.15
Elev	496	**Rwy/Length/ILS/ID**	01/10001/110.30/ISDF
Lat	N38°10'		19/10001/111.30/IADO
Long	W85°44'		11/7249
			29/7249/109.10/ILKS

VORs

Location/Name	Type	Ident	Freq	Lat	Long	Elev
Bowling Green	VORTAC	BWG	117.90	N36°55'	W86°26'	560
Bowman	VOR-DME	BQM	112.20	N38°13'	W85°39'	540
Central City	VORTAC	CCT	109.80	N37°22'	W87°15'	480
Cunningham	VORTAC	CNG	113.10	N37°00'	W88°50'	480
Falmouth	VOR-DME	FLM	117.00	N38°38'	W84°18'	810
Fort Knox	VOR-DME	FTK	109.60	N37°54'	W85°58'	740
Frankfort	VOR	FFT	109.40	N38°10'	W84°54'	805
Hazard	VOR-DME	AZQ	111.20	N37°23'	W83°15'	1247
Lexington	VORTAC	HYK	112.60	N37°57'	W84°28'	1040
London	VORTAC	LOZ	116.10	N37°01'	W84°06'	1250
Louisville	VORTAC	IIU	114.80	N38°06'	W85°34'	720
Mystic	VOR	MYS	108.20	N37°53'	W86°14'	790
New Hope	VOR-DME	EWO	110.80	N37°37'	W85°40'	960
Newcombe	VORTAC	ECB	110.40	N38°09'	W82°54'	1070
Owensboro	VOR-DME	OWB	108.60	N37°44'	W87°09'	400

NDBs

Location/Name	Ident	Freq	Lat	Long	Elev
Airbe (LOM/NDB)	FK	293	N36°44'	W87°24'	593
Bardstown	BRY	248	N37°50'	W85°28'	—
Beaver Creek	BVQ	260	N37°01'	W86°00'	745
Blayd (LOM/NDB)	LE	242	N37°59'	W84°39'	—
Claww (LOM/NDB)	SD	229	N38°05'	W85°45'	—
Cumberland River	CDX	388	N36°59'	W84°40'	955
Elk Spring	EKQ	290	N36°51'	W84°51'	950
Farrington	FIO	263	N36°58'	W88°34'	—
Flemingsburg	FGX	400	N38°32'	W83°44'	921
Frankfort	FKR	278	N40°16'	W86°33'	805
Geneva	GVA	224	N37°48'	W87°46'	450
Godman	GOI	396	N37°57'	W85°58'	—

Location/Name	Ident	Freq	Lat	Long	Elev
Goodall	DVK	311	N37°34'	W84°45'	1000
Higuy (LOM)	OW	341	N37°38'	W87°09'	—
Honey Grove	HIX	356	N36°52'	W87°20'	610
Jett	JET	365	N38°12'	W84°49'	—
Laang (LOM)	LK	414	N38°08'	W85°37'	624
Mayfield	GGK	401	N36°41'	W88°35'	490
Mount Sterling	IOB	210	N38°03'	W83°58'	1016
Muhlenberg	GMH	362	N37°13'	W87°09'	420
Seco	XYC	393	N37°45'	W84°01'	780
Springfield	IKY	429	N37°38'	W85°14'	927
Taylor Co	TYC	272	N37°24'	W85°14'	1053
Tradewater	TWT	276	N37°27'	W87°56'	402

Louisiana

Airports

New Orleans, LA – New Orleans Intl

Ident	MSY	**ATIS**	127.55
Elev	6	**Rwy/Length/ILS/ID**	01/7000/111.70/IJFI
Lat	N29°59'		19/7000
Long	W90°15'		06/4542
			24/4542
			10/10080/109.90/IMSY
			28/10080/109.90/IHOX

VORs

Location/Name	Type	Ident	Freq	Lat	Long	Elev
Alexandria	VORTAC	AEX	116.10	N31°15'	W92°30'	80
Barksdale	VOR	BAD	115.80	N32°30'	W93°40'	160
Baton Rouge	VORTAC	BTR	116.50	N30°29'	W91°17'	20
Downtown	VOR	DTN	108.60	N32°32'	W93°44'	180
Elm Grove	VORTAC	EMG	111.20	N32°24'	W93°35'	160
Esler	VORTAC	ESF	117.90	N31°26'	W92°19'	195
Hammond	VOR	HMU	109.60	N30°31'	W90°25'	40
Harvey	VORTAC	HRV	112.40	N29°51'	W90°00'	1
Lake Charles	VORTAC	LCH	113.40	N30°08'	W93°06'	20
Leeville	VORTAC	LEV	113.50	N29°10'	W90°06'	2
Monroe	VORTAC	MLU	117.20	N32°31'	W92°02'	80
New Orleans	VORTAC	MSY	113.20	N30°01'	W90°10'	1
Polk	VOR	FXU	108.40	N31°06'	W93°13'	310
Shreveport	VORTAC	SHV	117.40	N32°46'	W93°48'	—
Tibby	VORTAC	TBD	112.00	N29°39'	W90°49'	10
White Lake	VOR-DME	LLA	111.40	N29°39'	W92°22'	5

NDBs

Location/Name	Ident	Freq	Lat	Long	Elev
Acadi (LOM/NDB)	AR	269	N29°57'	W91°51'	—
Andra (LOM)	ANDRA	223	N31°23'	W92°10'	—
Anger (LOM)	HP	212	N30°36'	W90°25'	94
Bastrop	BQP	329	N32°45'	W91°53'	—
Campi (LOM/NDB)	IE	407	N31°39'	W93°04'	—
Carma (LOM/NDB)	BX	353	N30°52'	W89°51'	14
Crakk (LOM/NDB)	SH	230	N32°30'	W93°52'	—
De Quincy	DQU	410	N30°26'	W93°28'	82
Florenville	FNA	371	N30°24'	W89°49'	—
Gator	GUV	359	N31°01'	W93°11'	—
Grand Isle	GNI	236	N29°11'	W90°04'	—
Hazer (LOM/NDB)	HZ	356	N30°37'	W91°29'	—
Hodge	JBL	256	N32°12'	W92°43'	240
Homer	HMQ	212	N32°47'	W93°00'	—
Houma (LOM)	HU	219	N29°39'	W90°39'	6
Idder (LOM/NDB)	DR	385	N30°45'	W93°20'	160
Keyli (LOM)	LC	353	N30°11'	W93°15'	—
Kinte (LOM/NDB)	MS	338	N30°01'	W90°23'	—
Laffs (LOM)	LF	375	N30°17'	W91°54'	—
Lake Providence	BLE	278	N32°49'	W91°11'	—
Leesville	VED	247	N31°06'	W93°20'	250
Mansfield	MSD	414	N32°03'	W93°45'	—
Many	MMY	272	N31°34'	W93°32'	324
Marksville	MKV	347	N31°05'	W92°04'	78
Minden	MNE	201	N32°38'	W93°18'	—
Molly Ridge	MRK	338	N32°24'	W91°46'	75
Mossy (LOM)	CW	418	N30°18'	W93°11'	23
Nados (LOM/NDB)	OC	253	N31°29'	W94°43'	360
Patterson	PTN	245	N29°42'	W91°20'	—
Rundi (LOM)	BT	284	N30°34'	W91°12'	—
Sabar (LOM)	ML	219	N32°27'	W92°06'	—
Saint Landry	OPL	335	N30°39'	W92°05'	57
Slidell	DEF	256	N30°17'	W89°50'	15
Springhill	SPH	375	N32°58'	W93°24'	—
Vivian	VIV	284	N32°51'	W94°00'	250
Winnfield	IFJ	402	N31°57'	W92°39'	153

Maine

Airports

Portland, ME – Portland Intl Jetport

Ident	PWM	ATIS	119.05
Elev	74	Rwy/Length/ILS/ID	11/6800/109.90/IPWM
Lat	N43°38'		29/6800/109.90/IGCS
Long	W70°18'		18/5001
			36/5001

VORs

Location/Name	Type	Ident	Freq	Lat	Long	Elev
Augusta	VORTAC	AUG	111.40	N44°19'	W69°47'	350
Bangor	VORTAC	BGR	114.80	N44°50'	W68°52'	360
Brunswick	VOR	NHZ	115.20	N43°54'	W69°56'	75
Houlton	VOR-DME	HUL	116.10	N46°02'	W67°50'	860
Kennebunk	VORTAC	ENE	117.10	N43°25'	W70°36'	190
Millinocket	VORTAC	MLT	117.90	N45°35'	W68°30'	550
Presque Isle	VORTAC	PQI	116.40	N46°46'	W68°05'	590

NDBs

Location/Name	Ident	Freq	Lat	Long	Elev
Belfast	BST	278	N44°24'	W69°00'	195
Bracy (LOM/NDB)	RL	399	N44°27'	W69°44'	335
Burnham	BUP	348	N44°41'	W69°21'	—
Dunns (LOM)	AU	366	N44°24'	W69°51'	239
Eastport	EPM	260	N44°54'	W67°00'	46
Excal (LOM)	PQ	278	N46°36'	W68°01'	—
Frenchville	FVE	257	N47°16'	W68°15'	—
Lewie (LOM)	LE	240	N43°57'	W70°20'	310
Lincoln	LRG	216	N45°21'	W68°32'	204
Machias	MVM	251	N44°42'	W67°28'	97
Milnot	LNT	344	N45°38'	W68°33'	—
Old Town	OLD	272	N45°00'	W68°38'	—
Orham (LOM)	PW	394	N43°39'	W70°26'	—
Rangeley	RQM	221	N44°56'	W70°45'	1560
Sanfd (LOM)	SF	349	N43°20'	W70°50'	—
Sebago	SZO	227	N43°54'	W70°46'	950
Sprucehead	SUH	356	N43°59'	W69°07'	—
Squaw	XQA	236	N45°31'	W69°40'	1185
Surry (LOM/NDB)	BH	330	N44°32'	W68°18'	55
Totte (LOM)	BG	227	N44°43'	W68°42'	—
Wiscasset	ISS	407	N43°58'	W69°38'	160

Maryland

Airports

Baltimore, MD – Baltimore/Wash Intl

Ident	BWI	ATIS	115.1
Elev	146	Rwy/Length/ILS/ID	04/6005
Lat	N39°10'		22/6005
Long	W76°40'		10/9452/109.70/IBAL
			28/9452/109.70/IOEH
			15R/9519/111.70/IFND
			33L/9519/111.70/IRUX
			15L/5000/111.95/IUQC
			33R/5000/111.95/IBWI

Camp Springs, MD – Andrews AFB

Ident	ADW	ATIS	113.1
Elev	281	Rwy/Length/ILS/ID	01L//110.5/IRWS
Lat	N38°48'		19R//111.5/IMXK
Long	W76°52'		

College, MD – College Park

Ident	CGS	ATIS	—
Elev	50	Rwy/Length	—
Lat	N38°58'		
Long	W76°55'		

VORs

Location/Name	Type	Ident	Freq	Lat	Long	Elev
Andrews	VORTAC	ADW	113.10	N38°48'	W76°51'	260
Baltimore	VORTAC	BAL	115.10	N39°10'	W76°39'	140
Frederick	VOR	FDK	109.00	N39°24'	W77°22'	300
Grantsville	VOR-DME	GRV	112.30	N39°38'	W79°03'	2640
Hagerstown	VOR	HGR	109.80	N39°41'	W77°51'	560
Nottingham	VORTAC	OTT	113.70	N38°42'	W76°44'	210
Patuxent	VORTAC	PXT	117.60	N38°17'	W76°24'	18
Phillips	VOR	PPM	108.40	N39°28'	W76°10'	41
Salisbury	VORTAC	SBY	111.20	N38°20'	W75°30'	50
Snow Hill	VORTAC	SWL	112.40	N38°03'	W75°27'	40
Test Test	VOR-DME	ESN	112.80	N38°48'	W76°04'	58
Westminster	VORTAC	EMI	117.90	N39°29'	W76°58'	820

NDBs

Location/Name	Ident	Freq	Lat	Long	Elev
Aberdeen	APG	349	N39°32'	W76°06'	45
Cambridge	CGE	257	N38°32'	W76°01'	—
Colbe (LOM)	SB	278	N38°16'	W75°24'	—
Cresap	RYP	339	N39°30'	W78°46'	589
Cumberland	CBE	317	N39°38'	W78°44'	—
Easton	ESN	212	N38°48'	W76°04'	58
Ellicott	FND	371	N39°17'	W76°46'	—
Fort Meade	FME	353	N39°05'	W76°45'	—
Gaithersburg	GAI	385	N39°10'	W77°09'	540
Kirby (LOM)	RW	360	N38°42'	W76°52'	—
Landy (LOM/NDB)	OX	407	N38°21'	W75°11'	33
Martin	MTN	342	N39°17'	W76°22'	20
Patuxent River	NHK	400	N38°17'	W76°24'	18
Potomac	VKX	241	N38°44'	W76°57'	115
Zoote (LOM)	MX	232	N38°55'	W76°52'	74

Massachusetts

Airports

Boston, MA – General E.L. Logan Intl

Ident	BOS	ATIS	135.00
Elev	20	Rwy/Length/ILS/ID	4R/10005/110.3/IBOS
Lat	N42°21'		22L/10005/110.3/ILQN
Long	W71°00'		4L/7860
			22R/7860
			9/7000
			27/7000/111.3/IDGU
			15R/10081/110.7/IMDC
			33L/10081/110.7/ILIP
			15L/2557
			33R/2557

Edgartown, MA – Katama Airpark

Ident	1B2	ATIS	—
Elev	20	Rwy/Length	—
Lat	N42°21'		
Long	W70°31'		

Martha's Vineyard, MA – Martha's Vineyard

Ident	MVY	ATIS	126.25
Elev	68	Rwy/Length/ILS/ID	06/5500
Lat	N41°23'		24/5500/108.70/IMVY
Long	W70°36'		15/3297
			33/3297

Southbridge, MA – Southbridge Muni

Ident	3B0	ATIS	—
Elev	697	Rwy/Length	02/3500
Lat	N42°06'		20/3500
Long	W72°02'		10/1450 Grass
			28/1450 Grass

VORs

Location/Name	Type	Ident	Freq	Lat	Long	Elev
Barnes	VORTAC	BAF	113.00	N42°09'	W72°42'	—
Boston	VORTAC	BOS	112.70	N42°21'	W70°59'	20
Chester	VOR-DME	CTR	115.10	N42°17'	W72°56'	1600
Gardner	VORTAC	GDM	110.60	N42°32'	W72°03'	1280
Lawrence	VOR-DME	LWM	112.50	N42°44'	W71°05'	300
Marconi	VORTAC	LFV	114.70	N42°01'	W70°02'	152
Marthas Vineyard	VOR-DME	MVY	114.50	N41°23'	W70°36'	60
Nantucket	VORTAC	ACK	116.20	N41°16'	W70°01'	100
Westover	VOR	CEF	114.00	N42°11'	W72°31'	820

NDBs

Location/Name	Ident	Freq	Lat	Long	Elev
Bedds (LOM)	BE	332	N42°28'	W71°23'	—
Bogey (LOM)	HYX	342	N41°42'	W70°12'	—
Crow Hill	CLY	392	N42°15'	W71°46'	—
Dalton	DXT	370	N42°28'	W73°10'	1082
Dickinson	DKO	352	N42°38'	W71°43'	501
Dunca (LOM)	RS	279	N42°16'	W72°01'	—
Fall River	FLR	406	N41°45'	W71°06'	—
Fitchburg	FIT	365	N42°33'	W71°45'	—
Great Barrington	GBR	395	N42°10'	W73°24'	—
Haget (LOM)	LW	402	N42°38'	W71°11'	130
Hullz (LOM)	LI	346	N42°18'	W70°55'	—
Lyndy (LOM/NDB)	LQ	382	N42°27'	W70°57'	8
Mansfield	IHM	220	N42°00'	W71°11'	120
Marshfield	IMR	368	N42°05'	W70°40'	64
Miltt (LOM)	BO	375	N42°16'	W71°02'	6
Nantucket	TUK	194	N41°16'	W70°10'	—
Nauset	CQX	279	N41°41'	W69°59'	40
Nefor (LOM)	EW	274	N41°37'	W71°01'	—
Orange	ORE	205	N42°33'	W72°12'	—
Otis (LOM)	FMH	362	N41°43'	W70°26'	80
Palmer	PMX	212	N42°13'	W72°18'	—
Plymouth	FFF	257	N41°50'	W70°48'	140
Provincetown	PVC	389	N42°04'	W70°13'	43
Shaker Hill	SKR	251	N42°27'	W71°10'	345

Location/Name	Ident	Freq	Lat	Long	Elev
Stoge (LOM)	OW	397	N42°07'	W71°07'	178
Taunton	TAN	227	N41°52'	W71°01'	—
Topsfield	TOF	269	N42°37'	W70°57'	—
Waivs (LOM)	AC	248	N41°18'	W69°59'	—
Wesie (LOM)	BA	230	N42°14'	W72°41'	—

Michigan

Airports

Grand Rapids, MI – Kent County Intl

Ident	GRR	ATIS	127.10
Elev	794	Rwy/Length/ILS/ID	8R/10000/108.30/ICYZ
Lat	W42 53		26L/10000/109.70/IGRR
Long	W85°31'		8L/3918
			26R/3918
			18/3400
			36/3400

Marquette, MI – Marquette County

Ident	MQT	ATIS	123.00
Elev	1419	Rwy/Length/ILS/ID	01/3000
Lat	N46°32'		19/3000
Long	W87°33'		08/6500/110.50/IMQT
			26/6500

VORs

Location/Name	Type	Ident	Freq	Lat	Long	Elev
Alpena	VORTAC	APN	108.80	N45°04'	W83°33'	680
Au Sable	VORTAC	ASP	116.10	N44°26'	W83°24'	620
Bad Axe	VOR-DME	BAX	108.20	N43°46'	W82°59'	755
Battle Creek	VORTAC	BTL	109.40	N42°18'	W85°15'	930
Carleton	VORTAC	CRL	115.70	N42°02'	W83°27'	630
Detroit	VOR-DME	DXO	113.40	N42°12'	W83°22'	640
Escanaba	VORTAC	ESC	110.80	N45°43'	W87°05'	600
Flint	VORTAC	FNT	116.90	N42°57'	W83°44'	770
Gaylord	VOR-DME	GLR	109.20	N45°00'	W84°42'	1320
Giper	VORTAC	GIJ	115.40	N41°46'	W86°19'	800
Grand Rapids	VOR-DME	GRR	110.20	N42°47'	W85°29'	800
Grayling	VOR	CGG	109.80	N44°40'	W84°43'	1153
Houghton	VORTAC	CMX	112.80	N47°10'	W88°28'	1072
Houghton Lake	VOR-DME	HTL	111.60	N44°21'	W84°39'	1145
Iron Mountain	VORTAC	IMT	111.20	N45°48'	W88°06'	1130

Location/Name	Type	Ident	Freq	Lat	Long	Elev
Ironwood	VORTAC	IWD	108.80	N46°31'	W90°07'	1230
Jackson	VOR-DME	JXN	109.60	N42°15'	W84°27'	1000
K I Sawyer	VORTAC	SAW	116.30	N46°21'	W87°23'	1170
Kalamazoo	VOR-DME	AZO	109.00	N42°14'	W85°33'	870
Keeler	VORTAC	ELX	116.60	N42°08'	W86°07'	800
Lansing	VORTAC	LAN	110.80	N42°43'	W84°41'	880
Litchfield	VORTAC	LFD	111.20	N42°03'	W84°45'	1040
Manistee	VOR-DME	MBL	111.40	N44°16'	W86°13'	620
Marquette	VOR-DME	MQT	116.80	N46°31'	W87°35'	1450
Menominee	VOR-DME	MNM	109.60	N45°10'	W87°38'	650
Mount Pleasant	VOR-DME	MOP	110.60	N43°37'	W84°44'	760
Muskegon	VORTAC	MKG	115.20	N43°10'	W86°02'	660
Newberry	VOR-DME	ERY	108.20	N46°18'	W85°27'	870
Peck	VORTAC	ECK	114.00	N43°15'	W82°43'	810
Pellston	VORTAC	PLN	111.80	N45°37'	W84°39'	840
Pontiac	VORTAC	PSI	111.00	N42°42'	W83°31'	1150
Pullman	VORTAC	PMM	112.10	N42°27'	W86°06'	640
Saginaw	VORTAC	MBS	112.90	N43°31'	W84°04'	670
Salem	VORTAC	SVM	114.30	N42°24'	W83°35'	950
Sault Ste Marie	VORTAC	SSM	112.20	N46°24'	W84°18'	690
Schoolcraft Co	VOR-DME	ISQ	110.4	N45°58'	W86°10'	684
Traverse City	VORTAC	TVC	114.60	N44°40'	W85°32'	910
West Branch	VOR-DME	BXZ	113.20	N44°14'	W84°11'	805
White Cloud	VORTAC	HIC	117.60	N43°34'	W85°42'	920

Location/Name	Ident	Freq	Lat	Long	Elev
Gwenn (LOM/NDB)	TV	365	N44°44'	W85°25'	—
Hardwood	BHW	236	N44°14'	W84°05'	800
Holland	HLM	233	N42°47'	W86°09'	—
Howell	OZW	242	N42°38'	W83°59'	951
Jakso (LOM)	JX	212	N42°19'	W84°21'	—
Knobs (LOM)	GR	263	N42°53'	W85°22'	—
Koloe (LOM/NDB)	CI	400	N46°19'	W84°32'	696
Litchfield	LTD	371	N39°09'	W89°40'	1040
Ludington	LDM	341	N43°57'	W86°24'	642
Madds (LOM)	DE	338	N42°29'	W83°05'	—
Mally (LOM)	BE	397	N42°07'	W86°18'	—
Musko (LOM)	MK	219	N43°07'	W86°10'	—
Olste (LOM)	MB	257	N43°27'	W84°10'	200
Ontonagon	OGM	375	N46°51'	W89°21'	882
Petli (LOM)	FN	269	N42°58'	W83°53'	—
Phurn (LOM)	PH	332	N42°50'	W82°35'	635
Revup (LOM)	DT	388	N42°07'	W83°25'	631
Rogers City	PZQ	215	N45°24'	W83°49'	665
Spenc (LOM)	DM	223	N42°13'	W83°12'	—
Sturgis	IRS	382	N41°48'	W85°26'	—
Three Rivers	HAI	407	N41°57'	W85°35'	—
Tribe (LOM)	TN	239	N45°03'	W87°41'	613
Watersmeet	RXW	407	N46°17'	W89°16'	1625
Wiggins	GDW	209	N43°58'	W84°28'	—
Yipps (LOM)	YI	359	N42°10'	W83°37'	—

NDBs

Location/Name	Ident	Freq	Lat	Long	Elev
Adrian	ADG	278	N41°52'	W84°04'	—
Alma	AMN	329	N43°19'	W84°47'	—
Alpine	ALV	375	N45°00'	W84°48'	—
Artda (LOM)	LA	206	N42°46'	W84°29'	841
Austn (LOM)	AZ	371	N42°07'	W85°31'	—
Batol (LOM/NDB)	BTI	272	N42°21'	W85°11'	—
Berz	UIZ	215	N42°39'	W82°57'	—
Boyne Falls	BFA	263	N45°10'	W84°55'	707
Browne	HYX	385	N43°25'	W83°51'	600
Cadillac	CAD	269	N44°16'	W85°24'	1295
Cargl (LOM/NDB)	VQ	230	N42°21'	W82°57'	580
Charlevoix	CVX	222	N45°18'	W85°15'	655
Clam Lake	CXK	251	N44°53'	W85°14'	799
Deckerville	DQV	378	N43°34'	W82°39'	750
Drummond Island	DRM	218	N46°00'	W83°44'	580
Felps (LOM)	APH	206	N44°57'	W83°33'	750
Galey (LOM/NDB)	CM	275	N47°06'	W88°24'	—
Grayling	GYG	359	N44°44'	W84°49'	1178
Grosse Ile	RYS	419	N42°06'	W83°09'	577

Minnesota

Airports

Duluth, MN – Duluth Intl

Ident	DLH	ATIS	124.10
Elev	1428	Rwy/Length/ILS/ID	03/5699
Lat	N46°50'		21/5699
Long	W92°11'		09/10152/110.30/IDLH
			27/10152/108.70/IJUD

Minneapolis, MN – Minneapolis-St. Paul

Ident	MSP	ATIS	135.35
Elev	841	Rwy/Length/ILS/ID	04/8256/109.30/IAPL
Lat	N44°53'		22/8256/110.50/ISIJ
Long	W93°13'		11R/10000/110.30/IHKZ
			29L/10000/110.30/IMSP
			11L/8200/110.70/IPJL
			29R/8200/109.90/IINN

VORs

Location/Name	Type	Ident	Freq	Lat	Long	Elev
Albert Lea	VOR-DME	AEL	109.80	N43°40'	W93°22'	1253
Alexandria	VORTAC	AXN	112.80	N45°57'	W95°13'	1380
Austin	VOR-DME	JAY	108.20	N43°34'	W92°55'	1232
Baudette	VOR-DME	BDE	111.60	N48°43'	W94°36'	1080
Bemidji	VORTAC	BJI	108.60	N47°34'	W95°01'	1410
Brainerd	VORTAC	BRD	116.90	N46°20'	W94°01'	1250
Camp Ripley	VOR	RYM	111.10	N46°05'	W94°21'	1154
Darwin	VORTAC	DWN	109.00	N45°05'	W94°27'	1130
Detroit Lakes	VOR-DME	DTL	111.20	N46°49'	W95°52'	1390
Duluth	VORTAC	DLH	112.60	N46°48'	W92°12'	1430
Ely	VOR-DME	ELO	109.60	N47°49'	W91°49'	1490
Eveleth	VOR-DME	EVM	108.20	N47°25'	W92°30'	1380
Fairmont	VOR-DME	FRM	110.20	N43°38'	W94°25'	1160
Farmington	VORTAC	FGT	115.70	N44°37'	W93°10'	930
Fergus Falls	VOR-DME	FFM	110.40	N46°17'	W96°09'	1190
Flying Cloud	VOR-DME	FCM	111.80	N44°49'	W93°27'	900
Gopher	VORTAC	GEP	117.30	N45°08'	W93°22'	880
Grand Rapids	VOR-DME	GPZ	111.40	N47°09'	W93°29'	1400
Halfway	VOR-DME	FOW	111.20	N44°12'	W93°22'	1099
Hibbing	VOR-DME	HIB	110.80	N47°18'	W92°42'	1350
Humboldt	VORTAC	HML	112.40	N48°52'	W97°07'	800
Intl Falls	VORTAC	INL	111.00	N48°33'	W93°24'	1180
Mankato	VOR-DME	MKT	110.80	N44°13'	W93°54'	1020
Marshall	VOR-DME	MML	111.00	N44°26'	W95°49'	1180
Minneapolis	VORTAC	MSP	115.30	N44°52'	W93°13'	850
Montevideo	VOR-DME	MVE	111.60	N44°58'	W95°42'	1030
Morris	VOR-DME	MOX	109.60	N45°33'	W95°58'	1130
Nodine	VORTAC	ODI	117.90	N43°54'	W91°28'	1280
Park Rapids	VOR-DME	PKD	110.60	N46°53'	W95°04'	1440
Princeton	VOR-DME	PNN	114.30	N45°19'	W67°42'	979
Redwood Falls	VORTAC	RWF	113.30	N44°28'	W95°07'	1060
Rochester	VOR-DME	RST	112.00	N43°46'	W92°35'	1380
Roseau	VOR-DME	ROX	108.80	N48°51'	W95°41'	1060
Saint Cloud	VOR-DME	STC	112.10	N45°32'	W94°03'	1020
Thief River Falls	VOR-DME	TVF	108.4	N48°04'	W96°11'	1110
Willmar	VOR-DME	ILL	113.70	N45°07'	W95°05'	1120
Winona	VOR-DME	ONA	111.40	N44°04'	W91°42'	650
Worthington	VOR-DME	OTG	110.60	N43°38'	W95°34'	1570

NDBs

Location/Name	Ident	Freq	Lat	Long	Elev
Aitkin	AIT	397	N46°32'	W93°40'	1207
Andri	AJW	281	N45°47'	W95°18'	1404

Location/Name	Type	Ident	Freq	Lat	Long	Elev
Appleton		AQP	356	N45°13'	W96°00'	1018
Babco (LOM)		BA	385	N44°51'	W92°59'	957
Benson		BBB	239	N45°19'	W95°39'	1080
Blue Earth		SBU	332	N43°35'	W94°05'	1083
Bunan (LOM)		MD	371	N47°26'	W94°50'	1350
Caledonia		CHU	209	N43°35'	W91°29'	1130
Cambridge		CBG	350	N45°33'	W93°15'	935
Cloquet		COQ	335	N46°41'	W92°30'	—
Cook		CQM	233	N47°49'	W92°41'	1322
Cook Co		CKC	358	N47°50'	W90°23'	1762
Crookston		CKN	400	N47°50'	W96°36'	895
Dawson-Madison		DXX	227	N44°59'	W96°10'	1077
Fosston		FSE	224	N47°35'	W95°46'	1276
Galex (LOM)		GP	272	N47°07'	W93°28'	1310
Glenwood		GHW	346	N45°38'	W95°19'	1385
Hamre (LOM)		FF	337	N46°13'	W96°03'	1160
Harvi (LOM)		HY	260	N48°00'	W96°05'	1114
Hopey		PPI	400	N44°52'	W92°56'	—
Humbolt		HXM	366	N40°59'	W75°59'	800
Hussk (LOM)		ST	342	N45°28'	W93°58'	980
Hutchinson		HCD	209	N44°51'	W94°22'	1060
Jackson		MJQ	353	N43°38'	W94°59'	1480
Larew (LOM)		BR	251	N46°27'	W94°01'	1259
Little Falls		LXL	359	N45°56'	W94°20'	1120
Mingo (LOM)		RS	329	N43°51'	W92°24'	1263
Mora		JMR	327	N45°53'	W93°16'	997
Narco (LOM/NDB)		MS	266	N44°49'	W93°05'	880
New Ulm		ULM	272	N44°19'	W94°29'	1010
Orr		ORB	341	N48°01'	W92°51'	1309
Ortonville		VVV	332	N45°18'	W96°25'	1050
Piney Pinecreek		PFT	342	N48°59'	W95°58'	1060
Pipestone		PQN	284	N43°59'	W96°17'	1778
Princeton		PNM	368	N45°33'	W93°36'	979
Pykla (LOM/NDB)		DL	379	N46°50'	W92°21'	—
Raize (LOM/NDB)		IN	353	N48°28'	W93°16'	—
Red Wing		RGK	248	N44°35'	W92°29'	782
Ripley		XCR	404	N46°04'	W94°20'	—
Roadd (LOM)		SW	360	N48°51'	W95°14'	—
Scott		SCG	385	N48°15'	W92°28'	—
Silver Bay		BFW	350	N47°15'	W91°24'	—
Spida (LOM/NDB)		PK	269	N46°50'	W94°58'	1412
Staples		SAZ	257	N46°22'	W94°48'	1285
Two Harbors		TWM	243	N47°03'	W91°44'	1071
Vagey (LOM)		AP	338	N44°49'	W93°18'	—
Waseca		ACQ	371	N44°04'	W93°33'	1120
Wheaton		ETH	326	N45°46'	W96°32'	1225
Windom		MWM	203	N43°54'	W95°06'	—

Mississippi

Airports

Jackson, MS – Allen C. Thompson Fld

Ident	JAN	ATIS	—
Elev	349	Rwy/Length/ILS/ID	15R/8501
Lat	N32°19'		33L/8501/109.30/IFRL
Long	W90°04'		15L/8500/110.50/IJAN
			33R/8500

VORs

Location/Name	Type	Ident	Freq	Lat	Long	Elev
Bigbee	VORTAC	IGB	116.20	N33°29'	W88°30'	240
Caledonia	VORTAC	CBM	115.20	N33°38'	W88°26'	220
Eaton	VORTAC	LBY	110.60	N31°25'	W89°20'	290
Greene Co	VORTAC	GCV	115.70	N31°05'	W88°29'	300
Greenville	VOR-DME	GLH	110.20	N33°31'	W90°58'	130
Gulfport	VORTAC	GPT	109.00	N30°24'	W89°04'	20
Holly Springs	VORTAC	HLI	112.40	N34°46'	W89°29'	630
Jackson	VORTAC	JAN	112.60	N32°30'	W90°10'	360
Kewanee	VORTAC	EWA	113.80	N32°22'	W88°27'	300
Mc Comb	VORTAC	MCB	116.70	N31°18'	W90°15'	440
Meridian	VORTAC	MEI	117.00	N32°22'	W88°48'	580
Natchez	VOR-DME	HEZ	110.00	N31°37'	W91°17'	280
Picayune	VORTAC	PCU	112.20	N30°33'	W89°43'	70
Sidon	VORTAC	SQS	114.70	N33°27'	W90°16'	125
Tupelo	VOR-DME	TUP	109.80	N34°13'	W88°47'	360

NDBs

Location/Name	Ident	Freq	Lat	Long	Elev
Allen (LOM)	JA	365	N32°24'	W90°07'	—
Bayou (LOM)	GP	360	N30°29'	W89°09'	—
Brenz (LOM/NDB)	JH	260	N32°24'	W90°15'	314
Brookhaven	BVV	407	N31°36'	W90°24'	485
Bryan	STF	281	N33°25'	W88°51'	333
Clarksdale	CKM	341	N34°17'	W90°30'	—
Corinth	CRX	338	N34°54'	W88°36'	—
Ferni (LOM/NDB)	MC	413	N31°15'	W90°30'	480
Foxworth	FOH	331	N31°17'	W89°49'	—
Hanco	AYI	221	N30°27'	W89°27'	90
Indianola	IDL	284	N33°28'	W90°40'	126

Location/Name	Ident	Freq	Lat	Long	Elev
Kosciusko	OSX	269	N33°05'	W89°32'	—
Louisville	LMS	212	N33°08'	W89°03'	—
Marks	MMS	391	N34°13'	W90°17'	—
Meridian	MPA	238	N43°35'	W116°34'	580
Metcalf	MTQ	359	N33°25'	W90°58'	120
Natchez-Adams Co	HAH	388	N31°41'	W91°17'	142
Olive Branch	OLV	275	N34°58'	W89°47'	401
Philadelphia	MPE	219	N32°47'	W89°07'	440
Prentiss	PJR	252	N31°35'	W89°54'	460
Raymond	RYB	375	N32°18'	W90°24'	257
Renova	RNV	272	N33°48'	W90°45'	—
Savoy (LOM/NDB)	ME	356	N32°14'	W88°46'	318
Scobey	SBQ	245	N33°53'	W89°52'	410
Tallahala	THJ	346	N31°41'	W89°11'	250
Teock (LOM)	GW	349	N33°35'	W90°05'	138
Tunng (LOM)	UV	426	N34°23'	W89°37'	410
Veron (LOM)	TU	420	N34°10'	W88°46'	325
Vicksburg	VKS	382	N32°13'	W90°55'	95

Missouri

Airports

Kansas City, MO – Kansas City Intl

Ident	MCI	ATIS	128.35
Elev	1026	Rwy/Length/ILS/ID	1L/10801/110.50/IDOT
Lat	N39°18'		19R/10801/109.10/IPAJ
Long	W94°43'		1R/5950
			19L/5950/109.55/IDYH
			09/9500/109.70/IRNI
			27/9500

St. Louis, MO – Lambert Intl

Ident	STL	ATIS	120.45
Elev	605	Rwy/Length/ILS/ID	06/7602
Lat	N38°44'		24/7602/110.30/ISTL
Long	W90°21'		12R/11019/109.70/ILMR
			30L/11019/111.50/IBKY
			30L/11019/110.55/IFXD
			12L/9003/108.90/ILDZ
			12L/9003/110.1/IABW
			30R/9003/111.30/ISJW
			13/6289
			31/6289
			17/3008
			35/3008

St. Louis, MO – Spirit of St. Louis

Ident	SUS	ATIS	134.8
Elev	463	Rwy/Length/ILS/ID	08R/111.9/ISUS
Lat	N38°39'		26L/111.9/IFZU
Long	W90°39'		

VORs

Location/Name	Type	Ident	Freq	Lat	Long	Elev
Butler	VORTAC	BUM	115.90	N38°16'	W94°29'	890
Cape Girardeau	VOR-DME	CGI	112.90	N37°13'	W89°34'	340
Columbia	VOR-DME	COU	110.20	N38°48'	W92°13'	883
Dogwood	VORTAC	DGD	109.40	N37°01'	W92°52'	1600
Farmington	VORTAC	FAM	115.70	N37°40'	W90°14'	1220
Foristell	VORTAC	FTZ	110.80	N38°41'	W90°58'	817
Forney	VOR	TBN	110.00	N37°44'	W92°08'	1160
Hallsville	VORTAC	HLV	114.20	N39°06'	W92°07'	920
Higginsville	VOR	HIG	110.60	N39°04'	W93°40'	—
Kansas City	VORTAC	MKC	112.60	N39°16'	W94°35'	1060
Macon	VORTAC	MCM	112.90	N39°39'	W92°28'	870
Malden	VORTAC	MAW	111.20	N36°33'	W89°54'	280
Maples	VORTAC	MAP	113.40	N37°35'	W91°47'	1370
Napoleon	VORTAC	ANX	114.00	N39°05'	W94°07'	878
Neosho	VORTAC	EOS	116.60	N36°50'	W94°26'	1195
Riverside	VOR-DME	RIS	111.40	N39°07'	W94°35'	740
Saint Joseph	VORTAC	STJ	115.50	N39°57'	W94°55'	1159
Saint Louis	VORTAC	STL	117.40	N38°51'	W90°28'	450
Springfield	VORTAC	SGF	116.90	N37°21'	W93°20'	1240
Sunshine	VOR-DME	SHY	108.40	N38°02'	W92°36'	910
Vichy	VORTAC	VIH	117.70	N38°09'	W91°42'	1110

NDBs

Location/Name	Ident	Freq	Lat	Long	Elev
Amazon	AZN	233	N39°53'	W94°54'	—
Bilmart	AOV	341	N36°58'	W92°40'	1302
Brookfield	BZK	383	N39°45'	W93°06'	845
Buckhorn	BHN	391	N37°41'	W92°06'	1098
Cameron	EZZ	394	N39°43'	W94°16'	1042
Charleston	CHQ	208	N36°50'	W89°21'	—
Chillicothe	CHT	375	N39°46'	W93°29'	—
Coole (LOM)	SG	404	N37°10'	W93°25'	—
Cuba	UBX	380	N38°03'	W91°25'	990
Dexter	DXE	423	N36°47'	W89°56'	308
Dotte (LOM/NDB)	DO	359	N39°13'	W94°44'	—
Dutch (LOM)	CG	248	N37°15'	W89°42'	—
Earli	FD	278	N36°40'	W90°19'	315

Location/Name	Ident	Freq	Lat	Long	Elev
Eaves (LOM/NDB)	FZ	227	N38°40'	W90°32'	458
Emville	EVU	317	N40°20'	W94°54'	1130
Festus	FES	269	N38°11'	W90°23'	475
Golden Valley	GLY	388	N38°21'	W93°41'	818
Guthrie	FTT	317	N38°50'	W92°00'	877
Hannibal	HAE	411	N39°43'	W91°26'	760
Huggy (LOM)	RN	242	N39°18'	W94°51'	—
Kaiser	AIZ	272	N38°05'	W92°33'	863
Kennett	TKX	358	N36°13'	W90°02'	258
Kenzy (LOM)	MK	344	N39°13'	W94°33'	—
Lebanon	IEB	414	N37°34'	W92°39'	1325
Lunns (LOM)	JL	344	N37°12'	W94°33'	910
Marshall	PUR	371	N39°02'	W93°11'	779
Memorial	MEO	397	N38°33'	W92°04'	—
Moberly	MBY	302	N39°27'	W92°25'	866
Mountain View	MNF	365	N36°59'	W91°42'	1165
Nevada	EAD	209	N37°51'	W94°18'	878
New Madrid	EIW	314	N36°32'	W89°36'	285
Noah	ONH	515	N38°38'	W92°14'	545
Norge (LOM)	GQ	517	N39°03'	W94°39'	955
Oblio (LOM/NDB)	LM	338	N38°48'	W90°28'	446
Perrine	PRI	367	N37°45'	W90°25'	916
Point Lookout	PLK	326	N36°37'	W93°13'	933
Pomona	UNO	335	N36°52'	W91°54'	1260
Sedalia	DMO	281	N38°42'	W93°10'	880
Sikeston	SIK	272	N36°53'	W89°33'	350
Snoop (LOM)	SU	326	N38°38'	W90°46'	461
Spring River	LLU	356	N37°29'	W94°18'	1009
Sullivan	UUV	356	N38°14'	W91°09'	906
Tario (LOM)	ST	260	N39°40'	W94°54'	—
Trenton	TRX	400	N40°04'	W93°35'	758
Viertel	VER	347	N38°56'	W92°41'	—
Willard	ILJ	254	N37°17'	W93°26'	—
Zodia (LOM)	CO	407	N38°42'	W92°16'	850
Zumay (LOM)	ST	404	N38°47'	W90°16'	—

Montana

Airports

Billings, MT – Logan Intl

Ident	BIL	ATIS	126.30
Elev	3649	Rwy/Length/ILS/ID	07/5500
Lat	N45°48'		25/5500
Long	W108°32'		10R/3800
			28L/3800
			10L/10528/110.30/IBIL
			26R/10528
			16/4945
			34/4945

Great Falls, MT – Great Falls Intl

Ident	GTF	ATIS	126.60
Elev	3674	Rwy/Length/ILS/ID	03/10502/111.30/ISMR
Lat	N47°28'		21/10502
Long	W111°22'		07/4294
			25/4294
			16/6357
			34/6357

VORs

Location/Name	Type	Ident	Freq	Lat	Long	Elev
Billings	VORTAC	BIL	114.50	N45°48'	W108°37'	3800
Bozeman	VOR-DME	BZN	112.20	N45°47'	W111°09'	4430
Coppertown	VORTAC	CPN	111.60	N46°01'	W112°44'	5780
Cut Bank	VORTAC	CTB	114.40	N48°33'	W112°20'	3780
Dillon	VORTAC	DLN	113.00	N45°14'	W112°32'	5260
Drummond	VOR	DRU	117.10	N46°38'	W113°11'	4150
Glasgow	VOR-DME	GGW	113.90	N48°12'	W106°37'	2280
Great Falls	VORTAC	GTF	115.10	N47°26'	W111°24'	3670
Havre	VOR-DME	HVR	111.80	N48°32'	W109°46'	2580
Helena	VORTAC	HLN	117.70	N46°36'	W111°57'	3820
Kalispell	VOR-DME	FCA	108.40	N48°12'	W114°10'	2980
Lewistown	VORTAC	LWT	112.00	N47°03'	W109°36'	4130
Livingston	VORTAC	LVM	116.10	N45°42'	W110°26'	4650
Miles City	VORTAC	MLS	112.10	N46°22'	W105°57'	2640
Missoula	VORTAC	MSO	112.80	N46°54'	W114°05'	3200
Whitehall	VORTAC	HIA	113.70	N45°51'	W112°10'	5530

NDBs

Location/Name	Ident	Freq	Lat	Long	Elev
Broadus	BDX	335	N45°26'	W105°24'	2992
Capitol	CVP	317	N46°36'	W111°56'	—
Choteau	CII	269	N47°49'	W112°10'	3938
Conrad	CRD	293	N48°11'	W111°54'	—
Forsyth	FOR	236	N46°16'	W106°31'	2715
Glendive	GDV	410	N47°08'	W104°48'	2518
Harlowton	HWQ	242	N46°26'	W109°49'	—
Hauser	HAU	386	N46°34'	W111°45'	—
Horton	HTN	320	N46°24'	W105°56'	—
Jordan	JDN	263	N47°20'	W106°56'	—
Kona	INE	521	N47°05'	W114°23'	3720
Leeds	LDS	389	N48°32'	W109°41'	—
Lewistown	LWT	353	N47°04'	W109°32'	4100
Malta	MLK	272	N48°21'	W107°53'	—
Manni (LOM)	BZ	266	N45°52'	W111°17'	—

Location/Name	Ident	Freq	Lat	Long	Elev
Milk River	MKR	339	N48°12'	W106°37'	—
Plentywood	PWD	251	N48°47'	W104°31'	—
Polson	PLS	275	N47°41'	W114°11'	2936
Red Lodge	RED	203	N45°14'	W109°15'	5467
Roundup	RPX	362	N46°28'	W108°34'	—
Saige (LOM)	BI	251	N45°51'	W108°41'	—
Scobey	SCO	283	N48°48'	W105°26'	2416
Shelby	SBX	347	N48°32'	W111°51'	3434
Sidney	SDY	359	N47°42'	W104°10'	—
Smith Lake	SAK	515	N48°06'	W114°27'	—
Targy (LOM/NDB)	LO	415	N44°34'	W111°11'	7000
Timber	BKU	344	N46°20'	W104°15'	—
Truly	ITU	371	N47°21'	W111°22'	4201
Wolf Point	OLF	404	N48°06'	W105°36'	—
Wondd (LOM)	OT	277	N43°36'	W95°27'	1515
Yellowstone	ESY	338	N44°41'	W111°07'	6697

Nebraska

Airports

Lincoln, NE – Lincoln Muni

Ident	LNK	ATIS	118.08
Elev	1214	Rwy/Length/ILS/ID	14/8620
Lat	N40°51'		32/8620
Long	W96°45'		17R/12901/111.10/IOCZ
			35L/12901/109.90/ILNK
			17L35R/5500

VORs

Location/Name	Type	Ident	Freq	Lat	Long	Elev
Ainsworth	VOR-DME	ANW	112.70	N42°34'	W99°59'	2582
Alliance	VOR-DME	AIA	111.80	N42°03'	W102°48'	3925
Beatrice	VOR	BIE	110.60	N40°18'	W96°45'	1300
Chadron	VOR-DME	CDR	113.40	N42°33'	W103°18'	4630
Columbus	VOR-DME	OLU	111.80	N41°27'	W97°20'	1442
Cozad	VOR	OZB	109.00	N40°52'	W100°00'	2518
Custer Co	VOR	CUZ	108.20	N41°29'	W99°41'	2850
Grand Island	VORTAC	GRI	112.00	N40°59'	W98°18'	1840
Hastings	VOR-DME	HSI	108.80	N40°36'	W98°25'	1950
Hayes Center	VORTAC	HCT	117.70	N40°27'	W100°55'	3010
Kearney	VOR	EAR	111.20	N40°43'	W99°00'	2130
Lincoln	VORTAC	LNK	116.10	N40°55'	W96°44'	1370
Mc Cook	VOR-DME	MCK	116.50	N40°12'	W100°35'	2570

Location/Name	Type	Ident	Freq	Lat	Long	Elev
Norfolk	VOR-DME	OFK	109.60	N41°59'	W97°26'	20
North Platte	VORTAC	LBF	117.40	N41°02'	W100°44'	3050
O Neill	VORTAC	ONL	113.90	N42°28'	W98°41'	2030
Omaha	VORTAC	OMA	116.30	N41°10'	W95°44'	1300
Pawnee City	VORTAC	PWE	112.40	N40°12'	W96°12'	1360
Scottsbluff	VORTAC	BFF	112.60	N41°53'	W103°28'	4170
Scribner	VOR	SCB	111.00	N41°36'	W96°37'	1317
Searle	VOR	SAE	110.20	N41°07'	W101°46'	3256
Sidney	VORTAC	SNY	115.90	N41°05'	W102°58'	4300
Tekamah	VOR	TQE	108.40	N41°45'	W96°10'	1030
Thedford	VOR-DME	TDD	108.60	N41°58'	W100°43'	3180
Wolbach	VORTAC	OBH	114.80	N41°22'	W98°21'	2010

NDBs

Location/Name	Ident	Freq	Lat	Long	Elev
Alaby	BVN	332	N41°43'	W98°03'	1796
Anoke (LOM)	EA	272	N40°37'	W99°01'	2128
Antioch	AOQ	287	N42°00'	W102°46'	—
Aurora	AUH	278	N40°53'	W97°59'	1801
Beklof	FMZ	392	N40°35'	W97°34'	1634
Big Blue	BJU	248	N40°21'	W96°48'	1352
Brenner	FNB	404	N40°04'	W95°35'	976
Broken Bow	BBW	290	N41°26'	W99°38'	2532
Burwell	BUB	362	N41°46'	W99°08'	2180
Chappell	CNP	383	N41°04'	W102°27'	3671
Crete	CEK	420	N40°37'	W96°55'	1479
Darr	RRX	326	N40°50'	W99°51'	2455
Dawes (LOM)	CD	362	N42°45'	W103°10'	3505
Fairbury	FBY	293	N40°10'	W97°09'	1450
Flick (LOM)	PP	513	N41°24'	W95°53'	—
Fremont	FET	311	N41°27'	W96°31'	1256
Gerfi (LOM/NDB)	OM	320	N41°22'	W95°57'	987
Gering	GIG	341	N41°56'	W103°40'	4050
Gordon	GRN	414	N42°48'	W102°10'	3540
Grant	GGF	359	N40°52'	W101°43'	3412
Harry Strunk	CSB	389	N40°18'	W100°09'	2392
Hebron	HJH	323	N40°09'	W97°35'	1523
Holdrege	HDE	396	N40°26'	W99°20'	2310
Imperial	IML	283	N40°30'	W101°37'	3268
Kehoe (LOM)	GR	380	N40°52'	W98°18'	1850
Kimball	IBM	317	N41°11'	W103°40'	4897
Mc Coy	CMY	412	N43°56'	W90°38'	1020
Millard	MLE	371	N41°11'	W96°06'	1051
Ord	ODX	356	N41°37'	W98°56'	2057
Oshkosh	OKS	233	N41°24'	W102°21'	3382
Panbe (LOM/NDB)	LB	416	N41°04'	W100°34'	2722
Platte Center	PLT	407	N41°29'	W97°22'	—

Location/Name	Ident	Freq	Lat	Long	Elev
Plattsmouth	PMV	329	N40°57'	W95°54'	1180
Potts (LOM/NDB)	LN	385	N40°44'	W96°45'	—
Prosser	PSS	338	N40°41'	W98°28'	1974
Rikky (LOM)	EN	426	N41°13'	W95°49'	983
Rock Co	RBE	341	N42°34'	W99°34'	2345
Seward	SWT	269	N40°51'	W97°06'	1500
Shaw	HWB	263	N40°15'	W96°45'	1250
Valentine	VTN	314	N42°51'	W100°32'	2586
Wahoo	AHQ	400	N41°14'	W96°35'	1221
Wayne	LCG	389	N42°14'	W96°59'	1431
Whitney	HIN	275	N42°49'	W103°05'	3312
Willow	DWL	353	N40°52'	W100°04'	2569
York	JYR	257	N40°53'	W97°37'	1665

Nevada

Airports

Carson City, NV – Carson

Ident	004	ATIS	—
Elev	4697	Rwy/Length	—
Lat	N39°11'		
Long	W119°44'		

Carson City, NV – Dayton Valley

Ident	NV11	ATIS	—
Elev	4412	Rwy/Length	—
Lat	N39°14'		
Long	W119°33'		

Carson City, NV – Parker Carson

Ident		ATIS	—
Elev	4900	Rwy/Length	—
Lat	N39°12'		
Long	W119°41'		

Las Vegas, NV – McCarran Intl

Ident	LAS	ATIS	125.60
Elev	2175	Rwy/Length/ILS/ID	1R/9776
Lat	N36°05'		19L/9776
Long	W115°09'		1L/5001
			19R/5001
			7R/8900
			25L/8900/111.75/IRLE
			7L/14405
			25R/14405/110.30/ILAS

Minden, NV – Douglas County

Ident	MEV	ATIS	—
Elev	4718	Rwy/Length	12/5289
Lat	N39°00'		30/5289
Long	W119°45'		16/7395
			34/7395

Reno, NV – Reno Cannon Intl

Ident	RNO	ATIS	124.35
Elev	4412	Rwy/Length/ILS/ID	07/6101
Lat	N39°29'		25/6101
Long	W119°46'		16L/9000
			34R/9000
			16R/10002/110.90/IRNO
			34L/10002/110.90/IRNO

Reno, NV – Nevada Flyers

Ident	NV18	ATIS	—
Elev	4600	Rwy/Length	—
Lat	N39°40'		
Long	W119°43'		

Reno, NV – Reno/Stead

Ident	4SD	ATIS	—
Elev	5046	Rwy/Length	08/7600
Lat	N39°40'		26/7600
Long	W119°52'		14/8080
			32/8080

Reno, NV – Reno/Tahoe Intl.

Ident	RNO	ATIS	135.8
Elev	4412	Rwy/Length/ILS/ID	16R//110.9/IRNO
Lat	N39°29'		
Long	W119°46'		

Tonopah, NV – Tonopah Test Range

Ident	XSD	ATIS	—
Elev	5549	Rwy/Length	—
Lat	N38°03'		
Long	W117°05'		

VORs

Location/Name	Type	Ident	Freq	Lat	Long	Elev
Battle Mountain	VORTAC	BAM	112.20	N40°34'	W116°55'	4536
Beatty	VORTAC	BTY	114.70	N36°48'	W116°44'	2930
Boulder City	VORTAC	BLD	116.70	N35°59'	W114°51'	3650
Bullion	VORTAC	BQU	114.50	N40°45'	W115°45'	6460

Location/Name	Type	Ident	Freq	Lat	Long	Elev
Coaldale	VORTAC	OAL	117.70	N38°00'	W117°46'	4800
Ely	VOR-DME	ELY	110.60	N39°17'	W114°50'	6250
Las Vegas	VORTAC	LAS	116.90	N36°04'	W115°09'	2140
Lovelock	VORTAC	LLC	116.50	N40°07'	W118°34'	4784
Mina	VORTAC	MVA	115.10	N38°33'	W118°01'	7860
Mormon Mesa	VORTAC	MMM	114.30	N36°46'	W114°16'	2120
Mustang	VORTAC	FMG	117.90	N39°31'	W119°39'	5940
Sod House	VORTAC	SDO	114.30	N41°24'	W118°01'	4130
Tonopah	VORTAC	TPH	117.20	N38°01'	W117°02'	5330
Wells	VOR	LWL	114.20	N41°08'	W114°58'	5910
Wilson Creek	VORTAC	ILC	116.30	N38°15'	W114°23'	9318
Winnemucca	VOR-DME	INA	108.20	N40°53'	W117°48'	4299

NDBs

Location/Name	Ident	Freq	Lat	Long	Elev
Mercury	MCY	326	N36°37'	W116°01'	—
Sparks	SPK	254	N39°41'	W119°46'	4570
Winnemucca	EMC	375	N40°57'	W117°50'	4303

New Hampshire

Airports

Berlin, NH – Berlin Muni

Ident	BML	ATIS	122.70
Elev	1158	Rwy/Length	18/4900
Lat	N44°34'		36/4900
Long	W71°10'		

Manchester, NH – Manchester

Ident	MHT	ATIS	119.55
Elev	234	Rwy/Length/ILS/ID	06/5847/109.10/IMHT
Lat	N42°56'		24/5847/109.10/IMHT
Long	W71°26'		17/7001
			35/7001/109.1/IMHT

VORs

Location/Name	Type	Ident	Freq	Lat	Long	Elev
Berlin	VOR-DME	BML	110.40	N44°38'	W71°11'	1685
Concord	VORTAC	CON	112.90	N43°13'	W71°34'	710

Location/Name	Type	Ident	Freq	Lat	Long	Elev
Keene	VORTAC	EEN	109.40	N42°47'	W72°17'	1380
Lebanon	VOR-DME	LEB	113.70	N43°40'	W72°12'	1460
Manchester	VORTAC	MHT	114.40	N42°52'	W71°22'	470
Pease	VORTAC	PSM	116.50	N43°05'	W70°49'	100

NDBs

Location/Name	Ident	Freq	Lat	Long	Elev
Belknap	BLO	328	N43°32'	W71°32'	—
Chern (LOM/NDB)	AS	359	N42°49'	W71°36'	218
Claremont	CNH	233	N43°22'	W72°22'	565
Derry	DRY	338	N42°52'	W71°23'	—
Epsom (LOM/NDB)	CO	216	N43°07'	W71°27'	390
Hanover	LAH	276	N43°42'	W72°10'	—
Hornebrook	HXK	281	N44°34'	W71°10'	1158
Mahn	GMA	386	N44°21'	W71°41'	1395
Rollins	ESG	260	N43°13'	W70°49'	77
White River	IVV	379	N43°33'	W72°27'	1125

New Jersey

Airports

Atlantic City, NJ – Atlantic City Intl

Ident	ACY	ATIS	120.30
Elev	76	Rwy/Length/ILS/ID	04/6144
Lat	N39°27'		22/6144
Long	W74°34'		13/10000/109.10/IPVO
			31/10000

Caldwell, NJ – Essex Co.

Ident	CDW	ATIS	135.5
Elev	173	Rwy/ILS/ID	22/109.35/ICDW
Lat	N40°52'		
Long	W74°16'		

Lincoln Park, NJ – Lincoln Park

Ident	N07	ATIS	—
Elev	182	Rwy/Length	—
Lat	N40°56'		
Long	W74°18'		

Linden, NJ – Linden

Ident	LDJ	ATIS	—
Elev	23	Rwy/Length	—
Lat	N40°37'		
Long	W74°14'		

Matawan, NJ – Marlboro

Ident	2N8	ATIS	—
Elev	122	Rwy/Length	—
Lat	N40°21'		
Long	W74°15'		

Morristown, NJ – Morristown Muni.

Ident	MMU	ATIS	124.25
Elev	187	Rwy/Length/ILS/ID	23//110.3/IMMU
Lat	N40°47'		
Long	W74°25'		

Newark, NJ – Newark Intl.

Ident	EWR	ATIS	132.45
Elev	18	Rwy/ILS/ID	04R/108.7/IEZA
Lat	N40°47'		04L/110.75/IEWR
Long	W74°25'		22L/108.7/ILSQ
			11/109.15/IGPR

Old Bridge, NJ – Old Bridge

Ident	3N6	ATIS	—
Elev	87	Rwy/Length	—
Lat	N40°19'		
Long	W74°20'		

Teterboro, NJ – Teterboro

Ident	TEB	ATIS	132.02
Elev	9	Rwy/Length/ILS/ID	06//108.9/ITEB
Lat	N40°51'		
Long	W73°03'		

VORs

Location/Name	Type	Ident	Freq	Lat	Long	Elev
Atlantic City	VORTAC	ACY	108.60	N39°27'	W74°34'	70
Broadway	VOR-DME	BWZ	114.20	N40°47'	W74°49'	1048
Cedar Lake	VORTAC	VCN	115.20	N39°32'	W74°58'	120
Colts Neck	VOR-DME	COL	115.40	N40°18'	W74°09'	120
Coyle	VORTAC	CYN	113.40	N39°49'	W74°25'	210
Mc Guire	VORTAC	GXU	110.60	N40°00'	W74°35'	120

Location/Name	Type	Ident	Freq	Lat	Long	Elev
Robbinsville	VORTAC	RBV	113.80	N40°12'	W74°29'	250
Sea Isle	VORTAC	SIE	114.80	N39°05'	W74°48'	10
Solberg	VORTAC	SBJ	112.90	N40°34'	W74°44'	190
Sparta	VORTAC	SAX	115.70	N41°04'	W74°32'	1410
Stillwater	VOR-DME	STW	109.60	N40°59'	W74°52'	920
Teterboro	VOR-DME	TEB	108.40	N40°50'	W74°03'	10
Woodstown	VORTAC	OOD	112.80	N39°38'	W75°18'	140

NDBs

Location/Name	Ident	Freq	Lat	Long	Elev
Chatham	CAT	254	N40°44'	W74°25'	255
Chesa (LOM)	EW	241	N40°35'	W74°13'	—
Lakehurst	NEL	396	N40°02'	W74°20'	144
Lizah (LOM)	EZ	204	N40°36'	W74°13'	10
Moree (LOM)	MM	392	N40°52'	W74°20'	—
Naada (LOM)	PV	336	N39°29'	W74°40'	54
Palisades Park	PPK	233	N40°49'	W73°58'	—
Paterson	PNJ	347	N40°56'	W74°09'	72
Rainbow	RNB	363	N39°25'	W75°08'	—
Torby (LOM)	TE	214	N40°48'	W74°07'	—
Trenn (LOM)	TT	369	N40°12'	W74°53'	137

New Mexico

Airports

Albuquerque, NM – Albuquerque Intl

Ident	ABQ	ATIS	118.00
Elev	5352	Rwy/Length/ILS/ID	03/9000
Lat	N35°01'		21/9000
Long	W106°37'		08/13775/111.90/ISPT
			26/13775
			12/5142
			30/5142
			17/10000
			35/10000

Santa Fe, NM – Santa Fe County Muni

Ident	SAF	ATIS	128.55
Elev	6344	Rwy/Length/ILS/ID	02/8324/111.70/ISGB
Lat	N35°37'		20/8324
Long	W106°05'		15/6304
			33/6304
			10/2905
			28/2905

VORs

Location/Name	Type	Ident	Freq	Lat	Long	Elev
Albuquerque	VORTAC	ABQ	113.20	N35°02'	W106°48'	5740
Anton Chico	VORTAC	ACH	117.80	N35°06'	W105°02'	5450
Boles	VOR-DME	BWS	109.60	N32°49'	W106°00'	4100
Carlsbad	VORTAC	CNM	116.30	N32°15'	W104°13'	3250
Chisum	VORTAC	CME	116.10	N33°20'	W104°37'	3770
Cimarron	VORTAC	CIM	116.40	N36°29'	W104°52'	6550
Columbus	VOR-DME	CUS	111.20	N31°49'	W107°34'	4010
Corona	VORTAC	CNX	115.50	N34°22'	W105°40'	6410
Deming	VORTAC	DMN	108.60	N32°16'	W107°36'	4200
Farmington	VORTAC	FMN	115.30	N36°44'	W108°05'	5820
Gallup	VORTAC	GUP	115.10	N35°28'	W108°52'	7050
Hobbs	VORTAC	HOB	111.00	N32°38'	W103°16'	3660
Las Vegas	VORTAC	LVS	117.30	N35°39'	W105°08'	6870
Otto	VOR	OTO	114.00	N35°04'	W105°56'	6290
Pinon	VOR-DME	PIO	110.40	N32°31'	W105°18'	6580
Santa Fe	VORTAC	SAF	110.60	N35°32'	W106°03'	6260
Silver City	VORTAC	SVC	110.80	N32°38'	W108°09'	5420
Socorro	VORTAC	ONM	116.80	N34°20'	W106°49'	4910
Taos	VORTAC	TAS	117.60	N36°36'	W105°54'	7860
Truth Or Conseq	VORTAC	TCS	112.7	N33°16'	W107°16'	4900
Tucumcari	VORTAC	TCC	113.60	N35°10'	W103°35'	4070
Zuni	VORTAC	ZUN	113.40	N34°57'	W109°09'	6550

NDBs

Location/Name	Ident	Freq	Lat	Long	Elev
Alamogordo	ALM	341	N32°51'	W105°58'	4210
Artesia	ATS	414	N32°51'	W104°27'	3532
Capitan	CEP	278	N33°29'	W105°24'	6561
Carlz (LOM)	CV	402	N32°16'	W104°20'	3840
Cozey (LOM)	SV	251	N32°37'	W108°03'	5350
Doman (LOM)	SG	341	N35°33'	W106°08'	5970
Dudle (LOM)	AE	308	N35°13'	W106°42'	—
Florida	FIA	329	N34°06'	W106°54'	4660
Hawke (LOM)	LR	206	N32°13'	W106°50'	4180
Hisan (LOM)	CV	335	N34°21'	W103°10'	4155
Isleta	ILT	247	N34°59'	W106°37'	5304
Lovington	LGX	396	N32°56'	W103°24'	—
Maxwell	MXR	284	N36°42'	W104°32'	6245
Portales	PRZ	407	N34°09'	W103°24'	4044
Ski	SKX	414	N36°27'	W105°40'	—
Topan (LOM/NDB)	RO	305	N33°21'	W104°26'	—

New York

Airports

Bethpage, NY – Grumman (CLOSED)

Ident		ATIS	—
Elev	132	Rwy/Length	—
Lat	N40°45'		
Long	W73°30'		

Calverton, NY – NAVWPS

Ident	CTO	ATIS	—
Elev	75	Rwy/Length	—
Lat	N40°54'		
Long	W72°48'		

East Hampton, NY – East Hampton

Ident	HTO	ATIS	—
Elev	55	Rwy/Length	—
Lat	N40°57'		
Long	W72°15'		

East Moriches, NY – Lufker

Ident	4NY7	ATIS	—
Elev	50	Rwy/Length	—
Lat	N40°49'		
Long	W72°45'		

East Moriches, NY – Spadaro

Ident	1N2	ATIS	—
Elev	50	Rwy/Length	—
Lat	N40°49'		
Long	W72°44'		

Farmingdale, NY – Farmingdale/Republic

Ident	FRG	ATIS	126.65
Elev	82	Rwy/Length/ILS/ID	01/5516
Lat	N40°43'		19/5516
Long	W73°24'		14/6827/111.9/IFRG
			32/6827

Flushing, NY – Flushing Meadows (CLOSED)

Ident	FLU	ATIS	—
Elev	22	Rwy/Length	—
Lat	N40°46'		
Long	W73°50'		

Islip, NY – Islip/Long Island MacArthur

Ident	ISP	ATIS	128.45
Elev	99	Rwy/Length/ILS/ID	06/7002/108.3/IISP
Lat	N40°47'		24/7002/108.3/IRXN
Long	W73°06'		15R/5186
			33L/5186
			15L/3212
			33R/3212
			10/5036
			28/5036

Mattituck, NY – Mattituck

Ident	21N	ATIS	—
Elev	30	Rwy/Length	—
Lat	N40°59'		
Long	W72°31'		

Montauk, NY – Montauk

Ident	MTP	ATIS	—
Elev	20	Rwy/Length	—
Lat	N41°04'		
Long	W71°55'		

New York, NY – Brooklyn CGAS (CLOSED)

Ident		ATIS	—
Elev	16	Rwy/Length	—
Lat	N40°34'		
Long	W73°53'		

New York City, NY – JF Kennedy Intl

Ident	JFK	ATIS	128.72
Elev	13	Rwy/Length/ILS/ID	4R/8400/109.5/IJFK
Lat	N40°38'		22L/8400/110.9/IIWY
Long	W73°46'		4L/11351/110.9/IHIQ
			22R/11351/109.5/IJOC
			13R/14572
			31L/14572/111.35/IMOH
			13L/10000/111.5/ITLK
			34R/10000

New York City, NY – La Guardia

Ident	LGA	ATIS	127.05
Elev	22	Rwy/Length/ILS/ID	04/7000/110.5/ILGA
Lat	N40°46'		22/7000/111.15/ITKD
Long	W73°52'		13/7000/108.5/IGDI
			31/7000/108.5/IPZV

Shirley, NY – Brookhaven

Ident	HWV	**ATIS**	—
Elev	82	**Rwy/ILS/ID**	06/108.95/IHWV
Lat	N40°49'		
Long	W72°52'		

Westhampton Beach, NY – The Gabreski

Ident	FOK	**ATIS**	—
Elev	67	**Rwy/ILS/ID**	24/111.7/IFOK
Lat	N40°50'		
Long	W72°38'		

White Plains, NY – White Plains Westchester Cty

Ident	HPN	**ATIS**	133.8
Elev	439	**Rwy/Length/ILS/ID**	11/4451
Lat	N41°03'		29/4451
Long	W73°42'		16/6548/109.7/IHPN
			34/6548/109.7/IOJZ

VORs

Location/Name	Type	Ident	Freq	Lat	Long	Elev
Albany	VORTAC	ALB	115.30	N42°44'	W73°48'	275
Binghamton	VORTAC	CFB	112.20	N42°09'	W76°08'	1570
Buffalo	VORTAC	BUF	116.40	N42°55'	W78°38'	730
Calverton	VORTAC	CCC	117.20	N40°55'	W72°47'	86
Cambridge	VORTAC	CAM	115.00	N42°59'	W73°20'	1490
Canarsie	VOR-DME	CRI	112.30	N40°36'	W73°53'	10
Carmel	VORTAC	CMK	116.60	N41°16'	W73°34'	690
De Lancey	VOR-DME	DNY	112.10	N42°10'	W74°57'	2560
Deer Park	VORTAC	DPK	117.70	N40°47'	W73°18'	120
Dunkirk	VORTAC	DKK	116.20	N42°29'	W79°16'	680
Elmira	VOR-DME	ULW	109.65	N42°05'	W77°01'	1620
Geneseo	VORTAC	GEE	108.20	N42°50'	W77°43'	990
Georgetown	VORTAC	GGT	117.80	N42°47'	W75°49'	2040
Glens Falls	VORTAC	GFL	110.20	N43°20'	W73°36'	320
Hampton	VORTAC	HTO	113.60	N40°55'	W72°19'	30
Hancock	VORTAC	HNK	116.80	N42°03'	W75°18'	2070
Huguenot	VORTAC	HUO	116.10	N41°24'	W74°35'	1300
Ithaca	VOR-DME	ITH	111.80	N42°29'	W76°27'	1110
Jamestown	VOR-DME	JHW	114.70	N42°11'	W79°07'	1790
Kennedy	VORTAC	JFK	115.90	N40°37'	W73°46'	11
Kingston	VORTAC	IGN	117.60	N41°39'	W73°49'	580
La Guardia	VOR-DME	LGA	113.10	N40°47'	W73°52'	15
Massena	VORTAC	MSS	114.10	N44°54'	W74°43'	200
Pawling	VORTAC	PWL	114.30	N41°46'	W73°36'	1250
Plattsburgh	VORTAC	PLB	116.90	N44°41'	W73°31'	344
Rochester	VORTAC	ROC	110.00	N43°07'	W77°40'	550
Rockdale	VORTAC	RKA	112.60	N42°27'	W75°14'	2032

Location/Name	Type	Ident	Freq	Lat	Long	Elev
Romulus	VOR-DME	RYK	108.40	N42°42'	W76°52'	635
Saranac Lake	VOR-DME	SLK	109.20	N44°23'	W74°12'	1650
Syracuse	VORTAC	SYR	117.00	N43°09'	W76°12'	420
Utica	VORTAC	UCA	111.20	N43°01'	W75°09'	1420
Watertown	VORTAC	ART	109.80	N43°57'	W76°03'	370
Wellsville	VORTAC	ELZ	111.40	N42°05'	W77°59'	2300

NDBs

Location/Name	Ident	Freq	Lat	Long	Elev
Alpine	ALP	245	N42°14'	W76°45'	—
Avon	AVN	344	N43°00'	W77°46'	—
Babylon	BBN	275	N40°40'	W73°23'	—
Bethpage	BPA	248	N40°45'	W73°26'	—
Breit (LOM)	RO	400	N43°07'	W77°33'	—
Bridge	OGY	414	N40°34'	W73°52'	10
Briel (LOM)	SL	395	N44°28'	W74°07'	1677
Clay	CJY	275	N43°03'	W75°15'	—
Conda (LOM/NDB)	JF	373	N40°35'	W73°47'	12
Drum	GTB	257	N44°04'	W75°44'	609
Frikk (LOM)	FR	407	N40°46'	W73°28'	146
Ganse	GF	209	N43°15'	W73°36'	—
Grimm (LOM)	RT	268	N40°35'	W73°39'	—
Halos (LOM/NDB)	EL	269	N42°06'	W77°54'	2103
Hawky (LOM)	AL	219	N42°49'	W73°48'	—
Hestr (LOM)	HP	281	N41°08'	W73°45'	501
Hunter	HEU	356	N42°51'	W73°56'	378
Johnstown	JJH	523	N42°59'	W74°19'	867
Kathi (LOM)	IA	329	N43°06'	W78°50'	—
Kirki (LOM)	SY	242	N43°06'	W76°00'	403
Klump (LOM)	BU	231	N43°00'	W78°39'	630
Kring (LOM)	OZ	279	N42°35'	W74°59'	1573
Lokks (LOM)	IS	366	N40°43'	W73°11'	78
Lorrs (LOM)	IW	226	N40°43'	W73°41'	—
Meier (LOM/NDB)	PO	403	N41°34'	W73°57'	9
Misse (LOM)	MS	278	N44°51'	W74°54'	240
Monga (LOM/NDB)	MS	359	N41°45'	W74°51'	1330
Neely (LOM/NDB)	SW	335	N41°29'	W74°13'	420
Ogive (LOM)	OG	358	N44°42'	W75°21'	355
Olean	LYS	360	N42°17'	W78°20'	—
Orchy (LOM)	UR	385	N40°51'	W73°48'	10
Otims (LOM)	MG	353	N41°26'	W74°17'	378
Peconic	PIC	339	N40°48'	W72°54'	—
Penn Yan	PYA	260	N42°38'	W77°03'	858
Peths (LOM)	LG	332	N40°42'	W73°55'	—
Philmont	PFH	272	N42°15'	W73°43'	—
Plazz (LOM)	GB	204	N42°52'	W78°48'	—
Plein (LOM/NDB)	BK	329	N43°13'	W75°28'	450
Potsdam	PTD	400	N44°43'	W74°52'	—

Location/Name	Type	Ident	Freq	Lat	Long	Elev
Seneca	SSN	208		N42°44'	W76°54'	—
Smite (LOM)	BG	332		N42°06'	W75°53'	860
Squir (LOM)	FO	400		N40°54'	W72°33'	—
Stanwyck	SKU	261		N41°31'	W74°02'	520
Varna (LOM)	IT	266		N42°25'	W76°22'	1504

North Carolina

Airports

Raleigh/Durham, NC – Raleigh-Durham

Ident	RDU	ATIS	123.80
Elev	436	Rwy/Length/ILS/ID	5R/7500/109.50/IRDU
Lat	N35°53'		23L/7500/108.50/ILEI
Long	W78°47'		5L/10000/109.10/IGKK
			23R/10000/111.70/IDMP
			14/3700
			32/3700

VORs

Location/Name	Type	Ident	Freq	Lat	Long	Elev
Barretts Mountain	VOR-DME	BZM	110.80	W81°14'	N35°52'	1880
Charlotte	VOR-DME	CLT	115.00	N35°11'	W80°57'	733
Cherry Point	VOR	NKT	112.80	N34°54'	W76°52'	72
Cofield	VORTAC	CVI	114.60	N36°22'	W76°52'	70
Elizabeth City	VOR-DME	ECG	112.50	N36°15'	W76°10'	10
Fayetteville	VOR-DME	FAY	108.80	N34°59'	W78°52'	180
Greensboro	VORTAC	GSO	116.20	N36°02'	W79°58'	880
Kinston	VORTAC	ISO	109.60	N35°22'	W77°33'	70
Kirksville	VORTAC	IRK	114.60	N40°08'	W92°35'	70
Liberty	VORTAC	LIB	113.00	N35°48'	W79°36'	830
Lumberton	VOR	LBT	110.00	N34°36'	W79°03'	130
New Bern	VOR-DME	EWN	113.60	N35°04'	W77°02'	10
Raleigh/Durham	VORTAC	RDU	117.20	N35°52'	W78°46'	430
Rowan	VOR-DME	RUQ	111.00	N35°38'	W80°31'	770
Sandhills	VORTAC	SDZ	111.80	N35°12'	W79°35'	590
Simmons	VOR	FBG	109.80	N35°07'	W78°54'	240
Sugarloaf	VORTAC	SUG	112.20	N35°24'	W82°16'	3970
Tar River	VORTAC	TYI	117.80	N35°58'	W77°42'	70
Wilmington	VORTAC	ILM	117.00	N34°21'	W77°52'	20
Wright Brothers	VOR-DME	RBX	111.60	N35°55'	W75°41'	10

NDBs

Location/Name	Ident	Freq	Lat	Long	Elev
Ahoskie	ASJ	415	N36°17'	W77°10'	218
Airli (LOM)	IL	281	N34°11'	W77°51'	—
Alwood	AQE	230	N35°42'	W77°22'	—
Anson Co	AFP	283	N35°01'	W80°04'	302
Ashee (LOM/NDB)	JU	410	N36°26'	W81°19'	3123
Broad River	BRA	379	N35°16'	W82°28'	—
Burlington	BUY	329	N36°02'	W79°28'	605
Camp	CPC	227	N34°16'	W78°42'	90
Carolina Beach	CLB	216	N34°06'	W77°57'	—
Cherry Point Mc	NKT	245	N34°50'	W76°48'	—
Chocowinity	RNW	388	N35°30'	W77°06'	40
City Lake	CQJ	266	N35°42'	W79°51'	750
Clinton	CTZ	412	N34°58'	W78°21'	—
Davie	DVZ	354	N35°54'	W80°27'	810
Dixon	DIW	198	N34°34'	W77°27'	54
Doone (LOM)	GR	367	N34°54'	W78°56'	170
Dorchester Co	DYB	365	N33°03'	W80°16'	100
Edenton	EDE	265	N36°01'	W76°33'	—
Elizabethtown	TGQ	398	N34°31'	W78°30'	115
Ellas (LOM)	OA	261	N34°45'	W77°42'	65
Fiddlers	FIQ	391	N35°42'	W81°40'	1140
First River	SLP	368	N35°15'	W81°35'	850
Fort Bragg	FGP	393	N35°08'	W78°48'	—
Greon (LOM)	RD	382	N35°47'	W78°52'	—
Harnett	HQT	417	N35°25'	W78°40'	—
Hemlock	BAR	320	N36°09'	W81°52'	—
Huntsboro	HXO	271	N36°18'	W78°37'	491
Jambe (LOM/NDB)	RW	235	N35°46'	W77°57'	150
Jigel	JB	384	N34°32'	W79°08'	135
Jnall	EUU	251	N35°36'	W78°21'	250
Katfi (LOM)	EW	362	N35°01'	W77°04'	35
Keans (LOM)	IM	357	N35°31'	W82°35'	2165
Kenan	DPL	344	N35°02'	W77°56'	—
Lee Co	EEJ	428	N35°22'	W79°13'	—
Leevy (LOM/NDB)	LE	350	N35°55'	W78°43'	500
Lincolnton	IZN	432	N35°32'	W81°05'	910
Mackall	HFF	278	N35°01'	W79°29'	—
Manteo	MQI	370	N35°54'	W75°41'	10
Marky (LOM)	GS	254	N36°10'	W80°02'	938
Maxtn	ME	257	N34°44'	W79°26'	200
Mohall	HBC	350	N48°45'	W101°32'	1648
Morehead	MRH	269	N34°43'	W76°39'	5
Mount Airy	AXI	284	N36°27'	W80°33'	1037
New River (Marine)	NCA	356	N34°43'	W77°25'	—
Pamlico	OUC	404	N35°06'	W75°59'	9
Pendy	ACZ	379	N34°42'	W78°00'	30
Person (LOM/NDB)	HUR	220	N36°13'	W79°03'	625
Plymouth	PMZ	221	N35°48'	W76°45'	38
Pope (LOM/NDB)	POB	338	N35°13'	W78°57'	—

Location/Name	Ident	Freq	Lat	Long	Elev
Rapids	RZZ	407	N36°26'	W77°42'	259
Reeno (LOM)	IN	317	N36°04'	W80°10'	—
Robeson	RSY	359	N34°36'	W79°03'	—
Roscoe	RCZ	375	N34°51'	W79°41'	350
Rutherford	RFE	344	N35°20'	W81°57'	925
Salisbury	SRW	233	N35°40'	W80°30'	771
Slammer	SIF	423	N36°22'	W79°45'	856
Stals (LOM)	IS	401	N35°14'	W77°41'	40
Stanly Co	SWY	362	N35°24'	W80°09'	602
Statesville	SVH	404	N35°50'	W80°55'	—
Stonia	GHJ	293	N35°11'	W81°09'	750
Swearing	SEN	260	N35°46'	W80°17'	685
Tawba (LOM/NDB)	HK	332	N35°47'	W81°18'	975
Tomotla	TTQ	335	N35°06'	W83°57'	1855
Tryon (LOM)	CL	242	N35°09'	W81°01'	691
Wayne (LOM/NDB)	JYN	208	N35°31'	W77°54'	126
Wesley	TWL	204	N34°57'	W80°42'	660
Wilki (LOM/NDB)	UK	209	N36°06'	W81°05'	1380
Williamston	MCZ	336	N35°51'	W77°10'	76
Woodville	LLW	254	N36°15'	W76°17'	—
Yaupon	SUT	233	N33°55'	W78°04'	20
Zephyr	ZEF	326	N36°18'	W80°43'	—

North Dakota

Airports

Bismark, ND – Bismark Muni

Ident	BIS	ATIS		119.35
Elev	1677	Rwy/Length/ILS/ID		03/5107
Lat	N46°46'			21/5107
Long	W100°44'			13/8794/111.50/IBZX
				31/8794/110.30/IBIS
				17/4009
				35/4009

Grand Forks, ND – Grand Forks Intl

Ident	GFK	ATIS		119.40
Elev	844	Rwy/Length/ILS/ID		08/4200
Lat	N47°57'			26/4200
Long	W97°10'			17R/1349
				35L/1349/109.10/IFGK
				17L/3900
				35R/3900

VORs

Location/Name	Type	Ident	Freq	Lat	Long	Elev
Bismarck	VOR-DME	BIS	116.50	N46°45'	W100°39'	1840
Deering	VOR	MIB	114.90	N48°24'	W117°25'	1668
Devils Lake	VORTAC	DVL	111.00	N48°06'	W98°54'	1450
Dickinson	VORTAC	DIK	112.90	N46°51'	W102°46'	2520
Fargo	VORTAC	FAR	116.20	N46°45'	W96°51'	910
Grand Forks	VOR-DME	GFK	114.30	N47°57'	W97°11'	840
Hazen	VORTAC	HZN	114.10	N39°30'	W118°59'	1786
Jamestown	VOR-DME	JMS	114.50	N46°55'	W98°40'	1490
Minot	VORTAC	MOT	117.10	N48°15'	W101°17'	1690
Williston	VORTAC	ISN	116.30	N48°15'	W103°45'	2372

NDBs

Location/Name	Ident	Freq	Lat	Long	Elev
Bowman	BOD	374	N46°11'	W103°25'	2960
Breckenridge-Wa	BWP	233	N46°14'	W96°36'	966
Colij (LOM/NDB)	BI	230	N46°41'	W100°38'	—
Gwinner	GWR	278	N46°13'	W97°38'	1250
Hazen	HZE	205	N47°17'	W101°34'	1786
Hettinger	HEI	392	N46°01'	W102°38'	2714
Kenie (LOM/NDB)	AA	365	N47°00'	W96°48'	887
Noson (LOM)	DI	353	N46°41'	W102°42'	2527
Parshall	PSH	379	N47°56'	W102°08'	1998
Rugby	RUG	212	N48°23'	W100°01'	—
Sabon (LOM)	JM	395	N46°51'	W98°34'	—
Valley City	VCY	382	N46°52'	W97°54'	1440
Watford City	AFD	400	N47°47'	W103°15'	2066
Yuson (LOM)	SF	275	N48°07'	W103°30'	2264

Ohio

Airports

Cincinnati, OH – Cincinnati Muni-Lunken Field

Ident	LUK	ATIS		120.25
Elev	484	Rwy/Length/ILS/ID		2R/6102/110.90/ILUK
Lat	N39°06'			20L/6102
Long	W84°25'			2L/3802
				20R/3802
				06/5128
				24/5128

Columbus, OH – Port Columbus Intl

Ident	CMH	ATIS	124.60
Elev	815	Rwy/Length/ILS/ID	05/4483
Lat	N39°59'		23/4483
Long	W82°52'		10R/10250/108.70/IAQI
			28L/10250/108.70/ICMH
			10L/6000/109.10/ICBP
			28R/6000

VORs

Location/Name	Type	Ident	Freq	Lat	Long	Elev
Akron	VOR-DME	ACO	114.40	N41°06'	W81°12'	1200
Allen Co	VORTAC	AOH	108.40	N40°42'	W83°58'	980
Appleton	VORTAC	APE	116.70	N40°09'	W82°35'	1360
Bellaire	VORTAC	AIR	117.10	N40°01'	W80°49'	1290
Briggs	VORTAC	BSV	112.40	N40°44'	W81°25'	1230
Buckeye	VOR	BUD	109.80	N40°36'	W83°03'	991
Chardon	VORTAC	CXR	112.70	N41°31'	W81°09'	1330
Cincinnati	VORTAC	CVG	117.30	N39°00'	W84°42'	880
Dayton	VOR-DME	DQN	114.50	N40°00'	W84°23'	990
Dryer	VORTAC	DJB	113.60	N41°21'	W82°09'	780
Findlay	VORTAC	FDY	108.20	N40°57'	W83°45'	820
Jefferson	VORTAC	JFN	115.20	N41°45'	W80°44'	900
Lost Nation	VOR-DME	LNN	110.20	N41°41'	W81°23'	624
Mansfield	VORTAC	MFD	108.80	N40°52'	W82°35'	1210
Marathon	VOR	MAH	114.90	N41°00'	W83°39'	812
Midwest	VOR-DME	MXQ	112.90	N39°25'	W83°48'	1050
Newcomerstown	VORTAC	CTW	111.80	N40°13'	W81°28'	1180
Patterson	VORTAC	FFO	115.20	N39°49'	W84°03'	810
Rosewood	VORTAC	ROD	117.50	N40°17'	W84°02'	1083
Sandusky	VOR-DME	SKY	109.20	N41°26'	W82°39'	580
Springfield	VOR-DME	SGH	113.20	N39°50'	W83°50'	1050
Tiverton	VOR-DME	TVT	116.50	N40°27'	W82°07'	1340
Waterville	VOR-DME	VWV	113.10	N41°27'	W83°38'	660
Yellow Bud	VOR	XUB	112.50	N39°31'	W82°58'	690
Youngstown	VORTAC	YNG	109.00	N41°19'	W80°40'	1140
Zanesville	VOR-DME	ZZV	111.40	N39°56'	W81°53'	900

NDBs

Location/Name	Ident	Freq	Lat	Long	Elev
Addys (LOM)	SI	351	N39°07'	W84°40'	—
Airbo (LOM/NDB)	IL	407	N39°29'	W83°44'	1056
Akron (LOM/NDB)	AK	362	N41°04'	W81°23'	—
Ashland	AAU	329	N40°57'	W82°15'	1206
Benton Ridge	BNR	209	N41°01'	W83°39'	800
Boutn (LOM/NDB)	BU	230	N39°49'	W83°12'	900
Bruny (LOM)	AT	315	N39°50'	W84°20'	934

Location/Name	Ident	Freq	Lat	Long	Elev
Bryan	BYN	260	N41°28'	W84°27'	—
Burke Lakefront	BKL	416	N41°31'	W81°39'	581
Burln (LOM/NDB)	UR	321	N39°02'	W84°46'	—
Cadiz	CFX	239	N40°14'	W81°00'	1158
Cambridge	CDI	223	N39°57'	W81°35'	855
Caser (LOM)	LH	338	N39°44'	W82°32'	960
Cincinnati	LUK	335	N39°09'	W84°20'	871
Cincinnati-Blue	ISZ	388	N39°14'	W84°23'	839
Circleville	CYO	366	N39°31'	W82°58'	680
Clark Co	CCJ	341	N39°52'	W83°46'	1012
Cobbs (LOM)	DD	253	N39°44'	W83°01'	732
Court House	CSS	414	N39°35'	W83°23'	993
Cubla (LOM/NDB)	HW	299	N39°21'	W83°52'	998
Defiance	DFI	246	N41°20'	W84°25'	—
Delaware	DLZ	215	N40°16'	W83°06'	945
Don Scott	DKG	348	N40°04'	W83°04'	—
East Liverpool	EVO	385	N40°40'	W80°38'	1099
Engel	EZE	226	N41°29'	W81°43'	617
Fetch (LOM)	YN	338	N41°12'	W80°35'	1127
Fostoria	FZI	379	N41°11'	W83°23'	—
Fuler (LOM/NDB)	OS	515	N40°04'	W83°11'	940
Fulton	USE	375	N41°36'	W84°07'	779
Gallipolis	GAS	420	N38°50'	W82°09'	560
Georgetown	GEO	219	N38°52'	W83°53'	954
Grens (LOM)	CB	272	N40°00'	W83°01'	—
Hamilton	HAO	260	N39°22'	W84°34'	668
Harri (LOM/NDB)	CL	344	N41°20'	W81°57'	800
Hillsboro	HOC	278	N39°11'	W83°32'	923
Hogaf (LMM)	GF	521	N41°34'	W81°28'	870
Hook Fld	HKF	239	N39°29'	W84°26'	651
Hubbard	HBD	408	N41°09'	W80°31'	—
Lakefield	CQA	205	N40°28'	W84°33'	892
Lima	LYL	362	N40°42'	W84°01'	971
London	UYF	284	N39°56'	W83°27'	1070
Madeira	MDE	379	N39°13'	W84°21'	790
Manns (LOM/NDB)	MF	372	N40°45'	W82°26'	—
Marion	MNN	201	N40°37'	W83°04'	991
Marysville	MRT	303	N40°13'	W83°20'	1284
Millersburg	MLR	382	N40°32'	W81°52'	1145
Newark	HEH	524	N40°01'	W82°27'	875
Onida (LOM)	MW	223	N39°34'	W84°19'	685
Ottawa	PDR	233	N41°01'	W83°58'	760
Oxford	OXD	282	N39°30'	W84°46'	1030
Pickl (LOM)	LC	376	N39°52'	W82°50'	—
Port Clinton	PCW	423	N41°31'	W82°52'	586
Portsmouth	PMH	373	N38°46'	W82°50'	664
Ross Co	RZT	236	N39°26'	W83°01'	724
Rushsylvania	RUV	326	N40°27'	W83°40'	1220
Smithville	SLW	400	N40°52'	W81°49'	1140
Sportys	PWF	245	N39°04'	W84°12'	848
Stanley	VFU	411	N40°51'	W84°36'	780
Sumie (LOM/NDB)	CM	391	N39°59'	W82°45'	—
Tabey (LOM)	BF	248	N41°34'	W81°34'	—
Tiffin	TII	269	N41°05'	W83°12'	784

Location/Name	Ident	Freq	Lat	Long	Elev
Tolson	TSO	395	N40°33'	W81°04'	—
Tophr (LOM)	TO	219	N41°33'	W83°55'	—
University	UGS	250	N39°15'	W82°07'	754
Versailles	VES	356	N40°12'	W84°31'	1005
West Union	AMT	359	N38°51'	W83°33'	886
Xenia	XEN	395	N39°42'	W83°55'	—
Zanesville	ZZV	204	N39°54'	W81°55'	850

Oklahoma

Airports

Oklahoma City, OK – Will Rogers World

Ident	OKC	ATIS	125.85
Elev	1295	Rwy/Length/ILS/ID	13/7800
Lat	N35°23'		31/7800
Long	W97°36'		17R/9800/110.70/IOKC
			35L/9800
			17L/9802
			35R/9802/110.90/IRGR
			18/3077
			36/3077

Oklahoma City, OK – Page Muni.

Ident	F29	ATIS	—
Elev	1353	Rwy/Length	—
Lat	N35°29'		
Long	W97°49'		

Oklahoma City, OK – Wiley Post

Ident	PWA	ATIS	128.72
Elev	1299	Rwy/Length/ILS/ID	03/3409
Lat	N35°32'		21/3409
Long	W97°38'		13/4213
			31/4213
			17R/4232
			35L/4232
			17L/7198/108.70/IPWA
			35R/7198

Tulsa, OK – Tulsa Intl

Ident	TUL	ATIS	124.90
Elev	677	Rwy/Length/ILS/ID	08/7695
Lat	N36°11'		26/7695
Long	W95°53'		18L/10000/109.70/IDWE
			36R/10000/110.30/ITUL
			18R/6101/111.10/ITJY
			36L/6101/111.10/ITJY

VORs

Location/Name	Type	Ident	Freq	Lat	Long	Elev
Ada	VOR-DME	ADH	117.80	N34°48'	W96°40'	987
Altus	VORTAC	LTS	109.80	N34°39'	W99°16'	1370
Ardmore	VORTAC	ADM	116.70	N34°12'	W97°10'	925
Bartlesville	VOR-DME	BVO	117.90	N36°50'	W96°01'	940
Burns Flat	VORTAC	BFV	110.00	N35°14'	W99°12'	1780
Davis	VOR	MEE	108.60	N35°39'	W95°22'	932
Duncan	VOR-DME	DUC	111.00	N34°23'	W97°55'	1090
Gage	VORTAC	GAG	115.60	N36°20'	W99°52'	2430
Glenpool	VOR-DME	GNP	110.60	N35°55'	W95°58'	810
Hobart	VORTAC	HBR	111.80	N34°51'	W99°03'	1460
Kingfisher	VORTAC	IFI	114.70	N35°48'	W98°00'	1112
Lawton	VOR-DME	LAW	109.40	N34°29'	W98°24'	1100
Mc Alester	VORTAC	MLC	112.00	N34°50'	W95°46'	820
Okmulgee	VOR	OKM	112.20	N35°41'	W95°51'	766
Pioneer	VORTAC	PER	113.20	N36°44'	W97°09'	1060
Rich Mountain	VORTAC	PGO	113.50	N34°40'	W94°36'	2700
Sayre	VORTAC	SYO	115.20	N35°20'	W99°38'	1990
Stillwater	VOR-DME	SWO	108.40	N36°13'	W97°04'	1020
Tinker	VORTAC	TIK	115.80	N35°26'	W97°22'	1283
Tulsa	VORTAC	TUL	114.40	N36°11'	W95°47'	790
Vance	VORTAC	END	115.40	N36°20'	W97°55'	1304
Wiley Post	VOR-DME	PWA	113.40	N35°31'	W97°38'	1270
Will Rogers	VORTAC	IRW	114.10	N35°21'	W97°36'	1230
Woodring	VOR-DME	ODG	109.00	N36°22'	W97°47'	1150

NDBs

Location/Name	Ident	Freq	Lat	Long	Elev
Ada	AMR	302	N34°48'	W96°40'	1008
Addmo (LOM)	AI	400	N34°13'	W96°55'	715
Alva	AVK	203	N36°46'	W98°40'	—
Antlers	AEE	391	N34°11'	W95°39'	569
Arbuckle	AUV	284	N34°09'	W97°07'	840
Blaki (LOM)	SW	255	N36°14'	W97°05'	975
Bristow	TZO	251	N35°46'	W96°25'	929
Buffalo	BFK	215	N36°51'	W99°37'	1819
Chickasha	OLR	290	N35°06'	W97°58'	1142
Clinton	CLK	320	N35°32'	W98°56'	—
Cushing	CUH	242	N35°53'	W96°46'	—
Dewie (LOM)	BV	201	N36°50'	W96°00'	893
Durant	DUA	359	N33°56'	W96°23'	684
El Reno	RQO	335	N35°28'	W98°00'	1418
Elk City	EZY	241	N35°25'	W99°23'	1971
Fairview	FAU	246	N36°17'	W98°28'	—
Fossi (LOM/NDB)	BZ	393	N35°27'	W99°12'	1740

Location/Name	Ident	Freq	Lat	Long	Elev
Frederick	FDR	222	N34°21'	W98°59'	—
Gally (LOM/NDB)	RG	350	N35°17'	W97°35'	1198
Garfy (LOM)	EI	341	N36°16'	W97°47'	1100
Guymon	GUY	275	N36°42'	W101°30'	—
Henryetta	HET	267	N35°24'	W96°00'	—
Holdenville	HDL	411	N35°05'	W96°24'	862
Hugo	HHW	323	N34°02'	W95°32'	546
Idabel	IBO	271	N33°54'	W94°50'	508
Logan Co	LCY	326	N35°50'	W97°24'	1074
Miami	MMW	317	N36°54'	W94°53'	—
Mooreland	MDF	284	N36°29'	W99°11'	1955
Muskogee	MKO	306	N35°35'	W95°17'	—
Norman	OUN	260	N35°14'	W97°28'	—
Owaso (LOM/NDB)	DW	375	N36°18'	W95°52'	—
Pauls Valley	PVJ	384	N34°42'	W97°13'	—
Ponca (LOM/NDB)	PN	275	N36°49'	W97°06'	1038
Post	PFL	308	N34°36'	W98°24'	—
Prague	GGU	314	N35°31'	W96°43'	925
Preso (LOM)	OK	388	N35°45'	W95°56'	740
Sallisaw	IQS	520	N35°23'	W94°47'	805
Seminole	SRE	278	N35°16'	W96°40'	1007
Shawnee	SNL	227	N35°21'	W96°56'	1055
Tahlequah	TQH	215	N35°55'	W95°00'	—
Thorp	BCY	212	N36°45'	W102°32'	4172
Tilghman	CQB	396	N35°43'	W96°49'	967
Trail	OFZ	388	N34°46'	W98°24'	—
Tuloo (LOM/NDB)	OK	406	N35°28'	W97°36'	—
Wampa (LOM)	ML	344	N34°47'	W95°49'	739
Watonga	JWG	299	N35°51'	W98°25'	1530
Weatherford	OJA	272	N35°31'	W98°40'	1581
West Woodward	OWU	329	N36°26'	W99°31'	2167
William Pogue	OWP	362	N36°10'	W96°09'	878

Oregon

Airports

Portland, OR – Portland Intl

Ident	PDX	ATIS	128.35
Elev	26	Rwy/Length/ILS/ID	02/7000
Lat	N45°35'		20/7000/108.90/IGPO
Long	W122°36'		10R/11000/109.90/IPDX
			28L/11000
			10L/8000
			28R/8000/111.30/IIAP

VORs

Location/Name	Type	Ident	Freq	Lat	Long	Elev
Astoria	VOR-DME	AST	114.00	N46°09'	W123°52'	10
Baker	VORTAC	BKE	115.30	N44°50'	W117°48'	3361
Columbia	VOR	CBU	109.20	N45°35'	W122°36'	19
Corvallis	VOR-DME	CVO	115.40	N44°29'	W123°17'	250
Deschutes	VORTAC	DSD	117.60	N44°15'	W121°18'	4100
Eugene	VORTAC	EUG	112.90	N44°07'	W123°13'	360
Kimberly	VORTAC	IMB	115.60	N44°38'	W119°42'	5220
Klamath Falls	VORTAC	LMT	115.90	N42°09'	W121°43'	4087
Klickitat	VORTAC	LTJ	112.30	N45°42'	W121°06'	3220
Lakeview	VORTAC	LKV	112.00	N42°29'	W120°30'	7460
Newberg	VORTAC	UBG	117.40	N45°21'	W122°58'	1440
Newport	VORTAC	ONP	117.10	N44°34'	W124°03'	150
North Bend	VORTAC	OTH	112.10	N43°24'	W124°10'	680
Pendleton	VORTAC	PDT	114.70	N45°41'	W118°56'	1556
Portland	VOR-DME	PDX	111.80	N45°35'	W122°36'	20
Rogue Valley	VORTAC	OED	113.60	N42°28'	W122°54'	2080
Rome	VORTAC	REO	112.50	N42°35'	W117°52'	4040
Roseburg	VOR-DME	RBG	108.20	N43°10'	W123°21'	1320
Wildhorse	VOR-DME	ILR	113.80	N43°35'	W118°57'	4140

NDBs

Location/Name	Ident	Freq	Lat	Long	Elev
Abate (LOM)	HI	356	N45°37'	W123°02'	208
Bodey (LOM/NDB)	RD	411	N44°18'	W121°01'	3009
Emire (LOM/NDB)	OT	378	N43°23'	W124°18'	30
Foris (LOM/NDB)	PD	230	N45°41'	W118°43'	1185
Frakk (LOM)	EU	260	N44°12'	W123°13'	—
Gold Beach	GOL	396	N42°25'	W124°25'	—
Goose	GOS	278	N42°09'	W120°24'	4717
Karpen	PEN	201	N46°08'	W123°35'	722
La Grande	LGD	296	N45°22'	W117°59'	2735
Laker (LOM/NDB)	IA	332	N45°32'	W122°27'	—
Lewisburg	LWG	225	N44°36'	W123°16'	330
Mc Dermitt State	RMD	204	N42°00'	W117°43'	4430
Merrill	LFA	347	N41°59'	W121°38'	4090
Minne (LOM)	MM	383	N45°14'	W123°01'	159
Ontario	ONO	305	N44°01'	W117°00'	—
Prahl	PLV	366	N45°17'	W122°46'	157
Pumie (LOM)	MF	373	N42°27'	W122°54'	1175
Roseburg	RBG	400	N43°14'	W123°21'	—
Turno (LOM)	SL	266	N44°50'	W122°56'	—
Viole (LMM)	FR	356	N42°23'	W122°52'	—
Wilson	TKW	271	N45°29'	W123°51'	20

Pennsylvania

Airports

Philadelphia, PA – Philadelphia Intl

Ident	PHL	ATIS	133.40
Elev	21	Rwy/Length/ILS/ID	9R/10499/109.30/IPHL
Lat	N39°52'		27L/10499/109.30/IGLC
Long	W75°14'		9L/9500/108.95/IVII
			27R/9500/108.95/IPDP
			17/5459
			35/5459

Pittsburgh, PA – Pittsburgh Intl

Ident	PIT	ATIS	127.25
Elev	1203	Rwy/Length/ILS/ID	10R/11500/108.90/IGUT
Lat	N40° 29'		28L/11500/108.90/IPFS
Long	W80°13'		10C/8039
			28C/8039
			10L/10502/111.70/ILXB
			28R/10502/111.70/IHFE
			14/8100
			32/8100

VORs

Location/Name	Type	Ident	Freq	Lat	Long	Elev
Allegheny	VORTAC	AGC	110.00	N40°16'	W80°02'	1290
Allentown	VORTAC	FJC	117.50	N40°43'	W75°27'	680
Altoona	VOR	AOO	108.80	N40°19'	W78°18'	1630
Bradford	VORTAC	BFD	116.60	N41°47'	W78°37'	2100
Clarion	VORTAC	CIP	112.90	N41°08'	W79°27'	1530
East Texas	VORTAC	ETX	110.20	N40°34'	W75°41'	750
Ellwood City	VORTAC	EWC	115.80	N40°49'	W80°12'	1220
Erie	VORTAC	ERI	109.40	N42°01'	W80°17'	800
Franklin	VOR	FKL	109.60	N41°26'	W79°51'	1530
Harrisburg	VORTAC	HAR	112.50	N40°18'	W77°04'	1301
Hazleton	VOR	HZL	109.40	N40°58'	W76°07'	1710
Indian Head	VORTAC	IHD	108.20	N39°58'	W79°21'	2820
Johnstown	VORTAC	JST	113.00	N40°19'	W78°50'	2280
Keating	VORTAC	ETG	116.00	N41°12'	W78°08'	2250
Lake Henry	VORTAC	LHY	110.80	N41°28'	W75°28'	2320
Lancaster	VORTAC	LRP	117.30	N40°07'	W76°17'	400
Milton	VORTAC	MIP	109.20	N41°01'	W76°39'	1000
Modena	VORTAC	MXE	113.20	N39°55'	W75°40'	474
Montour	VORTAC	MMJ	112.00	N40°29'	W80°11'	1200
North Philadelphi	VOR	PNE	112.00	N40°04'	W75°00'	110

Location/Name	Type	Ident	Freq	Lat	Long	Elev
Pennridge	VOR-DME	CKZ	108.85	N40°23'	W75°17'	552
Philipsburg	VORTAC	PSB	115.50	N40°54'	W77°59'	2450
Pottstown	VORTAC	PTW	116.50	N40°13'	W75°33'	290
Ravine	VORTAC	RAV	114.60	N40°33'	W76°35'	1750
Revloc	VOR-DME	REC	110.60	N40°32'	W78°44'	2340
Saint Thomas	VORTAC	THS	115.00	N39°56'	W77°57'	2338
Selinsgrove	VORTAC	SEG	110.40	N40°47'	W76°53'	620
Slate Run	VORTAC	SLT	113.90	N41°30'	W77°58'	2310
Stoneyfork	VORTAC	SFK	108.60	N41°41'	W77°25'	1990
Tidioute	VORTAC	TDT	117.60	N41°42'	W79°25'	10
Tyrone	VORTAC	TON	114.90	N40°44'	W78°19'	2630
Wilkes Barre	VORTAC	LVZ	111.60	N41°16'	W75°41'	2120
Williamsport	VORTAC	FQM	114.40	N41°20'	W76°46'	2090
Yardley	VORTAC	ARD	108.20	N40°15'	W74°54'	300

NDBs

Location/Name	Ident	Freq	Lat	Long	Elev
Ambler	ING	275	N40°07'	W75°17'	—
Barty (LOM)	AV	257	N41°16'	W75°46'	994
Bellgrove	BZJ	328	N40°26'	W76°33'	518
Benje	BHU	382	N40°22'	W79°16'	1180
Brafo (LOM/NDB)	BF	224	N41°45'	W78°34'	2143
Camor (LOM/NDB)	VV	299	N39°52'	W79°44'	1020
Carbon	LQX	339	N40°48'	W75°45'	512
Cascade	CQD	372	N42°07'	W80°06'	—
Castle	UCP	272	N41°01'	W80°24'	—
Corry	ORJ	258	N41°54'	W79°38'	—
Crystal Lake	CYE	410	N41°12'	W75°49'	—
Doylestown	DYL	237	N40°20'	W75°07'	—
Enola (LOM)	MD	204	N40°14'	W76°54'	—
Esmer (LOM)	ER	349	N42°02'	W80°15'	—
Googl (LOM)	PT	264	N40°14'	W75°26'	330
Indiana	INP	242	N40°37'	W79°03'	—
Latle (LOM)	CX	219	N40°10'	W77°00'	—
Leehi (LOM)	AB	400	N40°35'	W75°32'	—
Penue (LOM)	UN	388	N40°54'	W77°44'	943
Picture Rocks	PIX	344	N41°16'	W76°42'	—
Ports (LOM)	PS	275	N40°59'	W78°08'	—
Quakertown	UKT	208	N40°25'	W75°17'	—
Shapp (LOM)	RD	356	N40°18'	W75°56'	—
Speez (LOM)	PD	222	N39°54'	W75°05'	—
Stoystown	SYS	209	N40°05'	W78°54'	—
Stroh (LOM/NDB)	RV	407	N40°36'	W77°43'	—
Washington Co	PNU	255	N40°08'	W80°09'	1363
Willow Grove	NXX	388	N40°11'	W75°08'	350
York	EUD	285	N39°55'	W76°52'	523

Rhode Island

Airports

Block Island, RI – Block Island State

Ident	BID	ATIS	—
Elev	109	Rwy/Length	10/2501
Lat	N41°10'		28/2501
Long	W71°34'		

Providence, RI – T Francis Green

Ident	PVD	ATIS	124.20
Elev	55	Rwy/Length/ILS/ID	05/7166/109.30/IPVD
Lat	N41°43'		23/7166/109.30/IARJ
Long	W71°25'		16/6081
			34/6081/111.50/IUNQ

VORs

Location/Name	Type	Ident	Freq	Lat	Long	Elev
Providence	VORTAC	PVD	115.60	N41°43'	W71°25'	50
Sandy Point	VOR-DME	SEY	117.80	N41°10'	W71°34'	100

NDBs

Location/Name	Ident	Freq	Lat	Long	Elev
Armin (LOM)	AR	356	N41°48'	W71°21'	65
Block Island	BID	216	N41°09'	W71°34'	125
Central	SFZ	241	N41°55'	W71°29'	455
Rench (LOM)	PV	335	N41°38'	W71°29'	—
Westerly	RLS	264	N41°20'	W71°48'	35

South Carolina

Airports

Charleston, SC – Charleston AFB/Intl

Ident	CHS	ATIS	124.75
Elev	46	Rwy/Length/ILS/ID	03/7000
Lat	N32°54'		21/7000
Long	W80°02'		15/9001/109.70/ICHS
			33/9001/108.90/ICCI

Hilton Head, SC – Hilton Head

Ident	49J	ATIS	21
Elev	20	Rwy/Length/ILS/ID	03/4300/111.30/IHXD
Lat	N32°13'		21/4300/111.30/IHXD
Long	W80°41'		

VORs

Location/Name	Type	Ident	Freq	Lat	Long	Elev
Allendale	VOR	ALD	116.70	N33°00'	W81°17'	190
Beaufort	VOR	NBC	110.50	N32°28'	W80°43'	49
Charleston	VORTAC	CHS	113.50	N32°53'	W80°02'	40
Chesterfield	VOR-DME	CTF	108.20	N34°39'	W80°16'	610
Colliers	VORTAC	IRQ	113.90	N33°42'	W82°09'	428
Columbia	VORTAC	CAE	114.70	N33°51'	W81°03'	410
Edisto	VOR-DME	EDS	111.40	N33°27'	W80°51'	201
Electric City	VORTAC	ELW	108.60	N34°25'	W82°47'	740
Florence	VORTAC	FLO	115.20	N34°13'	W79°39'	110
Fort Mill	VORTAC	FML	112.40	N34°59'	W80°57'	650
Grand Strand	VORTAC	CRE	117.60	N33°48'	W78°43'	20
Greenwood	VORTAC	GRD	115.50	N34°15'	W82°09'	630
Mc Entire	VORTAC	MMT	113.20	N33°55'	W80°48'	298
Spartanburg	VORTAC	SPA	115.70	N35°02'	W81°55'	910
Vance	VORTAC	VAN	110.40	N33°28'	W80°26'	140

NDBs

Location/Name	Ident	Freq	Lat	Long	Elev
Aiken	AIK	347	N33°39'	W81°40'	529
Alcot (LOM)	FL	335	N34°10'	W79°51'	140
Anderson Co	AND	230	N34°29'	W82°42'	760
Ashly (LOM/NDB)	CH	329	N32°58'	W80°05'	36
Barnwell	BNL	260	N33°15'	W81°22'	—
Bennettsville	BES	230	N34°37'	W79°43'	146
Benton	BEZ	347	N34°05'	W78°51'	95
Calab (LOM)	CR	267	N33°53'	W78°37'	—
Camden	CDN	263	N34°17'	W80°33'	303
Cheraw	CQW	409	N34°44'	W79°51'	179
Clemson	CEU	257	N34°40'	W82°53'	—
Coronaca	GIW	239	N34°15'	W82°05'	550
Darlington	UDG	245	N34°26'	W79°53'	184
Dillon	DLC	274	N34°27'	W79°22'	122
Dyana (LOM/NDB)	GY	338	N34°41'	W82°26'	—
Enoree	EOE	278	N34°18'	W81°38'	558
Evans	CFY	420	N33°51'	W79°45'	80
Fairmont	FRT	248	N34°54'	W81°59'	—

Location/Name	Ident	Freq	Lat	Long	Elev
Georgetown	GGE	242	N33°18'	W79°19'	—
Greer (LOM)	GS	287	N34°48'	W82°16'	—
Hartsville	HVS	341	N34°24'	W80°06'	—
Horry	HYW	370	N33°49'	W79°07'	55
Johns Island	JZI	283	N32°42'	W80°00'	—
Judky (LOM)	GM	521	N34°46'	W82°20'	—
Kingstree	CKI	404	N33°43'	W79°51'	66
Lake Keowee	LQK	408	N34°48'	W82°42'	970
Lancaster	LKR	400	N34°43'	W80°51'	—
Laurens	LUX	307	N34°30'	W81°56'	695
Manning	MNI	381	N33°35'	W80°12'	—
Marion	MAO	388	N34°11'	W79°19'	113
Mc Entire	MMT	427	N33°56'	W80°47'	298
Moncks Corner	MKS	354	N33°11'	W80°02'	—
Murry (LOM)	CA	362	N33°58'	W81°14'	330
Orangeburg	OYI	226	N33°25'	W80°54'	200
Pageland	PYG	270	N34°44'	W80°20'	569
Rally	UZ	227	N34°53'	W81°04'	523
Siler City	TOX	371	N35°45'	W79°27'	670
Stuckey	HEK	236	N33°43'	W79°31'	—
Sumter	SMS	252	N33°59'	W80°21'	—
Union Co	UOT	326	N34°41'	W81°38'	580
Walterboro	RBW	221	N32°55'	W80°38'	98
Winnsboro	FDW	414	N34°18'	W81°06'	55

South Dakota

Airports

Rapid City, SD – Rapid City Regional

Ident	RAP	ATIS	118.70
Elev	3202	Rwy/Length/ILS/ID	05/3600
Lat	N44°03'		23/3600
Long	W103°03'		14/8701
			32/8701/109.30/IRAP

Sioux Falls, SD – Joe Foss Field

Ident	FSD	ATIS	126.60
Elev	4129	Rwy/Length/ILS/ID	03/8999/109.90/IFSD
Lat	N43°34'		21/8999/111.10/IJOU
Long	W96°44'		09/3152
			27/3152
			15/6658
			33/6658

VORs

Location/Name	Type	Ident	Freq	Lat	Long	Elev
Aberdeen	VOR-DME	ABR	113.00	N45°25'	W98°22'	1300
Brookings	VOR-DME	BKX	108.80	N44°18'	W96°48'	1640
Buffalo	VOR	BUA	109.40	N45°32'	W103°28'	3020
Dupree	VORTAC	DPR	116.80	N45°04'	W101°42'	2530
Huron	VORTAC	HON	117.60	N44°26'	W98°18'	1300
Lemmon	VOR	LEM	111.40	N45°55'	W102°06'	2572
Mitchell	VOR-DME	MHE	109.20	N43°46'	W98°02'	1300
Mobridge	VOR	MBG	108.60	N45°33'	W100°21'	1925
Philip	VOR-DME	PHP	108.40	N44°03'	W101°39'	2340
Pierre	VORTAC	PIR	112.50	N44°23'	W100°09'	1790
Rapid City	VORTAC	RAP	112.30	N43°58'	W103°00'	3150
Sioux Falls	VORTAC	FSD	115.00	N43°38'	W96°46'	1570
Watertown	VORTAC	ATY	116.60	N44°58'	W97°08'	1750
Winner	VOR	ISD	112.80	N43°29'	W99°45'	2355
Yankton	VOR-DME	YKN	111.40	N42°55'	W97°23'	1300

NDBs

Location/Name	Ident	Freq	Lat	Long	Elev
Beady (LOM)	HO	302	N44°26'	W98°20'	1313
Belle Fourche	EFC	269	N44°44'	W103°51'	3189
Black Hills	SPF	300	N44°29'	W103°47'	3885
Britton	BTN	386	N45°48'	W97°44'	—
Cagur (LOM)	YK	347	N42°50'	W97°18'	1215
Flying T	FTA	388	N43°23'	W103°26'	3440
Hand	MKA	371	N44°31'	W98°57'	1568
Lican (LOM)	AT	215	N44°48'	W97°09'	—
Ranch (LOM/NDB)	RA	254	N43°57'	W102°59'	2994
Reney (LOM)	AB	203	N45°23'	W98°19'	—
Riverbend	RVB	407	N45°32'	W100°24'	1702
Rokky (LOM/NDB)	FS	245	N43°29'	W96°49'	1526
Vermillion	VMR	375	N42°45'	W96°56'	1143
Wagner	AGZ	392	N43°03'	W98°17'	1462
Wentworth	MDS	400	N44°00'	W97°05'	1714

Tennessee

Airports

Memphis, TN – Memphis Intl

Ident	MEM	ATIS	127.75
Elev	332	Rwy/Length/ILS/ID	09/8936/109.50/IMEM
Lat	N35°03'		27/8936/108.70/IJIM
Long	W89°58'		18L/8400/108.30/ISDU
			36R/8400/110.50/ITSE
			18R/9319/109.90/IOOI
			36L/9319/108.90/IOHN

Nashville, TN – Nashville Intl

Ident	BNA	ATIS	135.67
Elev	599	Rwy/Length/ILS/ID	2R/8000/111.75/IUQU
Lat	N36°07'		20L/8000/109.35/ISSX
Long	W86°40'		2C/8000/110.75/IIAX
			20C/8000
			2L/7702/109.90/IBNA
			20R/7702/111.30/IVIY
			13/11029
			31/11029/109.70/IPNO

VORs

Location/Name	Type	Ident	Freq	Lat	Long	Elev
Arnold Afs	VOR	AYX	112.50	N35°23'	W86°05'	1070
Choo Choo	VORTAC	GQO	115.80	N34°57'	W85°09'	1030
Clarksville	VOR-DME	CKV	110.60	N36°37'	W87°24'	540
Dyersburg	VORTAC	DYR	116.80	N36°01'	W89°19'	380
Graham	VORTAC	GHM	111.60	N35°50'	W87°27'	770
Hinch Mountain	VORTAC	HCH	117.60	N35°46'	W84°58'	3040
Holston Mountain	VORTAC	HMV	114.60	N36°26'	W82°07'	4321
Jacks Creek	VORTAC	JKS	109.40	N35°35'	W88°21'	630
Lafayette	VORTAC	LFT	109.80	N30°11'	W91°59'	985
Livingston	VORTAC	LVT	108.40	N36°35'	W85°09'	1020
Mc Kellar	VOR-DME	MKL	112.00	N35°36'	W88°54'	410
Memphis	VORTAC	MEM	117.50	N35°03'	W89°58'	250
Nashville	VORTAC	BNA	114.10	N36°08'	W86°41'	620
Shelbyville	VOR-DME	SYI	109.00	N35°33'	W86°26'	810
Snowbird	VORTAC	SOT	108.80	N35°47'	W83°03'	4239
Volunteer	VORTAC	VXV	116.40	N35°54'	W83°53'	1290

NDBs

Location/Name	Ident	Freq	Lat	Long	Elev
Aulon (LOM/NDB)	ME	287	N35°03'	W90°04'	—
Benfi (LOM)	TY	353	N35°44'	W84°04'	—
Boiling Fork	BGF	263	N35°10'	W86°04'	979
Booie (LOM/NDB)	BO	221	N36°23'	W82°29'	1600
Burwi	ULH	332	N35°27'	W86°14'	810
Covington	COO	326	N35°35'	W89°35'	270
Daisy	CQN	341	N35°09'	W85°09'	—
Dickson	DMZ	203	N36°07'	W87°25'	852
Dobbs (LOM)	BN	304	N36°01'	W86°43'	985
Dulaney	DYQ	263	N36°08'	W82°53'	1550
Elizabethton	EZT	275	N36°18'	W82°16'	1722
Elvis (LOM/NDB)	TS	371	N34°57'	W89°58'	—
Gallatin	GYN	214	N36°22'	W86°24'	560
Gibson	TGC	378	N35°56'	W88°51'	—
Giles	GZS	375	N35°09'	W87°03'	659
Graham	GHX	371	N33°09'	W98°29'	—
Hardeman	BAV	404	N35°12'	W89°02'	500
Hardwick	HDI	369	N35°09'	W84°54'	—
Huntingdon	HZD	217	N36°05'	W88°27'	485
Hurricane	SKN	256	N35°59'	W85°48'	1050
Hutchins	HEM	233	N35°59'	W85°35'	1086
Jacksboro	JAU	204	N36°20'	W84°09'	1170
Jasper	APT	382	N35°03'	W85°35'	—
Jefferson	JXT	346	N36°06'	W83°28'	1218
Kelso	TNY	358	N35°08'	W86°32'	—
Lafayette	LFB	245	N36°30'	W86°03'	985
Lascassas	MBT	317	N35°52'	W86°22'	—
Lawrenceburg	LRT	269	N35°14'	W87°15'	941
Lebanon	LDQ	414	N36°11'	W86°18'	570
Loosahatchie	LHC	265	N35°17'	W89°40'	308
Madisonville	MNV	361	N35°32'	W84°22'	1005
Mark Anton	DTE	394	N35°28'	W84°55'	710
Maury County	PBC	365	N35°36'	W87°05'	730
Mc Minn Co	MMI	242	N35°23'	W84°33'	840
Mersy (LOM)	MK	394	N35°30'	W88°57'	—
Millington	MIG	232	N35°16'	W89°55'	—
Mocca (LOM)	TR	299	N36°33'	W82°19'	—
Mountain City	JJO	396	N36°24'	W81°49'	2247
Nally Dunston	DNT	343	N35°59'	W89°24'	370
Needmore	PED	221	N36°32'	W86°55'	706
Obion	OQZ	212	N36°17'	W88°59'	305
Opery (LOM/NDB)	VI	344	N36°12'	W86°39'	433
Piney Grove	BPO	403	N36°32'	W84°28'	1460
Pinhook	HHY	242	N35°13'	W88°12'	395
Rogersville	RVN	329	N36°27'	W82°53'	1248
Sewanee	UOS	277	N35°12'	W85°53'	—

Location/Name	Ident	Freq	Lat	Long	Elev
Sewart	SWZ	391	N35°57'	W86°27'	—
Sibley	SZY	386	N35°14'	W88°30'	550
Snuff (LOM)	CK	335	N36°31'	W87°23'	501
Spain	SPQ	414	N35°12'	W90°03'	—
Trainer	TIQ	410	N36°14'	W88°24'	450
Verona	LUG	251	N35°30'	W86°48'	—
Warri (LOM/NDB)	RN	209	N35°45'	W85°45'	992
Waverly	AEY	329	N36°06'	W87°44'	708

Texas

Airports

Dallas-Ft Worth, TX – DFW Intl

Ident	DFW	ATIS	135.50
Elev	603	Rwy/Length/ILS/ID	13L/9300
Lat	N32°54'		31R/9300/110.90/IRRA
Long	W97°00'		13R/9000/109.50/ILWN
			31L/9000
			17L/11388/110.30/IFLQ
			35R/11388/110.30/IPKQ
			17R/13400/111.35/IJHZ
			35L/13400/111.35/IUWX
			18L/11387/110.55/ICIX
			36R/11387/110.55/IFJN
			18R/11388/111.90/IVYN
			36L/11388/111.90/IBXN

Houston, TX – Houston Intercontinental

Ident	IAH	ATIS	124.05
Elev	98	Rwy/Length/ILS/ID	08/9401/109.70/IIAH
Lat	N29°59'		26/9401/109.70/IJYV
Long	W95°20'		09/9999/110.90/IUYO
			27/9999/110.90/IGHI
			14L/12001/111.90/IHSQ
			32R/12001/111.90/ICDG
			14R/6038
			32L/6038

San Antonio, TX – San Antonio Intl

Ident	SAT	ATIS	118.90
Elev	809	Rwy/Length/ILS/ID	03/7505/109.70/ISAT
Lat	N29°31'		21/7505
Long	W98°28'		12R/8502/110.90/IANT
			30L/8502/110.90/IIZR
			12L/5519
			30R/5519

Waco, TX – James Connally (TSTC-Waco)

Ident	CNW	ATIS	124.00
Elev	590	Rwy/Length/ILS/ID	17R/6291
Lat	N31°38'		35L/6291
Long	W97°04'		17L/8600/110.70/ICNW
			35R/8600

VORs

Location/Name	Type	Ident	Freq	Lat	Long	Elev
Abilene	VORTAC	ABI	113.70	N32°28'	W99°51'	1810
Acton	VORTAC	AQN	110.60	N32°26'	W97°39'	850
Alice	VOR	ALI	114.50	N27°44'	W98°01'	168
Amarillo	VORTAC	AMA	117.20	N35°17'	W101°38'	3550
Arvilla	TACAN	MJF	109.60	—	—	550
Austin	VORTAC	AUS	117.10	N30°17'	W97°42'	630
Beaumont	VORTAC	BPT	114.50	N29°56'	W94°00'	10
Bergstrom	VOR	BSM	109.80	N30°11'	W97°41'	509
Big Spring	VORTAC	BGS	114.30	N32°23'	W101°29'	2670
Blue Ridge	VORTAC	BUJ	114.90	N33°16'	W96°21'	610
Borger	VORTAC	BGD	108.60	N35°48'	W101°22'	3130
Bridgeport	VORTAC	BPR	116.50	N33°14'	W97°45'	890
Brownsville	VORTAC	BRO	116.30	N25°55'	W97°22'	10
Brownwood	VOR-DME	BWD	108.60	N31°53'	W98°57'	1570
Carswell	VOR	FWH	108.70	N32°46'	W97°26'	663
Center Point	VORTAC	CSI	117.50	N29°55'	W99°12'	2080
Childress	VORTAC	CDS	117.60	N34°22'	W100°17'	1920
College Station	VORTAC	CLL	113.30	N30°36'	W96°25'	370
Corpus Christi	VORTAC	CRP	115.50	N27°54'	W97°26'	54
Cotulla	VORTAC	COT	115.80	N28°27'	W99°07'	520
Cowboy	VOR-DME	CVE	116.20	N32°53'	W96°54'	450
Daisetta	VORTAC	DAS	116.90	N30°11'	W94°38'	74
Dalhart	VORTAC	DHT	112.00	N36°05'	W102°32'	4020
Dallas	VOR	NBE	108.30	N32°44'	W96°58'	463
Dallas-Ft Worth	VORTAC	DFW	117.00	N32°51'	W97°01'	560
Eagle Lake	VOR-DME	ELA	116.40	N29°39'	W96°19'	190
El Paso	VORTAC	ELP	115.20	N31°48'	W106°16'	4020
Ellington	VORTAC	EFD	109.40	N29°36'	W95°09'	30
Fort Stockton	VORTAC	FST	112.80	N30°57'	W102°58'	3160
Frankston	VOR-DME	FZT	111.40	N32°04'	W95°31'	305
Gray	VOR-DME	GRK	111.80	N31°01'	W97°48'	980
Gregg Co	VORTAC	GGG	112.30	N32°25'	W94°45'	320
Guthrie	VORTAC	GTH	114.50	N33°46'	W100°20'	1940
Harlingen	VOR-DME	HRL	108.80	N26°17'	W97°47'	50
Hobby	VOR-DME	HUB	117.60	N29°39'	W95°16'	50
Hondo	VOR	HDO	109.40	N29°21'	W99°10'	933
Hudspeth	VORTAC	HUP	115.00	N31°34'	W105°22'	4390
Humble	VORTAC	IAH	116.60	N29°57'	W95°20'	90
Industry	VORTAC	IDU	110.20	N29°57'	W96°33'	419
Junction	VORTAC	JCT	116.00	N30°35'	W99°49'	2280
Lampasas	VORTAC	LZZ	112.50	N31°11'	W98°08'	1200

Location/Name	Type	Ident	Freq	Lat	Long	Elev
Laredo	VORTAC	LRD	117.40	N27°28'	W99°25'	583
Laughlin	VORTAC	DLF	114.40	N29°21'	W100°46'	1070
Leona	VORTAC	LOA	110.80	N31°07'	W95°58'	350
Llano	VORTAC	LLO	108.20	N30°47'	W98°47'	1200
Lubbock	VORTAC	LBB	109.20	N33°42'	W101°54'	3310
Lufkin	VORTAC	LFK	112.10	N31°09'	W94°43'	290
Marfa	VOR-DME	MRF	115.90	N30°17'	W103°57'	4830
Mc Allen	VOR-DME	MFE	117.20	N26°10'	W98°14'	100
Midland	VORTAC	MAF	114.80	N32°00'	W102°11'	2850
Millsap	VORTAC	MQP	117.70	N32°43'	W97°59'	890
Navasota	VORTAC	TNV	115.90	N30°17'	W96°03'	240
Newman	VORTAC	EWM	112.40	N31°57'	W106°16'	4040
Palacios	VORTAC	PSX	117.30	N28°45'	W96°18'	20
Paris	VOR-DME	PRX	113.60	N33°32'	W95°26'	655
Pecos	VOR-DME	PEQ	111.80	N31°28'	W103°34'	2620
Plainview	VOR-DME	PVW	112.90	N34°05'	W101°47'	3400
Quitman	VORTAC	UIM	114.00	N32°52'	W95°22'	520
Randolph	VOR	RND	112.30	N29°31'	W98°17'	773
Reese	VORTAC	RVO	108.80	N33°35'	W102°02'	3338
Robinson	VOR-DME	RSV	108.40	N39°01'	W87°38'	394
Rocksprings	VORTAC	RSG	111.20	N30°00'	W100°17'	2320
Sabine Pass	VOR-DME	SBI	115.40	N29°41'	W94°02'	10
Salt Flat	VORTAC	SFL	113.00	N31°44'	W105°05'	3730
San Angelo	VORTAC	SJT	115.10	N31°22'	W100°27'	1890
San Antonio	VORTAC	SAT	116.80	N29°38'	W98°27'	1160
Scholes	VORTAC	VUH	113.00	N29°16'	W94°52'	10
Scurry	VORTAC	SCY	112.90	N32°27'	W96°20'	435
Stinson	VOR	SSF	108.40	N29°15'	W98°26'	540
Stonewall	VORTAC	STV	113.10	N30°12'	W98°42'	1530
Sulphur Springs	VOR-DME	SLR	109	N33°11'	W95°32'	480
Temple	VOR-DME	TPL	110.40	N31°12'	W97°25'	710
Texico	VORTAC	TXO	112.20	N34°29'	W102°50'	4060
Three Rivers	VORTAC	THX	111.40	N28°30'	W98°09'	270
Traux	VORTAC	NGP	114.00	N27°41'	W97°17'	10
Trinity	VOR-DME	MHF	113.60	N29°32'	W94°44'	38
Tuscola	VOR-DME	TQA	111.60	N32°14'	W99°49'	2020
Tyler	VOR-DME	TYR	114.20	N32°21'	W95°24'	540
Victoria	VOR-DME	VCT	109.00	N28°54'	W96°58'	130
Waco	VORTAC	ACT	115.30	N31°39'	W97°16'	510
Wichita Falls	VORTAC	SPS	112.70	N33°59'	W98°35'	1100
Wink	VORTAC	INK	112.10	N31°52'	W103°14'	2870

NDBs

Location/Name	Ident	Freq	Lat	Long	Elev
Alamo (LOM/NDB)	AN	368	N29°36'	W98°34'	—
Alibi (LOM/NDB)	CX	281	N30°25'	W95°28'	370
Amason	CZJ	341	N31°50'	W94°08'	312
Ambassador	ABG	404	N32°35'	W95°06'	—
Anahuac	CBC	413	N29°46'	W94°39'	21

Location/Name	Ident	Freq	Lat	Long	Elev
Andrau	AAP	269	N29°44'	W95°35'	80
Andrews	ANR	245	N32°20'	W102°32'	3170
Athens	AHX	269	N32°09'	W95°49'	455
Atlanta	ATA	347	N33°06'	W94°11'	271
Austi (LOM/NDB)	AU	353	N30°14'	W97°37'	—
Ballinger	UBC	239	N31°40'	W99°58'	1735
Bay City	BYY	344	N28°58'	W95°51'	41
Beeville	BEA	284	N28°22'	W97°47'	269
Bluie (LOM)	SA	219	N29°28'	W98°31'	—
Bonham	HJM	415	N33°36'	W96°10'	607
Brady	BBD	380	N31°10'	W99°19'	1816
Brashear	BHG	338	N33°09'	W95°37'	483
Brazos River	GZV	280	N32°57'	W98°24'	1003
Breckenridge	BKD	245	N32°44'	W98°53'	1282
Brenham	BNH	362	N30°13'	W96°22'	274
Brewster Co	BWR	201	N30°27'	W103°38'	4200
Brons (LOM)	AD	407	N33°02'	W96°52'	585
Brooks Co	BKS	353	N27°12'	W98°07'	115
Brownfield	BFE	311	N33°10'	W102°11'	—
Burnet	BMQ	341	N30°44'	W98°14'	—
Caddo Mills	MII	316	N33°02'	W96°14'	541
Carthage	RPF	332	N32°10'	W94°17'	242
Cash	SYW	428	N32°58'	W96°04'	493
Castroville	CVB	338	N29°20'	W98°50'	—
Chaparrosa Ranc	CPZ	385	N28°54'	W100°00'	700
Cherokee Co	JSO	263	N31°52'	W95°12'	670
Clarendon	CNZ	281	N34°54'	W100°52'	2825
Coffi (LOM)	AC	242	N31°41'	W97°12'	—
Coleman	COM	385	N31°50'	W99°24'	88
Conis (LOM)	LV	275	N32°46'	W96°46'	—
Conor (LOM/NDB)	CR	382	N27°50'	W97°34'	68
Corsicana	CRS	396	N32°01'	W96°23'	440
Crosbyton	CZX	332	N33°37'	W101°14'	3012
David Hooks	DWH	521	N30°07'	W95°33'	—
Denison	DNI	341	N33°49'	W96°40'	—
Depoo (LOM)	BR	393	N25°59'	W97°30'	—
Devine	HHH	359	N29°08'	W98°56'	698
Dimmit Co	DMD	343	N28°31'	W99°49'	612
Durrett	DUX	414	N35°51'	W102°00'	3693
Farly (LOM/NDB)	MA	326	N31°59'	W102°19'	—
Fluet (LOM)	EF	421	N33°15'	W96°35'	642
Flufy (LOM)	LF	350	N31°13'	W94°49'	205
Fostr (LOM)	VC	226	N28°54'	W97°00'	138
Freep (LOM)	LB	263	N29°11'	W95°27'	35
Gaines Co	GNC	344	N32°40'	W102°38'	3271
Gainesville	GLE	330	N33°43'	W97°11'	860
Galveston	GLS	206	N29°20'	W94°45'	—
Garys (LOM)	RU	272	N29°57'	W97°56'	790
Georgetown	GUO	332	N30°41'	W97°40'	779
Goodhue	GDE	368	N30°04'	W94°12'	—
Grindstone Mtn	GMZ	356	N33°36'	W97°46'	1097
Hamilton	MNZ	251	N31°37'	W98°08'	1268
Hardin Co	HRD	524	N30°20'	W94°15'	68

Location/Name	Ident	Freq	Lat	Long	Elev
Haskell	AKL	407	N33°11'	W99°43'	1622
Hebbronville	HBV	266	N27°21'	W98°44'	657
Hemphill Co	HHF	400	N35°53'	W100°24'	—
Henderson	HNO	371	N32°11'	W94°51'	461
Hereford	HRX	341	N34°51'	W102°19'	3781
Hondo	HMA	329	N29°22'	W99°10'	933
Hood	HLR	347	N31°07'	W97°42'	—
Hull	SGR	388	N29°37'	W95°39'	98
Humphrey	HPY	275	N29°47'	W94°57'	35
Huntsville	UTS	308	N30°44'	W95°35'	943
Iresh (LOM/NDB)	IL	278	N31°01'	W97°42'	857
Issue (LOM)	PK	233	N32°48'	W97°01'	499
Jackson Co	EDX	201	N29°00'	W96°35'	—
Jasper	JAS	344	N30°57'	W94°02'	641
Jecca	JUG	388	N32°40'	W96°31'	420
Jiffy (LOM)	FL	219	N32°59'	W97°01'	525
Kazoo (LOM)	BP	257	N29°59'	W94°06'	—
Kleberg Co	TKB	347	N27°36'	W98°05'	—
Kotti (LOM)	DR	335	N29°26'	W100°59'	1148
La Fonda Ranch	BRX	269	N29°12'	W100°37'	1018
Lakeside	LYD	249	N29°48'	W95°40'	126
Lamesa	LSA	338	N32°45'	W101°54'	2997
Lancaster	LNC	239	N32°34'	W96°43'	495
Lee Co	GYB	385	N30°10'	W96°58'	464
Leroi (LOM)	CN	283	N31°44'	W97°04'	570
Levelland	LLN	266	N33°33'	W102°22'	3503
Littlefield	LIU	212	N33°55'	W102°23'	3602
Lone Star	LST	305	N32°55'	W94°44'	—
Lubbi (LOM)	LD	272	N33°39'	W101°43'	3197
Major (LOM)	GV	201	N33°09'	W96°03'	515
Marathon	IMP	388	N30°15'	W103°14'	4274
Marbe (LOM)	HS	379	N30°04'	W95°24'	—
Mesquite	PQF	248	N32°48'	W96°31'	445
Mexia	LXY	329	N31°38'	W96°30'	533
Mineral Wells	MWL	266	N32°47'	W98°03'	—
Missi (LOM)	MF	388	N26°15'	W98°18'	—
Monahans	OHE	214	N31°34'	W102°54'	2613
Mount Pleasant	MSA	381	N33°07'	W94°58'	390
Mufin (LOM/NDB)	FT	365	N32°53'	W97°22'	—
Nacogdoches	GXD	391	N31°38'	W94°42'	445
New Braunfels	BAZ	212	N29°42'	W98°02'	—
Nixin (LOM)	JY	326	N29°59'	W95°12'	75
Old Rip	OIP	410	N32°23'	W98°48'	1428
Olney	ONY	272	N33°21'	W98°48'	—
Orange	ORG	211	N30°04'	W93°47'	14
Palestine	PSN	375	N31°46'	W95°42'	—
Pampa	PPA	368	N35°36'	W100°59'	—
Pande (LOM/NDB)	AM	251	N35°08'	W101°48'	3623
Pekks (LOM)	LR	405	N27°38'	W99°27'	675
Perryton	PYX	266	N36°24'	W100°44'	—
Pinck (LOM)	DT	257	N33°16'	W97°11'	—
Pleasanton	PEZ	275	N28°57'	W98°31'	—
Pollo (LOM)	LB	219	N33°44'	W101°49'	—

Location/Name	Ident	Freq	Lat	Long	Elev
Port Lavaca	PKV	515	N28°39'	W96°40'	26
Powell	CGQ	344	N32°03'	W96°25'	394
Pyramid	PYF	418	N31°51'	W96°11'	350
Reagan Co	LUJ	341	N31°11'	W101°28'	2698
Redbird	RBD	287	N32°40'	W96°52'	—
Robinson	ROB	400	N31°30'	W97°04'	394
Rockport	RKP	391	N28°05'	W97°02'	25
Rosanky	RYU	266	N29°53'	W97°20'	498
Rowdy (LOM)	CL	260	N30°29'	W96°20'	—
Sandy Point	SYG	338	N29°30'	W95°28'	65
Sanjac	JPA	347	N29°40'	W95°04'	24
Scotland	SKB	344	N33°47'	W98°29'	985
Sebas (LOM/NDB)	HR	338	N26°18'	W97°39'	—
Shawn (LOM/NDB)	SP	296	N33°54'	W98°27'	—
Shein (LOM/NDB)	ER	263	N29°54'	W99°00'	1592
Snyder	SDR	359	N32°42'	W100°56'	2434
Sonora	SOA	371	N30°34'	W100°38'	2139
Spofford	PFO	356	N29°08'	W100°25'	967
Stamford	TMV	290	N32°52'	W99°43'	1541
Starn (LOM/NDB)	GR	323	N31°10'	W97°52'	877
Sweetwater	SWW	275	N32°27'	W100°27'	2360
Tomball	TMZ	408	N30°04'	W95°33'	—
Tomhi (LOM)	AB	353	N32°17'	W99°40'	1950
Travis	AVZ	299	N32°45'	W96°14'	491
Tutte (LOM)	HU	395	N29°35'	W95°20'	—
Tyler (LOM/NDB)	TY	320	N32°24'	W95°28'	—
Uvalde	UVA	281	N29°10'	W99°43'	—
Valtr (LOM/NDB)	EL	242	N31°51'	W106°19'	3940
Van Horn	VHN	233	N31°03'	W104°47'	3955
Veels (LOM)	GG	410	N32°27'	W94°47'	—
Weiser	EYQ	286	N29°56'	W95°38'	138
Wharton	ARM	245	N29°15'	W96°09'	97
Wilbarger	VRT	230	N34°13'	W99°16'	1250
Winters	IEW	396	N31°57'	W99°59'	1862
Woole (LOM)	SJ	356	N31°16'	W100°34'	2140
Yoakum	OKT	350	N29°18'	W97°08'	348

Utah

Airports

Salt Lake City, UT – Salt Lake City Intl

Ident	SLC	ATIS		124.75
Elev	4227	Rwy/Length/ILS/ID		14/4758
Lat	N40°46'			32/4758
Long	W111°58'			16/12003/110.70/IMOY
				34/12003/109.50/ISLC
				17/9596/111.50/IBNT
				35/9596/110.10/IUTG

VORs

Location/Name	Type	Ident	Freq	Lat	Long	Elev
Bonneville	VORTAC	BVL	112.30	N40°43'	W113°45'	4220
Bryce Canyon	VORTAC	BCE	112.80	N37°41'	W112°18'	9040
Carbon	VOR-DME	PUC	115.50	N39°36'	W110°45'	5890
Cedar City	VOR-DME	CDC	108.60	N37°47'	W113°04'	5460
Delta	VORTAC	DTA	116.10	N39°18'	W112°30'	4600
Fairfield	VORTAC	FFU	116.60	N40°16'	W111°56'	7690
Hanksville	VORTAC	HVE	115.90	N38°25'	W110°41'	4430
Logan	VOR-DME	LGU	109.80	N41°50'	W111°51'	4450
Lucin	VORTAC	LCU	113.60	N41°21'	W113°50'	4400
Milford	VORTAC	MLF	112.10	N38°21'	W113°00'	4980
Moab	VOR-DME	OAB	109.80	N38°45'	W109°44'	4570
Myton	VORTAC	MTU	112.70	N40°08'	W110°07'	5332
Ogden	VORTAC	OGD	115.70	N41°13'	W112°05'	4220
Provo	VOR-DME	PVU	108.40	N40°12'	W111°43'	4490
Saint George	VOR-DME	OZN	109.80	N37°05'	W113°35'	2898
Salt Lake City	VORTAC	SLC	116.80	N40°51'	W111°58'	4220
Vernal	VOR-DME	VEL	108.20	N40°22'	W109°29'	5340

NDBs

Location/Name	Ident	Freq	Lat	Long	Elev
Blanding	BDG	340	N37°31'	W109°29'	—
Brigham City	BMC	294	N41°30'	W112°04'	—
Dugway	DPG	284	N40°10'	W112°56'	—
Kernn (LOM)	SL	338	N40°40'	W111°57'	4310
Meggi (LOM)	EC	217	N37°47'	W113°01'	—
Tooele	TVY	371	N40°36'	W112°20'	4293

Vermont

Airports

Burlington, VT – Burlington Intl

Ident	BTV	ATIS	123.80
Elev	334	Rwy/Length/ILS/ID	01/3602
Lat	N44°28'		19/3602
Long	W73°09'		15/7807/110.30/IBTV
			33/7807

VORs

Location/Name	Type	Ident	Freq	Lat	Long	Elev
Burlington	VORTAC	BTV	117.50	N44°23'	W73°10'	420
Montpelier	VOR-DME	MPV	110.80	N44°05'	W72°26'	2080

NDBs

Location/Name	Ident	Freq	Lat	Long	Elev
Dyer	DYO	239	N43°35'	W72°57'	630
Herro (LOM)	BT	219	N44°31'	W73°14'	293
Ira	IRA	398	N43°41'	W72°59'	—
Lyndonville	LLX	353	N44°30'	W72°01'	1058
Morrisville-Stowe	JRV	375	N44°34'	W72°35'	830
Mount Mansfield	VKN	268	N44°23'	W72°41'	—
Mount Snow	VWD	224	N42°55'	W72°51'	1290
Newport	EFK	242	N44°57'	W72°10'	—
Springfield	SXD	265	N43°16'	W72°35'	—
Williams	MWX	257	N44°07'	W72°31'	—

Virginia

Airports

Norfolk, VA – Norfolk Intl

Ident	ORF	ATIS	127.15
Elev	27	Rwy/Length/ILS/ID	05/9000/109.10/IORF
Lat	N36°53'		23/9000/109.10/IJZQ
Long	W76°11'		14/4876
			32/4876

Richmond, VA – Richmond Intl-Byrd Field

Ident	RIC	ATIS	119.15
Elev	168	Rwy/Length/ILS/ID	02/6607/110.90/IEZD
Lat	N37°30'		20/6607
Long	W77°19'		07/5316
			25/5316
			16/9003/110.70/IRGJ
			34/9003/110.70/IBNE

Washington, VA – Washington Dulles Intl.

Ident	3VA5	**ATIS**		134.85
Elev	313	**Rwy/ILS/ID**		01R/110.1/IIAD
Lat	N38°56'			01L/111.3/IOSZ
Long	W77°27'			19R/111.3/IDLX
				19L/110.1/ISGC
				12/109.3/IAJU

VORs

Location/Name	Type	Ident	Freq	Lat	Long	Elev
Armel	VORTAC	AML	113.50	N38°56'	W77°28'	297
Brooke	VORTAC	BRV	114.50	N38°20'	W77°21'	120
Cape Charles	VORTAC	CCV	112.20	N37°20'	W75°59'	10
Casanova	VORTAC	CSN	116.30	N38°38'	W77°51'	450
Chambers	VOR	NGU	111.10	N36°56'	W76°16'	45
Danville	VOR	DAN	113.10	N36°34'	W79°20'	570
Flat Rock	VORTAC	FAK	113.30	N37°31'	W77°49'	460
Franklin	VORTAC	FKN	110.60	N36°42'	W77°00'	90
Glade Spring	VOR-DME	GZG	110.20	N36°49'	W82°04'	4200
Gordonsville	VORTAC	GVE	115.60	N38°00'	W78°09'	380
Harcum	VORTAC	HCM	108.80	N37°26'	W76°42'	10
Hopewell	VORTAC	HPW	112.00	N37°19'	W77°06'	70
Lawrenceville	VORTAC	LVL	112.90	N36°49'	W77°54'	350
Linden	VORTAC	LDN	114.30	N38°51'	W78°12'	2440
Lynchburg	VORTAC	LYH	109.20	N37°15'	W79°14'	880
Montebello	VOR-DME	MOL	115.30	N37°54'	W79°06'	3460
Norfolk	VORTAC	ORF	116.90	N36°53'	W76°12'	20
Pulaski	VORTAC	PSK	116.80	N37°05'	W80°42'	2120
Richmond	VORTAC	RIC	114.10	N37°30'	W77°19'	160
Roanoke	VORTAC	ROA	109.40	N37°20'	W80°04'	3060
South Boston	VORTAC	SBV	110.40	N36°40'	W79°00'	530
Washington	VOR-DME	DCA	111.00	N38°51'	W77°02'	10
Woodrum	VOR	ODR	114.90	N37°19'	W79°58'	1160

NDBs

Location/Name	Ident	Freq	Lat	Long	Elev
Ashey	LJK	280	N37°46'	W77°28'	220
Azalea Park	AZS	336	N38°00'	W78°31'	378
Bales (LOM/NDB)	UV	396	N36°35'	W79°55'	1080
Blackstone	BKT	326	N37°07'	W78°02'	419
Bojar (LOM/NDB)	LY	385	N37°15'	W79°14'	—
Bridgewater	VBW	241	N38°21'	W78°57'	—
Callahan	CNQ	379	N37°15'	W80°09'	1245
Caverns	LUA	245	N38°41'	W78°28'	—
Chase City	CXE	342	N36°47'	W78°30'	520

Location/Name	Ident	Freq	Lat	Long	Elev
Cogan	TZ	364	N39°05'	W78°04'	550
Culpeper	CJR	252	N38°31'	W77°51'	310
Davee (LOM)	DA	223	N38°39'	W77°06'	54
Emporia	EMV	346	N36°40'	W77°28'	—
Farmville	FVX	367	N37°21'	W78°26'	412
Felker	FAF	226	N37°08'	W76°37'	—
Fort A P Hill	APH	396	N38°05'	W77°19'	284
Georgetown	GTN	323	N38°55'	W77°07'	—
Goodwin Lake	GDX	227	N38°57'	W77°49'	505
Henry	PJS	375	N37°07'	W76°29'	39
Hillsville	HLX	269	N36°45'	W80°49'	2737
Ingle (LOM)	OR	329	N36°50'	W76°15'	5
Long Hollow	LQV	252	N36°42'	W83°04'	1670
Louisa	IQK	382	N38°01'	W77°51'	475
Mecklenburg	MBV	356	N36°41'	W78°03'	430
Melfa	MFV	388	N37°39'	W75°45'	48
Orange	COG	428	N38°13'	W78°08'	760
Oxonn (LOM/NDB)	DC	332	N38°45'	W77°01'	—
Petersburg	PTB	284	N37°07'	W77°34'	—
Portsmouth	PVG	241	N36°46'	W76°26'	23
Pubbs (LOM/NDB)	CF	392	N37°19'	W77°27'	180
Shannon	EZF	237	N38°15'	W77°26'	123
Staut (LOM)	SH	375	N38°12'	W78°57'	—
Suffolk	SFQ	203	N36°40'	W76°36'	—
Suzze (LOM/NDB)	MK	335	N36°55'	W81°14'	—
Tech	TEC	257	N37°12'	W80°24'	—
Tille (LOM)	IA	346	N38°50'	W77°26'	242
Vinton	VIT	277	N37°12'	W79°52'	913
Wakefield	AKQ	274	N36°58'	W77°00'	115
Whine (LOM)	VJ	236	N36°44'	W81°56'	—

Washington

Airports

Alderwood Manor, WA – Martha Lake

Ident	S13	**ATIS**	—
Elev	500	**Rwy/Length**	16/3000
Lat	N47°51'		34/3000
Long	W122°14'		

Arlington, WA – Arlington Muni

Ident	AWO	**ATIS**	—
Elev	137	**Rwy/Length/ILS/ID**	11/3500
Lat	N48°09'		29/3500
Long	W122°09'		16/5333
			34/5333/111.5/IAWO

Auburn, WA – Auburn Muni

Ident	S50	ATIS	—
Elev	57	Rwy/Length	16/3400
Lat	N47°19'		34/3400
Long	W122°13'		

Bremerton, WA – Bremerton National

Ident	PWT	ATIS	—
Elev	439	Rwy/Length/ILS/ID	01/6200
Lat	N47°29'		19/6200/111.1/IPWT
Long	W122°45'		

Chelan, WA – Chelan Muni

Ident	S10	ATIS	—
Elev	1263	Rwy/Length	—
Lat	N47°51'		
Long	W119°56'		

Everett, WA – Everett/Snohomish/Paine Field

Ident	PAE	ATIS	128.65
Elev	606	Rwy/Length/ILS/ID	11/4514
Lat	N47°54'		29/4514
Long	W122°16'		16R/9010/109.30/IPAE
			34L/9010
			16L/3000
			34R/3000

Monroe, WA – First Air Field

Ident	WA38	ATIS	—
Elev	50	Rwy/Length	07/2092
Lat	N47°52'		25/2092
Long	W121°59'		

Olympia, WA – Olympia

Ident	OLM	ATIS	124.40
Elev	206	Rwy/Length/ILS/ID	08/5001
Lat	N46°58'		26/5001
Long	W122°54'		17/5419/111.9/IOLM
			35/5419

Port Angeles, WA – Wm R Fairchild Intl

Ident	CLM	ATIS	134.15
Elev	288	Rwy/Length/ILS/ID	08/6349/108.9/ICLM
Lat	N48°07'		26/6349
Long	W123°29'		13/3245
			31/3245

Port Orchard, WA – Port Orchard

Ident	OS8	ATIS	—
Elev	370	Rwy/Length	18/2460
Lat	N47°25'		36/2460
Long	W122°39'		

Puyallup, WA – Pierce County-Thun Field

Ident	1S0	ATIS	—
Elev	534	Rwy/Length	16/3650
Lat	N47°06'		34/3650
Long	W122°17'		

Renton, WA – Renton Muni

Ident	RNT	ATIS	—
Elev	29	Rwy/Length	15/5379
Lat	N47°29'		33/5379
Long	W122°12'		

Seattle, WA – Boeing Field/King County Intl

Ident	BFI	ATIS	127.75
Elev	18	Rwy/Length/ILS/ID	13R/10001/110.90/IBFI
Lat	N47°32'		31/10001
Long	W122°18'		13L/3710
			31R/3710

Seattle, WA – Seattle-Tacoma Intl

Ident	SEA	ATIS	118.00
Elev	429	Rwy/Length/ILS/ID	16R/9425/111.70/ISZI
Lat	N47°26'		34L/9425/111.70/ITUC
Long	W122°18'		16L/11900
			34R/11900/110.30/ISEA

Shelton, WA – Sanderson

Ident	SHN	ATIS	—
Elev	269	Rwy/Length	—
Lat	N47°14'		
Long	W123°08'		

Snohomish, WA – Harvey Field

Ident	S43	ATIS	—
Elev	16	Rwy/Length	13/2660
Lat	N47°54'		31/2660
Long	W122°06'		

Spanaway, WA – Shady Acres

Ident	WA16	ATIS	—
Elev	445	Rwy/Length	16/1800
Lat	N47°04'		34/1800
Long	W122°22'		

Spanaway, WA – Spanaway

Ident	S44	ATIS	—
Elev	373	Rwy/Length	16/2700
Lat	N47°05'		34/2700
Long	W122°25'		

Spokane, WA – Felts Field

Ident	SFF	ATIS	—
Elev	1953	Rwy/Length	3L/4500
Lat	N47°40'		21R/4500
Long	W117°19'		3R/3059
			21L/3059

Tacoma, WA – Tacoma Narrows

Ident	TIW	ATIS	124.05
Elev	292	Rwy/Length/ILS/ID	17/5002/109.1/ITIW
Lat	N47°16'		35/5002
Long	W122°34'		

VORs

Location/Name	Type	Ident	Freq	Lat	Long	Elev
Battle Ground	VORTAC	BTG	116.60	N45°44'	W122°35'	250
Bellingham	VORTAC	BLI	113.00	N48°56'	W122°34'	80
Ellensburg	VORTAC	ELN	117.90	N47°01'	W120°27'	1770
Ephrata	VORTAC	EPH	112.60	N47°22'	W119°25'	1250
Hoquiam	VORTAC	HQM	117.70	N46°56'	W124°08'	10
McChord	VORTAC	TCM	109.60	N47°08'	W122°28'	280
Moses Lake	VOR-DME	MWH	115.00	N47°12'	W119°19'	1177
Olympia	VORTAC	OLM	113.40	N46°58'	W122°54'	200
Paine	VOR-DME	PAE	110.60	N47°55'	W122°16'	674
Pasco	VOR-DME	PSC	108.40	N46°15'	W119°06'	400
Pullman	VOR-DME	PUW	109.00	N46°40'	W117°13'	2720
Seattle	VORTAC	SEA	116.80	N47°26'	W122°18'	350
Spokane	VORTAC	GEG	115.50	N47°33'	W117°37'	2760
Tatoosh	VORTAC	TOU	112.20	N48°17'	W124°37'	1652
Walla Walla	VOR-DME	ALW	116.40	N46°05'	W118°17'	1150
Wenatchee	VOR-DME	EAT	111.00	N47°23'	W120°12'	1220
Yakima	VORTAC	YKM	116.00	N46°34'	W120°26'	980

NDBs

Location/Name	Ident	Freq	Lat	Long	Elev
Abern (LOM)	HQ	414	N46°59'	W123°47'	366
Benza (LOM)	BL	338	N48°53'	W122°32'	44
Carney	CAN	274	N47°24'	W122°50'	—
Deerpark	DPY	216	N47°58'	W117°25'	2250

Location/Name	Ident	Freq	Lat	Long	Elev
Dondo	ODD	224	N47°21'	W122°18'	320
Donny (LOM)	YK	371	N46°31'	W120°22'	—
Dunez (LOM)	PS	331	N46°20'	W119°00'	651
Elwha (LOM/NDB)	CL	515	N48°09'	W123°40'	1069
Felts	SFF	365	N47°41'	W117°18'	1950
Friday Harbor	FHR	284	N48°31'	W123°01'	180
Graye (LOM/NDB)	GR	216	N47°09'	W122°36'	343
Ione	ION	379	N48°42'	W117°24'	2107
Kelso	LSO	256	N46°09'	W122°54'	—
Kitsap	PWT	206	N47°29'	W122°45'	492
Lacomas	LAC	328	N47°00'	W122°33'	—
Lopez Island	OPZ	356	N48°28'	W122°55'	198
Mason Co	MNC	348	N47°14'	W123°05'	210
Neah Bay	EBY	391	N48°21'	W124°33'	—
Nolla (LOM)	BF	362	N47°37'	W122°23'	142
Omak	OMK	396	N48°27'	W119°31'	1303
Parkk (LOM)	SZ	281	N47°31'	W122°18'	17
Pelly (LOM/NDB)	MW	408	N47°06'	W119°16'	1186
Phort (LOM)	GE	388	N47°40'	W117°27'	—
Renton	RNT	353	N47°29'	W122°12'	20
Riboo (LOM)	RLL	260	N46°22'	W119°15'	395
Ritts (LOM)	PA	396	N48°03'	W122°17'	10
Skagit/Bay View	BVS	240	N48°28'	W122°25'	93
Toledo	TDO	219	N46°28'	W122°49'	371
Trina (LOM)	AL	353	N46°10'	W118°11'	—
Waton (LOM)	AW	382	N48°04'	W122°09'	61

West Virginia

Airports

Huntington, WV – Tri-State/Walker

Ident	HTS	ATIS	125.20
Elev	828	Rwy/Length/ILS/ID	03/3007
Lat	N38°21'		21/3007
Long	W82°33'		12/6509/109.90/IHTS
			30/6509/108.70/ITUU

VORs

Location/Name	Type	Ident	Freq	Lat	Long	Elev
Beckley	VORTAC	BKW	117.70	N37°46'	W81°07'	2500
Bluefield	VORTAC	BLF	110.00	N37°18'	W81°11'	2900
Charleston	VORTAC	HVQ	117.40	N38°20'	W81°46'	1100
Clarksburg	VOR-DME	CKB	112.60	N39°15'	W80°16'	1430
Elkins	VORTAC	EKN	114.20	N38°54'	W80°05'	2160
Henderson	VORTAC	HNN	115.90	N38°45'	W82°01'	860

Location/Name	Type	Ident	Freq	Lat	Long	Elev
Kessel	VOR-DME	ESL	110.80	N39°13'	W78°59'	2590
Martinsburg	VORTAC	MRB	112.10	N39°23'	W77°50'	600
Morgantown	VORTAC	MGW	111.60	N39°33'	W79°51'	2340
Parkersburg	VORTAC	JPU	108.60	N39°26'	W81°22'	1030
Rainelle	VOR	RNL	116.60	N37°58'	W80°48'	3350
Wheeling	VORTAC	HLG	112.20	N40°15'	W80°34'	1270
Wht Sulphur Sprng	VOR	SSU	108.4	N37°45'	W80°18'	3330

NDBs

Location/Name	Ident	Freq	Lat	Long	Elev
Bushi (LOM/NDB)	LW	346	N37°46'	W80°28'	2160
Dorch (LOM)	HL	212	N40°06'	W80°41'	1270
Guyandot	GTC	293	N37°46'	W81°54'	2121
Huntt (LOM)	HTN	226	N38°23'	W82°39'	758
Nicholas	IJZ	272	N38°10'	W80°55'	1880
Randolph Co	RQY	284	N38°53'	W79°51'	—
Versi (LOM)	PK	388	N39°15'	W81°29'	797

Wisconsin

Airports

Milwaukee, WI – Gen Mitchell International

Ident	MKE	ATIS	126.40
Elev	723	Rwy/Length/ILS/ID	1R/4182
Lat	N42°56'		19L/4182
Long	W87°53'		1L/9690/110.30/IMKE
			19R/9690/110.30/IBLY
			7R/8011/111.50/IGMF
			25L/8011/111.50/IPXY
			7L/3163
			25R/3163
			13/5868
			31/5868

Oshkosh, WI – Wittman Regional

Ident	OSH	ATIS	125.80
Elev	808	Rwy/Length/ILS/ID	04/3424
Lat	N43°59'		22/3424
Long	W88°33'		09/6166
			27/6166
			13/3008
			31/3008
			18/8001
			36/8001/110.50/IOSH

VORs

Location/Name	Type	Ident	Freq	Lat	Long	Elev
Ashland	VOR-DME	ASX	110.20	N46°32'	W90°55'	820
Badger	VORTAC	BAE	116.40	N43°07'	W88°17'	1080
Burbun	VOR	BUU	114.50	N42°41'	W88°18'	770
Dells	VORTAC	DLL	117.00	N43°33'	W89°45'	1020
Eau Claire	VORTAC	EAU	112.90	N44°53'	W91°28'	900
Falls	VOR	FAH	110.00	N43°46'	W87°50'	—
Green Bay	VORTAC	GRB	115.50	N44°33'	W88°11'	760
Hayward	VOR-DME	HYR	113.40	N46°01'	W91°26'	1207
Horlick	VOR	HRK	117.70	N42°45'	W87°48'	669
Janesville	VORTAC	JVL	114.30	N42°33'	W89°06'	900
Kenosha	VOR	ENW	109.20	N42°35'	W87°55'	730
La Crosse	VOR-DME	LSE	108.40	N43°52'	W91°15'	650
Lone Rock	VORTAC	LNR	112.80	N43°17'	W90°07'	—
Madison	VORTAC	MSN	108.60	N43°08'	W89°20'	860
Manitowoc	VOR-DME	MTW	111.00	N44°07'	W87°40'	650
Oshkosh	VORTAC	OSH	111.80	N43°59'	W88°33'	780
Rhinelander	VORTAC	RHI	109.20	N45°38'	W89°27'	1590
Rice Lake	VOR-DME	IKE	110.00	N45°28'	W91°43'	1130
Siren	VOR-DME	RZN	109.40	N45°49'	W92°22'	987
Stevens Point	VORTAC	STE	110.60	N44°32'	W89°31'	1110
Timmerman	VOR-DME	LJT	112.50	N43°06'	W88°02'	750
Wausau	VORTAC	AUW	111.60	N44°50'	W89°35'	1202
West Bend	VOR	BJB	109.80	N43°25'	W88°07'	870

NDBs

Location/Name	Ident	Freq	Lat	Long	Elev
Ameron	AHH	278	N45°16'	W92°22'	—
Antigo	AIG	347	N45°09'	W89°06'	1518
Arbor Vitae	ARV	221	N45°55'	W89°43'	1627
Big Doctor	BXR	203	N45°49'	W92°21'	998
Black River Fal	BCK	362	N44°15'	W90°50'	835
Bong	SUW	260	N46°41'	W92°06'	675
Calin (LOM)	DU	266	N44°34'	W90°09'	1170
Cappy (LOM)	MK	410	N42°50'	W87°54'	678
Central Wiscons	HWS	377	N44°46'	W89°40'	1264
Clintonville	CLI	209	N44°37'	W88°43'	865
Codee (LOM)	EN	389	N42°33'	W88°01'	—
Cumberland	UBE	375	N45°30'	W91°58'	1239
Danci (LOM)	CW	275	N44°45'	W89°47'	1235
Depre (LOM/NDB)	SG	332	N44°23'	W88°07'	637
Eagle River	EGV	341	N45°55'	W89°15'	1644
Famis (LOM)	GR	356	N44°26'	W88°14'	—
Fichy (LOM)	II	224	N44°45'	W87°26'	700
Fond Du Lac	FLD	248	N43°46'	W88°29'	—
Gamie (LOM)	AT	230	N44°09'	W88°35'	—
Hartford	HXF	200	N43°20'	W88°23'	1032
Janesville	JVL	375	N42°36'	W89°02'	900

Location/Name	Ident	Freq	Lat	Long	Elev
Juneau	UNU	344	N43°25'	W88°42'	968
Kennedy	ENY	254	N46°33'	W90°54'	826
Kettle Moraine	LLE	329	N43°25'	W88°07'	—
Kickapoo	HBW	251	N43°39'	W90°19'	—
Kooky	AKT	407	N44°12'	W88°23'	753
Lake Lawn	LVV	404	N42°42'	W88°35'	—
Land O Lakes	LNL	396	N46°09'	W89°12'	1706
Maggs (LOM)	EA	239	N44°56'	W91°22'	—
Manitowish	MHA	364	N46°07'	W89°52'	1610
Marshfield	MFI	391	N44°38'	W90°11'	1261
Medford	MDZ	335	N45°06'	W90°18'	1461
Merrill	RRL	257	N45°11'	W89°42'	1316
Mindi (LOM)	LS	272	N44°00'	W91°15'	—
Mineral Point	MRJ	365	N42°53'	W90°13'	1157
Monah (LOM/NDB)	MS	400	N43°03'	W89°20'	—
Necedah	DAF	233	N44°02'	W90°04'	914
Neillsville	VIQ	368	N44°33'	W90°30'	1204
Nepco (LOM)	EK	326	N44°15'	W89°53'	925
New Richmond	RNH	257	N45°08'	W92°32'	995
Oconto	OCQ	388	N44°52'	W87°54'	603
Osceola	OEO	233	N45°18'	W92°41'	896
Paser (LOM/NDB)	RA	206	N42°40'	W87°53'	710
Phillips	PBH	263	N45°42'	W90°24'	1463
Platteville	PVB	203	N42°41'	W90°26'	—
Pober (LOM)	OS	395	N43°52'	W88°33'	—
Rice Lake	RIE	407	N45°28'	W91°43'	1130
Rock River	RYV	371	N43°10'	W88°43'	822
Rusk Co	RCX	356	N45°30'	W91°00'	1241
Seeley	SLY	344	N46°06'	W91°23'	1200
Shebb (LOM)	HE	338	N43°50'	W87°46'	693
Shell Lake	SSQ	212	N45°43'	W91°55'	1232
Solon Springs	OLG	388	N46°19'	W91°48'	1099
Sturgeon Bay	SUE	414	N44°50'	W87°25'	771
Teels (LOM/NDB)	GM	242	N42°54'	W88°02'	—
Waukesha	UES	359	N43°02'	W88°14'	905
Waupaca	PCZ	382	N44°19'	W89°00'	804
Wausau	FZK	243	N44°55'	W89°37'	1202
Wisconsin Rapids	ISW	215	N44°21'	W89°50'	1069
Yanks (LOM/NDB)	BL	260	N43°03'	W87°52'	—

Wyoming

Airports

Cheyenne, WY – Cheyenne

Ident	CYS	ATIS	134.42
Elev	6156	Rwy/Length/ILS/ID	08/9200/110.10/ICYS
Lat	N41°09'		26/9200
Long	W104°48'		12/6691
			30/6691

Jackson, WY – Jackson Hole

Ident	JAC	ATIS	122.80
Elev	6445	Rwy/Length/ILS/ID	18/6299/109.10/IJAC
Lat	N43°36'		36/6299
Long	W110°44'		

VORs

Location/Name	Type	Ident	Freq	Lat	Long	Elev
Big Piney	VOR-DME	BPI	116.50	N42°34'	W110°06'	6949
Boysen Reservoir	VORTAC	BOY	117.80	N43°27'	W108°17'	7550
Cherokee	VORTAC	CKW	115.00	N41°45'	W107°34'	7050
Cheyenne	VORTAC	CYS	113.10	N41°12'	W104°46'	6210
Cody	VOR-DME	COD	111.80	N44°37'	W108°57'	4790
Crazy Woman	VORTAC	CZI	117.30	N43°59'	W106°26'	4800
Douglas	VOR-DME	DGW	108.60	N42°40'	W105°13'	4900
Dunoir	VOR-DME	DNW	113.40	N43°49'	W110°20'	7720
Evanston	VOR-DME	EVW	110.00	N41°16'	W111°01'	7187
Fort Bridger	VORTAC	FBR	108.60	N41°22'	W110°25'	7060
Gillette	VOR-DME	GCC	114.60	N44°20'	W105°32'	4335
Jackson	VOR-DME	JAC	108.40	N43°36'	W110°44'	6430
Laramie	VORTAC	LAR	117.60	N41°20'	W105°43'	7280
Medicine Bow	VORTAC	MBW	111.60	N41°50'	W106°00'	7000
Muddy Mountain	VORTAC	DDY	116.20	N43°05'	W106°16'	5860
Newcastle	VOR	ECS	108.20	N43°52'	W104°18'	4210
Rawlins	VOR-DME	RWL	109.40	N41°48'	W107°12'	6750
Riverton	VOR-DME	RIW	108.80	N43°03'	W108°27'	5540
Rock Springs	VORTAC	OCS	116.00	N41°35'	W109°00'	6780
Sheridan	VORTAC	SHR	115.30	N44°50'	W107°03'	4410
Worland	VOR-DME	RLY	114.80	N43°57'	W107°57'	4190

NDBs

Location/Name	Ident	Freq	Lat	Long	Elev
Antelope	AOP	290	N41°36'	W109°00'	—
Cowley	HCY	257	N44°54'	W108°26'	4082
Deryk (LOM/NDB)	GC	380	N44°16'	W105°31'	—
Greybull	GEY	275	N44°30'	W108°04'	3917
Horse (LOM)	CY	353	N41°08'	W104°40'	—
Johno (LOM)	CP	375	N42°54'	W106°34'	—
Kemmerer	EMM	407	N41°49'	W110°33'	—
Klint (LOM)	RI	217	N43°00'	W108°18'	5045
Powell	POY	344	N44°52'	W108°47'	5070
Sinclair	SIR	368	N41°48'	W107°05'	—
Torrington	TOR	293	N42°03'	W104°09'	—
Wenz	PNA	392	N42°47'	W109°48'	7073

Glossary

Ailerons The moveable surfaces on the trailing outer edges of the wings. They control the bank of the aircraft.

Airfoil Any surface or structure on the aircraft that is specifically designed to garner a reaction from air moving over its surface.

Airspeed indicator This indicator displays the aircraft's current speed through the air.

Altimeter This indicator displays the aircraft's current altitude. This is usually calibrated to show the altitude over sea level, or mean sea level (MSL) altitude.

Angle of attack The angle between the relative wind and the wing's chord line. *See also* **Chord**.

Approach lighting system The approach lighting system is designed to aid the pilot with visual references when landing. These lights are usually color coded and flashing in sequence for easy recognition.

Artificial horizon This instrument shows the bank and pitch attitudes of the aircraft with respect to the ground. *See also* **Attitude indicator**.

Aspect ratio The ratio between the chord of the wings and the wingspan.

Atmospheric pressure The pressure exerted by the atmosphere on the earth. At higher elevations, where the air is thinner, the atmospheric pressure is lower.

Attitude This term describes the aircraft's pitch and bank position with regard to the horizon or ground.

Attitude indicator This instrument displays the aircraft's pitch and bank position with regard to the horizon or ground. *See also* **Artificial horizon**.

Auto-coordination When auto-coordination is on, the rudders and ailerons automatically move together to provide turns with no "slips."

Automatic direction finder (ADF) This is a navigational instrument used with nondirectional radio beacons to determine relative headings.

Automatic terminal information service (ATIS) This is a continuously played recording that gives weather and other important information for airfields. It is broadcast by airports on a set frequency and is continually updated.

Autopilot This will fly the aircraft at a set altitude and heading so that the pilot can spend more time on other activities.

Axis indicator This instrument indicates the current axis of the aircraft, which is the direction or aim of the center of the aircraft.

Balloon Ballooning occurs when you increase the angle of attack and pitch attitude too quickly. This can cause a stall.

Bank Rotation around the horizontal axis of the plane; it's also called roll. Tilt your head from side to side to get an idea of bank.

Canopy relative work (CRW) The art of maneuvering your canopies side-by-side or in formation.

Ceiling The altitude of the lowest solid cloud layer. This does not apply to broken or scattered clouds.

Centrifugal force Outward force exerted on an object spun from a central location.

Chord The distance between the leading and trailing edges of the wing.

Collective Controls the pitch of a helicopter's rotor's blades and is used to climb or descend.

COM An abbreviation for "communication."

Course deviation indicator (CDI) This is a vertical indicator on the omnibearing indicator (OBI) that displays your deviation from the very-high-frequency omnidirectional range (VOR) radial set. If the indicator is to the left of center, the radial is to the left, and likewise.

Course selector This number on the OBI indicates which VOR radial is being tracked.

Crab angle The difference between the aircraft's ground track and its heading, or when the aircraft's nose is at an angle to its direction of travel. Crab angles are necessary whenever a wind is not blowing directly at or behind an airplane.

Cruise speed The average speed calculated during normal level flight.

Cyclic Controls a helicopter's pitch and bank angle, similar to the flight yoke in an airplane.

Dead reckoning Navigation of the aircraft by calculations of airspeed, heading, course, wind and ground speed, and time.

Decision altitude The moment or altitude during a landing approach when a pilot must make the decision whether to land the plane or abort and retry.

Distance measuring equipment (DME) Measures distance in nautical miles from VOR stations.

Drag The retarding force exhibited on the aircraft as it moves through the air.

Electronic flight instrument system (EFIS) Used with CFPD (command flight path display), this displays a proper glide slope for landing.

Elevator Pulling back or pushing forward on the yoke controls the elevator, which controls the pitch of the aircraft.

Federal Aviation Administration (FAA) This agency is the U.S. government body responsible for establishing rules and regulations governing the safe passage of aircraft.

Flaps Flaps increase lift by changing the wing surface. This also has the effect of slowing your stall speed, so you can make a landing approach at a lower airspeed.

Flare A maneuver that slows your descent rate just before touchdown. This is accomplished by pulling back on the yoke.

G Force The force induced on the aircraft as various maneuvers are performed.

Glide slope The path an aircraft takes as it approaches the runway. A proper glide slope minimizes the vertical descent rate and ensures that the plane doesn't overshoot or undershoot the runway.

Ground speed An aircraft's airspeed relative to the ground. Headwinds or tailwinds affect the ground speed of the aircraft.

Heading indicator This indicator displays what direction the plane is facing with respect to the earth's magnetic field.

Horizontal situation indicator (HSI) An instrument on the 737-400 and JetRanger III that provides a top-down view of your location relative to a radio beacon.

Indicated airspeed The airspeed of your airplane, without compensating for air density at altitude. *See also* **True airspeed**.

Instrument flight rules (IFR) A method of navigation that uses an aircraft's instruments to navigate, such as the VOR indicator and the automatic direction finder. *See also* **VFR**.

Instrument landing system (ILS) This system coordinates signals from marker beacons, the localizer, and the glide slope to project the proper orientation and descent rate for a landing. The plane's deviation from the proper glide slope is reflected on the needle.

Instrument rating This rating is awarded to pilots who have completed IFR training and have passed the FAA written exam.

Knots Nautical miles per hour. One nautical mile is equivalent to 1.15 statute miles.

Landing gear Wheels that are raised after takeoff and lowered before landing.

Lift The upward force on an airplane wing created by the curved surface of the wing and the deflection of air downward.

Localizer A radio beam oriented along the runway heading that helps a pilot stay on course during an ILS approach.

Mach number The ratio of your current true airspeed with the current speed of sound.

Magnetic compass This is the only direction-seeking instrument in the plane, and it serves primarily to set the heading indicator and verify its accuracy.

Magnetic heading The orientation of the plane with respect to the earth's magnetic field. The heading is expressed in degrees.

Magneto A device that makes the engine run by providing an electrical current to the spark plug.

Minimum controllable airspeed (MCA) Just above the stall speed, MCA is the lowest speed at which an airplane can fly and still be controllable. MCA varies for different types of aircraft.

Manifold pressure gauge This indicates the power output of the engine by measuring the air pressure in the engine induction system.

Marker beacons Outer, middle, and inner marker beacons are set up at specific distances from the airport and sound a tone in the cockpit when the aircraft crosses over them.

Mixture control This adjusts the air/fuel mixture, allowing you to operate the engine more efficiently.

Navigational radio (NAV) This radio works with the OBI to display your position relative to a ground-based station. Each plane usually has two, labeled NAV 1 and NAV 2.

Nondirectional radio beacon (NDB) This is a ground-based station that broadcasts a signal that can be picked up by your automatic direction finder (ADF).

Omnibearing indicator (OBI) An instrument that works in conjunction with your NAV 1 radio to display your current position relative to a VOR station.

Performance boosters Files that are located on your FS98 CD that are read into the cache to speed access times. You can modify, edit, or delete these files in the scenery library.

Phonetic alphabet A system that replaces each letter of the alphabet with a word signifying that letter. The phonetic alphabet is used by pilots to avoid verbal miscommunication.

Pilotage A method of navigation using visible landmarks and an aeronautical chart.

Pitch Rotation around the lateral axis of the plane. Nod your head up and down to get an idea of pitch.

Primary flight instruments The six main instruments used for flight—the airspeed indicator, the attitude indicator, the altimeter, the turn coordinator, the heading indicator, and the vertical speed indicator.

Radials Signals emitted from a VOR station that radiate outward, like spokes of a wheel. By tuning in a VOR station on the OBI, the pilot can select a radial using the course selector, and the OBI will display the aircraft's position relative to that particular radial.

Rate of climb Change in altitude over time. This is represented by the vertical speed indicator (VSI) in hundreds of feet per minute.

Relative wind Air flowing over the object going through the air. The flight path of an airplane is directly opposite the relative wind.

Ridge lift Air currents deflected upward as wind hits the side of a ridge. Sailplanes use this lift to gain altitude. *See also* **Thermal**.

Rotate Pulling back on the yoke to raise the plane's nose off the ground during takeoff.

Rotation speed The speed at which the pilot should start to pull back on the yoke during takeoff. On the Cessna, this is generally around 70 knots.

Rudder A moveable control surface located on the tail that compensates for the plane's yaw and allows you to control the airplane in a turn.

Slip In a slip, opposite rudder is added to a turn, making it possible to bank the plane while keeping a consistent heading. This comes in handy when landing in a crosswind.

Skid In a skid, the rate of turn is not sufficient for the bank angle. You can compensate for a skid by increasing the bank angle or reducing the amount of rudder.

Spoilers Spoilers are used on the sailplane to increase your rate of descent without increasing speed.

Spool up The process by which jet engines power up to full.

Stall A stall occurs when an aircraft's angle of attack is too great for the wings to continue to provide lift. Any airplane will stall if the wing's critical angle of attack is exceeded—regardless of airspeed.

Stall speed The stall speed is the speed at which the critical angle of attack is exceeded.

Taxi The movements of airplanes on the ground, usually guided by the air traffic control tower.

Thermal Warm currents of air that rise up from dark patches of ground. Sailplanes can rise on these thermals.

Throttle This controls the amount of air that enters the engine.

Thrust The force produced by the engine or propeller.

Traffic pattern A defined pattern that all airplanes fly when approaching an airport.

Transponder Radio equipment in an aircraft that broadcasts information about the aircraft to air traffic control.

Trim Trim tabs allow you to make slight adjustments to the wing surfaces to relieve you from having to maintain constant pressure on the yoke.

True airspeed An airplane's airspeed that compensates for changes in air density at altitude. Because the air is thinner as you gain altitude, indicated airspeed will read a little lower than true airspeed, which needs to be taken into account when planning flight plans and navigation.

Turn coordinator This instrument indicates the bank of the plane. A small ball in the turn coordinator also indicates whether you are making a coordinated turn.

Uncoordinated flight In this mode of flight, the rudder moves independently of the yoke; you will need to control both the rudder and the yoke to get a smooth turn.

Visual flight rules (VFR) A set of rules you have to follow to fly in good weather. *See also* **Instrument flight rule**.

Yaw Rotation around the vertical axis of the plane. Shake your head from side to side to get an idea of yaw.

Index

COMPUTER GAME BOOKS

688 (I) Hunter/Killer: The Official Strategy Guide	$19.99
Betrayal In Antara: The Official Strategy Guide	$19.99
Birthright: The Official Strategy Guide	$19.99
Blood: The Official Strategy Guide	$19.99
CD-ROM Classics Vol. 2	$19.99
Command & Conquer: Red Alert Secrets & Solutions—The Unauthorized Edition	$19.99
Command & Conquer: Red Alert—Unauthorized Advanced Strategies	$19.99
Command & Conquer: Red Alert-Counterstrike—Unauthorized Secrets and Solutions	$19.99
Dark Earth: The Official Strategy Guide	$19.99
Diablo: The Official Strategy Guide	$19.99
Diablo battle.net Advanced Strategies: The Official Strategy Guide	$16.99
DOOM II: The Official Strategy Guide	$19.95
Duke Nukem 3D: Unauthorized Secrets & Solutions	$14.99
Dungeon Keeper Official Secrets	$19.99
Ecstatica II: The Official Strategy Guide	$19.99
Fighters Anthology: The Official Strategy Guide	$24.99
Final Doom: Unauthorized Game Secrets	$19.99
Heroes of Might and Magic II: The Price of Loyalty—The Official Strategy Guide	$14.99
Imperalism: The Official Strategy Guide	$19.99
Interstate '76: The Official Strategy Guide	$19.99
Links LS 98: The Official Strategy Guide	$19.99
MDK: The Official Strategy Guide	$12.99
Microsoft Flight Simulator for Win95: The Official Strategy Guide	$19.99
Myst: The Official Strategy Guide	$19.95
NASCAR Racing 2: The Official Strategy Guide	$19.99
OddWorld: Abe's Oddysee—The Official Strategy Guide	$12.99
Online Games Guide: The Official Strategy Guide	$19.99
Outlaws: The Official Strategy Guide	$19.99
Pacific General: The Official Strategy Guide	$16.99
Phantasmagoria: Puzzle of Flesh—The Official Strategy Guide	$19.99
Quake Strategy Guide: Unauthorized	$19.99
Quake Unauthorized Map Guide	$14.99
Rebel Moon Rising: The Official Strategy Guide	$19.99
Shadows of the Empire, PC Version: The Official Strategy Guide	$19.99
Shivers Two: Harvest of Souls—The Official Strategy Guide	$19.99
Sid Meier's Civilization II: The Official Strategy Guide	$19.99
The Games Troubleshooting Guide: Simple Solutions to Common Problems	$7.99
The Last Express: The Official Strategy Guide	$19.99
Timelapse: The Official Strategy Guide	$19.99
Ultima Online: The Official Strategy Guide	$19.99
WarCraft II: Beyond the Dark Portal Official Secrets & Solutions	$14.99
WarCraft II: Tides of Darkness—The Official Strategy Guide	$19.99

To Order Call 1-800-531-2343

Warlords III: The Official Strategy Guide $19.99
Wing Commander IV: The Unauthorized Strategy Guide $14.99
X-COM Apocalypse: The Official Strategy Guide $19.99

VIDEO GAME BOOKS

Beyond the Beyond: Unauthorized Game Secrets	$14.99
Blast Corps Unauthorized Game Secrets	$12.99
Blood Omen: Legacy of Kain—Official Game Secrets	$14.99
Dark Rift: Official Secrets & Solutions	$12.99
Doom 64 Official Game Secrets: Official Secrets & Solutions	$12.99
Dynasty Warriors: Official Secrets & Solutions	$12.99
Game Boy Pocket Power Guide: Unauthorized	$7.99
GoldenEye 007: Unauthorized Game Secrets	$12.99
Hexen 64: Official Secrets & Solutions	$12.99
Killer Instinct Gold: The Unauthorized Guide	$12.99
MDK: The Official Strategy Guide	$12.99
Mortal Kombat 3: Official Power Play Guide	$9.95
Mortal Kombat Trilogy Official Game Secrets	$9.99
Nintendo 64 Pocket Power Guide Volume 2: Unauthorized	$7.99
Nintendo 64 Unauthorized Game Secrets Volume 2	$12.99
OddWorld: Abe's Oddysee—The Official Strategy Guide	$12.99
Ogre Battle: The Official Strategy Guide	$12.99
PlayStation Game Secrets Unauthorized Volume 4	$12.99
PlayStation Pocket Power Guide Volume 2: Unauthorized	$7.99
Shadows of the Empire Game Secrets	$12.99
Sports Pocket Power Guide—Authorized	$7.99
Star Fox 64: Unauthorized Game Secrets	$12.99
Super Mario 64 Game Secrets: Unauthorized	$12.99
Tomb Raider Game Secrets	$14.99
Twisted Metal 2 Unauthorized Game Secrets	$12.99
Vandal Hearts Unauthorized Secrets & Solutions	$14.99
Warcraft II: Dark Saga—Official Game Secrets	$12.99
War Gods Official Arcade Game Secrets	$9.99
War Gods Official Game Secrets	$12.99
WCW Vs. the World: Official Secrets & Solutions	$3.99
Wild Arms: Unauthorized Game Secrets	$12.99
Castlevania: Symphony of the Night—Unauthorized Secrets & Solutions	$12.99
Sega Saturn Pocket Power Guide Volume 2: Authorized	$7.99
GameShark Pocket Power Guide: Authorized	$7.99
Croc: Legend of the Gobbos: Authorized	$12.99

To Order Call 1-800-531-2343

Prima
The World Leader in

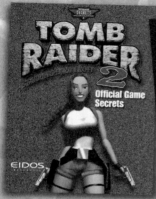

Tomb Raider™ II
The Official Strategy Guide
$12.99

Tomb Raider™
Game Secrets
$12.99

OddWorld™:
Abe's Oddysee
The Official Strategy Guide
$12.99

Dungeon Keeper™
Official Secrets
$19.99

**Shadows of
the Empire™**
Game Secrets
$12.99

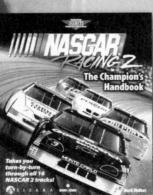

Nascar Racing™ II:
The Champion's Handbook
$19.99

Myst™
The Official Strategy Guide
$19.95

Dark Earth™
The Official Strategy Guide
$19.99

PRIMA'S
SECRETS
OF THE GAMES

Prima Publishing
PO Box 629000 • El Dorado Hills, CA 95762
To Order Call 1•800•531•2343
Secrets of the Games® is a registered trademark of Prima Publishing, a division of Prima Communications, Inc.

Publishing
Electronic Entertainment Books!

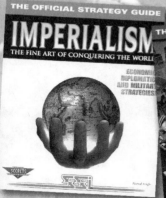

Imperialism™
The Official Strategy Guide
$19.99

X-COM Apocalypse™
The Official Strategy Guide
$19.99

Betrayal in Antara™
The Official Strategy Guide,
$19.99

WarCraft II™:
Dark Saga
Official Game Secrets
$12.99

Diablo™
The Official Strategy Guide
$19.99

MDK™
The Official Strategy Guide
$12.99

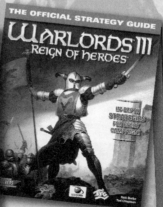

Warlords™ III:
Reign of Heroes
The Official Strategy Guide
$19.99

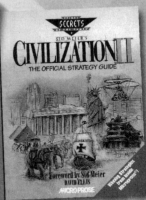

Sid Meier's Civilization II™
The Official Strategy Guide
$19.99

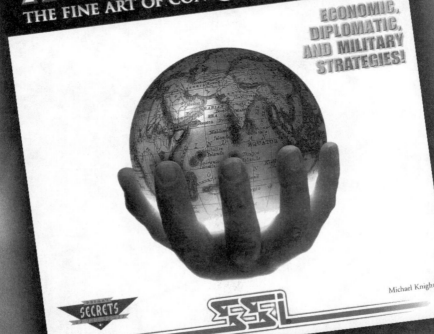

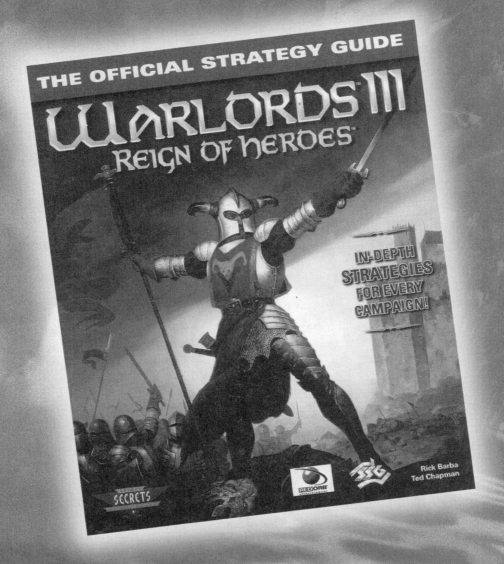

THE OFFICIAL STRATEGY GUIDE

X·COM

APOCALYPSE

ALL THE INFORMATION YOU NEED TO
DEFEAT
THE ALIEN THREAT!

PRIMA'S SECRETS

MICROPROSE

David Ellis

to order, call prima at
1-800-531-2343

PRIMA PUBLISHING

To Order Books

Please send me the following items:

Quantity	Title	Unit Price	Total
_____	_____	$ _____	$ _____
_____	_____	$ _____	$ _____
_____	_____	$ _____	$ _____
_____	_____	$ _____	$ _____
_____	_____	$ _____	$ _____

Subtotal	$ _____
Deduct 10% when ordering 3-5 books	$ _____
7.25% Sales Tax (CA only)	$ _____
8.25% Sales Tax (TN only)	$ _____
5.0% Sales Tax (MD and IN only)	$ _____
7.0% G.S.T. Tax (Canada only)	$ _____
Shipping and Handling*	$ _____
Total Order	$ _____

*Shipping and Handling depend on Subtotal.

Subtotal	Shipping/Handling
$0.00–$14.99	$3.00
$15.00–$29.99	$4.00
$30.00–$49.99	$6.00
$50.00–$99.99	$10.00
$100.00–$199.99	$13.50
$200.00+	Call for Quote

Foreign and all Priority Request orders:
Call Order Entry department
for price quote at 916-632-4400

This chart represents the total retail price of books only
(before applicable discounts are taken).

By Telephone: With MC or Visa, call 800-632-8676 or 916-632-4400. Mon–Fri, 8:30-4:30.

WWW: http://www.primapublishing.com

By Internet E-mail: sales@primapub.com

By Mail: Just fill out the information below and send with your remittance to:

Prima Publishing
P.O. Box 1260BK
Rocklin, CA 95677

My name is _____

I live at _____

City_____ State _____ ZIP _____

MC/Visa#_____ Exp._____

Check/money order enclosed for $ _____ Payable to Prima Publishing

Daytime telephone _____

Signature _____